AESTHETIC DISTANCE
IN
CHRETIEN DE TROYES:

IRONY AND COMEDY IN

CLIGES
AND
PERCEVAL

PETER HAIDU

AESTHETIC DISTANCE
IN
CHRETIEN DE TROYES:
IRONY AND COMEDY IN
CLIGES
AND
PERCEVAL

GENÈVE
LIBRAIRIE DROZ
11, RUE MASSOT

1968

1ʳᵉ édition : août 1968

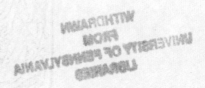

*To my mother
and the memory of my father*

CONTENTS

PREFACE

To some extent, this dissertation may be viewed as presenting the report of an experiment. In its early stages, it was conceived of as the study of a certain aspect of style in Chrétien de Troyes: irony. It was clear from the outset that such a study would have to take into account elements which are not stylistic in themselves but which provide the context in which stylistic irony operates. Though some forms of irony appear to be more or less self-sufficient in that they contain all that is required to reveal the intended meaning, the more frequent case is that the ironic statement does not obtain its meaning (and irony) unless it is seen as located within a specific narrative situation. Nevertheless, it seemed originally that such contextual material could easily be sketched in to form the background of particular stylistic ironies. This turned out to be true for the simpler forms of irony, those defined in medieval school-books. Even here, however, it quickly became apparent that this manner of presentation imposed limits which would distort the intention of my author. The romance which, for reasons to be cited later, was to be the first approach to the study of stylistic irony—*Cligès*—is renowned for its monologues. These are long: one continues for over two hundred and fifty lines. On close examination, it yielded a number of small-scale examples; more than that, it turned out to be ironic both in internal structure and in relationship to the character whose thought it revealed. Furthermore, I found that this character was juxtaposed to another in the romance, and that this juxtaposition was ironic. Finally, I found that certain developments in the plot could be accounted for only in terms of what I had already concluded was a structural method essentially ironic.

In brief, the study of stylistic irony led to the discovery that irony was the basic method of composition used in *Cligès*.

It also led to some speculation as to the nature and function of this irony. Much of the time, this irony had the effect of placing the reader in a privileged position vis-à-vis the story. It revealed aspects of character or situation unknown to one or more characters in the situation— as in dramatic irony. It allowed the reader certain insights into the narrative and the values implied by the narrative which were not available to the characters of the romance. It frequently seemed to range the reader with the author as against the characters, as if Chrétien de Troyes were offering a guided tour through a living laboratory of charming foolishness: with a sideward wink or a meaningful nudge, he would suggest comparisons which both brought together certain aspects of his story and provided the observer with material for instructive meditation. It defined one's relationship to the text, a relationship both sympathetic and reserved; this was not a story to become "involved" in, these were not characters with whom a reader might identify himself; one was to keep one's aesthetic distance.

Could this lesson, and the ironic techniques which had taught it, be applied to Chrétien's other romances? The first, *Erec et Enide,* proved to use irony only as an occasional stylistic ornament, with no effort that I could see to employ it for the general purposes I had found in *Cligès.* Another, the famous *Lancelot,* offered a highly ambiguous hero with occasional ironic and even farcical turns. These, however, were best accounted for as subversive protests by a writer annoyed at a patroness who had given him a distasteful task. *Yvain* and *Perceval* remained. The first was particularly attractive as the object of extended analysis: generally acknowledged as the most accomplished production of Chrétien's art, it had already been the main subject of my Master's Essay. There were two difficulties, however. The first was that the matter had been largely pre-empted by the dean of Chrétien scholarship, Jean Frappier, in the publication of his lectures on *Yvain* at the Sorbonne: I found that the little I might add to his judicious discussion would not balance the large amount of repetition of his work which would be necessary. Furthermore, much of what had been learned from *Cligès* would not be useful to an analysis of *Yvain,* while the fact that both Chrétien's second and last romances dealt with two heroes was encouraging. I was also greatly attracted by the conjunction of two elements in *Perceval*: the obvious and frequent comedy, and the apparent incongruity of this comedy with the religious, not to say mystical concerns, some scholars had found there. [1]

The choice of *Perceval* was also made attractive when I realized that a careful analysis of the function of its irony and comedy could contribute to the vexed discussions which surround the unfinished romance—discussions which often exist at some remove from the text. This analysis would affect the interpretation of the hero and the structure of his adventures; the technique of suggested juxtaposition of characters I had found in *Cligès* seemed also applicable to Perceval and Gauvain, which in turn affected the interpretation of the structure and meaning of the two parts of the work. Thus, what had originally been conceived as a study in stylistic analysis led me to questions of wider relevance and perhaps greater importance. This meant abandoning the plan of a purely stylistic study; I felt the loss would be compensated by the fact that the new work might be of greater service and interest. However, I have retained the original basis in so far as the entire dissertation is based on careful (and therefore sometimes lengthy) analysis of the manner in which Chrétien de Troyes used certain resources of language to indicate by incongruity a meaning he did not state.

---

[1] I must also acknowledge some subtle urging from Professor W.T.H. Jackson.

But the choice of *Perceval* also raised some delicate problems of literary theory. Even more than irony, the comic is difficult of analysis While it is possible to demonstrate at least a probability of ironic intent in a given case, nothing in the world will persuade a man to laugh where he has not done so of his own accord: the effect of an attempt to prove that something is comic usually leads to one rebuttal; *viz.*, that the author was no great shakes as a comic writer. I have dealt with this problem as legend claims Alexander disposed of the Gordian knot. In doubtful situations where authority could be invoked, I have done so. Elsewhere, I have reduced comedy to one element it shares with irony: incongruity. Finally, I have drawn sometimes on general, popular recognition of comic patterns, and occasionally on the most widely known theory of laughter, that of Henri Bergson. The tools of analysis, then, are elementary, for irony as well: there, I have used the traditional definitions of tropes and figures found in schoolbooks. To possible objections to such methodological looseness, I can only answer that my primary purpose throughout has been to serve the writer who is my subject, and to avoid theoretical entanglements which, however interesting, would not aid in that purpose.

It is a pleasure to acknowledge certain debts. The first is to David B. Truman, then Dean of Columbia College, for the award of a Lawrence H. Chamberlain Fellowship in the Spring Semester of 1965, as well as to Professors Bert M.-P. Leefmans of the French Department and Howard A. Porter of the Greek and Latin Department and then Chairman of the Humanities A course, on whose recommendations the award was made: this dissertation could not have been completed at this time without that award. I owe Professor Michael Riffaterre a number of techniques in stylistic analysis, above all the idea of convergence which will frequently be used in these pages. [2] I am grateful to Professor Jean Hytier for his willingness to read a dissertation in a subject far removed from his own interests.

Above all, however, I wish to express my warmest gratitude to my first two readers, whose patience, understanding and advice have helped shape this dissertation well beyond its original merits. Professor W. T. H. Jackson, with whom I studied Medieval Latin and Medieval Comparative Literature, has been a living example of that courtesy and scholarly humanism which is so often the subject of our common studies. In addition to saving me from several *gaffes,* Professor Lawton P. G. Peckham, my first and continuing mentor in Old French and the sponsor of this dissertation, has offered practical help, encouragement, and a lesson of scholarly restraint I have attempted to follow.

---

[2] See his *Le style des Pléiades de Gobineau, Essai d'application d'une méthode stylistique* (New York: Columbia, 1957), pp. 2 f., 190-210.

INTRODUCTION

Our first step in the study of the techniques by which Chrétien de Troyes obtained the effect of aesthetic distance will be the analysis of certain stylistic devices in terms of the grammatical and rhetorical theories inherited by the Middle Ages from classical antiquity. It must be said immediately that these terms—the definitions of tropes and figures—are quite unprepossessing. The works in which they are found were designed for the education of the young toward the end of the Empire; the same texts were used for the same purpose in the Middle Ages. [1] Minimal definitions and simple examples are to be expected, nothing more, even when the subjects are as far-reaching in literary implications as allegory and irony. In addition, the reduction of style

---

[1] On classical education, the works of Henri-Irénée Marrou are authoritative: *Histoire de l'éducation dans l'Antiquité* (Paris: Seuil, 1948), and his *Saint Augustin et la fin de la culture antique*, 2nd. ed. in *Bibliothèque des Ecoles Françaises d'Athènes et de Rome*, vol. 145bis (Paris: De Boccard, 1949); see also Aubrey Gwynn, *Roman Education from Cicero to Quintilian* (New York: Russell & Russell, 1926 & 1964). Older but still useful on details not covered by Marrou and Gwynn is Emile Jullien, *Les professeurs de littérature dans l'ancienne Rome et leur enseignement depuis l'origine jusqu'à la mort d'Auguste* (Paris: Leroux, 1885).

For the period of transition into the early Middle Ages, see Theodore Haarhof, *Schools of Gaul: A Study of Pagan and Christian Education in the Last Century of the Western Empire* (Oxford: Milford, 1920); M. Roger, *L'Enseignement des lettres classiques d'Ausone à Alcuin: Introduction à l'histoire des écoles carolingiennes* (Paris: Picard, 1905); and especially Pierre Riché, *Education et culture dans l'occident barbare, Ve-VIIIe siècles*, in *Patristica Sorboniensia*, Vol. IV (Paris: Seuil, 1962).

On literary education in the twelfth century, the following works are useful: Paul Abelson, *The Seven Liberal Arts, A Study in Medieval Culture* (New York: Columbia, 1906); A. Clerval, *Les écoles de Chartres au Moyen Age, du Ve au XVIe siècle* (Paris: Picard, n. d., 1895?); Louis John Paetow, *The Arts Course at Medieval Universities with Special Reference to Grammar and Rhetoric*, in *The University of Illinois Studies*, Vol. III, (Urbana-Champaign: University Press, 1910); G. Paré, A. Brunet, & P. Tremblay, *La renaissance du XIIe siècle: les écoles et l'enseignement*, in *Publications de l'Institut d'Etudes Médiévales d'Ottawa*, Vol. III (Paris & Ottawa: Vrin & Institut d'Etudes Médiévales, 1933). These are largely concerned with the higher potentials of medieval intellectual education; a brief survey of more mundane realities is provided by Philippe Delhaye, "L'organisation scolaire au XIIe siècle," *Traditio*, V (1947), 211-268.

Mention must be made of Charles Thurot's pioneering work, *Notices et extraits de divers manuscrits latins pour servir à l'histoire des doctrines grammaticales au Moyen Age*, in *Notices et extraits des manuscrits*, Vol. XXII, part 2 (1868). Though still useful for both earlier and later periods, it is particularly weak on the twelfth century.

to the compartmentalized system of tropes and figures is foreign to modern taste. Nevertheless, it provides a fairly objective means of dealing with the minutiae of style—minutiae which can lead to larger understanding.

GRAMMATICA: ALLEGORIA

Among the tropes, one in particular was considered appropriate for the indirect and ironic revelation of thought: *allegoria.* It is discussed by a group of grammarians from the Late Empire: Sacerdos (third century), Donatus, Charisius, Diomedes (all three from the fourth century), and Pompeius (fifth century). [2] Except for Sacerdos—the least important for the Middle Ages—their treatments are basically identical. The minor variations in definitions or choice of examples change nothing in the basic structure or content of their material. We will follow Donatus, amplifying his treatment with that of the others when necessary.

Allegoria

This is both a trope in its own right and the generic designation of seven subtypes: *ironia, antiphrasis, aenigma, charientismos, paroemia, sarcasmos,* and *asteismos.*

As a trope, it simply means something other than is said: *tropus quo aliud significatur quam dicitur.* [3] Pompeius expands this slightly by explaining that the words say one thing but the matter encloses something else. [4] The possibility of irony is only suggested by Charisius and Diomedes who add that it operates *per similitudinem aut contrarium.*

---

[2] The texts are to be found in Heinrich Keil, *Grammatici Latini,* 8 vols. (Leipzig: Teubner, 1857-1880): Sacerdos in vol. VI, p. 261 f.; Donatus in vol. IV, p. 401 f.; Charisius in vol. I, p. 276 f.; Diomedes in vol. I, p. 461 ff.; Pompeius in vol. V, p. 310 ff. Since these sections are short, and since we will follow the grammarians' own order, further page references to this material will be omitted.

Quintilian also deals with *allegoria* in the *Institutes* (VIII, vi, 44-59; he also discusses *ironia* independently: IX, ii, 44-51). However, the grammarians were far better known in the Middle Ages; on the question of Quintilian's influence, see below, p. 20, n. 35.

[3] Donatus' entire treatment: "Allegoria est tropus, quo aliud significatur quam dicitur, ut
            et iam tempus equum fumantia solvere colla,
hoc est 'carmen finire'." The example is the concluding line of Virgil's second *Georgics.*

[4] "... verba nostra aliud sonant et res aliud habet."

Ironia

The classical definition is the narrowest possible: irony is the trope which attempts to express something by its contrary. [5] The example used by most of the grammarians is from the fourth book of the *Aeneid*. Juno reproaches Venus for using Cupid in order to make Dido fall in love with Aeneas:

> *"egregiam vero laudem et spolia ampla refertis*
> *tuque puerque tuus*; magnum et memorabile numen,
> una dolo divum si femina victa duorum est..." [6]

All the grammarians add that this trope is particularly difficult unless it is assisted by an appropriate delivery: otherwise, it will seem to affirm what the speaker wishes to deny. [7] Pompeius makes an interesting distinction: saying one thing and meaning another is equally descriptive of allegory and irony. As he states it, the allegorically used words refer to something quite different from the apparent meaning, while the ironically used words can both affirm and deny what they state. [8] In other words, allegory has reference to a reality other than that indicated by its words, while irony hovers about the same reality but sees it from two different points of view.

Antiphrasis

This is speedily dispatched by Donatus with the definition: *unius verbi ironia*. His own examples and the other grammarians' definitions indicate that one can be more precise. Diomedes distinguishes it from *ironia*: while the latter changes its meaning by the tone and manner of delivery, antiphrasis actually gives a thing a different name. [9] The examples elucidate the definitions. They are all words whose irony is derived from a supposed etymology: *bellum* (war, but also a form of *bellus*, "beautiful") is so named because it is least beautiful; the *Parcae* are so named because they spare (*parcant*) no one; *lucus* (a grove), is so named because no light shines there (*non luceat*). [10]

---

[5] Donatus: "ironia est tropus per contrarium quod conatur ostendens..."

[6] "A praise-worthy feat, I must say, a fine achievement you've brought off,
You and your boy: it should make a great, a lasting name for you—
One woman mastered by the arts of two immortals."
The translation is that of C. Day Lewis, *The Aeneid of Virgil* (Garden City, N.Y.: Doubleday Anchor, 1952), p. 84. The grammarians normally quote only the italicized words.

[7] Donatus: "... hanc nisi gravitas pronuntiationis adiuverit, confiteri videbitur quod negare contendit."

[8] "ironia est, quotienscumque re vera aliud loquimur et aliud significamus in verbis; non ita, ut diximus de allegoria, quando aliud dicimus et aliud significamus, non, sed isdem verbis potes et negare et confirmare; sola autem pronuntiatione discernitur."

[9] "... dictio e contrario significans ... haec ab ironia differt quod ironia pronuntiando et adfectu mutat significationem, antiphrasis vero diversitatem rei nominat."

[10] Donatus, *in toto*: "antiphrasis est unius verbi ironia, ut [bellum lucus et Parcae] bellum, hoc est minime bellum, et lucus eo quod non luceat, et Parcae eo quod nulli parcant."

Aenigma

Donatus defines this as "an obscure formula [which operates] by a hidden similarity in things." [11] Diomedes adds that it is an allegory so obscure as to be unintelligible, [12] a comment justified by the example:

> mater me genuit, eadem mox gignitur ex me.

In fact, as Pompeius explains, it is a riddle, a child's game in which silly questions are asked which no one understands. [13] Fortunately, the answer is provided: it means that water hardens into ice and flows thence again.

Charientismos

This trope is a kindly one, or seems to be at first sight. For Donatus, it is a way of saying harsh things in a more agreeable way, [14] but Charisius' emphasis is different: it is a way of speaking which says one thing but means something else through the use of agreeable words. [15] The example both use suggests that the second definition is more appropriate. When we inquire whether anyone has asked for us and are told "You're lucky," that is *charientismos*: we understand that no one was looking for us. [16]

Paroemia

The definitions of this trope also vary somewhat. For Donatus, it is simply the adaptation of proverbs to particular occasions and situations. [17] Sacerdos and Charisius emphasize that it is the appropriation of a popular proverb but with a certain twist in implication. [18] While Donatus merely states the contextual use of a proverb without specifying its provenance, the other two add the notion of a transference from a popular linguistic context to a literary one. Donatus simply offers two examples: "don't kick against the pricks" and "talk of the devil, and he appears." [19] Sacerdos explains the first as meaning that it is foolish to be courageous against evil or stronger men; Pompeius

---

11 "... obscura sententia per occultam similitudinem rerum..."

12 "... dictio obscuritate allegoriae non intelligibilis..."

13 "aenigma est, quo ludunt etiam parvuli inter se, quando sibi proponunt quaestiunculas, quas nullus intellegit." Sacerdos is quite disdainful: "...dictio obscura, quaestio vulgaris, allegoria difficilis, antequam fuerit intellecta, postea ridicula."

14 "... tropus quo dura dictu gratius proferentur..."

15 "... dictio per ea quae grata sunt alius dicens aliud significans..."

16 Donatus: "... ut cum interrogantibus nobis, numquis nos quaesierit, respondetur 'bona fortuna'; exinde intellegitur neminem nos quaesisse."

17 "... adcommodatum rebus temporibusque proverbium."

18 Charisius: "... vulgaris proverbi usurpatio cum aliqua diversitate..."

19 "adversum stimulum calces» and "lupus in fabula." The translations are from Charleţjn T. Lewis and Charles Short, *A Latin Dictionary* (Oxford: 1958), under 1 *calx* I, 2, and 1 *lupus* I.

explains that the second is used when the person one is talking about suddenly appears. [20]

Sarcasmos

This is stronger than the English "sarcasm". It is a "hostile mockery full of hate," [21] "it insults mockingly." [22] Sacerdos differentiates between irony and sarcasm as follows: "irony contains a mocking meaning contrary to the words, while sarcasm must be understood in the way in which it was said, with a great deal of mockery." [23] The point seems to be that sarcasm is immediately understood as such, while irony may require a little thought. The usual example is from the *Aeneid*. In the last book, Turnus has downed the Trojan Eumedes with his javelin; wresting the victim's sword from his hand, he plunges it into his throat:

> *"en agros et quam bello, Troiane, petisti,*
> *Hesperiam metire iacens*: haec praemia, qui me
> ferro aussi temptare, ferunt, sic moenia condunt." [24]

Asteismos

One of the most interesting tropes appears last in the discussion of allegory. As Donatus says, it is a manifold trope with many applications. [25] Charisius is curiously restrained in his definition, remaining content with a mere "allegoria cum urbanitate." Donatus is more expansive—surprisingly so, for his definition seems very general by contrast to his usual precision: whatever is lacking in coarse simplicity and embellished with a fair amount of elegant refinement is considered *asteismos*. [26] Sacerdos, though briefer, is equally vague: it is a compound of urbanity and witty charm. [27] The vagueness is not dispelled by the Virgilian example, an ironic *allegoria*:

> qui Bavium non odit amet tua carmina, Maevi
> atque idem iungat vulpes et mulgeat hircos. [28]

---

[20] "puta de nescio quo loquebaris, et subito venit is, dicis tu 'lupus in fabula'..."

[21] Donatus: "... plena odio atque hostilis inrisio..."

[22] Pompeius: "... ironia cum inrisione hostili..."

[23] "inter ironiam ergo et sarcasmon hoc est, quod ironia contrarium dictioni continet sensum cum inrisione, sarcasmo vero eodem modo quo dicitur intellegatur necesse est, quamvis cum inrisione."

[24] "Lie there, measure out with your length, you Trojan, the land of Hesperia
You wanted to grab by aggression. This is the pay-off they get
Who dare to take arms against me: thus do they found their city.
(*Aen.* XII, 359 f.; Lewis, p. 300). The grammarians quote only the italicized words.

[25] "... tropus multiplex numerosaeque virtutis."

[26] "... astismos putatur quidquid simplicitate rustica caret et faceta satis urbanitate expolitum est..."

[27] "... urbanitate et faceta gratia composita..."

[28] *Buc.* 3, 90 f.: "Let him who hates not Bavius love your songs, Maevius, and let him also yoke and milk hegoats." *Virgil*, tr. H. Rushton Frairclough, rev. ed., 2 vols., (London & Cambridge, Mass.: Harvard & Heinemann, 1955); vol. I, p. 25.

Pompeius, whose commentary is a transcription of classroom lectures, exclaims: "nothing is more delightful, nothing more urbane. The two were terrible poets: he says that whoever likes this one should endure the punishment of liking the other one too: for no punishment were comparable." [29]

A brief historical excursus may explain the ambiguity. [30] Historically, the Greek ἀστεῖον was used in two senses: as the equivalent of *urbanum* etymologically and semantically, it stood for a general contrast between city and country manners; thence it came to mean refined, clever, elegant, witty. It also developed a more specific literary meaning, that of brief, clever, and pungent remarks. The same ambiguity— urbane tone present through a speech as opposed to specific, localized sharpness of wit—is present in Roman usage. Quintilian disagrees with Domitius Marsus, who restricted *urbanitas* to the latter meaning: "... to my thinking, *urbanity* involves the total absence of all that is incongruous, coarse, unpolished and exotic whether in thought, language, voice or gesture, and resides not so much in isolated sayings as in the whole complexion of our language, just as for the Greeks *Atticism* means that elegance of taste which was peculiar to Athens." [31]

The ambiguity is also inherent in the very attempt to define irony in terms of tropes. Although there is no question but that poets and narrative writers use the methods of indirection in such localized, "tropical" ways, they are even more crucial as structure and spirit. The notion of dramatic irony—a knowledge possessed by the audience but not by the character concerned—reveals the breadth of irony disregarded by the attempt to restrict it in the bounds of a trope. And when such structural techniques are used in conjunction with ironic tropes, does not a certain all-pervasive attitude result which colors every part of the work we are reading?

I would suggest that Charisius, by his unaccustomed brevity, and Donatus, by his unaccustomed vagueness, were accounting for the same intellectual recognition: that the whole idea of "literary tone," crucial in our encounter with imaginative literature, had not found a place in the stylistic tradition their grammars represented; that, in fact, such an idea *could* not find its place within a tradition of stylistic analysis cast in terms of tropes and figures. This seems to be confirmed by a linguistic and theoretical development from Quintilian to our grammarians. Quintilian does not know the word *charientismos*. He assigns

---

[29] "nihil suavius, nihil urbanius. Duo fuerunt pessimi poetae: dicit, qui istum amat, illud pro poena contingat, ut et illum amet: alia enim poena illi nulla talis erit."

[30] This entire paragraph is a summary of Mary A. Grant, *The Ancient Rhetorical Theories of the Laughable: The Greek Rhetoricians and Cicero*, in *University of Wisconsin Studies in Language and Literature*, vol. XXI (Madison: Wisconsin, 1924), pp. 123 ff.

[31] *The Institutio oratoria of Quintilian*, trans. H.E. Butler, 4 vols. (Cambridge, Mass., & London: Harvard & Heinemann, 1960), VI, iii, 107; vol. II, p. 499.

its function to *asteismos*: for Quintilian, it is *asteismos* that "urbanely says harsh things in gentle words," [32] not *charientismos*. Sacerdos, the earliest of our grammarians, notes that *asteismos* is called *charientismos* by others. [33] By the fourth century, however, all the grammarians agree in the basic definitions of the two terms we have given. These three steps trace a process in which the localized aspect of *urbanitas* was removed from *asteismos* and assigned to *charientismos*, which is then established as a trope; *asteismos*, still in the disguise of a trope, becomes the acknowledgement of the tropical system's insufficiency when confronted with the idea of ironic tone. [34]

---

[32] "... tristia dicamus mollioribus verbis urbanitatis gratia..." (*Inst.*, VIII, vi, 57; my translation).

[33] "Astimos, quem quidam charientismon dicunt..."

[34] It should also be noted that Donatus, in listing the subtypes of allegoria, explains that it has many forms of which he gives only the most prominent: "huius species multae sunt, ex quibus eminent... [etc.]."

It is hardly necessary to amass evidence that Donatus was well-known in the Middle-Ages: "c'est par centaines qu'il faudrait compter les manuscrits subsistants, malgré les destructions opérées par l'usage et la disparition des anciennes bibliothèques." (Paré *et al.*, *La renaissance du XII⁰ siècle...*, p. 152, referring to both Donatus and Priscian).

The distinction between Donatus' *Ars minor* (which deals only with the eight parts of speech) and the *Ars maïor* (a text for the whole course in *grammatica*) must be observed. The third book of the latter, *Barbarismus*, was frequently used as an independent book on style (*ibid.*, p. 151, n. 3).

On the specific matter of *allegoria* (the trope, not the four-fold system), a number of Christian writers used Donatus and other grammarians as the basis of further work. Cassiodorus used their definitions in his *Expositio in Psalterium* (Migne, *Patrologia latina*, Vol. LXX) to illustrate the thesis that the liberal arts antedate paganism and that all forms of figurative language exist in the Bible; his commentary is no more than "un exercice littéraire" (Riché, *Education et culture...*, p. 209). Isidore of Seville transmitted the doctrine of *allegoria* and its subtypes intact, although he reworded the definitions and substituted other pagan examples for those of the pagan grammarians (*Isidori Hispalensis Episcopi Etymologiarum sive Originum Libri XX*, ed. W.M. Lindsay, 2 vols. [Oxford 1911], I, xxxvii, 22-30); his definitions and examples will be found in the footnotes of the next chapter, at the beginning of the section on each trope. His work was amplified by Julian of Toledo whose general practice (in the section on *allegoria*) is to quote Donatus *verbatim*, then to quote Isidore *verbatim*, and finally to add examples of his own which are drawn both from Virgil and the Bible (Julian of Toledo, *De vitiis et figuris*, ed. W.M. Lindsay, in *St. Andrews University Publications*, vol. XV [Oxford, 1922], pp. 36 ff.). Bede's *De schematibus et tropis* takes the definitions of *allegoria* and its subtypes *verbatim* from Donatus (except *antiphrasis*, taken *verbatim* from Isidore), but the examples are taken exclusively from the Bible (text in Karl Felix von Halm, *Rhetores latini minores* [Leipzig: Teubner, 1863], pp. 615-618, as well as in Migne, *P.L.* XC, 175 ff.). In the twelfth century, however, Hugh of St. Victor returns to Donatus and pagan examples in his *De grammatica* ("Le *De grammatica* de Hugues de Saint-Victor," ed. Jean Leclerq, in *Archives d'Histoire Doctrinale et Littéraire du Moyen Age* [Paris: Vrin, 1943], vol. XVIII, pp. 263-322).

RHETORIC: SIGNIFICATIO

The theory of *allegoria* was expounded in texts belonging to the sphere of grammar, the secondary level of classical education whose main concern was the analysis of traditional literary works. The third and culminating level was that of rhetoric, which added a different set of techniques by which meaning could be indirectly revealed for ironic purposes: *significatio,* and its several forms. This is discussed in the *Rhetorica ad Herennium,* which the Middle Ages, following St. Jerome, attributed to Cicero, as one of the figures of thought. [35]

Significatio

The figure is described in general terms as leaving "more to be suspected than has been actually asserted." Its five forms are pro-

---

[35] [Cicero], *Ad C. Herennium: De ratione dicendi (Rhetorica ad Herennium),* ed. & trans. Harry Caplan (Cambridge, Mass., & London: Harvard & Heinemann, 1954). *Significatio* is the Latin equivalent of the Greek εμψασις ; Caplan uses the latter's English derivative "emphasis", which is somewhat inappropriate, since the "emphasis" is not obtained by obvious stress but by suggestion or insinuation (the terms used by Charles Sears Baldwin, *Medieval Rhetoric and Poetic* [New York: Macmillan], 1928, p. 185). Unless otherwise noted, translations in quotes are Caplan's.

Quintilian also deals with *significatio,* but his treatment, scattered throughout the *Institutes,* is less systematic than the *ad Herennium's.* He considers it one of the essential qualities of style (VII, iii, 61 ff.) and a *sine qua non* of rhetoric (IX, ii, 65). Nevertheless, he objects to the fact that the name *schema* (figure) has been almost entirely restricted to this technique by contemporary rhetoricians (IX, ii, 65). This seeming disparity may be explained by distinguishing an occasional, localized use of the device from its adoption as the basic strategy of an entire speech: Quintilian seems to reserve his objections for the latter (Richard Volkmann, *Hermagoras oder Elemente der Rhetorik* [Stettin: Nahmer, 1865], p. 288 f.).

On the possible influence of Quintilian on the Middle Ages (especially the twelfth century), compare Paul Lehmann, "Die *Institutio oratoria* des Quintilians im Mittelalter," *Philologus,* LXXXIX, Neue Folge (1934), 349-383, for whom Quintilian played only a *Nebenrolle,* to the articles of A. Mollard: "L'imitation de Quintilien dans Guibert de Nogent," *Moyen Age,* V (1934), 81-87, and "La diffusion de l'*Institution oratoire* au XIIᵉ siècle," *Ibid.,* 161-175, and VI (1935), 1-9.

The expansion of indirection as basic rhetorical strategy can be seen in two late rhetoricians, C. Julius Victor and especially C. Chirius Fortunantianus. The former's *Ars rhetorica* (Halm, *Rhetores latini...,* pp. 434 ff.) contains two chapters, "De figuratis" and "De obliquitate" which are almost entirely a pastiche of Quintilian's discussion of the *controversiae figuratae (Inst.,* IX, ii, 65-99). Fortunantianus, in his *Ars rhetorica,* systematically elaborates the subject in his section on *ductus* (Halm, *op. cit.,* pp. 84-6), which is later summarized by Martianus Capella in *De nuptiis Philologiae et Mercurii* (ed. Adolphus Dick [Leipzig: Teubner, 1925], p. 235 f.).

These two rhetoricians appear to have had some influence in the Middle Ages (Abelson, *The Seven Liberal Arts,* p. 56 f.). Their discussion, however, is too broad for use in stylistic analysis.

duced by exaggeration, ambiguity, (logical) consequence, a breaking off in the middle of a speech, and analogy. [36]

Significatio per exsuperationem

That this is hyperbole is clear from the definition: it is produced "when more is said than the truth warrants." The *auctor ad Herennium* also discusses hyperbole as a figure of diction under the name *superlatio*; a comparison of his examples is instructive. The first in *superlatio* is: "But if we maintain concord in the state, we shall measure the empire's vastness by the rising and the setting of the sun." Another, taken from Homer, is: "From his mouth speech flowed sweeter than honey." [37] Both of these, as well as the other examples of *superlatio,* are clearly intended to praise or augment their subject. As a form of *significatio,* however, hyperbole has a different function, as the *auctor's* example shows: "Out of so great a patrimony, in so short a time, this man has not laid by even an earthen pitcher wherewith to seek a fire for himself." [38] There is hyperbole and hyperbole: "straight", where the intention is to augment and praise, ironic, where exaggeration is a means of subtracting from the subject.

Significatio per ambiguum

Or, as we say in English, the pun: *significatio* "is produced through ambiguity when a word can be taken in two or more senses, but yet is taken in that sense which the speaker intends..." The example is: "Prospice tu, qui plurimum cernis." [39] As Caplan explains, "the play is upon the double meaning of *cernere*: to 'discern' and, in judicial language, 'to enter upon an inheritance;' thus: 'you who know exceedingly well how to enter upon bequests.' " [40]

Significatio per consequentiam

The next two forms of *significatio* are closely related. The first states a symbolic fact and a practical conclusion, suggesting a general principle; the second states a symbolic fact, but stresses the withholding of the conclusion. *Significatio* "is produced by Logical Consequence when one mentions the things that follow from a given

---

[36] "Significatio est res quae plus in suspicione relinquit quam positum est in oratione. Ea fit per exsuperationem, ambiguum, consequentiam, abscisionem, similitudinem." The section on *significatio* is in IV, liii, 67; Caplan, pp. 400-403.

[37] *Iliad* I, 249; *superlatio* is in IV, xxxiii, 44; Caplan, pp. 338-41.

[38] "Per exsuperationem [significatio fit], cum plus est dictum quam patitur veritas, augendae suspicionis causa, sic: 'Hic de tanto patrimonio tam cito testam qui sibi petat ignem non reliquit."

[39] "Per ambiguum [significatio fit], cum verbum potest in duas pluresve sententias accipi, sed accipitur tamen in eam partem quam vult is qui dixit; ut de eo si dicas qui multas hereditates adierit: "Prospice tu, qui plurimum cernis.'"

[40] *Op. cit.,* p. 401, n. g.

circumstance, thus leaving the whole matter in distrust; for example, if you should say to the son of a fish-monger: 'Quiet, you whose father used to wipe his nose with his forearm.' " [41] The fact of base descent and its implication of untrustworthiness or lack of qualification for discussion is not stated, merely suggested.

Significatio per abscisionem

This is structurally the same as aposiopesis: both work by a statement that the speaker is not pursuing his thought to its inevitable conclusion. *Significatio* "is produced through Aposiopesis if we begin to say something and then stop short, and what we have already said leaves enough to arouse suspicion, as follows: 'He who so handsome and so young, recently at a stranger's house—I am unwilling to say more.' " [42]

Significatio per similitudinem

The last form of *significatio* "is produced through Analogy, when we cite some analogue and do not amplify it, but by its means intimate is what we are thinking, as follows: 'Do not, Saturnius, rely too much on the popular mob—unavenged lie the Gracchi.' " [43]

The *auctor* concludes his discussion of *significatio* with the comment that "this figure possesses liveliness and distinction in the highest degree; indeed, it permits the hearer himself to guess what the speaker has not mentioned. [44]

---

[41] "Per consequentiam significatio fit cum res quae sequantur aliquam rem dicuntur, ex quibus tota res relinquitur in suspicione; ut si salsamentarii filio dicas: 'Quiesce tu, cuius pater cubito se emungere solebat.'"

[42] "Per abscisionem [significatio fit], si, cum incipimus aliquid dicere, deinde praecidamus, et ex eo quod iam diximus satis relinquitur suspicionis, sic: 'Qui ista forma et aetate nuper alienae domi—nolo plura dicere.'"

[43] "Per similitudinem [significatio fit], cum aliqua re simili allata nihil amplius dicimus, sed ex ea significamus quid sentiamus, hoc modo: 'Noli, Saturnine, nimium populi frequentia fretus esse; inulti iacent Gracci.'"

[44] "Haec exornatio plurimum festivitatis habet interdum et dignitatis; sinit enim quiddam tacito oratore ipsum auditorem suspicari."

Although the *ad Herennium* was one of the major authorities for rhetorical and poetic theory in the Middle Ages (Edmond Faral, *Les Arts poétiques du XIIᵉ et du XIIIᵉ siècle, Recherches et documents sur la technique littéraire du moyen âge*, in *Bibliothèque de l'Ecole des Hautes Etudes*, vol. 238 [Paris: Champion, 1958], pp. 99-103), its influence in the twelfth century as measured by surviving manuscripts and the number of imitations is not to be compared with that of Donatus. Its *Fortleben* is traced by Karl Manitius, "Zur Überlieferung des sogenannten Auctor ad Herennium," *Philologus*, C (1956), 62-66, and by Dorothy Grosser's unpublished dissertation, "Studies in the Influence of the *Rhetorica ad Herennium* and Cicero's *De Inventione*," (Cornell, 1953), especially chapters 4 ("The Arts of Poetry of the Twelfth Century," pp. 128-168) and 5 ("MSS. of *De Inventione* and the *Rhetorica ad Herennium* in Medieval Catalogues"). She concludes that the twelfth century marks the beginning of

It is obvious that the techniques of *allegoria* and *significatio* represent minimal forms of literary indirection, such as might appropriately be taught to schoolboys. Their very simplicity, however, gives them a certain serviceability as the first step in investigating a medieval author's use of stylistic resources to suggest ironic meanings and interpretations of his characters' words and actions. The importance of such techniques in medieval education is indicated by two remarks, one from the seventh century, the other from the twelfth. For Isidore of Seville, obliquity is an essential characteristic of poetic language:

> Officium autem poetae in eo est ut ea, quae vere gesta sunt, *in alias species obliquis figurationibus* cum decore aliquo conversa transducant. [45]

And, in the century of Chrétien de Troyes, Matthew of Vendome will discuss the trope *allegoria*. Mentioning the fact that it has seven subtypes, he explains that he will deal only with the least known (*de minus ventilata*), *aenigma*. The implication is that *allegoria* was too important to be omitted, but that it and its subtypes were so well-known, with one exception, that it was unnecessary to discuss them in detail. [46]

---

more extensive use of the *ad Herennium,* though it is considered secondary to *De Inventione* (p. 288).

As far as *significatio* is concerned, the first use of the *ad Herennium* I have found is that of Geoffroi de Vinsauf in his *Poetria Nova* (in Faral, *op. cit.,* p. 244 f.); this, dated by Faral between 1208 and 1213 (*ibid.,* p. 33), postdates Chrétien de Troyes. Geoffroi's text on *significatio* will be found in the footnotes of the next chapter under each of its forms.

[45] *Etym.* VIII, vii, 10. Isidore probably had this notion from Servius, who stated it often; see Charles de Trooz, "La critique de Virgile dans les Commentaires de Servius," *Musée Belge,* XXXIII (1929), 229-261; p. 244.

[46] *Ars versificatoria* III, 43; Faral, p. 177. There are a number of studies dealing with the style of Chrétien de Troyes to which I have not had occasion to refer in this thesis. I list them in chronological order: R.G. Grosse, *Der Stil des Crestiens von Troies,* in *Französische Studien,* XXV (1908), 127-260; Gunnar Biller, *Etude sur le style des premiers romans français en vers (1150-75),* in *Göteborg Högskolas Arsskrift,* IV (1916); Tatiana Fotich, *The Narrative Tenses in Chrétien de Troyes, A Study in Style and Stylistics,* in *Catholic University of America: Studies in Romance Languages and Literature,* vol. XXXVII (Washington, D.C., 1950); Jean Frappier, "Le tour je me sui chez Chrétien de Troyes," *Romance Philology* IX (1955-6) 126-33; S. Heinimann, "Zur stilgeschichtlichen Stellung Chrétiens," in *Mélanges de linguistique et de littérature romanes à la mémoire d'Istvan Frank,* in *Annales Universitatis Saraviensis,* VI (1957), pp. 235-49; Helmut Hatzfeld, "Deuten Stilelemente in Chrétiens Perceval auf eine strukturelle Einheit?" in *Medium Aevum Romanicum, Festschrift für Hans Rheinfelder,* ed. Heinrich Bihler and Alfred Noyer-Weidner (München: Hueber, 1963).

CHAPTER I

CLIGES

The special character of *Cligès* among Chrétien's romances has often been remarked, sometimes pejoratively. [1] While the action of the truly Arthurian romances is generally bathed in a strange atmosphere of mystery varied by the unexplained entrances of intriguing personages whose presence seems to suggest a meaning always beyond our intellectual grasp, *Cligès* shines with such a brilliance of dialectically deployed reasoning, of clearly defined motivation and plot-structure, of unmistakable literary reference and adaptation of available sources, that it has given rise to as many contradictory interpretations as any of Chrétien's other works. [2] Alternately praised and damned for its "artificiality", [3] one of the few notes of agreement to which *Cligès* has brought at least some of its critics is that it should be a locus for a study of its author's literary techniques: "Any study of the person,

---

[1] The harshest criticism is that of Gaston Paris: "Cligès est celui de tous les poèmes de Chrétien qui a pour nous le moins d'attraits; le style en est particulièrement pénible et maniéré; les sentiments y sont décrits et exprimés avec une froide subtilité; les caractères y sont faiblement ou banalement tracés; le vieux motif oriental sur lequel le roman est construit y est, peu heureusement, altéré dans le détail (le changement que le poète a introduit dans l'esprit même de ce motif est au contraire très admissible), et une introduction inutile et parfaitement ennuyeuse, sortie de l'invention du poète, fait attendre trop longtemps au lecteur le vrai commencement de l'action." *Mélanges de littérature française du moyen âge* (Paris: Champion, 1912), pp. 229-327; p. 309; reprinted from the *Journal des Savants,* (1902), 57-69, 289-309, 345-357, 438-458, 641-655. Even the most recent and sympathetic treatment of the romance, that of Jean Frappier, is frequently defensive: *Le roman breton; Chrétien de Troyes: Cligès* (Paris: Centre de Documentation Universitaire, 1958).

[2] Most of these have centered around the relation of *Cligès* to *Tristan.* For Wendelin Foerster, it was an anti-*Tristan* (Introduction to his edition of *Cligès* in *Romanische Bibliothek,* No. 1 [Halle: Niemeyer, 1901]; for Alexandre Micha, a *Tristan revue et corrigé* ("Tristan et Cligès," *Neophilologus,* XXXVI [1952], 1-10); for Frappier, a neo-*Tristan* or a transposition of the *Tristan* (*op. cit.,* and *Chrétien de Troyes, l'homme et l'œuvre,* in *Connaissance des Lettres,* Vol. 50 [Paris: Hatier, 1957]). Further references in this last work, pp. 249 ff. I have generally avoided consideration of the relation between *Cligès* and *Tristan* for the sake of clarity and simplicity. However, see below, pp. 56 f., 80 f., 89 f., 100, 103, 106.

[3] For damnation, see the quotation from G. Paris in fn. 1 to this chapter; for praise, the references to van Hamel and Frappier in the footnote below.

talent, or work of Chrétien must be based on a detailed analysis of
Cligès ... nowhere else than in *Cligès* is revealed more clearly the
moralist, the psychologist, the artist—let us add, the plagiarist—that
was Chrétien de Troyes." [4]

It is, of course, its very "artificiality"—a term pejorative only to the
narrowest interpretations of the artistic *mimesis*—which renders the
romance so apt for stylistic and technical analysis. To a large extent,
it is a bravura display by a young writer confident enough in the
admiration of his audience to rehearse, at the opening of a new work,
the bibliography of his former publications, and to pit against these
former achievements the present evidence of his creative powers. This
beginning in itself is already a recognition by the author and an
indication to his audience that the romance to follow is intended to
impress by skill and literary prowess rather than affect and mystery.
It is artificial in the admirable sense of the word, suggesting a compact
between author and audience at the very entrance to the aesthetic
world, a compact in which both writer and reader agree to a large
measure of gratuitous adventure which, without denying the possibility of serious concerns and implication, is directed primarily to
aesthetic delight in the tools of literature themselves. Chrétien opens
his romance by calling attention to himself as a literary creator; he
invites us to enjoy his creation at the same level that he enjoyed writing
it; *Cligès* is a *romancier*'s romance.

Our procedure in this chapter will be to begin with the most elementary forms of irony, the stylistic devices defined under *allegoria*
and *significatio*. As might be expected in a narrative, the study of
style will inevitably involve us in considerations of character portrayal
and structure as contextual to particular stylistic effects. In each case,
we will start with a fairly obvious and low-level example of the technique, and then move on to variations from the formal norm represented
by the grammatical and rhetorical definitions which are the individual
writer's adaptation of school formulae to literary art. In the second
section, we will examine a few literary elements (primarily grammatical
structures and traditional literary materials) which are ironized. The
third section will consider large-scale structural ironies, and will
approach—though by no means embrace—the relation between Chrétien's
constant use of irony in *Cligès* and the meaning of the romance.

---

    [4] "Toute étude de la personne, du talent, de l'œuvre de Chrétien devra
prendre pour base une analyse minutieuse de *Cligès* ... nulle part ne se révèle
plus clairement que dans *Cligès,* le moraliste, le psychologue, l'artiste—ajoutons,
le plagiaire—qu'a été Chrétien de Troyes."   A.G. van Hamel, "Cligès et Tristan," *Romania,* XXXIII (1904), 465-489; p. 486.   See also Paris, *loc. cit.,* and
Frappier, *Cligès,* pp. 89-103.

ALLEGORIA

Allegoria [5]

The first example of *allegoria* is also an example of a frequent technique in the *chansons de geste,* that of epic irony. Alexander attacks a man in battle:

> Si cruelment le fiert an haste
> Que l'ame de son cors li oste,
> Et li ostex remest sanz oste. (1752-4) [6]

This is a remarkably compact allegory: both the literal and figurative levels are stated in two lines, and include three reinforcing devices: the chiastic inversion between the two levels (contained, container/ container, contained—the allegory is based on a metonymic relationship); this allows the poet an end-stopped rhyme on one of the figurative words, which, since they are homonyms, is also paranomasia. In so far as the allegory communicates an unpleasant reality in apparently pleasant words, we might also consider this an example of *charientismos.*

An allegorically described battle can have a more humorous effect when its vocabulary is taken from a lower social register:

> Molt sont andui li vasal large
> De cos doner a grant planté,
> S'a chascuns boene volanté
> De tost randre ce qu'il acroit,
> Ne cil ne cist ne s'an recroit,
> Que tot sanz conte et sanz mesure
> Ne rande chetel et ousure
> Li uns a l'autre sanz respit. (4034-41)

---

[5] As a reminder, the definition of these terms will be provided in the first footnote to the section on each trope; for variety's sake, the definitions will be Isidore's (*Etymologiarum* I, xxxvii, 22-30). "Allegoria est alieniloquium. Aliud enim sonat, et aliud intelligitur, ut (Virg. Aen. I, 184):

> Tres litore cervos
> conspicit errantes.

Vbi tres duces belli Punici, vel tria bella Punica significantur. Et in Bucolicis (3, 71):
> Aurea mala decem misi,

id est ad Augustum decem eglogas pastorum." (*Etym.,* I, xxxvii, 22).

[6] Unless otherwise specified, all references to the romances of Chrétien de Troyes (except the *Perceval*) are to the editions of the *Classiques Français du Moyen Âge,* all published in Paris by Champion under the general editorship of Mario Roques: *Erec et Enide,* ed. Mario Roques, in *CFMA,* Vol. 80 (1955); *Cligès,* ed. Alexandre Micha, *CFMA,* Vol. 84 (1957); *Le chevalier au lyon (Yvain),* ed. Mario Roques, *CFMA,* Vol. 89 (1960); *Le chevalier de la charrete,* ed. Mario Roques, *CFMA,* Vol. 86 (1958). For the *Perceval,* I have used *Der Percevalroman (Li Contes del Graal),* ed. Alfons Hilka, which is Vol. 5 in Foerster's *Grosse Aufgabe* (Halle: Niemeyer, 1932). For the sake of convenience, I refer to the romances by the name of the hero.

The basic allegory of these lines is the idea of exchange, peaceful rather than warlike, but it does not actually take allegorical form until the last lines. Each of the first three lines contains an example of *ironia* (generosity, plentiful giving, good will; all terms of peaceful exchange, perhaps of gifts), but these are too imprecise to form an allegory. It is only in the last two lines, where the non-warring form of exchange is specified as money-lending with technical terms of capital and usurious profit, that the passages retroactively takes form as an allegory. A further irony is that the passage begins with the metaphoric invocation of the courtly virtue of *largesce* but degenerates into the uncourtly metaphor of money-lending.

From death and battle, we move to marriage. Alexander having conquered Windsor castle in which the traitor Angrès and his men had taken refuge, Arthur grants him a kingdom and the Queen takes upon herself the role of marriage broker. So the young hero had three joys and three honors: the castle he took, the kingdom promised him, but

> La graindre joie fu la tierce,
> De ce que s'amie fu fierce*   *queen, in chess
> De l'eschaquier don il fu rois. (2333-5)

The marriage, which is the reward of Alexander's knightly exploits, is figuratively portrayed under the integument of the most exciting and least bloody war-game, chess; the game is over, and has been won by Alexander. It should be noted that this last implication is available to us only from our knowledge of the context, not from the quotation itself. We know that this is the climax of the hero's adventures—knightly and amorous—at Arthur's court, and are able to provide the context for this particular allegory.

This principle of contextuality is crucial for the analysis of irony. Though certain occasional ironies, such as the first two examples of epic irony, are fairly obvious in immediate terms (i.e., their context is immediately present), it is often necessary to recall a larger context for the placement of ironic tone. The context may extend to a speech or monologue, a given scene or section of the work, or indeed, to the work as a whole. [7] This is the source of the error made by those critics who have treated the admittedly lengthy monologues of *Cligès* as theoretical arguments in the doctrine of courtly love, rather than as expressions of particular characters in particular situations. As doctrine, they are unutterably tiresome; as a combination of character portrayal and literary virtuosity, they are revealing and delightful.

Alexander, in love, thinks he is ill. The Ovidian metaphor was hardly new at the time Chrétien wrote *Cligès*: a good case has been made for the Old French *Eneas* as Chrétien's source for both the form of the monologue and many of the Ovidian metaphors with which the

---

[7] For an example of a particular irony using the entire work—or at least two thirds of it—as its context, see below, p. 57 f.

form is filled. [8]   It has even been suggested that not only Chrétien, but the author of his source, the *Eneas,* was already using these ironically. [9] This would indicate that by the middle of the XIIth century, the introspective courtly character had already become sufficiently commonplace to make it difficult for an author to take his introspection seriously:

> "A chascun mal n'a pas mecine.
> Li miens est si anracinez,
> Qu'il ne puet estre mecinez.
> Ne puet? Je cuit que j'ai manti.
> Des que primes cest mal santi,
> Se l'osasse mostrer et dire,
> Poïsse je parler au mire,
> Qui de tot me porroit eidier.
> Mes molt m'est grief a empleidier,
> Espoir n'i daigneroit antendre,
> Ne nul loier n'an voldroit prandre." (642-52)

If love is an illness according to the traditional metaphor, we provide a doctor to cure it.   Paradoxically, the doctor, if we recall the context, is the cause of the illness.   Alexander, timid despite his prowess as a knight, was unable to speak his love to Soredamors, and starts his monologue by ridiculing himself for being unable to say what he thinks (618-24).   The illness is not only love, but his inability to verbalize this emotion when it counts: to Soredamors.   The scene these lines portray is a fantasied one in which Alexander declares his love, not as a proud knight, but as a patient pleading for help from his doctor.   This fantasy is not an entirely gratuitous renovation of a tired metaphor, however: as is true of the entire monologue, it embodies a perfectly sound psychological principle, as any shy man who has cursed himself for not speaking to an attractive woman at the first possible opportunity can testify. [10]   But we are not allowed to commiserate too long or deeply with shy Alexander. [11]   The last line quoted carries the extension of the cliché one allegorical step further.   We started with an illness, then found a doctor.   But doctors are paid a

---

[8] Alexandre Micha, *"Eneas et Cligès,"* in *Mélanges de philologie romane et de littérature médiévale offerts à Ernest Hoeppfner,* (Paris: Les Belles-Lettres, 1949), pp. 237-43.   It is not necessary to posit Ovid and *Eneas* as exclusive alternatives.   Chrétien had undoubtedly read Virgil and Ovid.   As a professional writer, he was equally undoubtedly interested in his predecessors' adaptations and translations of Latin works into Old French.   Like any professional writer, he was indebted to these predecessors.

[9] Frappier, *Cligès,* p. 73.

[10] Compare Frappier's fine comments on the *refoulement amoureux, ibid.,* p. 88.

[11] This oxymoron—"shy Alexander"—is an irony of character Chrétien does not use stylistically.   Nevertheless, in so far as he is shy, the character whose name is that of Alexander the Great bears an ironic relationship to his name.

fee (*loier*), and if we recall the context of the allegory, what is the fee a lover can pay his lady commensurate with her efforts? [12]

Later in the monologue, the illness is metamorphosed into a wound caused by love's arrow which has paradoxically left no sign of a wound. After nearly a hundred lines of variations on this theme, Alexander describes the arrow itself (762ff.), but does it so ambiguously at first that we are quite uncertain of the allegory's referent:

> "La floiche et li penon ansanble
> Sont si pres, qui bien les ravise,
> Que il n'i a c'une devise
> Ausi con d'une greve estroite;
> Mes ele est si polie et droite
> Qu'an la rote sanz demander
> N'a rien qui face a amander."   (770-6) [13]

It is only when Alexander begins to describe the *penon* as golden (778) and identifies them as *treces sores* (782) that we understand him to be referring to Soredamors' golden hair, its part in the middle, and the long tresses hanging down her side. [14] But Alexander is no mere stand-in for "Chrétien the rhetorician": he is a young man in love, and so desirous of physical possession that he quite forgets the distinction between the metaphorical and literal levels to launch into a description of the arrow's forehead, eyes, mouth, nose, teeth, chin and ears! He saw the breast as far as the fastener; it was whiter than snow ... but this glimpse of a white heaven was only a teaser:

> "Bien fust ma dolors alegiee,
> Se tot le dart veü eüsse.
> Molt volantiers, se je seüsse,
> Deïsse quex an est la floiche:
> Ne la vi pas, n'an moi ne poiche,*   *that's not my
> Se la façon dire n'an sai   fault
> De chose que veüe n'ai.

---

[12] Chrétien's source for the theme of love as illness and love as its own cure is Lavinia's monologue in the *Eneas* (see note 11 above, and Edmond Faral, *Recherches sur les sources latines des contes et romans courtois du moyen âge* [Paris: Champion, 1913] p. 144 j.; the monologue is ll. 8083ff. in *Eneas, roman du XIIe siècle*, 2 vols. ed. J.-J. Salverda de Grave, in *CFMA*, vols. 44 and 62 [Paris: Champion, 1964 and 1929]; see also the preceding conversation between Lavinia and her mother, ll. 7857ff.). There, however, love is the personification *Amors, qui navre et sane an un jor* (7992). In Alexander's case, the passage with which we have dealt occurs at the beginning of the monologue, before the personification *Amors* enters his day-dream: it is still Soredamors herself who is the referent of this allegory. In these lines, the change Chrétien has wrought on his material from *Eneas* is individuation. In the monologue as a whole, however, the basic technical difference is that the *Eneas* monologue remains within the *Amors* allegory throughout, while Chrétien delights in shifting from the figurative (allegorical) level to the literal: see the following paragraphs.

[13] In so far as this allegory is incomprehensible until explained, it is an example of *aenigma*; cf. *infra*, p. 34 f.

[14] Fappier, *op. cit.*, p. 86.

Ne m'an mostra Amors adons
Fors que la coche* et les penons,   *notch in the
Car la fleche ert el coivre mise: arrow's base
C'est li bliauz et la chemise,
Don la pucele estoit vestue." (838-49)

This is the direction of a young man's thoughts wandering about his "Lady" in a pleasantly sensual way, and of older men too, if we can take Andrew Marvell's "To His Coy Mistress" as evidence. But what might be the occasion for unease among readers too delicate for such indulgence is saved by an amazing *tour de force*: having spent forty-five lines (800-44) describing the bust of a person and disregarding the distinction between the allegorical and literal levels altogether, Chrétien returns us to that distinction with a shock. The referent for this entire description was the little bit of the arrow that is left in sight when the arrow is stored in the quiver: streamers, and a small length of the shaft with a notch at its base, *i.e.*, Soredamors' golden hair, its part, and her neck and the exposed part of her bosom, are shrunk to the size of a miniature or medallion in a sudden reduction of scale. The length and detail of the description serve not only to make us forget the original metaphorical basis, but by doing so, create the surprise of its remainder. At the same time the unease or—in the case of less delicate readers—the pleasure caused by the suggestiveness of Alexander's direction of thought is transmuted into aesthetic awareness and delight.

Ironia [15]

The simplest form of irony described by the grammarians—meaning the precise opposite of what is said—is comparatively infrequent in *Cligès*. Certain examples of epic irony can be accommodated in this category. Alexander, having disposed of one opponent in battle,

A un autre offre son servise... (1750);

he wreaks havoc on the field of battle, and

Si conpaignon resont si large
De sanc et de cervele espandre.... (1766 f.)

---

[15] "Ironia est sententia per pronuntiationem contrarium habens intellectum. Hoc enim tropo callide aut per accusationem, aut per insultationem aliquid dicitur, ut est illud (Virg. Aen. I, 140):

Vestras, Eure, domos; illa se iactet in aula
Aeolus, et clauso ventorum carcere regnet.

Et quomodo aula, si carcer est? Solvitur enim pronuntiatione. Nam carcer pronuntiatio est: iactet et aula ironia est; et totum per contrariam pronuntiationem adnuntiatur per ironiae speciem, quae laudando deridet." (*Etym.*, I, xxxvii, 23.)

The qualification, universal among the grammarians, that it is by the manner of speaking that irony is indicated, is useless to us: we obviously have no information as to the manner in which Chrétien read his text, either to himself, or perhaps, to an intimate audience.

3

Though equally valid as examples of *charientismos,* these can be considered *ironia* in so far as the tone of the words (offering one's service, being generous) is directly contrary to the fact they communicate.

Nevertheless, there are quite a few pungent examples of *ironia* in this romance. When the ladies of the palace in Constantinople are spying on the *troi fisicïen de Salerne,* they realize the atrocious torture to which the "corpse" of Fénice is being subjected:

> ... les dames vont lor desserte
> As trois mires doner et rendre... (5958 f.)

The doctors' "reward" is to be thrown out the window into the palace courtyard:

> Si que tuit troi ont peçoiez
> Cos, et costez, et braz, et james.
> Einz mialz nel firent nules dames.
> Or ont eü molt malemant
> Li troi mire lor paiemant,
> Car les dames les ont paiez. (5964-9)

The irony here seems to be weakened by the adverb *malemant,* a rather unnecessary qualifier. However, it leads by rhyme into the reinforcing paranomasia of *paiemant: paiez.*

An extensive *ironia* is Thessala's speech in which she persuades Cligès to serve the emperor Alis a magic potion which will safeguard Fénice's virginity by inducing her husband to dream of his conquest while, in fact, he leaves Fénice intact. Chrétien's audience has heard this potion described (3156-74), but Cligès knows nothing about it:

> "Amis, dist ele, a cest mangier
> Voel l'empereor losangier
> D'un boivre qu'il avra molt chier;
> ....
> Je cuit que molt amer le doive,
> C'onques de si boen ne gosta...
> ....
> Se par avanture l'enquiert,
> Sachiez que a tant peis en iert.*   *everything will
> ....   be fine
> ... li boivres est clers, et sains,
> Et de boenes espices plains..." (3239-64)

The irony of these lines, however, is addressed to the audience, not to Cligès, who, unaware of the true character of the drink, accepts Thessala's words literally. The *ironia,* therefore, is predicated on a dramatic irony in which we share knowledge with one character which is denied another character. Dramatic irony is not only a frequent technique in *Cligès*: it is so basic a strategy of Chréten's that it largely determines the tone of the romance. [16]

---

[16] *Infra,* pp. 43 f., 49 f., 86 f., 89, 91.

Another example of this double irony—tropical and dramatic—occurs when Alis orders a tomb for his "dead" wife. Cligès' servant, Jehan, describes a tomb he has already built and prepared at his master's order:

> "Or soit en leu de saintuaire
> L'empererriz dedanz anclose,
> Qu'ele est, ce cuit, molt sainte chose." (6010-2)

Both the reader and Jehan know that Fénice is neither "saintly" nor dead, that she is feigning death to escape her husband and belong entirely and exclusively to Cligès. Again, it is our privileged knowledge, not shared by Alis, which enables us to see Jehan's words as ironic. [17]

Earlier in the story, the same stratagem of the feigned death led the entire city to intone one of those *complaintes* against death so frequent in medieval literature. [18] Death was attacked in the harshest terms:

> "Dex, quel enui et quel contraire
> Nos a fet la morz deputaire*!   *despicable
> Morz, trop est male, et covoiteuse,
> Et sorprenanz, et envïeuse,
> Qui ne puez estre saoulee." (*etc.*) (5719-23)

Our knowledge that Fénice's death is feigned prevents identification with the mourners and enables us to appreciate the same irony noted in the previous example, when Fénice is first described as

> "La meillor chose et la plus sainte..." (5728),

and when she is clothed in an unmistakably religious light:

> "D'une clarté, d'une lumiere
> Avoit Dex le mont alumé." (5770 f.) [19]

The incongruity of the religious tone and imagery with the mundane fact of a deceitful young girl is obvious.

---

[17] Compare Erich Kohler: "Chrestien ist est zweifellos ernst damit; alles andere wäre nicht Ironie, sondern eine für ihn unverständliche Frivolität." *Ideal und Wirklichkeit in der höfischen Epik; Studien zur Form der frühen Artus- und Graldichtung,* in *Beihefte zur Zeitschrift für Romanische Philologie,* Heft 97 (Tübingen: Niemeyer, 1956), p. 162, n. 2.

[18] Chrétien himself had used the form before Cligès: once in *Philomena* (*Philomena, conte raconté d'après Ovide,* ed. Charles de Boer, [Paris: Geuthner, 1909], ll. 979-1004; and again in *Erec et Enide,* ll. 4570-4631. The latter has little of the accusatory nature common to the genre. Both, however, resemble the *complainte* in *Cligès* in being occasioned by "false deaths". However, there is little indication of ironic intent in either of these earlier versions.

[19] At this point, the *complainte* has become part of the conversation of the townspeople with the three Salernian doctors.

Antiphrasis [20]

For the classical grammarians and their medieval followers, this trope was defined by the contradiction between the current meaning of a word and the meaning of what was thought to be its etymon. Therefore the location of antiphrasis in the strict sense depends on knowledge by the critic of the etymological consciousness of the writer or speaker—a precondition we cannot meet in the case of a medieval writer unless he specifically indicates this conscious contradiction. Chrétien never does this, but there is one exceptional case in which the symbolic meaning of a word is clearly in contradiction with its use. As Soredamors herself informs us, her name means *sororee d'amors,* the Blonde of Love (972). Blondes are the best (962), and particularly appropriate to *fine amors* (963-6). Therefore, in so far as Soredamors remains *desdaigneuse d'amors* (440), she bears an antiphrastic relationship to her own name. [21]

It is possible that the name of *Cligès'* other heroine is similarly used. The phoenix, after whom Fénice is named, was used in clerical literature as a symbol of the faithful wife. [22] If Chrétien had this in mind—and it must be said that there is no verbal evidence comparable to that in Soredamors' case—he surely named the young girl who was to cheat ner husband of his first night's pleasure and marital rights, evade him with a lover, ridicule him in the eyes of the world, and eventually cause his death, with an ironic smile on his face.

Aenigma [23]

Truly enigmatic language is rare in *Cligès*; there are no riddles as such, and few statements of such obliquity that they have no meaning without explanation. We have already seen one of the latter in the

---

[20] "Antiphrasis est sermo e contrario intellegendus, ut 'lucus', quia caret lucem per nimiam nemorum umbram; et 'manes,' id est mites (quum sint inmites) et modesti, cum sint terribilis et inmanes; et 'Parcas' et 'Eumenides,' Furiae quod nulli parcant vel beneficiant. Hoc tropo et nani Athlantes et caecividentes et vulgo Aethiopes argentei appellantur. Inter ironia autem et antiphrasim hoc distat, quod ironia pronuntiatione sola indicat quod intellegi vult, sicut cum dicimus omnia agenti male: 'Bonum est, quo facis'; antiphrasis vero non voce pronuntiantis significat contrarium, sed suis tantum verbis, quorum origo contraria est." (*Etym.,* I, xxxvii, 24-5.)

[21] Compare my comments on "shy Alexander", above, p. 29, n. 11.

[22] Alexandre Micha, "Tristan et Cligès," *Neophilologus* XXXVI (1952), 1-10. He quotes St. Jerome: *"Optima femina, quae rarior est phenice."* (*P.L.* XXX, 264; Micha's article, p. 6, n. 2).

[23] "Aenigma est quaestio obscura quae difficile intellegitur, nisi aperiatur, ut est illud (Iudic. 14, 14): 'De comedente exivit cibus, et de forte egressa est dulcedo,' significans ex ore leonis favum extractum. Inter allegoriam autem et aenigma hoc interest, quod allegoriae vis gemina est et sub res alias aliud figuraliter indicat; aenigma vero sensus tantum obscurus est, et per quasdam imagines adumbratus." (*Eym.,* I, xxxvii, 26.)

first description of love's arrow. [24]   Another occurs during Fénice's ruminations after Cligès has taken leave of her with the words:

> "Mes droiz est qu'a vos congié praigne
> Com a celi cui ge sui toz." (4282f.)

She pensively mulls over the entire scene, recalling how Cligès' face paled from its usual bright and healthy color, his tears, his submissive behavior.

> Aprés, por boene boche feire,
> Met sor sa leingue un po d'espece:*... (4328f.)   *spice

The meaning of this gustatory enigma is not long hidden; in fact, it is slowly revealed by being elaborated into an allegory:

> Que ele, por trestote Grece
> An celui san qu'ele le prist,
> Ne voldroit que cil qui le dist
> L'eüst ja pansé par faintié,
> Qu'ele ne vit d'autre daintié,
> Ne autre chose ne li plest.
> Cil seus moz la sostient et pest,
> Et toz ses max li asoage.
> D'autre mes ne d'autre bevrage
> Ne se quiert pestre n'abevrer;
> Car quant ce vint au dessevrer,
> Dist Cligés qu'il estoit toz suens.
> Cist moz li est pleisanz et buens,
> Que de la leingue au cuer li toche,
> Sel met el cuer et an la boche,
> Por ce que mialz en est seüre. (4330-45)

Chrétien's consciousness of the enigmatic quality of the allegory, and its need for explanation, is marked by the conjunction *Car,* which introduces the explanation both of Fénice's rumination and of Chrétien's allegory.   The assimilation of sweet words to spices, which in the Middle Ages were precious as well as sweet, is both aesthetically true and appropriately naive for Fénice.   The hyperbolic extension, that she is so pleased by this spice as to wish no other food or drink, is an example of *significatio per exsuperationem.*   The last two lines affirm how precious the spice is to Fénice, since she is concerned about its "safekeeping", but, in also showing the pleasure she finds in keeping it safe, touch her meditation with a gentle irony.

Charientismos [25]

Having already noted that some of the examples of *allegoria* and *ironia* could equally well appear under this heading, it is only equitable

---

[24] *Supra,* p. 30.

[25] "Charientismos est tropus, quo dura dictu gratius proferentur, uti cum interrogantibus, 'numquid nos quaesierit aliquis?' respondetur: 'Bona Fortuna.' Vnde intellegitur neminem nos quaesisse." (*Etym.,* I, xxxvii, 27.).

to admit that some of the present examples could also be considered
under those headings. Our first two examples hinge on the use of a
single word (in substantive and verbal forms) out of its usual context.
Alexander and his companions are watching some of Angrès' knights
amusing themselves on their side of the Thames armed only with lances
and shields, to show how unafraid they are of the opposing army.
Alexander speaks to his men:

> "Seignor, fet il, talanz m'est pris
> Que de l'escu et de la lance
> Aille a cez faire une acointance
> Qui devant moi behorder vienent." (1280-3)

Alexander's words show his intention to emulate the opponents' style—
he will bring only lance and shield also—and carries it one step further
by referring to battle as *acointance*: a friendly meeting.

The same word is used later, in a description of Alexander attacking
a third knight:

> Apres ces deus au tierz s'acointe;
> Un chevalier molt noble et cointe
> Fiert si par anbedeus les flans
> Que d'autre part an saut li sans,
> Et l'ame prant congié au cors,
> Que cil l'a espiree fors. (1755-60)

Here, the tone of friendly social intercourse, representing an engage-
ment in which one man is killed, is extended by the phrase *prandre
congié* referring to the departure of the loser's soul in death.

The same tone is used again when Alexander and his companions
make their way into Angrès' castle by disguising themselves in enemy
armor. All those within the castle have disarmed, except for eight who
have just returned. Alexander and his men reveal themselves by dis-
patching twenty-one of the unarmed, and then turn to the eight:

> Lor espees bien i espruevent;
> Car les trois en ont si charmez,
> De ces qu'il troverent armez,
> Qu'il n'an i ont que cinc lessiez. (1870-73)

It is clear from these examples of *charientismos,* as well as from the
earlier examples of the same tone given under *allegoria* and *ironia,*
that Chrétien distinguishes his descriptions of warfare from that of
the true epic by stylistic means which, in the aggregate, reduce the
audience's awareness of battle as a serious event which results in loss
of blood and life, and which stress rather the pleasure derived from a
surprisingly mild metaphorical description of these events. [26]

---

[26] A. Franz, in "Die reflektierte Handlung im *Cligès,*" (*Zeitschrift für
Romanische Philologie* XLVII [1927] 61-86), developed a very interesting analysis of Chrétien's method of subordinating action to the reaction of the observers. Spitzer criticized Franz rather harshly for attributing the theatrical
"pose" implied by his analysis to the characters rather than the author (see his

Paroemia[27]

The use of proverbs, by nature popular, in a courtly romance, by nature elevated in style, would seem to present an obvious case of incongruity between the proverb and its context. However, proverbs as well as individual words change from one linguistic register to another: what was popular or vulgar in origin may have become acceptable and normalized in an elevated literary style through frequent use in various social and literary contexts. Since we are dealing with a phenomenon which is social as well as literary—how did people use particular words or locutions in daily conversation?—literary evidence alone is not sufficient to establish the linguistic level of any given word or locution. Unfortunately, material information for daily linguistic usage in the Middle Ages is simply not available to the extent necessary for a fair level of critical certainty.[28]

Therefore, it is only as a possible example of *paroemia* that the following use of a proverb can be offered. Soredamors, undergoing the pangs of what she thinks is unrequited love, admits that she knows nothing about love since she has always withheld herself from *Amors*:

> "Sel me fet si chier conparer
> C'or an sai plus que bués d'arer." (1023f.)

The degree of self-directed irony here depends on how foreign or acclimatized to the elevated style of courtly romance this particular proverb was felt to be. Though the general ironic intent is unmistakable, it is unclear to what extent Chrétien and his audience would actually have juxtaposed the mental image of a laboring, sweating beast in the field to that of Soredamors tossing in bed—in the eventuality that the proverb was experienced as shocking or surprising in its literary context; or whether the proverb was experienced as merely communicating the intellectual idea of "hard work" without calling up the precise image it denotes—the eventuality that the impact of the proverb, even in a high literary context, was dulled through frequent use and acceptance.

One means of determining the level of irony intended, not available in the previous example, lies in the principle of reinforcement: are

---

review of Kellerman's *Aufbaustil und Weltbild Chrestiens von Troyes im Percevalroman,* in *Modern Language Notes* LV [1940] 222-6; p. 225). While Spitzer's reservation must be admitted, it should not obscure the real interest of Franz's article.

[27] "Paroemia est rebus et temporibus adcommodatum proverbium. Rebus, ut: 'Contra stimulum calces,' dum significatur adversis resistendum. Temporibus, ut: 'Lupus in fabula.' Aiunt enim rustici vocem hominem perdere, si eum lupus prior viderit. Vnde et subito tacenti dicitur istud proverbium: 'Lupus in fabula.'" (*Etym.,* I, xxxvii, 28.)

[28] It is this methodological difficulty which limits the usefulness of those forms of modern stylistic analysis based on transferences from one linguistic register to another for medieval literature; a corollary is the increased importance of methods of stylistic analysis based on structural relationships within the work itself. The figures and tropes which the Middle Ages inherited from classical antiquity are one such method.

there other stylistic indications of such intent associated with the given passage? Soredamors is again the victim of our example. She has just been introduced as the one *Qui desdaigneuse estoit d'amors*, but who begins to suffer the pangs of love as soon as she sets eyes on Alexander:

> Chieremant achate et conpere
> Son grant orguel et son desdaing.
> Amors li a chaufé un baing
> Qui molt l'eschaufe et molt li nuist. (462-5)

The irony of the proverb *chaufer un baing* ("making it hot for someone") receives two convergences. The first is the paradoxical quality of *Amors* as a source of injury, a consideration not denied by the traditional character of this paradox since Chrétien stresses it in the following lines:

> Or li est boen, et or li nuist,
> Or le vialt, et or le refuse.. (466 f.),

itself reinforced by intertwined anaphora (*Or ... et or ... Or ... et or ...*). The second reinforcement consists of a dual principle Chrétien frequently uses. The proverb is taken literally and extended allegorically by *l'eschaufe*: to heat, in the obvious thermal sense, but also "to become excited, inflamed". [29] This last meaning is further reinforced by Soredamors' turning against her own eyes as traitors (468 ff.).

The convergence of stylistic effects at this point leaves no doubt of the lines' intention. It is not enough, however, to note the *soupçon d'humour* of the proverb itself, [30] for the irony is not entirely gratuitous. The lines we have quoted are not a self-sufficient literary composition: they serve as an introduction to Soredamors' long monologue (469-515), and the irony of the introduction colors what is introduced. If the monologue is presented as her reaction to becoming excited or inflamed, it seems wiser to read it as character portrayal rather than as cool, intellectually developed doctrine. The young girl, totally inexperienced in love, reacts to her confusion in cultural terms familiar

---

[29] Compare:

> "Si m'aïst Dex, traï vos ont
> li deable, li vif maufé;
> trop fustes enuit *eschaufé*,
> et por ce que trop vos grevastes,
> voz plaies sanz dote escrevastes." (*Lancelot*, 4876-80)

> Ensi trestuit d'ire *eschaufé*
> par mi la sale le queroient... (*Yvain*, 1132f.)

> De honte et de crieme *eschaufez*,
> se desfant de tote sa force;... (*Yvain*, 5582f.)

[30] Frappier, *Cligès*, p. 42. More than any other previous critic of Chrétien, Frappier has noted his irony and wit. Unfortunately, the necessities of a brief, general, introductory book (*Chrétien de Troyes*) and of university courses (the publications with the Centre de Documentation Universitaire) have prevented him from dealing with these as anything more than occasional ornaments, however frequent.

to her, those of courtly love with its hierarchical structure and sense of formal duties. But the manner in which she translates these terms into her personal problem reveals that the monologue is structured according to a clear and valid psychology. Love, a profound emotion caused but not defined by another person, an external event—perhaps that is why we hear her symptoms even before being told she has laid eyes on Alexander (450-9)—throws her into such confusion that she disowns it, making first her eyes and then her heart responsible and guilty for her distress. It is a naive psychological projection, but one entirely appropriate to a young, inexperienced girl, and one which, for a moment, enables her to still believe in her self-possession by personifying eyes and heart.

Needless to say, her respite is of short duration. If her heart brings her pain, she will affirm her sovereign will:

> "Cuide moi Amors metre an voie,
> Qui les autres sialt desveier?
> Autrui li covient aveier,
> Car je ne sui de rien a lui,
> Ja n'i serai n'onques n'i fui,
> Ne ja n'amerai s'acointance." (510-5)

It requires little experience in love or literary romances to smile at her determination. Her own words betray the paradox of her indecision: the paranomasia of *metre an voie* (to put on the *right* path)—*desveier* (turn off the right path)—*aveier* (also to put on the right path), indicates clearly enough that she has lost her way.

Sarcasmos [31]

I have found no examples of sarcasm in *Cligès*, though Keu, in *Yvain* and *Perceval*, does provide some. [32]

Asteismos [33]

Our discussion of this trope showed that its definition was vague, consisting essentially of adjectives such as "urbane, elegant, refined";

---

[31] "Sarcasmos est hostilis inrisio cum amaritudine, ut (Virg. Aen. 2, 547):
> Referes ergo haec, et nuntius ibis
> Pelidae genitoris; illi mea tristia facta
> degeneremque Neoptolemum narrare memento."
(*Etym.*, I, xxxvii, 29.)

[32] *Infra*, pp. 194, 196.

[33] "Huic (*i.e.*, sarcasm) contrarius est Astysmos, urbanitas sine iracundia, ut illud (Virg. Ecl. 3, 90):
> Qui Bavium non odit, amet tua carmina, Maevi,
> atque idem iungat vulpes et mulgeat hircos.

Id est: qui Bavium non odit, pro poena ei contingat ut diligat Maevium. Fuerunt autem Maevius et Bavius poetae pessimi, et inimici Vergilii. Qui hos ergo diligit, faciat quae contra naturam sunt, id est, iungat vulpes et mulgeat hircos." (*Etym.*, I, xxxvii, 30).

it seemed to imply a recognition that the system of tropes was insufficient to capture the idea of literary tone, especially irony. [34] Therefore, it will not be surprising to find here examples which, though
perhaps elegant in tone, could also find a place in another category.

Again, we start on a warlike note. Cligès has disposed of six
enemy knights:

> De cez nus ne se contretint;
> Toz les lesse teisanz et muz.
>
> ....
>
> Quant de cez fu asseürez,
> De honte et de maleürtez
> Vet presant feire au remenant. (3702-9)

A striking example in which elegant refinement of style is used to
describe combat occurs in the duel between Cligès and the Duke of
Saxony:

> As espees notent un lai
> Sor les hiaumes qui retantissent,
> Si que lor genz s'an esbaïssent. (4024-6)

The rapid crashing of sword on helmet is metamorphosed into the
playing of a musical composition ... well might the observers be amazed,
who expected an epic battle and were treated to aesthetic display
instead! And so might the reader be, who sees a lyric technique of
rich and feminine rhymes continued through the description of a hard-
fought battle:

> Il sanble a ces qui les esgardent
> Que li hiaume espraignent et ardent,
> Car quant les espees resaillent,
> Estanceles ardanz an saillent
> Ausi come de fer qui fume,
> Que li fevres bat sor l'anclume,
> Quant il le tret de la faunarge. (4027-33)

Repetition is essential to primitive poetry, where it has a magical or
incantatory intention, [35] and later poetry retains a minimal connection
with its source in part through its techniques of aural repetition, mainly
rhythm and rhyme. In so far as a repetitive technique is stressed, an
effect similar to that of primitive poetry may be intended. Thus, the
lyric impulse of spring or love and the profoundly religious intent tend
frequently to highly repetitive forms. [36] But so does, at the other end
of the poetic scale, the ironic poem, where the awareness of the tech-

---

[34] *Supra,* pp. 17 ff.
[35] C.M. Bowra, *Primitive Song* (New York: New American Library, 1963),
p. 80.
[36] For an example of repetitive rhyming in a spring lyric, see *Carmina
Burana* 118 (*Salve ver optatum*), in Helen Waddell, *Mediaeval Latin Lyrics*
(New York: Holt, 1929), p. 232. An obvious medieval example of the richly
rhymed religious lyric is the "Dies irae."

nique's origin is turned against its subject. [37] The incongruity between subject and style results in an ironic dissociation which precludes the identification we experience in the lyric or religious poem, but enhances our attitude toward the poem as an artistic object to be admired. In our passage, this aesthetic distance is already suggested by the interposition, between the description and the reader, of the amazed observers.

Another example of *asteismos* occurs in the scene where Thessala manages to have Cligès serve Alis her magic potion. This was not an idea which came to her immediately, however:

> Thessala covient qu'ele espit
> Par quel engin, par quel message
> Ele anvoiera son message.
> ....
> Puis s'apanse come cortoise
> Del boivre servir an fera
> Celui cui joie et preuz sera.... (3222-34),

which, of course, means Cligès himself. The irony of referring to her potion as a message, and the one who delivers it as a messenger, is slight enough to pass unnoticed except for the paranomasia. The description of Thessala, a Greek witch whose highest possible social description is as Fénice's governess, as *cortoise,* is more surprising. Is she worthy of the appellation because of her service in the cause of *Amors*? If we recall Chrétien's prejudice in favor of married love, and the fact that Thessala here is plotting to prevent the consummation of a marriage, two possible interpretations present themselves: either Chrétien believes Thessala to be courtly, in which case a conflict arises between his predilection for married love and Thessala's courtliness; or courtliness does not represent a real value for Chrétien, in which case the word is applied ironically to the witch. Either the value itself, or the word in this use, is being viewed ironically.

The most ironic aspect of the scene, however, is not revealed by the style, but by the action and situation themselves. As the passage points out, the "messenger" is the one who will be made happiest

---

[37] Compare Frappier, who finds an epic quality in this description: "... implicitement, la métaphore [of the musical lai] semble conférer à l'action guerrière le prestige de la poésie ... le jaillissement des étincelles autour de deux combattants leur donne une apparence fantastique qui s'accorde au mieux avec l'optique de l'épopée." (*Cligès,* p. 95; see also *Chrétien de Troyes,* p. 235). I have already commented on Chrétien's efforts to differentiate his battle descriptions from that of the epic (*supra,* p. 36). The technical problem for the critic is to decide whether the juxtaposition of two affective registers is intended to suggest assimilation or dissociation. The context indicates the latter intention. The present passage is immediately followed by:

> Molt sont andui li vasal large
> De cos doner a grant planté,...

and the following lines, which have already been considered an example of ironic *allegoria* (*supra,* p. 27).

and profit most by the outcome of Thessala's plan, Cligès. [38]   The
irony lies in that he will serve his happiness and profit unknowingly.

SIGNIFICATIO [39]

Litotes [40]

An occasional understatement is the easiest form of irony, and some
of Chrétien's uses of litotes are not very impressive.   This is particularly true when what is implied by the irony is immediately made
explicit.   Cligès, hearing that Fénice has been captured by the Saxons,
is displeased:

> N'en a mie son cuer riant
> Einz est mervoille qu'il n'enrage. (3656f.)

The Queen thinks of Soredamors as the one

> Qui Alixandre pas ne het,
> Einz l'aimme molt et loe et prise. (1140f.)

But the formula can be quite successful, even where, as in epic
irony, it is most expected.   Angrès de Guinesores and his followers
plan an attack for the following day:

---

[38] The word *preuz* here is being used in the sense of "profit, advantage," of
course, but Chrétien and his audience were probably not unaware of the pun
(*significatio per ambiguum*) it also represents.

[39] As with *allegoria*, a medieval definition will be provided for each figure.
Those of *significatio* are taken from Geoffroi de Vinsauf's *Poetria nova*, in
Faral's *Les arts poétiques...*, pp. 197-262; *significatio*, ll. 1531-87, pp. 244 f.
Geoffroi postdates Chrétien (Faral places the *Poetria nova* between 1208 and
1213: *op. cit.*, p. 33), but the tradition he represents—that of the *Rhetorica ad
Herennium*—was current during the XIIth century: *supra*, p. 22, n. 44.

[40] Litotes is not considered by the *ad Herennium* as part of *significatio*, but
"La forme naturelle de l'ironie est la litote," as the author of the most supple,
wide-ranging and perceptive book on irony I know of has said: Vladimir Jankélévitch, *L'ironie ou la bonne conscience*, 2nd ed., (Paris: Presses Universitaires,
1950), p. 70.   I have hardly used his work in this thesis, partly for historical reasons (the irony he treats of is primarily the contemporary, post-romantic sort),
and partly out of a fear of letting this thesis turn into a tissue of quotations from
Jankélévitch.

The *ad Herennium*'s omission of litotes is remedied by Geoffroi, who treats
it as the first form of *significatio*:

> Hoc ita proposito: *Non est mea parva potestas,*
> *Non exilis honor,* plus innuo quam loquor, et res
> Est ipso verbo major. Pro parte meorum
> Sive mea si fortasse loquor, modus iste loquendi
> Est sapor: et tali sermone modestius utor.
> Sic cooperta venit sententia: non aperitur
> Res plene: plus est in se quam sermo sit in re. (1531-7)

> Desperance, comant qu'il aille,
> Les anhardist de la bataille,
> Qu'il ne voient lor garison
> Fors que de mort ou de prison.
> Tex garisons n'est mie sainne... (1653-7)

It is equally expected and effective in matters of love. Chrétien uses litotes to introduce the mutual avowal of love between Cligès and Fénice. After Cligès returns from England,

> Un jor seus an la chanbre vint
> Celi qui n'ert pas s'anemie,
> Et bien sachiez, ne li fu mie
> Li huis a l'encontre botez. (5098-5101)

The last two lines are an extension of "she who was not his enemy," and part of the effect is to be found in the fact that the extension is also formulated negatively.

The next three examples of ironic litotes are from the Alexander section. The first occurs in Soredamors' monologue; since it caps a long development, some summary is required. We have already seen Soredamors experience the *coup de foudre* (450ff.) and begin her rationalizations in the first, shorter monologue (469-515), and heard Chrétien tell us of the wavering she undergoes, loving one hour, hating the next. There is no question in our minds of her love for Alexander. Now she starts off with an idea she has previously broached (503ff.; Alexander has also indulged in this thought: 618ff.): love is madness, and I am mad to love! What difference is it to me if he is of such fine appearance, and generous, and courtly, and noble? All this is fine for him: what is his beauty to me? Let his beauty go with him, since I can do nothing about it anyway. I certainly don't wish to detract from it. Detract? Hardly! I certainly don't want that. If he had the intelligence of Solomon, and if Nature had given him the perfection of human beauty, and if God had put in my hand the power of destroying it all, I would not seek to anger him, but most happily, if I knew how, I would make him wiser, and more handsome. My heavens, so then I don't hate him at all.

For all that, am I his *amie*? Not at all, no more than another's. And then why do I think so much about him, if he pleases me no more than another? I don't know, I'm all confused, for never did I think so much about any man in this world, and if I had my way, I would look at him the whole day, I would never seek to take my eyes off him, so happy am I, when I see him.

> Est ce Amors? Oïl, ce croi. (918) [41]

The young girl's helpless, humorous wanderings about the central point of her thoughts, repeatedly suggested by the mild understatements, is a triumph of technical delicacy. The ironic incongruity between the

---

[41] *Amors* should not be capitalized in this line: it is the emotion, not the god.

chaos of her emotions and their tentative, hesitant verbalization is especially gentle and sympathetic here, without for a moment allowing us to move from sympathy to empathy.

Chrétien is at pains to maintain this aesthetic distance between his characters and his audience, repeatedly intervening, subtly but firmly, to differentiate the two. The Queen has given Alexander a shirt sewn by Soredamors of gold and silver threads, to which she has added one of her own golden hairs. He is not aware of this origin, nor she that he has it:

> Mes cil ne cele ne le sot:
> C'est granz enuiz que il nel sevent. (1173f.)

"What a pity they don't know it."! For the reader has seen the two young people tortured at night by thoughts of the other, each thinking their love is unreturned. The reader knows what hero and heroine do not, and observes them stumbling in the dark of their emotions from his privileged place in the light of knowledge granted by the author.

The entire "romance" between Alexander and Soredamors is based on such incongruities of feeling and expression, between the character's doubts as to the other's feelings and the reality shared by the author with his reader. The impossibility the two young lovers feel of declaring their feelings until assured they are reciprocated is resolved by the Queen, who chides the hero for his silence. Even after this indirect assurance of Soredamors' feelings—and the three are together in the Queen's tent, apart from others in attendance—it is to the Queen that Alexander makes his declaration of love for Soredamors!:

> "S'ele de li rien ne m'otroie,
> Totevoies m'otroi a li."
> A cest mot cele tressailli,
> Qui cest presant pas ne refuse. (2290-3)

The effect of the understatement in the last line depends not only on the situation in this particular scene, but on the entire story of un-avowed love which has preceded: we smile in remembrance of the tormented but baseless self-doubts of Soredamors in filling the gap between the words and their meaning.

Significatio per exsuperationem [42]

Ironic hyperbole in rhetoric consists of a disparity between the facts and the words chosen to represent them. This adequately describes the

---

[42]   *Ex tot et ex opibus tantis a patre relictis*
         Dilapidator opum non habet quo tegmine velet
         Pauperiem, sed nec testam qua postulet ignem.
         Sic de re minima dico nimis; immoderate
         Arguo quod non est moderatum. Nec modus in re,

technique of our first example. Alexander and the Queen are sitting together; facing them is Soredamors:

> Qui si volantiers l'esgardoit
> Qu'an paradis ne volsist estre. (1544f.)

Chrétien more frequently adapts the rhetorical, verbal technique to his narrative by presenting the facts themselves as ironic. Thus, he describes Soredamors in the throes of love:

> Amors li est el cuer anclose,
> Une tançons et une rage
> Qui molt li troble son corage,
> Et qui l'angoisse, et destraint,
> Que tote nuit plore, et se plaint,
> Et se degiete, et si tressaut,
> A po que li cuers ne li faut. (870-6)

There is nothing in the text to make us doubt the "truth" of Chrétien's reporting: this is how Soredamors behaved, and if we find this portrait of love's symptoms ironic, it is on the basis of an incongruity between her behavior and her pride, or between her behavior and a concept of normal behavior, not between her behavior and the words which describe it. [43]

> Nec modus in verbo. Si res moderatior ore,
> Sermo tamen nimius in re minus innuit esse.
> (*Poetria nova*, 1538-44)

Geoffroi's example here is a considerable expansion of the example for *significatio per exsuperationem* in his source, the *Rhetorica ad Herennium*: cf. *supra*, p. 21, n. 38.

[43] D.W. Robertson has commented on these symptoms of love as follows: "Although we are usually urged to accept these things as 'conventions', if Professor Rand's general attitude [that Ovid, the source of these literary symptoms, was primarily a satirist of love: E.K. Rand, "Ovid and the Spirit of Metamorphosis," *Harvard Essays on Classical Subjects,* ed. Herbert W. Smyth (Boston: Houghton Mifflin, 1912)] was correct they are a part of Ovid's design to make love ridiculous. Chrétien does not lend them any greater dignity by adding yawning and sweating to the symptoms of love-sickness...." ("Chrétien's *Cligès* and the Ovidian Spirit," *Comparative Literature* VII [1955] 32-42 ; p. 38 f.) I obviously agree with Robertson on Chrétien's ironic intent, but his error in attributing the addition of yawning and sweating to Chrétien reveals the uncertainty of his method: these two symptoms already occur in the *Eneas* (ll. 8453-6, 8930-4; cf. Faral, *Recherches sur les sources latines...,* p. 133f.; Frappier, *Cligès,* p. 43, and "Vues sur les conceptions courtoises dans les littératures d'oc et d'oïl au XIIᵉ siècle," *Cahiers de civilisation médiévale* II [1959] 135-156; p. 150, n. 56).

As Robertson himself recognizes, two problems are posed by his method of comparing Chrétien to Ovid. First, what was the earlier poet's intention? "It must be admitted that it is possible to interpret Ovid in a number of different ways." (*loc. cit.,* p. 41). Even admitting Ovid's irony, there remains the question of how Chrétien interpreted him: "... it would be useful to know whether he regarded Ovid as a humorous mocker of a misdirected love ... but I do not propose to answer this question here." (*loc. cit.,* p. 37). In this particular instance, a third step is added, and we would have to ask: How did Chrétien

The reason for the change in the technique of hyperbole is fairly evident. While the orator has relatively little power over the facts of the case on which he is speaking, and is restricted to verbal variations from mere recital, the narrative poet's invention applies to the "facts" of his story as well. This freedom enables him to portray characters as engaged in exaggerated action, which can be recited in a perfectly straightforward manner. [44] It is the last three forms of *significatio* that deal more closely with the factual level of narrative, and it is under *significatio per consequentiam* that cases of exaggerated action will be considered. [45]

Significatio per ambiguum [46]

The true pun does not occur frequently in *Cligès*, though this may be a reflection of the modern critic's relative distance from the linguistic life of Old French rather than a fact of the text. Nonetheless, I have found only three puns in this romance. The first is famous. Soredamors, sitting alone next to Alexander, notices for the first time that he is wearing the shirt she made and into which she sewed one of her own blond hairs. Now she finally has an opportunity to open a conversation! But something holds her back. She is not certain of the proper form of address. Shall she call him by his name, or *ami*? She would try his name, but *trop i a letre* (1392), and she would stumble and stop in the middle... But she cannot call him *ami,* since this would be a lie, though it would be perfectly true if he called her *sa dolce amie....* And so on for twenty-seven lines (1372-98). The word is ambiguous, and Soredamors is so involved in her feelings for Alexander that it does not occur to her that he would interpret *ami* as a perfectly normal salutation.

Interestingly, Chrétien does not actually use the pun itself here, but exploits its potential use for psychological purposes. For Soredamors, concerned only with her own emotions, considers only the word's more intimate meaning, the meaning it would have for her if she used it. Calling Alexander *ami* would be tantamount to a unilateral declaration

---

interpret the *Eneas*? How did the author of the *Eneas* interpret Ovid? What did Ovid himself intend?

Since we are faced, at some point or another, with the problem of interpreting the work of one poet directly, it seems simpler and more efficient to interpret the one we are primarily concerned with, rather than his sources. This is what Robertson to a large extent has done convincingly with a number of Chrétien's classical references. Some of these will be considered under *significatio per similitudinem*: see below, pp. 55 ff.

[44] As in the "dead pan" technique of movie and stage comics.

[45] *Infra,* pp. 50-3.

[46]   *Ille vir egregius*: vox haec sonat *optimus.* Aut vir
           Pessimus oblique nos respicit; hic sonat. Haec vox
           Transvertit visum, vel peccat visus in istis
           Ambiguis. Res est cooperta, et risus apertus.
                                          (*Poetria nova,* 1545-8)

of love on her part, which neither her pride nor social mores allow.
A more profound fear is also present:

> "Ce que je cuit dire mançonge.
> Mançonge? Ne sai que sera,
> Mes se je mant, moi pesera." (1380-2)

In what sense can Soredamors be "lying" if she calls the man she
loves *ami*? It is certainly not an intentional lie, since there is nothing
she wants as much as to be his *amie*:

> "Dex, ja ne mantiroit il mie,
> S'il me clamoit sa dolce amie." (1385 f.)

She would be lying only if Alexander did not accept the appellation
ami in its more intimate sense, *i.e.*, if he did not love her. Thus, her
inability to address Alexander betrays not only the social and personal
principles governing the behavior of a young lady at court, but also a
deeper fear of rejection by the man she loves—totally groundless, of
course.

This analysis, however, paints the passage in far too serious a
light—it is only a poet of Chrétien's caliber who can combine psychological perception and light-hearted wit, and do justice to both. Soredamors' inner debate turns to fantasy, as she imagines a world where
proper names are proper indeed:

> "Voldroie avoir de mon sanc mis
> Qu'il eüst non 'mes dolz amis'." (1397 f.)

Which is immediately followed by the Queen's entrance and her perfectly casual address of Alexander:

> "Amis, fet ele..." (1406)

If that first pun—or putative pun—is most relevant to Chrétien as a
psychological writer, the second bears primarily on aesthetic attitudes
toward his work: his own attitude, that of his original audience, and
that of his historical audience, the modern reader. The latter has
generally been most strongly rebuffed by the lengthy monologues of
the heroes and heroines in *Cligès*. They are characterized by lengthy
self-concern and an extensively elaborated combination of allegory
and dialectic. [47] No aspect of *Cligès* has been more harshly criticized.
Even the most sympathetic scholar reveals an unease only partially
compensated by his insight that author and character are not identical,

---

[47] "... eine gewisse logische Tendenz zur dialektikspitzfindigen Methode
[kann] nicht geleugnet werden..." Alfons Hilka, *Die direkte Rede als stili-
stisches Kunstmittel in den Romanen des Kristian von Troyes*, (Halle: Niemeyer,
1903), p. 71. The same reaction is still present under the usual polite acknow-
ledgment of Chrétien's intent of virtuosity ... a more polite term, apparently,
than "rhetoric".

and that the former can portray his characters with sympathy and yet disapprove of them morally. [48]

It is our moral concerns, I believe, combined with the remains of the nineteenth century view of the Middle Ages as a monolith paralyzed by the institutional and intellectual structure of the Church, which hampers both our enjoyment and understanding of Chrétien. There is a large part of gratuitous aesthetic pleasure offered by his romances which we deny ourselves by insistence that all aspects of their affabulation contribute directly to a moral meaning or thesis. [49] His own attitude, presumably shared by the audience for which he wrote, seems to have been less stringently moral. The two most salient characteristics of these monologues are their length and convoluted style. Alexander's fills over 250 lines (618-864); it is the longest and the most "artificial" of the monologues. [50] Can we believe that so self-conscious a writer as Chrétien de Troyes was unaware of the length or style of this extraordinary display of virtuosity? I think he answers this question and implies an attitude toward his own work in the first line which follows the monologue. Let us abandon scholarly objectivity momentarily, and indulge in a brief historical fantasy. The audience is a small group of courtly ladies, attendant knights, and perhaps even the lord of the court. The author has just read to them Alexander's monologue: he raises his eyes from the text, the corner of his mouth twitches, and he speaks directly to his audience of friends after taking a long breath:

> Granz est la conplainte Alixandre... (865),

and pauses in his reading to allow the laughter to die down. As in modern French, *granz* can mean both quantitatively large and qualitatively great. [51] Here, it puns, and bears both meanings.

This kind of comment by the author on his own work, ironically self-congratulatory, reaffirms the compact with which the romance began. [52] The compact establishes the aesthetic distance the author and audience share as against the characters, and which allows us to enjoy the work as gratuitous aesthetic display. Again, this does not deny the implication of serious moral and psychological concerns, but it does tend to undermine such analyses as do not first take into account that aspect of the work which is most visible and striking. As

---

[48] Frappier, *Cligès*, p. 87: here, Frappier remarks that "... le langage précieux de *Cligès* est en somme moins celui de l'auteur que celui de ses personnages..."; in particular, Alexander's *préciosité* would be the result of a mental state Chrétien considers *fâcheux*. Elsewhere, however, Frappier believes that the characters who use this style "... sont des miroirs et des modèles de la société courtoise." (*op. cit.*, p. 75).

[49] See Robert Guiette, "D'une poésie formelle en France au moyen âge," *Revue des Sciences Humaines* LIV (1949) 61-68.

[50] Frappier, *Cligès*, p. 70.

[51] Compare *Cligès* 106, 396, 1243, 1256 for *granz*="large", to *Cligès* 150, 153, 1163, 1175 for *granz*="great".

[52] *Supra*, p. 26.

we will see, it is not only that the tone of irony at Alexander's expense seems to undermine the doctrinal content of his monologue, [53] but also that the functional value of the monologue—character portrayal—resides precisely in these "artificial" convolutions. [54]

More frequent than the simple pun is Chrétien's adaptation of its principle to ambiguity of statement. We have already seen a major example of this technique in the words with which Cligès takes leave of Fénice on his departure for England and Arthur's court:

> "Mes droiz est qu'a vos congié praigne
> Com a celi cui ge sui toz." (4282 f.) [55]

These words, which can be interpreted either as a normal form of social salutation or a covert declaration of love, make Fénice pensive as she ruminates the alternative interpretations. [56]

Chrétien sometimes manipulates these ambiguities quite obviously. After Alis has imbibed the potion which will preserve Fénice's virginity, it is time for the newly-weds to find each other in bed:

> Quant ore fu d'aler gesir
> L'empereres si com il dut
> La nuit avoec sa fame jut. (3290-2) [57]

The adverbial phrase *si com il dut* may modify the *fact* of the husband sleeping in the same bed as his new bride: they slept in the same bed, as is proper for a young couple; or it may describe the *manner* in which they behave while in bed: they slept in the same bed in the proper manner expected of newly-weds. Chrétien picks up this ambiguity to play with:

> Si com il dut? Ai ge manti,
> Qu'il ne la beisa ne santi;
> Mes an un lit jurent ansanble. (3293-5)

The last line reinforces the paradox of the couple in bed ... but *il ne la beisa ne santi*! Though the *fact* of the first sentence is "proper", the *manner* of it is not.

Many of these ambiguities, however, depend on the discrepancy between our knowledge of the situation and that of a character—a sort of small-scale dramatic irony. When Thessala, in a scene already discussed, [58] tells Cligès that the drink he is to serve Alis

> "Vos fera lié, si con je pans." (3266),

---

[53] I refer to the "doctrine" of love, of course. Not that this "doctrine" or theory is unimportant, but that it should be seen as a means of character portrayal, not as an end in itself.

[54] *Infra*, pp. 70 ff. The third pun, that on *la mer, amer, amour,* is treated below, pp. 89 ff.

[55] *Supra*, pp. 34 ff.

[56] Compare to Soredamors' similar difficulty with *ami*; above, p. 46 f.

[57] I have omitted Micha's punctuation within this sentence to show the ambiguity more clearly.

[58] *Supra*, p. 32.

Cligès understands by this that serving the Emperor this drink will be pleasurable for his uncle and therefore advantageous for the nephew. Our knowledge is that Cligès' advantage demands his uncle's loss. Our opinion will vary according to our evaluation of the entire situation. If we feel that Alis has abrogated all right to our friendlier feelings by breaking his promise not to marry—thereby endangering Cligès' inheritance of the throne—we regard the irony with pure enjoyment as a form of poetic justice. On the other hand, if we feel that there are excuses for Alis' behavior, and do not embrace whole-heartedly the purpose and means of Thessala's trickery, the irony cuts into Cligès' stature as well: a suggestion of ridicule attaches to a man whose success is due to luck or to having been used instrumentally "for his own good."

Significatio per consequentiam [59]

The unstated "consequence" derives from a stated fact. In the example of the *Rhetorica ad Herennium,* the relationship is a logical one: a man's father used to wipe his nose on his arm, *therefore* the man is of base descent and should keep silent. [60] The same is true of Geoffroi's example: the boy saw the switches, the color left his face and he was pale, *therefore* he was afraid. Chrétien uses the same pattern in the episode of Soredamors' shirt. When Alexander learns it was she who made it, and that she inserted one of her own hairs in it, he sleeps with it, spends the whole night embracing it and examining the single hair:

> Et quant il le chevol remire,
> De tot le mont cuide estre sire.
> Bien fet Amors d'un sage fol,
> Quant cil fet joie d'un chevol. (1619-22)

This observation of Chrétien's echoes Alexander's own exclamation at the beginning of his monologue:

> "Por fol, fet il, me puis tenir." (618)

That Chrétien reaffirms this observation should give us pause in taking too seriously the character's ruminations. In the present passage, the

---

59   *Inspectis virgis pueri rubor ora reliquit*
     Et facies exsanguis erat: talis color ipsum
     Significat timuisse. *Rubor perfuderat ora*
     Virginis: haec facies notat hanc puduisse. *Vagando*
     Crinibus incessit comptis: modus iste reportat
     Luxuriasse. Datae da signa sequentia formae;
     Praefer res ipsas, sed eas non praefer ut ipsas,
     Immo notas rerum solas: pallore timorem,
     Comptura Venerem, subitoque rubore pudorem,
     Remque notis certis ostende, sequente priorem:
     Hic color, hic sexus, haec aetas, ista figura.
                      (*Poetria nova*, 1549-59)

60 *Supra*, p. 22.

irony is stressed by two convergences: the oxymoron by position of
sage fol, and the end-stopped couplet, reinforcing the *fol/chevol* rhyme.

An interesting variation of this figure might be called *significatio
per falsam consequentiam.* Soredamors, earlier disdainful, is converted
and concerns herself with the proper observance of *Amors'* rules:

> "Amors voldroit, et je le vuel,
> Que sage fusse, et sanz orguel,
> Et deboneire, et acointable,
> Vers toz por un seul amïable.
> Amerai les ge toz por un?" (945-3)

Her former pride having left her totally inexperienced in the proper
behavior of a courtly beloved, her decision to accept these standards
leads her to ponder absurdities. [61]

A further variation ironizes the cause rather than its consequence.
The traitor Angrès and his men are being attacked within their castle
by Alexander and his men:

> Et cil fieremant les anchaucent,
> Qui les reoignent, et estaucent,
> Et detranchent, et escervelent,
> Et traïtor le conte apelent.
> Quant s'ot nomer de traïson,
> Vers sa tor cort a garison... (1911-6)

Angrès runs off to his tower, not out of fear, not because the enemy
within his gates is slashing his men, as Chrétien tells us in three verbs
meaning essentially the same thing, and literally knocking out their
brains, but because he has been called a traitor!

The same technique is used to undermine rationalizations. When
Soredamors is afraid to call Alexander by his own name, she ratio-
nalizes:

> "Ce m'est avis, trop i a letre,
> S'aresteroie tost en mi." (1391 f.)

The consequence—that she does not address him at all—is absurd in
itself, but has not yet occurred: we are still within her inner debate,
but the final irony is already indicated by her helpless rationalizing—
again a trait familiar to any shy person. Of course, the ironic twist to
which the entire episode leads is a narrative adaptation of this technique. The reader is aware of a logical relationship between the
Queen's use of *ami* and Soredamors' non-use, but the two linguistic
events do not bear the same relation to each other as in the rhetorical
examples. In the latter, facts are stated about a person which lead
to a logical inference about his background or emotions. Here, there
is no logical connection between the use and non-use of the same word
by two characters: one does not lead to the other. This adaptation is

---

[61] This might also be considered a narrative extension of *significatio per
exsuperationem,* a hyperbolic rhetorical question.

important: two events or episodes may be juxtaposed, even though separated by extensive intervening material, when some element common to them is identical. However, this exceeds the limits of stylistic analysis, and will be discussed later. [62]

But even on the immediate stylistic level, the technique is one of the most frequently used by Chrétien. Alexander has tricked his father into granting him an unspecified boon. The latter, on hearing that his son's wish is to go to Arthur's court to obtain his knighthood, offers to have Alexander knighted and crowned emperor the following day after mass.

> Li vaslez antant la promesse
> Que l'andemain aprés la messe
> Le vialt ses peres adober,
> Et dist qu'il iert malvés ou ber
> En autre païs que el suen. (133-7);

The offer is grandiose; the reaction to it, in objective indirect discourse, reveals Alexander's disdain and suggests something of his character. [63] We will go into this later in some detail; [64] for the moment, it is enough to say that the young man is impetuous, cunning, and rude to his father in forcing the latter to abide by his word. However, when the father, left with no choice, agrees to honor his promise,

> Or est li vaslez bien heitiez
> Et cortois et bien afeitiez,
> Quant ses peres tant li promet... (181-3)

In other words, his trick having worked, Alexander suddenly becomes everything he was not during the interview itself: happy, courtly, well brought up.

The entire scene is later paralleled when Cligès asks permission of Alis to do as his father did. [65] A clear echo of the last example occurs when Cligès obtains that permission:

> N'ot pas bien [Alis] la parole dite,
> Quant Cligés l'an ot mercié. (4233 f.)

---

[62] *Infra,* pp. 63 ff.

[63] In this case, it is possible to point to the obvious structural reinforcement of the irony: the three-line protasis, useless in itself since it merely repeats the content of the immediately preceding lines, exists only for the sake of the stylistic "fall" into the apodosis which contains the irony. In general, however, this kind of syntactical structural analysis is dangerous in Old French: "L'ancien français ... enchaîne les mots avec une liberté qui est inconnue à la langue moderne." (Lucien Foulet, *Petite syntaxe de l'ancien français,* 3d ed., in *CFMA* [Paris: Champion, 1958], p. 306). It would be extremely difficult to obtain standards by which to measure the probable effect of these structures on a medieval audience. Again it is the analysis of literary structures, in so far as these can be differentiated from the linguistic, that seems most appropriate; cf. *supra,* p. 37 and n. 28.

[64] *Infra,* pp. 64-73.

[65] The subject of parallelism is treated below, pp. 63 ff.

Though the stress here is on the fifteen year old boy's eagerness rather than the kind of trait Alexander revealed, this hardly obscures the similarity in the two situations.

Significatio per abscisionem [66]

Chrétien often comments in the first person on his narrative technique, and this is usually picked up as the basis for an elaboration of his theory of narrative. Sometimes, however, his interjections are more directed to humor, Gallic or other, than to theory. Fénice and Cligès have secreted themselves away in Jehan's hidden tower:

> Certes, de rien ne s'avilla
> Amors, quant il les mist ansanble;
> Car a l'un et a l'autre sanble,
> Quant li uns l'autre acole et beise,
> Que de lor joie et de lor eise
> Soit toz li mondes amandez;
> Ne ja plus ne m'an demandez. (6252-8)

If Chrétien does not delve into the details of the lovers' deportment, he does take care to inform us in the following lines that the pair spent fifteen months together, indoors.

A simple narrative adaptation is to have a character use this technique, hinting at what he might say were he free to do so. Cligès, having returned from England, asks Fénice:

> "Et vos comant a esté puis
> Qu'an cest païs fustes venue?
> Quel joie i avez puis eüe?
> Plest vos la gent, plest vos la terre?",

and adds :

> "Je ne vos doi de plus requerre,
> Fors tant se li païs vos plest." (5132-7)

Of course, *d'amors requerre* is a standard phrase, and one might ask what other subject for Fénice to like Cligès has in mind ... were one not sure of the answer.

A subtler adaptation of the rhetorical figure is to omit the *avis au lecteur*. Sometimes, the meaning is just as obvious:

> ... de toz amanz est costume
> Que volantiers peissent lor ialz
> D'esgarder, s'il ne pueent mialz... (584-6)

---

[66]   *Nuper in alterius thalamo ... sed dicere nolo.*
         Taliter abscindo vocem, nec dico quod iste,
         Immo quod istius aetatis, sive figurae.
              (*Poetria nova,* 1560-2)

Lines we have quoted in another context also belong here:

> "Bien fust ma dolors alegiee,
> Se tot le dart veü eüsse. (838 f.)
> ....
> Ne m'an mostra Amors adons
> Fors que la coche et les penons,
> Car la fleche ert el coivre mise... (845-7)

More is demanded of the reader when he is expected to juxtapose to the bare statement of fact another fact elsewhere stated or implied. The three doctors from Salerne obtain permission from the emperor Alis to examine the "corpse" of Fénice, and ask him to clear the palace:

> Ceste chose contredeïssent
> Cligés, Jehanz, et Tessala... (5852 f.)

which statement Chrétien leaves unamplified. He does, however, inform us that all the others present agree for fear that opposition might have bad results for the protestors. [67] But the greatest danger, of course, is for three conspirators named, and we may smile at our understanding of their "courage".

The subtlest use of *significatio per abscisionem* is that of the incomplete literary reference which the reader is expected to complete. When Fénice first appears on the scene, the emphasis is on her beauty, and it is in terms of beauty and uniqueness that her name is explained:

> Fenyce ot la pucele a non:
> Ce ne fu mie sanz reison.
> Car si con fenix li oisiax
> Est sor toz les autres plus biax,
> Ne estre n'an pot c'uns ansanble,
> Ice Fenyce me resanble:
> N'ot de biauté nule paroille.
> Ce fu miracles et mervoille
> C'onques a sa paroille ovrer
> Ne pot Nature recovrer. (2685-94)

The extraordinary aspect of this passage is not its content, but its omission. The distinctive aspect of the phoenix, its resurrection, is not even hinted at. Yet, certain associations are so essentially tied to words, and especially names, that they constitute inseparable elements of the word's usage. One cannot refer to Helen without thinking "beauty", Roland does not exist without "courage", Don Quixote without "chivalry", or the phoenix without its resurrection. At the risk of bad taste, the phoenix's resurrection is its *raison d'être*.

It is inconceivable that Chrétien was unaware of this, or "forgot" the essential association of the word *fenix*. Nor is it conceivable that

---

[67] "... tuit cil qui estoient la..." (5854) clearly refers to all the *others* who are there, since they either keep silent or praise the idea (5857 f.), while the three named oppose it.

a professional writer would disregard this association. In fact, this association has been assumed by scholars since Van Hamel, for the tale of the *fausse mort* which is the kernel of the second part of the romance constitutes a kind of resurrection. [68] The principle of importance here is the reliance of the author on the literary associations of certain proper names, even when, as here, there is a conscious avoidance of a specific indication of that association.

Significatio per similitudinem [69]

Although the last example was most interesting as a variation of *significatio per abscisionem,* it basically belongs in this section, where meaning is suggested by adducing a parallel. The cases we will study all include the use of a proper name out of an established literary tradition. It is with this form of reference that D.W. Robertson is mainly concerned in the previously cited article. [70] His first example is the comparison of Cligès to Narcissus:

> ... tant ert biax et avenanz [Cligès]
> Que Narcissus, qui desoz l'orme
> Vit an la fontainne sa forme,
> Si l'ama tant, si com an dit,
> Qu'il an fu morz, quant il la vit,
> Por tant qu'il ne la pot avoir. (2726-31)

---

[68] A.G. van Hamel, "Cligès et Tristan," p. 486.

[69] *Magnus es et genibus flexis tibi supplicat orbis.*
Cum possis, noli saevire: memento Neronis.
Sic re collata nihil amplius addo. Vel ecce
Exemplum vario clausum sermone sub isto:
Magnus Alexander, cum bella moveret Athenis,
Nulla reformandae placuerunt foedera pacis,
In pignus nisi forte datis sapientibus urbis.
Unus prudentum respondit ad istud et istis:
"Forte lupus bellum pastori movit. Utrimque
Tractatum de pace fuit; sed formula pacis
Nulla lupo placuit nisi pignus et obses amoris
Traditus esset ei custos gregis. Hoc ita facto,
Ante fuit timidus, sed post securior hostis."
Substitit hoc dicto. Rem voluit assimilari
Exemplo. Prudenter enim partem dedit auri,
Partem servavit animo. Modus iste periti,
Dimidio verbo totam vim claudere verbi.

Geoffroi de Vinsauf then concludes the section on *significatio* as follows:

Talibus egregium sententia nacta colorem
Non detecta venit, sed se per signa revelat.
Lucet ab obliquo, non vult procedere recte
In lucem. Species sunt quinque, sed est color idem.

(*Poetria nova,* 1563-83)

In the last line, Geoffroi numbers the species of this figure at five, even though he has given six. Perhaps he was following the *Rhetorica ad Herennium,* which has only five (Geoffroi added litotes: *supra,* p. 42, n. 40), too closely, and forgetting his own addition.

[70] "Chrétien's *Cligès* and the Ovidian Spirit;" *supra,* p. 45, n. 43.

The story of Narcissus, told and easily available in Ovid's *Metamorphoses,*[71] is a paradigm of the dangers of self-love, according to Robertson, and he shows that Chrétien's extensive allegorization on love entering through the eye has an ironic relation to the meaning of the story: "Chrétien shows his two young protagonists making eyes at each other, each falling hopelessly in love with the other's beauty, so that, without speaking, they come to have a common desire. In this sense their hearts are merged in one, a quaint device, we may observe, which arranges matters so that each in effect loves himself. Perhaps Chrétien intended his lovers to look a little foolish and reinforced this intention by referring to Narcissus."[72]

Another classical reference discussed by Robertson occurs in Cligès' proposal that he and Fénice solve their difficulty by leaving Greece for England and Arthur's court:

> "C'onques ne fu a si grant joie
> Eleinne reçeüe a Troie,
> Quant Paris li ot amenee,
> Que plus n'en soit de vos menee
> Par tote la terre le roi,
> Mon oncle, de vos et de moi." (5239-44)

As we have seen before, one of the modes of adaptation of rhetorical techniques is to assign them to characters, who then reveal themselves without, sometimes, being aware of it. As Robertson puts it, "... the suggestion that Cligès is like Paris, famous for his bad judgment (cf. Horace, *Epist.,* II, ii, 10-11) and that Fénice is like Helen, whose beauty leads only to misfortunes which she herself laments in the fifteenth book of the *Metamorphoses* (232-233), is not auspicious for our protagonists."[73] A further irony of the reference lies in that it is made by Cligès, thoughtless of the consequences of the famous pair's love affair, so that he condemns himself out of his own mouth.

Fénice rejects Cligès' proposal, substituting for his *significatio per similitudinem* another which puts his idea in a different light:

> "Ja avoec vos ensi n'irai,
> Car lors seroit par tot le monde
> Ausi come d'Ysolt la Blonde
> Et de Tristant de nos parlé..." (5250-3),

and this kind of reputation, of course, is very much what she wants to avoid. It does not suffice, however, to note these literary references and define their associations in respect to the characters involved: these associations are reflected in later turns of the action. Both the references to the Greek and the Celtic couples are picked up for further resonance later in the romance. After they are discovered, Fénice and

---

[71] III, 339-510.
[72] *Loc. cit.,* p. 37.
[73] *Loc. cit.,* p. 38.

Cligès wander under Thessala's guidance and magic protection until
they arrive at Arthur's court. There, Cligès brings a complaint against
his uncle;

> Qui por son desheritemant
> Avoit prise desleaumant
> Fame...   (6557-9)

Arthur immediately agrees to help Cligès: he will assemble a navy
before Constantinople, a thousand ships filled with knights, three
thousand with *sergenz,*

> Tex que citez, ne bors, ne vile,
> Ne chastiax, tant soit forz ne hauz,
> Ne porra sosfrir lor assauz.   (6566-8)

So that Cligès is in the position of bringing destruction to his homeland
as a result of his love, as did Paris. Worse, for it is Cligès himself
who would actually lead the invasion against his land.

The prophetic aspect of the Tristan reference is also fulfilled.
Fénice's refusal to accompany Cligès to England was based on concern
for her reputation. But when the young knight Bertrand brings back
the news to Alis that he has seen Fénice alive and lying naked next to
his nephew, the word spreads through the city:

> La vile an est tote esbolie
> De la novele, quant il l'oent;
> Li autre consoillent et loent
> L'empereor qu'a la tor voise.
> Molt est granz li criz et la noise
> Des genz qui apres lui s'esmuevent;... (6430-5)

Nor does the fame of the young lovers' exploit remain enclosed in
Constantinople. When he hears of the trick Thessala's potion played
on him, Alis wants revenge and orders the couple sought throughout
Europe:

> "Or tost, fet il, jusqu'a Pavie,
> Et de ça jusqu'an Alemaigne,
> Chastel, ne vile n'i remaigne,
> Ne cité, ou il ne soit quis.
> Qui andeus les amanra pris,
> Plus l'avrai que nul home chier.
> Or del bien querre, et del cerchier,
> Et sus, et jus, et prés, et loing." (6524-31)

Although Chrétien does not specify this, we may assume the searchers
will explain their mission as they go along.

And finally, it is not only throughout the Europe of their own time
that the story of their exploit spreads, but for all time that it will be
remembered. In the concluding lines of his romance, Chrétien explains
the institution of eunuchs in Constantinople as a result of Fénice's
reputation. From that time on, the emperors, remembering how she
deceived Alis, kept their empress, however high or noble, closely guarded

in her room as if she were in prison—it was not fear of sunburn—and no male approached her that was not castrated in childhood (6642-63). Thus, the entire romance, or the major part of it, becomes a *similitudo* whose moral has been learned by later emperors!

It does not seem hyperbolic to assert that the techniques described in the arts of grammar and the *Rhetorica ad Herennium* can usefully be applied to Chrétien's *Cligès*. The foregoing pages are by no means exhaustive of his stylistic irony in this romance: almost every page of his text can furnish examples. [74] Needless to say, the descriptions of tropes and figures found in school books are modified in their application to living literature—but so would they be if the text we were dealing with was the *Aeneid*. Given a certain degree of elasticity in the application of these stylistic structures to a work written centuries after the grammarians, in a different language, a different culture, and in a different genre, a sufficiently large degree of correlation between Chrétien's style and the traditional means of stylistic analysis has been demonstrated to reveal a large ironic intention on our author's part.

At the same time, it must be admitted that the limits of stylistic analysis have been passed. In the last example cited, some four thousand lines of narrative had to be invoked as the context for the irony of a few lines. Even in the discussion of examples of classical figurative ironies, we were some times led to consider extensive blocs of narrative developments. Though the present author will not deny a certain amount of premeditated guile in this respect, this tendency, deriving from the requirements of the text itself, is evidence that irony here is not an occasional ornament of style, but integral to character development and structure in *Cligès*. Before considering irony in the basic elements of narrative, however, we will consider certain forms of ironization on a fairly restricted scale which are not considered in traditional grammar or rhetoric.

IRONIZATION

Ironization of affirmation

The simplest statement is a bare affirmation, and one of the least obtrusive affirmations is the introductory phrase in indirect discourse: "he thinks" is totally uninteresting, and is tolerated in literary language merely for identification (often an unnecessary label), and out of a feeling of grammatical necessity. Insistence on this phrase is therefore surprising:

---

[74] Commenting on only one of these techniques, Kellermann remarks: "Alle verwendungen des Doppelsinns im Cligès aufzuführen, hiesse den ganzen Roman nacherzahlen." *Aufbaustil und Weltbild...*, p. 73.

Le dus cuide, et croit bien, et pansse
Que Cligés n'ait vers lui desfansse,
Que lués mort ou conquis ne l'ait. (3965-7) [75]

The repetition of the same, usually banal, word of introduction constitutes a principle of ironic insistence which, by a reverse logic normal in
irony, casts doubt on what is overly affirmed:

"Methinks the lady doth protest too much..."

Irony of fact

A simple statement of fact can be ironical, whether or not it is
supported by stylistic means, when it brings together certain aspects
of a situation which are incongruous. When we are told that

Alixandres aimme et desirre
Celi qui por s'amor sopire... (567 f.),

we may be aware of paranomasia (*aime/amor*), concretization (*sopire*
for "loves") at the rhyme, but these are weak and so common that they
bear comparatively little of the irony's weight, which resides simply
in the paradox that the two love each other and endure the torment of
doubt only because they are too timid to declare their love or even hint
at it.

An example completely bare of stylistic emphasis occurs when Alis
goes to Germany for a bride,

Et mainne avoec lui son neveu,
Por cui il avoit fet tel veu
Que ja n'avra fame an sa vie... (2649-51)

Every word is literal, the grammatical structure is perfectly normal,
but the juxtaposition of the vow and its denial by action constitute an
incongruity which gives rise to speculation about Alis' character and
Cligès' attitude toward the situation.

A similar irony is the wry, quasi-philosophical reflection of Fénice
when she awakens from her false death:

"Je me cuidai gaber et faindre,
Mes or estuet a certes plaindre,
Car la morz n'a soing de mon gap." (6187-9)

In this case, the character shares with the reader full awareness of
the irony: Fénice, though unable to speak during the tortures inflicted
on her by three doctors from Salerne, was conscious throughout.
However, her awareness of the discrepancy between intention and
actual result in this case has not taught her any lesson: she continues

---

[75] The subjunctive in indirect discourse after an affirmative word of thought
is normal in Old French (Foulet, *Petite syntaxe...*, p. 208 f.) and therefore stylistically valueless.

in a plan where her intention to save her reputation while enjoying illicit love is again frustrated.

Ironization of style

Style itself can be used ironically, by contradicting normal pre-suppositions or the associations which accompany its various forms. We have already seen an example of this under *asteismos,* where a lyric style was used to describe a battle scene. [76] Here is another example, slightly more complex. Angrès de Guinesores and his men sneak out for a night attack on a particularly dark night. But God hates traitors,

> Si comanda la lune luire,
> Por ce qu'ele lor deüst nuire.
> Molt lor est la lune nuisanz,
> Qui luist sor les escuz luisanz,
> Et li hiaume molt lor renuisent,
> Qui contre la lune reluisent:
> Car les eschargaites les voient,
> Qui l'ost eschargaitier devoient... (1685-92)

Again, the lyric technique of paranomasia, depicting the beauty of the night-shining moon reflected on the armor, is incongruous with the fact of their purpose. Another aspect of the ironic intent of the passage is its parodistic character. The motif of God's interference on the side of right is common in the *chanson de geste,* a genre from which Chrétien is often at pains to dissociate himself. However, this parodistic intent here depends on our acceptance of the stylistic irony. [77]

A facile form of ironization of style is taking a metaphor literally— a stylistic pun, as it were. Alexander, perplexed by the pain he feels in love, wonders at the fact that there is no wound on him. Is he wrong, then, to complain? No, for he personifies love as an archer, and allegorizes the cause of love—seeing Soredamors—as an arrow which has reached his heart. How does it happen that the wound is not visible?

> "Ce me diras: savoir le vuel!" (689)

"Solve *that* one: just show me how!" How did he do it? Alexander, confused by his emotions, challenges himself to solve the paradox of the arrow that reached his heart without leaving a visible sign, and accomplishes this by proposing an even more difficult paradox: the arrow pierced his eyes! ... and did not leave a wound there either. Few parts of the body are as sensitive as the eye, and to solve the first paradox by saying that the arrow went through the eye is hardly an "explanation", as Alexander's imaginary interlocutor exclaims:

> "Par l'uel? Si ne le t'a crevé?" (691)

---

[76] *Supra,* p. 40 f.
[77] Cf. Frappier, who stresses the feudal and mystical implications of God's intervention in this passage (*Cligès,* p. 52).

That the incongruity here is more humorous than ironic is indicated by Alexander's reply:

> "A l'uel ne m'a il rien grevé,
> Mes au cuer me grieve formant." (692 f.)

Alexander is so caught up in his metaphor as to forget its relation to reality. Rather than an explanation of reality, it has become a reality which itself must be explained.

Topos renversé

A traditional literary development may be ironized indirectly by first being used in the traditional manner, and then shown to be foolish or irrelevant. Cligès has just rescued Fénice from her Saxon kidnappers. He has demonstrated his knighthood by single-handedly killing off a dozen enemy knights with his Lady as the only spectator. Now, they are riding together, heading toward the Greek camp,

> C'or puet bien dire en audïance
> L'uns a l'autre sa concïance. (3779 f.)

However, they ride on without saying a word because, Chrétien informs us, each is afraid of the other's refusal. So far, this is a parallel to the Alexander-Soredamors story. Here, Chrétien dwells on the paradox of the brave young knight afraid, as we might say, of a simple slip of a girl: if she does not start the conversation,

> N'est mervoille, car sinple chose
> Doit estre pucele et coarde.
> Mes il qu'atant, de coi se tarde,
> Qui por li est par tot hardiz,
> S'est vers li seule acoardiz?
> Dex, ceste criemme don li vient,
> C'une pucele seule tient,
> Sinple et coarde, foible et quoie? (3794-3801)

The principle of ironic insistence makes us stop here to wonder about this point. On the surface, the irony seems to cut in Cligès' direction: if this is really so *sinple,* fearful, feeble, and quiet a girl, he should be able at least to engage in light conversation. On the other hand, we have seen that ironic insistence turns against the idea insisted on: is this truly Fénice's character? Is this really the way the Lady is in general? There is no answer yet, but it will not fail to come as the tale develops.

However, Chrétien does not dwell on the point, but continues the paradox of the young hero fearful of a simple slip of a thing by introducing a well-known *topos,* that of the world turned upside-down: [78]

---

[78] Ernst Robert Curtius, *La littérature européenne et le moyen âge latin,* trans. Jean Bréjoux (Paris: Presses Universitaires de France, 1956), pp. 117-22.

A ce me sanble que je voie
Les chiens foïr devant le lievre,
Et la turtre chacier le bievre,
L'aignel le lou, li colons l'aigle,
Et si fuit li vilains sa maigle,
Dom il vit et dom il s'ahane,
Et si fuit li faucons por l'ane,
Et li gripons por le heiron,
Et li luz fuit por le veiron,
Et le lyon chace li cers,
Si vont li choses a envers. (3802-12)

There is nothing very extraordinary about this example of the *topos,*
except perhaps for the note of realism of the peasant and the hoe with
which he earns his living and his weariness; but even that popular
note fits in the origin of this *topos.* [79] Nor is there anything extraordinary in the courtly clichés with which Chrétien explains the paradox
of the fearful hero: it is natural that he should shiver and pale in
love, for this relationship places the lover in the role of a *sergenz* who
must fear his *seignor* (3833 f.) ... nothing extraordinary in the clichés
themselves, that is, except for their application here. Fénice, the
feudal *seignor,* is just as frightened of speaking here as Cligès!

Nonetheless, Chrétien continues along the ironic road, the only one
to speak, as he develops the courtly theory, irrelevant as it may be to
the young couple in question:

Amors sanz criemme et sanz peor
Est feus ardanz et sanz chalor,
Jorz sanz soleil, cire sanz miel,
Estez sanz flor, yvers sanz giel,
Ciax sans lune, livres sanz letre. (3847-51)

This passage and the preceding *topos* have this in common, that they
are clichés, and that Chrétien is uniting them as elements of one development. The second is an answer to the first, and if both are paradoxes,
this need not worry us, for neither is really relevant to the situation,
neither explains it, as Chrétien indicates in the concluding lines of this
scene:

Donc ne fausse ne mesprant mie
Cligés, s'il redote s'amie.
Mes por ce ne leissast il pas
Qu'il ne l'eüst eneslepas
D'amors aresniee et requise,
Comant que la chose an fust prise,
S'ele ne fust fame son oncle.
Por ce sa plaie li reoncle,
Et plus li grieve et plus li dialt,
Qu'il n'ose dire ce qu'il vialt. (3859-68)

---

[79] *Ibid.,* p. 119.

Smilingly, Chrétien reveals he has, in the modern phrase, "put us on": he has led us through two well-developed literary clichés—one scholastic, the other fairly recently become fashionable—only to pull the rug slyly out from under us. If we have been taken in by his game, he has not. Neither raising the situation to a universal level in which the entire world partakes of the absurdity of the situation, nor the fashionable courtly theories of love have anything to do with Cligès' silence. He does not declare his love to Fénice for the very practical reason that she is his uncle's wife. Whether this is a moral problem for Cligès, or merely a tactical consideration, is not clear at this point of the story, but it is clear that courtly love has no more to do with Cligès' silence than it did with his father's.

PARALLELISM

The ironies examined so far have been localized: though the context of a given example might be extensive, the distinction between the particular stylistic effect and its background held true throughout. However, Chrétien's irony in *Cligès* reaches beyond the stylistic. The principle of incongruity which is operative on the level of words is also used to inform the structure of the romance. In scene after scene, there is a clear intent of parallelism, revealing itself sometimes in a word, sometimes in extended symmetry. The difference between this parallelism and the earlier ironies is that the two elements compared are no longer conceived as irony and background, but as two equal terms to be balanced and compared to each other. In this process of comparison, similarities and incongruities are found which suggest qualities and faults in each term. In the stylistic ironies considered up to now, one element criticized the other; here, criticism is mutual. [80]

A passage close to the beginning of *Cligès* suggests the theme of its major parallelistic structure. After the bibliography of his former works, Chrétien announces the subject of the present story, and explains that he found the *estoire* in a book in the church library of St. Peter's in Beauvais (1-24). This reference to his source enables Chrétien to modulate to the famous, oft-quoted theme of the *translatio studii:* we know from books that the first glory of *chevalerie* and *clergie* came from Greece, passed to Rome, and now honors France. May God grant

---

[80] My treatment of this technique has benefited from Kellermann's earlier discussion of *Wiederholung* and *Parallelismus* (*Aufbaustil und Weltbild...*, pp. 54-60). There is a basic difference in Kellermann's use of the term "parallelism" and mine. Whereas he stresses the identity of the parallel terms, I am primarily concerned with partial identities which reveal important differences between the two terms. This difference will explain the fact that, while he finds this technique to be least important in *Cligès* (and *Lancelot*) among Chrétien's romances (*ibid.*, p. 54), I consider it essential in *Cligès*.

it remain there, that the place pleases it: God (only) lent it to the others, for no one speaks of the Greeks and Romans any longer:

> D'ax est la parole remese
> Et estainte la vive brese. (41 f.)

Whether this should be considered a *profession de foi humaniste* or its reverse, [81] it is a striking passage to find at the beginning of a romance. But the beginning of a work is an important place for effects that will condition the reader's attitude toward what follows—it is not only rhetoric that says so—and our question is the function of this passage. Though there is a good deal of *chevalerie* in *Cligès, clergie* (knowledge, culture) does not play a major role. Nor does the sadness and sympathy of the closing couplet quoted above cohere with the tone of the romance: it is the first and the last time this note will be struck.

The basic idea of the "transfer", if one may be allowed the obvious, is the relationship between epochs. Each inherits from its predecessors and passes on to its own successors. Death intervenes, but the succession insures survival of achievements and ideals. The relationship is dual, as in the famous image Bernard of Chartres used to describe the same matter: dwarfs perched on the shoulders of giants see farther, but only because of their perch. The Romans whose works Chrétien read are dead, the Greeks he dimly perceives through their successors' works have long since disappeared, and the France he lives in has inherited their greatness by the grace of God. It is a gift all the more appreciated in that he knows it has been wrested from two nations. It is in France now:

> Dex doint qu'ele i soit maintenue
> Et que li leus li abelisse... (34 f.)

One the level of the individual, the "transfer" is that of the generations. As civilizations die and pass their riches on to other nations, so the generations within a civilization progress, sons assuming the inheritance transmitted by their father and building on it. *Cligès* has two distinct parts because it shows two generations, their behavior and ideals, as well as their equal but different foolishness. Although there are parallelisms which disregard the principle of the two generations, they are mostly secondary to the structure of the work, which separates into the stories of Alexander and his son Cligès. Both start as young men, leave their home and regent to gain knighthood and reputation at King Arthur's court, and fall in love with maidens whom, for different reasons, they have difficulty in obtaining.

Alexander-Cligès

In the great palace of the German emperor in Cologne, a great crowd has assembled to watch the encounters of two emperors, and the bride of one. Fénice enters first, and her beauty is described. Then the focus shifts to Cligès: his is the second panel of the pendant. He is introduced:

---

[81] Curtius, *op. cit.*, p. 476.

> Devant l'empereor son oncle
> Estoit Clygés desafublez. (2712 f.)

Why without a coat? Well, it was a matter of politeness not to wear
one's coat when meeting a great personage indoors ... as when, today,
a house or apartment provides a "foyer" in which to wipe one's feet
and hang one's coat. But why mention it? There is no development
to make us suspect that Cligès is lacking in manners. [82]

When Alexander and his companions land in England at South-
ampton, they sleep over the first night in that city, and are off to
Windsor the following morning, where they have been told that Arthur,
le meillor roi del mont/Qui onques fust ne ja mes soit (304 f.), is
holding court. Leaving their horses and squires in the courtyard, they
climb the steps of the great palace to see the great King.

> Mes ainz que devant lui venissent,
> Ostent les mantiax de lor cos,
> Que l'an ne les tenist por fos.
> Einsi trestuit desafublé
> An sont devant le roi alé. (308-12)

Que l'an ne les tenist por fos? Why should they fear being taken for
fools? Why are they so self-conscious that it is necessary to remark
that they do observe the proper rules of etiquette?

One of the essential characteristics of the twelfth-century knight is
largesce. When Cligès arrives in England, he lands at Wallingford:

> La s'est richemant contenuz
> A bel ostel, a grant despanse. (4532 f.)

Cligès behaves as a knight should, spending freely and affirming his
status. The fact is noted briefly as perfectly normal and according to
rule. Alexander had also spent greatly, though perhaps not as "freely".
Before he left Constantinople, his father delivered himself of a lecture
to his son on the subject of *largesce*—an appropriately "generous"
lecture. It began:

> "Biax filz, fet il, de ce me croi
> Que largesce est dame et reïne
> Qui totes vertuz anlumine,
> Ne n'est mie grief a prover..." (188-91)—

which he proceeds to do: however rich a man, what use is it *se il est
chiches*? (194). All the virtues (which are individually catalogued)
depend on *largesce,* which stands above all other virtues just as the
rose is more beautiful than all other flowers, and which increases
whatever other virtues it finds in a man five hundred fold.

> "Tant a en largesce a conter
> Que n'an diroie la mitié." (212 f.)

---

[82] A suggestion might be made that *desafublez* is an easy rhyme for the
enublez of the following line, but that is so inelegant a solution we shall not
consider it seriously except to note that the idea of cloudiness is hardly essential.

Alexander's immediate reaction is both obedient and profitable:

> Bien a li vaslez esploitié
> De quanqu'il a quis et rové,
> Car ses peres li a rové
> Tot ce qu'il li vint a creante. (214-7)

But there is a delayed reaction also. [83] In attendance at Arthur's court at Windsor, Alexander takes great pains to follow his father's advice:

> Molt i antant et met grant painne,
> Bele vie a son ostel mainne
> Et largemant done et despant,
> Si com a sa richesce apant
> Et si con ses cuers l'en consoille.

That this is more than the expected, normal generosity of a knight is shown by the court's reaction:

> Trestote la corz s'an mervoille
> Ou ce que il despant est pris,
> Qu'il done a toz chevax de pris
> Que de sa terre ot amenez. (403-11)

Again, Alexander is very conscious of the proper behavior expected of a knight. He has been told that a knight spends freely, and now that he is at the great King Arthur's court, he *applies* himself to following this rule. As in the matter of not wearing one's coat indoors, Chrétien suggests a self-consciousness in the observance of rules of behavior which might be effortless and performed with self-assurance—as does Cligès. But Cligès belongs to a later generation, brought up to accept these modes of behavior as the norm; Alexander seems to belong to a generation to which new social formulae have come in mid-course. [84]

It is not only in external behavior that the differences constitute ironic juxtaposition. Alexander's character, examined closely, is not quite that expected of a courtly knight. He is first characterized as *preuz et de fier corage* (14; cf. 63) which, though not unbefitting a courtly knight, is equally descriptive of the hero in a *chanson de geste*. A recurrent type of expression associated with his actions are varied equivalents of "come what may" (72 f.; 221 ff.; 1821). And the manner in which he obtains permission to leave Greece for England shows him to be shrewd, willful, and inconsiderate of others. The parallel episode in the Cligès story provides a standard of comparison. Cligès also

---

[83] Both the immediate and delayed reactions are *significatio per consequentiam*. The extent of narrative adaptation in the latter is obvious: the consequence comes nearly two hundred lines later.

[84] Chrétien is parodying the medieval reputation of Alexander the Great as "the type and model" of *largesse,* on which see Marian P. Whitney, "Queen of Mediaeval Virtues: Largesse," in *Vassar Mediaeval Studies,* ed. Christabel Forsyth Fiske (New Haven: Yale, 1923), pp. 181-215; on Alexander the Great, see pp. 199-202. Again, Alexander (in our romance) bears an ironic relation to his name; cf. *supra,* p. 29, n. 11.

faces the difficulty of a guardian who does not want him to leave, his uncle Alis. But he approaches this guardian in a straightforward way:

> Devant l'empereor s'aquialt,
> Et si li prie, se lui plest,
> Que an Bretaigne aler le lest
> Veoir son oncle* et ses amis. (4178-81),   *Arthur
>   GAUVAIN

and Chrétien comments:

> Molt sagemant l'en a requis... (4182)

Alis objects, and offers to make his nephew *conpainz et sires* of the empire along with himself. Cligès courteously and modestly declines— *Trop sui anfes et petit sai* (4201)—: first his prowess must be tested, and the place to do it is in Britain. He is no little Lord Fauntleroy, however:

> "Por ce le congié vos demant,
> Et sachiez bien certenemant
> Que, se vos ne m'an envoiez
> Et le don ne m'an otroiez,
> Que g'irai sanz vostre congié." (4217-21)

Alis consents, and Cligès reveals his enthusiasm:

> N'ot pas bien la parole dite,
> Quant Cligés l'en ot mercïé. (4234 f.) [85]

A straightforward, self-confident approach, then, enlivened by a youthful threat of disobedience and the touch of eagerness at the end.

Alexander behaves quite differently. First he decides to leave:

> Comant que la fins l'an responde
> Et comant qu'il l'en aveingne,
> N'est riens nee qui le deteingne
> El mont, que n'an voist an Breteingne. (72-5)

Having established his willfulness, Chrétien next shows us Alexander tricking his father into granting him an unspecified boon. When the latter accedes:

> Or a bien feite sa besoingne
> Li vaslez qui molt an fu liez.... (100 f.)

"Now the young man has pulled off his trick," and feels no compunction in showing his glee:

> Sire, fet il, volez savoir
> Que vos m'avez acreanté?
> Je vuel avoir a grant planté
> De vostre or, et de vostre argent,
> Et conpaignons de vostre gent
> Tex con je les voldrai eslire;
> Car issir vuel de vostre empire... (104-10)

---

[85] Again, *significatio per consequentiam.*

Can one be courtly without courtesy? This is a young man gloating over the success of the cunning trick he has played on his father, and rubbing it in! The impulse may certainly be ascribed to youthful enthusiasm, as with Cligès, but a comparison with the latter's words shows that the same impulse can be expressed with a politeness and straightforwardness which even include a threat of disobedience. [86]

If the role of Alexander's father here is more or less restricted to that of a "straight man" (or "fall guy"), his mother's reaction to Alexander's departure shows the effect of his character and behavior while reaffirming them:

> L'empereriz fut molt dolante,
> Quant de la voie oï parler
> Ou ses filz an devoit aler;
> Mes qui qu'an ait duel ne pesance,
> Ne qui que li tort a enfance,
> Ne qui que li blasme ne lot,
> Li vaslez au plus tost qu'il pot
> Comande ses nes aprester... (218-25)

It is hardly necessary to underline the anaphoric emphasis with which Chrétien describes the heedlessness of Alexander's departure to explain the grief caused his mother and others. [87]

Nor can it be said that Alexander gains polish at Arthur's court. His stay there is marred by two *faux-pas* toward the great king himself. In his first exploit, he has captured four of Angrès' men; *par corteisie* (1337), he offers his *première chevalerie* to the Queen,

> Car tost les feïst li rois pandre... (1341)

The king, however, "is not amused" (1345) : he demands the traitors be delivered over to him, and the Queen must tell Alexander:

> "De c'est li rois molt correciez
> Que je ne li ai ja bailliez... (1409 f.)

The Queen is truly courteous, taking on herself the responsibility which, in fact, is Alexander's. Without delving into the preferability of various executionary measures, it seems that his good but misplaced intentions have worsened the prisoners' fate: rather than being hung, as he had

---

[86] A repeated note on the verbal level suggests that even Alexander's motive is suspect: *"issir vuel de vostre empire"* (110); he says he will be *"malves ou ber/En autre païs"* than his father's (136 f.); and when he orders the ships readied, it is explained that *"il n'i vialt plus arester/An son païs plus longuemant."* (226 f.). In the last case, two emphases seem to suggest a lifetime of tiresome duty from which the speaker seeks earnestly to be relieved: the repetition of *plus,* and the unnecessary locative *i* which needlessly anticipates *an son païs* and thereby stresses that from which the brash, young, and quite unburdened Alexander feels impelled to escape: the adolescent wants to leave home!

[87] We know what Chrétien will do with the same theme, in a different affabulation, in the *Perceval.*

feared, they will be drawn and quartered by order of the angry king (1420 ff.).

Alexander's first blunder was *par corteisie*: his second is *par franchise.* [88] In so far as each of these terms includes the idea of correct behavior, they are ironic. Arthur has offered the prize of a cup as beautiful as it is valuable to the man—knight or *sergenz*—who captures the traitors' castle. The cup is described, and its workmanship, value, and beauty stressed (1518-34). And with the cup, if the conqueror is a knight, he will be granted any other reward he chooses, *Se el monde trover se lait.* [89] The fortunate man, of course, turns out to be Alexander. Since he is a knight, he has the choice, in addition to the cup, of any thing in the world he desires, *tant* [soit] *chiere* (2183).

This places Alexander in a problematic situation. The only thing he wants is Soredamors. But his lack of *savoir-faire* has up to now prevented him from so much as hinting at his feelings. Standing as he is in the middle of the court (2173 f.), he does not dare now to ask for her hand,

> Que molt mialz se vialt il doloir
> Que il l'eüst sor son voloir. (2193 f.)

His concern for her feelings is touching, but as Chrétien points out, irrelevant:

> Tant crient que il ne depleüst
> Celi qui grant joie en eüst... (2191f.) [90]

Alexander's first reaction is quite reasonable. Unable to declare at the moment the boon he desires, he asks for a postponement *Tant qu'il an sache son pleisir* (2197). His second reaction is stranger: he seizes the precious cup, and gives it in turn to Gauvain. The latter does not seem very pleased with the gift:

> Prie mon seignor Gauvain tant
> Que de lui cele cope prant
> Mes a molt grant paine l'a prise. [91]

That Alexander had to urge the gift on Gauvain might merely indicate a polite but temporary refusal; but the fact that the latter accepted the cup only *a molt grant paine* leads elsewhere. The gift of a king is not lightly disdained—especially so precious a gift from so great a king—and Gauvain's reluctance to accept the cup suggests that he views Alexander's gesture as close to *lèse-majesté.*

---

[88] I am drawing here on four verses omitted by Guiot and relegated by Micha to Appendix IV (p. 212). Micha comments on this omission: "vers non indispensables, mais bourdon probable." (Note to l. 2199).

[89] This is qualified at l. 2185: "Fors la corone et la reïne." Apparently, Arthur knew something at this time he was to forget by the time Lancelot arrived at court!

[90] This is an excellent example of a localized, factual irony summing up the irony of an extended situation; cf. *supra,* p. 79 f.

[91] See *supra,* n. 88.

Why should Alexander be displeasured by Arthur's rich gift? Why, if he is displeasured, does he show it? The second question is easily answered: willful people are likely to be impulsive also. The first may be explained by Alexander's state of mind. What he wants most in the world is being offered to him freely, but he feels he cannot claim it: we can sympathize with the frustration of a brash young man accustomed to having his own way, in this situation. By comparison to golden-haired Soredamors, the gold cup is worthless to him and nothing more than a distraction. His gesture reveals this, and implies that what he wants and plans to ask for later is worth far more than the fifteen marks at which the cup is appraised. [92]

Alexander's monologue

The same conflict between impulse and imposed modes of behavior and thought governs Alexander's immense monologue. It has already contributed several examples of particular ironies; [93] here, we will consider it as a whole. It divides into two roughly equal parts: the first half consists of the elaboration of four successive metaphorical analyses of love; the second half returns to the second metaphor, that of the arrow, and uses it as a pretext for the description of Soredamors.

The first two metaphors—love as illness and love as a harsh master who has shot his arrow through his servant's eye—have already been discussed. [94] In both cases, the same principle of elaboration was at work: the metaphor was spun out to the point of absurdity. Not surprisingly, the same thing is true of metaphors three and four. Rejecting the *dart d'amour* as an explanation for his troubles, since it does not explain why his heart grieves while his eye does not (692-700), Alexander next elaborates an allegory in which the heart is the candle in a lantern and the eye the glass door through which the light shines. Unfortunately, Alexander's attempt to compose courtly symbolic poetry is as ill-fated as his attempts at social courtliness: he confuses the allegory by combining the image of the glass door (the eye) with the image of a mirror, in which the heart looks both at itself and the outside world (724 ff.). We may assume, I think, that in Alexander's time, two-way mirrors were as yet nonexistent, as they were in Chré-

---

[92] The first lines following this scene are: *Quant Soredamors a aprise D'Alixandre voire novele, Molt li plot et molt li fu bele.* (2200-2; like everyone else, she had been grieving his "death".) She makes no mention of this scene. Is she so overwhelmed by the good news that he is alive, or does her omission of any reference to this scene in which Alexander was guilty of a blunder in etiquette constitue a case of *significatio per abscisionem*? Or is she unaware that it is a blunder, being "precourtly" herself?

Franz brackets this scene with that of Arioconde's message to Alis, considering both reversals of normal behavior (with which I agree entirely), and opines that the present gesture of Alexander is a "reine Schmuckgeste" for which there is no inner motivation; "Die reflektierte Handlung...", p. 84.

[93] *Supra,* pp. 28-31.

[94] *Supra,* pp. 28 f., 60 f.

tien's: a mirror was not yet to be seen through. The two metaphors combined in this allegory are contradictory, and the way Alexander deals with this difficulty is to indulge in a pretty little lyrical passage in which he describes the world the heart can see through its mirror-door, the eye:

> "Si voit maintes oevres diverses,
> Les unes verz, les autres perses,
> L'une vermoille, et l'autre bloe,
> L'une blasme, et l'autre loe,
> L'une tient vil, et l'autre chiere." (729-33),

which is indubitably true, but quite irrelevant to the experience which the metaphor originally intended to explain: the experience of love at first sight. [95]

And so also for the fourth metaphor. The eyes and heart are conceived as independent of Alexander: should he consider them friends or enemies? There is some psychological value in this translation of the feeling of helplessness and lack of self-confidence generally attested in such cases, [96] but the further development of the allegory, as in the former ones, is ludicrous. The idea of "friend or enemy" is modulated into a personification of these rebellious parts of the body as *sergent* (752 ff.), servants or military subordinates, who display far too much self-confidence in their cavalier handling of their lord and master, whose love for them will cease ... a slightly veiled threat Alexander makes to his eyes and heart.

Alexander's four attempts to analyze, explain, and deal with his feelings in metaphors which are medical, courtly, scholastic, and soldierly, lead him into successive absurdities which the audience can view either as the comedy of helplessness or the irony of the warrior handling delicate literary weapons so crudely that they turn against him. In spite of its incongruence with his own being, Alexander is willing and even eager to participate in the new culture. It is almost as if he were consciously playing a role which from time to time involves him enough

---

[95] Since the lyricism of these lines is irrelevant, this is another case of lyricism ironized; see *supra*, p. 60 f. Frappier seems to dismiss the possibility that Chrétien was "mi-sérieux mi-plaisant" in this passage, considering it rather a proto-scientific and symbolic "effort pour élucider un mystère de la vie intérieure" by means of "une transposition du sacré au profane: en effet la métaphore de la verrière traversée sans être rompue par le rayon du soleil symbolisait traditionnellement au Moyen Age le mystère virginal de l'Incarnation..." (*Cligès*, p. 84 f.). Given the questionable literary appropriateness of equating the birth of love in a man of Alexander's character with the presence of the Holy Ghost in the Virgin Mary, as well as the "faiblesse insigne" of Alexander's dialectic (*ibid.*, p. 84), it is difficult to accept the idea that Chrétien intended this passage to be taken at face value. Without denying either the religious provenance of the metaphor or its suggestiveness of religious origin (*ibid.*, p. 85 & n. 1), I would interpret this provenance as being suggested ironically: it is Alexander who takes himself so seriously, not his author. This would then be another example of a literary tradition (here symbolic and religious) being used for ironic purposes; cf. *supra*, pp. 61 ff.

[96] Compare the same transference in Soredamors, *infra*, p. 73.

to make him forget it is only a temporary role. He becomes so engrossed in the unaccustomed role of explaining things (to himself) that he begins to sound like a professor:

"Ce meïsmes sachiez des ialz,
Et del voirre et de la lanterne... (724 f.),

and traps himself into the over-elaboration of the outer world we have noted. It is as a lecturer closing an extensive parenthetical digression to return to his main subject that Alexander dismisses the preceding dialectal allegories and analyses:

"Or vos reparlerai del dart... (762) [97]

He seems to be returning to the same metaphor of love's arrow. In fact, it is a new metaphor in that the referent is new: "love's arrow" earlier referred to the experience of seeing Soredamors; now, it refers to Soredamors herself, and is no more than a pretext for Alexander's permission to his memory to rove over the details of the girl's appearance. The very ambiguity with which he starts off hints at the *trouble sensuel* [*qui*] *agite Alexandre*. [98] If this suggestion is correct, it is quite in the character of an older generation of warriors, those of the *chanson de geste*. Besides this introductory ambiguity, one characteristic opposes this final allegory to the four preceding: its clarity, as contrasted to their contradictory complexity. Indeed, the undeniable clarity of the allegory—an arrow with forehead, eyes, mouth, nose, etc...!—discards the allegorical integument altogether, and we understand that Alexander is on familiar territory again, presenting to the eye of his mind a young woman he urgently desires. [99]

In this reading, Alexander appears as the impulsive, willful, cunning warrior who is also the victim of a "cultural lag": a member of an older generation at a time when new ideals conquer society, his earnest

---

[97] It has become a cliché in Chrétien scholarship to cite this line as evidence that the author, bemused by his rhetorical virtuosity, has forgotten that it is his character speaking: Paris, *op. cit.*, p. 278; Frappier, *Cligès*, p. 70. Nothing of the kind: it is Alexander who forgets he is speaking to himself, taking his *dédoublement* quite seriously and imagining an audience.

I would not deny, however, that if Chrétien read his romance to an audience, he took advantage of the line for a "pun" bridging the illusion of art and the reality of his presence.

[98] Frappier, *Cligès*, p. 86.

[99] Chrétien used the same bi-partite structure for the same purpose in Yvain's monologue (*Yvain*, 1432-1510). Hilka criticized the first part (1432-67) for its "kühlen Erwägungen" (*Die direkte Rede...*, pp. 77 & 79), while Frappier commends the second part for its "fougue lyrique" (*Chrétien de Troyes*, p. 164). Both are correct as to fact: the first half contains what has come to be regarded as the typical casuistry of courtly love, the second a lyrical abandon to love. A modern psychology would speak of rational self-justification leading to a release of emotion and empathy. That Chrétien used the same structure twice indicates its inner relations are not accidental: I see no reason to deny Chrétien the perception of the relationship between rationalization and emotion. On this monologue of Yvain's, cf. Frappier, *Le roman breton: Yvain ou le Chevalier au Lyon* (Paris: Centre de Documentation Universitaire, 1958), p. 83 f.

attempts to adhere to the new etiquette make of him a self-conscious, timid, occasionally blundering and ostentatious immigrant to Arthur's court. ... This portrait is overdrawn, of course, as much as another which sees him as the perfect example of a courtly lover and a gentleman. [100] After all, Alexander is accepted and liked by Arthur's court, especially by Gauvain (391 f.) and the Queen. [101] The reason for the disparity between the present description and our experience of the character in the romance is that I have stated positively what is only suggested ironically by Chrétien, an author who never falters in his sympathy for his creation and victim. He is among those writers able to portray foolishness with sympathy and crudity with delicacy: his subjects are never "beyond the pale."

The portrait of Cligès is less interesting. As a fictional person, the youth, to borrow E.M. Forster's term, is a "flat" character. He is more important as a foil for Alexander and Fénice than for his own complexity. By contrast to his father, there is no difficulty, for Cligès, in adhering to courtly standards of behavior and feeling: he is to the "manner" born, and fully at ease in it. Courtliness, a goal for Alexander, is an assumption for Cligès. And this shift in the status of courtliness explains why Alexander is more interesting than Soredamors, and Fénice than Cligès. The new modes of thought and behavior which are established in the second part of *Cligès* enthrone the Lady as the "leading" character: in their relationship, it is Fénice who leads Cligès, who provides the motive power of the action which concerns their love. [102]

Soredamors' monologue

The tone of Soredamors' monologue differs from Alexander's. Though both are beset by a love they fear to express, their lonely lucubrations are cast in languages of different registers. Where Alexander turns to the stuff of dreams—images and metaphors—Soredamors deals with her experience in more intellectual terms. The prelude to the monologue, when she first lays eyes on Alexander, treats the question "Should I love?" in feudal terms (469-515). She accuses her eyes of treason (468 & ff.), asks herself whether she does not have control over them (475), and considers the possibility of forcing them to look elsewhere so as to guard herself against love. At this point, Soredamors sees love as a problem of sovereignty—hers over herself, and the threat of love's sovereignty over her. Briefly, she tries to relegate the responsibility for her emotions first to her eyes, then to her heart (496-501). [103]

---

[100] Frappier, *Cligès*, p. 63.

[101] Arthur's was a broad-minded court, which included such types as the ineffectual Calogrenant, a boor like Ké, and which wished to retain a bumptious youngster like the early Perceval.

[102] Further on Cligès below, p. 80 f.

[103] It will be noted that this stage recalls an extensive development in Alexander's monologue: *supra,* p. 71.

The prelude ends when she discards these relegations and assumes responsibility for herself. She reaffirms her sovereignty, locates it in her will (502-6), and decides that she will never love—a "decision" whose absurdity is underlined by Chrétien:

> Ensi a soi meïsmes tance,
> Une ore aimme, et autre het... (516 f.)—

her "decision" not to love, in the context Chrétien provides, is itself ironic proof that she does love.

In spite of the difference in tonality, Chrétien uses the same technique of ironic exaggeration here as in Alexander's metaphors. The first impulse continues the prelude as Soredamors attempts to convince herself that she does not love Alexander: she goes so far in her reasonable approach to say that, although she doesn't love him, she wishes him well nonetheless. In spite of herself, however, this leads to the timidly understated question: *Est ce Amors?*, to which, as we have seen, she hesitantly answers: *Oïl, ce croi*. [104] We have also seen the second development—Soredamors as a student at Love's school: *Or vuel amer, or sui a mestre* (938)—lead to the absurdity of "loving them all for the sake of [loving] one." [105] In the third section, she finds her essential nature and destiny in analyzing her own name in the medieval etymological method. [106] She takes such pride in the symbolic separation of the word into *sororee d'amors* (972), that in dedicating herself to the god she will gild his lily:

> "... je metrai an lui ma cure,
> Que de lui soie doreüre..." (977 f.)

and finally decides, in a declaration of regal absoluteness:

> "Or aim et toz jorz amerai." (980)

This decision, which concludes the third and begins the fourth development, is immediately undercut as she asks herself: *Cui?* whom will she love?, to which she answers with the reader's own comment: *Voir, ci a bele demande!* (981). In this last and longest development, Soredamors approaches the practical problem: granted that she loves Alexander, what good is it if he is not made to realize this? She cannot tell him herself, not out of modesty, [107] but because he would often reproach her for it:

---

[104] *Supra*, p. 43.

[105] *Supra*, p. 51 f.

[106] Frappier, *Cligès*, p. 76.

[107] Chrétien's reflection at the end of Soredamors' monologue distributes the irony evenly on both:

> Ensi se plaint et cil et cele,
> Et li uns vers l'autre se cele. (1039 f.)

This suggests that there are ways for a young girl to deal with this difficulty without losing her modesty ... as Soredamors realizes: see the following paragraphs.

> "Quant de ma boche le savroit,
> Je cuit que plus vil m'an avroit,
> Si me reprocheroit sovant
> Que je l'en ai proié avant." (997-1000) [108]

She first plans to wait until Alexander notices (1008), but then Soredamors stumbles on a doubt: what if he doesn't know anything about love?
He will not be able to perceive her feelings unless he has been in love
himself ... and we, the readers, know he is as much a novice in love (at
least of the courtly variety) as Soredamors herself.

Soredamors finds herself in an apparently insoluble dilemma. Having
finally come round to admitting her love—and the monologue ends on
this note: even if he does not return her feelings, she will love him
(1038)—she suspects that Alexander, ignorant of love, will not become
aware of these feelings. Her entire series of ratiocinations may be
useless, and her inner courage also. There is only one way out, a
solution which will do the job, safeguard her feelings, and preserve her
self-respect. She will let him know of her love, not directly, but *Par
sanblant et par moz coverz* (1033).

This is an eminently practical and appropriately subtle solution.
The only caveat is not theoretical: Soredamors fails to carry out this
plan. In fact, she never speaks to anyone in this romance. Only on
one occasion is she depicted as actually speaking to someone (when
the Queen orders her to explain to Alexander that she has sewn the
shirt he is wearing), but even here her speech is cast in indirect discourse (1591 ff.). We have seen her hesitate so long on one occasion,
when she and Alexander were sitting together and alone, that the
occasion was lost. [109] On another, when she hears the false report of
Alexander's death, she does not dare to show her grief (2084 ff.). It is
one of Chrétien's triumphs to have made her presence so convincing
through description and monologue that one hardly notices the absence
of actual conversation.

In part, this is a narrative adaptation of *significatio per abscisionem*:
an action is forecast, but never acted out. The principle applies to
Alexander as well. He postponed specification of Arthur's second prize
(after the gold cup) for capturing Angrès' castle, until he should learn
Soredamors' wishes. [110] This at least implies an effort to learn her
wishes and her feelings. As a matter of fact, of course, he does nothing
of the sort: it is the Queen who will finally bring the young pair
together and make their marriage possible. Their intentions, however
much mulled over in their monologues, are irrelevant to their actions.
The older generation, which the new mode of love at court has first

---

[108] Soredamors' objection to the solution of directly approaching Alexander
is the same as Fenice's objection to the "Iseut" solution of *her* problem: both
reject *vilenie*; cf. ll. 1001 f. and 3112.

[109] *Supra*, p. 46 f.

[110] *Supra*, p. 69 f.

reached, is really incapable of living that mode, and its desires and ideals must be brought to fruition, if at all, by external circumstance.

When we look at the entire romance of *Cligès,* however, Soredamors' plan of revealing her love indirectly is fulfilled, though by another character. It is Fénice who subtly leads on Cligès with a cunning equal to Alexander's in the scene with his father, though with a courtly elegance far different from his crudeness. Before discussing the scene in which this young couple of the new generation avow their feelings— a marked contrast to the mutism of the older pair—we will first examine the third, and last, major monologue of the romance, that of Fénice.

Fénice's monologue

We have already commented on the passage which, coming between the scene of leave-taking and Fénice's monologue, serves as an introduction to the latter. [111] She places his parting words on her tongue as a bit of spice, delicious and precious. So precious is it in fact that it is metamorphosed into a treasure to be hidden, for safe-keeping, in her heart (4346-9). But, continues Chrétien, her fear is baseless, for this treasure is like an edifice which cannot be destroyed by deluge or fire... (4352-8). *Mes ele n'an est pas certainne* (4359), and therefore examines this treasure of spice more closely. Thus, the introduction to the monologue and the monologue itself are related as description and the thing described. They are pendants, within the literary work itself, one panel bearing the object depicted, the other the painting of that object ... the art, and the reality, both within the work of art. Is their relationship ironic, or do they tend to the same point?

Let us first say what Fénice's monologue is not. It is not like Soredamors', in the prelude and beginning of her monologue, a defense against love. Fénice never doubts her feelings for Cligès. Indeed, Chrétien described her as "exchanging eyes" with Cligès when they first met (2760-9), and placing her heart with him already then (2773-6). Her concern is never with her own feelings, their naming and analysis, as was Soredamors', but with Cligès' feelings: she knows so well that she loves him that she need not even consider the question. But does he love her?, and she pensively weighs his parting words:

> "Mes droiz est qu'a vos congié praigne
> Com a celi cui ge sui toz." (4282 f.)

How can she possibly govern him (*"De quoi le puis je justisier?"* 4369), when he is more beautiful and noble than she? She does not deserve it, only *Amors* could grant this gift. And now Fénice must prove to herself that he would not have used that phrase—so ambiguous!—if he did not love her also. And so she weighs the alternative interpretations of the phrase—a merely social salutation, a personal declaration of love—the interpretation varying with the flux and reflux of

---

her emotions. [112] She becomes momentarily incensed at the thought that, like so many others, he may have said it to flatter her (4391-7), and then tenderly recalls his paleness as he knelt, his tears and sorrowful face:

> "Li oel ne me mantirent mie,
> Don je vi les lermes cheoir.
> Asez i poi sanblanz veoir
> D'amor, se je neant en sai." (4404-7)

And then turnabout again, as she moans that he has so flattered and tricked her that *"Morte sui"* (4412) since he has taken her heart with him. "My heart grows foreign to its house, And does not wish to remain with me, So does it hate me and my manor. In faith, he truly has mistreated me, Who has my heart in lordship, And does not love me—this I know well—who so steals and robs me mine." (4416-22) *Jel sai? Por coi ploroit il dons?* (4423) ... and Fénice turns about again. The themes already broached are picked apart and intertwined again—the heart has left her, and who will have lordship, and how badly Cligès mistreated her by making her fall in love!—for another fifty lines or so (4424-75), at which point a new image and theme are introduced. Her heart is away with its master (4476 ff.), and will serve this master as a *sergenz,* flattering him as one must in court, sitting at his right, removing the feather that stays in his hair from the pillow he sleeps on ... even when no feather is there! There is danger in such flattery: for he will smooth his hair, and if there be a touch of badness in him, no matter how courtly he speaks, he will boast he is unequalled in prowess and knowledge. For that is the way and effect of flatterers, to praise their masters when they do evil, and these believe them, and yet the flatterers praise their masters to their face and make faces behind their backs.... Whoever frequents the courts and lords must serve with lies. "So must my heart behave, if it wishes its master's grace: let it be a liar and flatterer. But Cligès is such a knight, so handsome, so noble, so loyal, that he will never be lying or false to me, however much I praise him, for in him there is nothing to correct. Because of this I want my heart to serve him, for the peasant says in his proverb: 'Whoever serves a good man is bad, if he does not improve.'" (4515-26).

I have paraphrased and translated this passage at length, not knowing a better way to counter one of the most puzzling misreadings to plague Chrétien. I confess to complete incomprehension of commentaries that assimilate this passage to the techniques of dialectics, which seems far more present in the monologue of Soredamors, which accuse it of pedanticism or *lourdeur,* and which label the final development of the heart as *sergenz* useless, absurd, and *fastidieux.* [113] This development is based on the techniques we have seen used in Alexander's

---

[112] Frappier, *Cligès,* p. 71.
[113] *Ibid., loc. cit.;* cf. Paris, *op. cit.,* p. 296, n. 3.

monologue: [114] the extensive development of a traditional image or metaphor, in this case that of the heart which has left its owner to accompany the man she loves, and the transmutation of this metaphor into a new integument, that of the distant heart as servant of the beloved. [115] To read the lines on the *sergenz* as criticism of flattering servants is simply not to read at all. Fénice, like Alexander, is bemused by her own musings, takes her metaphor literally, and, under the guise of a new integument. rejoins Cligès in England. The flattering servant who plucks a non-existent feather from Cligès' hair, who willingly demeans himself by flattering his master, relying on his master's goodness and incorruptibility, the creature so often criticized and damned in courtly poetry—this is the humbling role Fénice wishes and imagines for herself, at the right hand of Cligès! There is no question whatever of this identity. Fénice commands her heart to be a liar and flatterer (4517), and takes comfort in the thought that Cligès is so fine a knight

> "Que ja n'iert mançongiers ne fax
> Vers *moi*, tant le sache lober..." (4520 f.)

On the contrary, this seems to me a literary triumph, an extraordinary portrayal of a young girl's day-dreaming which, in its subtle use of stylistic devices to follow her thoughts and shifting moods of fear, hope, doubt, and the pleasure of her imagined service to the man she loves, verges on the stream-of-consciousness technique of modern novelists. The sentimentality which might be a danger is averted by a gentle suffusion of irony: the attentive reader, conscious of the stylistic devices being used, continually aware of the reality to which the metaphorical developments refer, finds himself by the very fact of this consciousness and awareness at a certain distance from the character. The metaphorical developments themselves are intentionally exaggerated, and there are other hyperbolic touches such as the frequent exclamations that "He has killed me! [with love?]", which we need not take too seriously since we recognize them as clichés.

---

114 *Supra,* pp. 70 ff.

115 Professor W.T.H. Jackson points out to me that the image of the heart in attendance with a distant lover is frequent in the crusading songs. It is difficult to evaluate whether this was an intentional reference on Chrétien's part, and if so, what his intention was. The crusading song soon merged with the love poem (among other lyric forms: see Jackson, *The Literature of the Middle Ages,* p. 255, and Paul Zumthor, *Histoire littéraire de la France médiévale, VIᵉ-XIVᵉ siècles* [Paris: Presses Universitaires de France, 1954], p. 149; Zumthor dates this merger ca. 1160-70 in Northern France [*loc. cit.*], the decade before Chrétien wrote *Cligès*: Frappier, *Chrétien de Troyes,* p. 12, and Micha, Introduction to the edition of *Cligès,* p. viii, both give 1176 as the most probable date). If Chrétien thought of the crusading song as merely another form of love poetry, the relationship is no more than that of a source for imagery; if he was thinking of the "pure" form of the crusade song, the intent may have been to ennoble even flattery, or to ironize Fénice's use of an image taken from a religious context for private, secular purposes.

The Avowals

And yet, such praise is insufficient. The monologue works not only as brilliant virtuosity at the service of character portrayal. It also lays the ground for a scene in which a different aspect of Fénice's character is revealed: the avowals. We have already seen that it is introduced on a note of light irony. [116] This tone is maintained throughout a dialogue whose key is the awareness described above: nearly all the words used by Cligès and Fénice in these sixty or so lines are allegorical, and continue the metaphor of the displaced heart. [117] It is a duet of tropes in which both participants speak according to an unspoken agreement, to declare their love in covert words and equally covert explanations. During the duet itself, the two operate as equals. Cligès is the first whose words are given in direct discourse:

> "Ausi com escorce sanz fust
> Fu mes cors sanz cuer an Bretaingne," (5120 f.)

since his heart remained in Greece. But he does not press Fénice to accept the metaphor. Instead, he courteously gives her the opportunity of carrying on the conversation on a social and innocuous level: [118] how do you like Greece, he asks ... since I may not ask more of you. [119]

---

[116] *Supra*, p. 43.

[117] The metaphor has been fixed in the reader's mind by its occurrence in other locations. Speaking in his own person, Chrétien made it the subject of a small dissertation (2779-2814) whose main feature is the appeal to common sense and physical reality in deciding a point of love-doctrine: one thing cannot be in two places at once (2800), and so one body can only have one heart (2814). In the present scene, Cligès and Fénice get around this objection: while her heart was with him in England, his was with her in Greece.

This "doctrinal question" is not to be taken with gravity, but a grain of salt. Its main points, the appeal to common sense and the equally simple and literal statement that what is involved is an exchange of wills rather than of hearts (2793-5), are minor by comparison to its functions: to fix in the audience's mind the fact that Cligès and Fénice, who exchanged eyes at their first encounter (2768 f.) are already in love, and to do this by indirect means which do not demand direct verbal expression of this by the two characters. It also provides a transition from the subject of love to the message of the Duke of Saxony's nephew (2817 ff.).

The importance of the doctrinal question is also reduced by the fact that it is, at least in part, a literary tradition. When Chrétien glosses the exchange of hearts as being in reality an exchange of wills, he is following Cicero, who, in *De amicitia* (highly prized in the XIIth century), spoke of the union of two wills in friendship: Faith Lyons, "Sentiment et rhétorique dans l'*Yvain*," *Romania*, LXXXIII (1962), 370-7.

[118] There is an obvious parallel and contrast here with Soredamors who, conscious of the different meanings *ami* acquired in the two levels of discourse, hesitated and (temporarily) lost. This linguistic dualism paralyzed her; our present pair take advantage of it to express their feeling with the least social and psychological danger to themselves.

[119] *Supra*, p. 53.

But Fénice is not in the least interested in small talk. She picks up his metaphor and makes it hers:

> "En moi n'a mes fors que l'escorce,
> Car sanz cuer vif et sanz cuer sui." (5144 f.)

She continues the parallel by explaining that, though she has never been in England, her heart has long sojourned there, and adds a note of maidenly timidity:

> "Ne sai s'il a bien ou mal fet." (5148)

And so the dialogue continues, each playing the other's "straight man", feeding each other lines which lead to the inevitable conclusion, still metaphorical, in which both join:

> "Dame, don sont ci avoec nos
> Endui li cuer, si con vos dites;
> Car li miens est vostres toz quites." [120]
> "Amis, et vos ravez le mien,
> Si nos antravenomes bien." (5170-4)

But this dialogue is only part of the scene. It is followed by an uninterrupted declaration of principles enunciated without hesitation by Fénice. At the beginning of the scene, it was also she who set the subject of the conversation. She first asked Cligès about England, then about Gauvain, *Tant qu'an la parole se fiert* (5110), and then led directly to the subject of love by asking Cligès if he loved an English lady or girl. Without accusing Fénice of hypocrisy in her indications of timidity, we can say that she is more self-willed and independent than appears on the surface. We have come a long way since she seemed *Sinple et coarde, foible et quoie.* [121] Though she submitted to her father's will that she marry Alis without a word of protest, this was a social obligation and a social helplessness in which she could change nothing. Now, however, her virginity unimpaired, sure of Cligès' love, she assumes the position of the leading determinant of action. There is no doubt or hesitation in her words or thought as she un-equivocally declares to Cligès that he will have no physical pleasure with her (*"Autre que vos or en avez,"* 5205) unless he can think of a way to separate her from Alis. [122] Like a teacher assigning homework, she orders him to think over the problem, and to come see her the fol-lowing morning.

The best he can come up with is to suggest they play the role of Helen and Paris by fleeing to England; she sees through the elegant classical integument of his suggestion, however, and replaces it by a

---

[120] This line clearly echoes Cligès' parting words (*supra*, p. 76); here, however, in spite of the metaphorical level of the dialogue, there is no ambiguity.
[121] *Supra*, p. 61.
[122] Interpreting *desasanblee* (5208) as meaning specifically "divorce" (as does Micha, "Tristan et Cligès," p. 6) is being overly precise: "separation" is closer.

reference to the other great love story which haunts her, that of Tristan and Iseut. [123] She will have none of either, and rejects his suggestion out of hand:

> "... Et je dirai:
> Ja avoec vos ensi n'irai..." (5249 f.)

Instead, she proceeds to outline, step by step, the well thought out plan devised with Thessala's help. [124] By contrast, Cligès has a restrained role. The previous evening, having heard his assignment, he reacted with complete acquiescence:

> Quant Cligés ot sa volanté
> Si li a tot acreanté
> Et dist que molt sera bien fet. (5221-3)

Now, although he has a long speech in which his serf Jehan is introduced, Cligès is dealing only with the means to carry out Fénice's proposal. Indeed, until the very end of the romance (when he obtains Arthur's promise of support in an invasion of Greece), Cligès is portrayed exclusively as following others' ideas, plans, and suggestions. He does not protest Alis' marriage to Fénice; he is tricked by Thessala into serving her potion to Alis; he is helpless when Fénice is tortured by the three doctors from Salerno—for his sake, as he later recognizes; he is completely awed by Jehan and his workmanship; unaware of the potion Fénice has drunk, he is deceived along with the rest of the people into mourning her "death"; when she revives in the cemetery, he is ready to leave her there while he goes chasing after Thessala, and it is Fénice, just "resurrected" from the grave, who suggests he send Jehan; he spends fifteen months shuttling back and forth between the city and the tower, never thinking that his mistress might like some air and sunshine until she requests it; and when they are discovered by Bertrand in their orchard, he does not move to chase the latter until Fénice explains the danger his discovery puts them into.

Fénice, first presented as helpless to alter her father's decision to marry her off for political reasons, soon appears as self-willed, imposing her will first on an unsuspecting Alis (thanks to Thessala's magic drink), and then on Cligès by force of argument as well as love. Her shrewdness and determination are demonstrated by the episode of the false death as well as in the scene of the avowals.

---

[123] *Supra*, p. 56 f.

[124] "... reconnaissons qu'elle prend l'initiative d'échapper à la vie conjugale et qu'elle échafaude le subterfuge qui doit la donner à celui qu'elle aime." Micha, *loc. cit.* I cannot follow Micha, however, when he makes of Fénice a figure of cruelty comparable to Racine's heroines, of determined and self-interested heroism for whom the end justifies the means. Without denying Fénice's moral culpability, the register of Micha's comparison seems to me to disregard the sympathetic and playful portrayal Chrétien has drawn of her.

REALITY AND ILLUSION

Things are rarely what they seem in *Cligès*. The hero after whom the novel is titled is weaker than his feminine counterpart, who in turn more resembles Alexander than Soredamors. This basic incongruity is not simply a result of the courtly theories in which the Lady has sovereignty over her lover. While it is possible to find support for such theories in the text, it is equally possible to find them contradicted. Indeed, support and contradiction both are found in one passage spoken by Fénice herself. The first sentence seems to contain the essence of this courtly relationship with a feudal background:

> "Ja mes an trestote ma vie
> Ne quier d'autre home estre servie.
> Mes amis, mes sergenz serez... (5289-91)

The doctrine of the roles here shines forth with unadulterated clarity, but the following lines invert the roles and their normal setting:

> "Boen m'iert quanque vos me ferez,
> Ne ja mes ne serai d'empire
> Dame, se vos n'en estes sire.
> Uns povres leus, oscurs et pales,
> M'iert plus clers que totes ces sales." (5292-6)

More important is the fact that this incongruity between appearance and reality is not simply a matter of doctrine, but is based on the very personality and character of the actors. Their traits, the depth of their being, are rarely stated, but suggested and revealed by indirection and action. There is one case where this is particularly true, since the character in question is not given any "doctrinal" speeches and monologues. A shadowy figure who at first seems nothing more than a convenient puppet to be managed according to the necessities of Chrétien's devious plot, Alis is nevertheless a pivotal figure for the plot itself and, more importantly, for an approach to what is both a pervasive literary technique of *Cligès* and its central intellectual concern.

Alis

From the point of view of the plot, there are only two links between the two parts of the romance. The first is Alexander's final recommendation to his son, that he prove himself as an unknown knight at Arthur's court. The second is the fact that Alis unintentionally usurps Alexander's throne, keeps it, and later breaks his promise to Alexander not to marry so that the throne will revert to Cligès when Alis dies. The manner of Alis' emperorship will lead us to that central intellectual concern.

Alis "inherits" the throne when a false report of Alexander's death reaches Constantinople. In fact, Alis is tricked into assuming the throne by a *felon* who preferred the younger to the elder brother (2365-8). We have observed before that a certain ironic doubt touches a man tricked into his own good: [125] he may be morally innocent, but he is hardly admirable. Though the manipulation may result in an advancement for the person concerned in reality, he has been deluded at least for a time. A related point seems to be made by another scene involving another secondary character, who also represents reality. Alexander is not dead after all, and his messenger Arioconde returns to claim his throne. The manner of his return, and the manner of his address to Alis, are curious: he performs his duty as a messenger in precisely the reverse of normal behavior: he does not answer the greetings of friends; he does not greet the emperor; he does not bow to the emperor; he does not call him by his title; in the ensuing diplomatic discussion, he does not yield to him in any way (2434-87). [126] And yet, Arioconde is called *riches de faconde* (2422), which is suggestive of manners as well as verbal copiousness. "The scene fascinates less through what happens and is discussed than through its divergence from the norm." [127] And, we may add, by its thematic implications. Arioconde, the messenger of the real world in which Alexander is still alive, discards the purely formal elements of his role as diplomatic ambassador, affirms the falseness of Alis' position, and presents him with a straightforward challenge:

> "De par ton frere te desfi, ..." (2480)

With this challenge, the messenger departs, leaving Alis to learn that his barons will not support him in a war against his older brother; they recall, by means of a *significatio per similitudinem,* the dangers of brotherly warfare:

> Tuit li dïent qu'il li soveingne
> De la guerre Polinicés
> Que il prist contre Etïoclés,
> Qui estoit ses freres germains:
> Si s'antrocistrent a lor mains. (2498-2502)

Alis' solution to the perplexing situation in which he and Alexander find themselves is to divide the role of emperor into two parts: Alis will keep the crown and name of emperor, while Alexander will, in reality, rule the country! Alexander agrees, with the proviso that Alis not marry so that Cligès will succeed to the throne, and then Chrétien underlines the absurdity of the "solution":

> Li baron grant joie demainnent;
> Alis por empereor tienent,

---

[125] *Supra,* pp. 41 f., 50.
[126] Franz, "Die reflektierte Handlung...", p. 83; cf. *supra,* p. 70, n. 92.
[127] "Die Scene fesselt weniger durch das, was geschieht und was verhandelt wird, als dadurch, dass sie von der Norm abweicht." (*loc. cit.,* p. 83).

> Mes devant Alixandre vienent
> Li grant afeire et li petit;
> Fet est ce qu'Alixandres dit,
> Et po fet an se por lui non.
> Alys n'i a fors que le non,
> Qui empereres est clamez... (2544-51)

In this respect, Cligès inherits his father's role *vis-à-vis* Alis. When the youth asks permission to prove his knighthood in England, his uncle offers to share the empire with him (4188-92); but this is a parallel as well to the scene between Alexander and his father. More telling is the extensive characterization of Cligès as the representative and hero of the Greeks against the Saxons, even before he has achieved knighthood at Arthur's court. Not only does he twice fight the saxon Duke's nephew, his equal; he also takes on the Duke himself twice, the equal rather of Alis. The inequality of Cligès and the Duke is stressed by Chrétien. When the challenge is received in the Greek camp,

> Tote l'oz an fremist et bruit,
> Et dïent que ja Deu ne place
> Que Cligés la bataille face... (3921-3),

and the following forty lines develop the fear of the Greeks, including the emperor, before this inequality. That a large part of this is a build-up for Cligès' climactic victory is undeniable, but it also forms part of the theme of reality and illusion which centers, in its most obvious form, about Alis.

In these cases, Alis is a man who prefers the name and symbols of being emperor to the reality of power and responsibility. He is the pivot of illusion against which are contrasted the "realities" of Alexander and Cligès. But the occasion most stressed by Chrétien in which Cligès represents reality and Alis illusion is in relation to Fénice. Thanks to Thessala's magic potion, Cligès will enjoy real possession of Fénice, for fifteen months and then for a lifetime, while Alis only possesses a dream. Chrétien, who otherwise expends little verbal irony at Alis' expense, makes up for this slight in a long development on the theme of erotic illusion:

> Il dort et songe, et veillier cuide,
> S'est an grant poinne et an estuide
> De la pucele losangier.
> Et ele li feisoit dongier,
> Et se desfant come pucele,
> Et cil la prie, et si l'apele
> Molt dolcement sa dolce amie;
> Tenir la cuide, n'an tient mie,
> Mes de *neant* est a grant eise,
> Car *neant* tient, et *neant* beise,
> *Neant* tient, a *neant* parole,
> *Neant* voit, et *neant* acole,
> A *neant* tance, a *neant* luite.

Molt fu la poisons bien confite
Qui si le travaille et demainne.
De *neant* est an si grant painne,
Car por voir cuide, et si s'an prise,
Qu'il ait la forteresce prise,
Et devient lassez et recroit,
Einsi le cuide, einsi le croit.
A une foiz vos ai tot dit,
C'onques n'en ot autre delit. (3309-30)

One such description is sufficient to plague a character the rest of his fictional life. It is this deception, rather than the later one in Jehan's tower and orchard, which wi!l call forth Alis' desire for vengeance (6511-24). And this passage will be recalled by a single word, when Jehan informs the emperor that he never did possess Fénice with the final and harshest irony Alis has to endure consciously:

"Mes de *neant* estes jalos." (6486)

We are, of course, partly in the territory of Gallic humor, in which no pleasure is as great as the first, and there can be no doubt as to the intention of mockery in the long passage quoted above. It is so strong as to obscure the factual irony that, while Alis' pleasure is entirely illusory, Fénice, on the other side of the same bed, is cowering with fear:

La pucele de peor tranble,
Qui molt se dote et molt s'esmaie
Que la poisons ne soit veraie. (3296-8)

—just as in Alis' dream! The details of this *ecphrasis* and the obvious, repetitious word-play, make one suspect that Chrétien preferred to drive the lesson home to his audience rather than indulge in his more usual suggestive irony.

The theme is a major one. Though Chrétien nowhere gives it such verbal stress as it has received here, it is the basis of nearly all the important action, war as well as love, in *Cligès*. Before examining it in the climactic episodes of the Cligès story—the "fausse mort" and the constructions of Jehan—we will backtrack to see it develop as ironic structure.

Alexander and Soredamors

Alis' dream of possessing Fénice is not the first example of erotic illusion in *Cligès*. It is a parallel to an earlier episode, that in which Alexander becomes ecstatic over the shirt into which Soredamors sewed one of her golden hairs. When Alexander hears the young girl reveal this, he experiences difficulty preventing himself from going down on his knees to adore the shirt: it is only the presence of his companions and the Queen which keeps him from touching the hair with his eyes and mouth (1597-1604).

Nequedant quant il est an eise,
Plus de .C^m. foiz la beise.
Molt an fet tote nuit grant joie,
Mes bien se garde qu'an nel voie.
Quant il est colchiez an son lit,
A ce ou n'a point de delit
Se delite, anvoise, et solace.
Tote nuit la chemise anbrace,
Et quant il le chevol remire,
De tot le mont cuide estre sire.
Bien fet Amors d'un sage fol,
Quant cil fet joie d'un chevol ; ... (1610-22)

Alexander's pleasure in this gift is almost as great as Alis' in his dream, and Chrétien's comment on the effect of Love leaves no doubt that the illusion to which Alexander is subject is as great, and as foolish, as his younger brother's.

But this episode is only the surfacing to the verbal level of the very basis of the Alexander-Soredamors romance. Both of them, in their timidity, in their mistaken concern with social rules of behavior quite foreign to their essential being, in their mutual fears of rejection by the other, are perpetually wrapped up in an illusory world whose imaginary borders prevent them from contact with the one being they treasure above all others. So distant are they from the normal world of social intercourse that it is only by transcribing for us their un-expressed thoughts and feelings that the author can make us acquainted with their emotional life. This—and not a vain display of his rhe-torical prowess—is the reason for Chrétien's extraordinary use of the monologue in *Cligès.* Neither in *Erec et Enide,* nor in the later romances, does he use a similar technique. [128] Having proposed to himself as subject a pair of young lovers whose socialization (in con-temporaneous terms) is so little advanced that their behavior toward each other can give even the reader no clue as to their feelings—except the negative one of silence—Chrétien adapt the monologue from earlier writers and develops essentially the same technique as modern novelists intent on portraying the inner life of their characters, the private monologue which sometimes hovers close to a stream-of-consciousness technique.

However, Chrétien's reader is never caught in the illusions of the characters' world. Chrétien—we have seen it again and again—con-tinually reminds us of the absurdity of their fears, of their social shib-boleths. We are always, in *Cligès,* fully informed observers watching the helpless foolishness of deluded characters. The reader is always

---

[128] Enide's monologues are of a different kind: she is faced with a practical problem, whether or not to warn Erec. Her monologues are inner debates on a matter of action, not character portrayal impossible by other means. Chrétien reverts to this use of the monologue in a similar situation in *Yvain,* when the hero, falling in love with the widow of the man he has just killed and who is hunting the killer, obviously cannot express his feelings directly.

in the privileged role which dramatic irony grants the spectator. Whether it is a matter of knowing facts or feelings, the reader never shares the ignorance which betrays the characters.

Reality and Illusion in War

The same play of reality and illusion is operative in the crucial battle episodes of the romance. Both Alexander and his son disguise themselves in enemy armor, obtain victory thanks to their deception, but because they have left their own armor on the field, are supposed dead by their side and mourned. The emphasis on intentional deception is clear when Alexander and his companions enter Windsor castle disguised as some of Angrès' rebels:

> Et li portiers les portes oevre,
> Si les a dedanz receüz.
> De c'est gabez et deceüz,
> Car de rien ne les areisone,
> Ne uns de cez mot ne li sone,
> Et vont outre mu et teisant,
> Et tel sanblant de duel feisant
> Qu'aprés aus lor lances traïnent
> Et desoz les escuz s'anclinent,
> Et molt sanble que il se duellent. (1838-47)

An equal emphasis on the unintended victims of the deception is clear in Chrétien's description of the Greeks who grieve the "death" of Alexander and his companions. The description of their sorrow is long (2036-2112), but it is interspersed with reminders that the grief is meaningless:

> Mes por neant se desconfortent... (2057)
> ....
> Mes trestuit li escu lor mantent... (2064)
> ....
> Mes de toz fors d'un ont mespris;
> Mes autresi con cil qui songe,
> Qui por verité croit mançonge,
> Les boisent li escu boclé,
> Car la mançonge font verté.
> Par les escuz sont deçeü. (2072-7)

It is here that Soredamors, hearing the report of Alexander's death, seems by her coloring to be *fame morte* (2088), without daring to express her grief openly. But, as Chrétien points out, she need not really have been concerned: everyone else was so busy with their own grief that they would not have cared! (2097-9).

Cligès uses the same idea of disguise and deception. The main differences are that he embarks on his deception alone, he is a little more thorough (he doesn't exchange lances, but in addition to the enemy's shield appropriates his horse and helmet), and quite intentionally leaves his own horse behind to frighten his own people (3479 f.). The deception works well:

> D'anbes parz cuident qu'il soit morz
> Et Sesne, et Greu, et Alemant;
> S'an sont cil lié, et cil dolant...   (3514-6),

but it does not lead to the same kind of verbal and stylistic emphasis Alexander's ruse received. Instead, we are offered the hair-raising, melodramatic climax in which Cligès, still bearing an enemy head on his lance, attacks the nearest Saxon and runs him through the chest with his lance—enemy head and all!—yelling to his own side:

> "... Baron ferez!
> Je sui Cligés que vos querez..." (3523 f.)

But the deception does not cease here. Still disguised, Cligès spots some Saxons fleeing the Greek camp. Unaware that they have kidnapped Fénice, he follows them "on suspicion", *Car por neant ne fuient pas* (3624). As we have seen, he approaches them, picks off the first half dozen one by one without difficulty thanks to his disguise, and then goes on to the remaining six, with Fénice watching the proceedings.

As in the Alexander parallel, Chrétien uses the situation of deception for psychological purposes. In both cases, the disguised knight's beloved is involved. [129] The situations are different, though: Soredamors is seen reacting to Alexander's supposed death, but Fénice is merely wondering as to the identity of the knight fighting to deliver her, hoping it is Cligès who fights so bravely, fearing it is Cligès in danger. The substantive (rather than formal) parallel to Soredamors' unexpressed grief occurs later, during Cligès' battle with the Duke of the Saxons. The Duke strikes him a mighty blow which sends Cligès to his knees, the which seeing Fénice *tant fu esbahie* she could not help but cry out "*Sainte Marie!*" (4053-6) before fainting dead away. We recall Soredamors' baseless self-restraint in the same situation. But when Fénice cried out, all praised her, thinking she would do as much for any of them (4070-2)! What is more, Cligès heard her cry and was inspired by it:

> Sa voiz force et cuer li randi. (4076)

It must not be thought, however, that Cligès is merely a slightly varied carbon copy of his father: he showed a certain ingenuity in deception. Following Alexander's advice to prove himself at Arthur's court before disclosing his identity, he arrives at the tournament the King is holding at Oxford well prepared for his deception. He has brought along four horses from Greece, and has his companions buy extra suits of armor of varying colors. By changing armor every day, Cligès makes his mark first as the Black Knight, then successively as

---

[129] Cf. Franz, "Die reflektierte Handlung...", p. 70, on Cligès and Fénice.

the Green, the Red, and the White, without losing his anonymity. By the end of the tournament, the spectators realize they have been tricked, but before that, they have compared the merits of all these unknown Knights. On the second day, they compare Cligès Green to Cligès Black:

> "... Cist est an toz endroiz
> Plus gent assez et plus adroiz
> De celui d'ier as noires armes,
> Tant con pins est plus biax que charmes,
> Et li loriers plus del seü." (4721-5) [130]

And the following day, when Cligès is Red:

> Lors l'esgarderent a mervoille
> Trestuit, plus c'onques mes ne firent,
> Et dïent c'onques mes ne virent
> Un chevalier si avenant...." (4782-5)

How easy it would have been for Chrétien to structure this episode for our mystery and suspense, by bringing Cligès to Oxford, and then describing the events without identifying the hero of the tournament. But irony is the reigning tone of the romance, the play between reality and illusion its stuff, and the reader the privileged observer for whom its world is spread out without secrets.

There are number of these ironic parallels, each of whose parts depends on the reader's knowledge of a reality hidden from the characters. I will cite only one more, which will also serve to bring us back to the subject of love from the fields of war. When the Queen sees Alexander and Soredamors grow pale, we know it is for love, but she ascribes it to the sea:

> Ne set don ce puet avenir,
> Ne ne set por coi il le font
> Fors que por la mer ou il sont. (536-8)

This leads into Chrétien's imitation of Thomas' play on *la mer, amer* (*amare*), and *amer* (*amarum*), an imitation which has been criticized on two grounds: first, that it misunderstands Thomas' text (which, be it noted, we do not have, since the passage survives only in Gottfried von Strassbourg's *Tristan*); second, that while the play on words has a real function in the *Tristan,* it is only a personal *jeu d'esprit* on the part of Chrétien. [131]

It is perhaps hazardous for a modern scholar to claim a better knowledge of Old French than a professional writer of Old French. Rather than slip into such comfortable conclusions, it is more advisable to study the text:

---

[130]Another example of lyric techniques ironized by their context: the redoubled natural comparison is absurd, since, as we know, the same referent is being compared to himself!

[131] Paris, *Mélanges...*, p. 281; cf. Frappier, *Cligès,* p. 48.

> Mais *la mer* l'engigne* et deçoit,   *the Queen
> Si qu'en *la mer* l'*amer* ne voit:
> Qu'en *la mer* sont, et d'*amer vient,*
> Et s'est *amers* li maus quis tient;
> Et de ces trois ne set blasmer
> La reïne fors que *la mer*... [132]

G. Paris' first criticism was that Chrétien " n'a pas bien su se tirer de l'*amer* (*amarum*), qu'il a rapporté à l'*amer* (*amare*) et non au vent..." [133] Chrétien, it is true, does not mention the wind, but there is no reason to disregard the possibility of a pun in d'*amer vient*: their paleness comes from *amer,* the harshness of the sea, the bitterness of love. It is also possible to read *Et s'est amers li maus quis tient* as a pun on *amer* (*amare*) and *amer* (*amarum*). [134] In this reading, rather than an inept imitator of Thomas' wordplay, Chrétien goes him one or two better.

In his second criticism, Paris was half right. It is true that Chrétien's pun(s) here has no bearing on the development of the plot; Thomas used the word-play to bring about the scene of the avowals. However, whether the positivistic standards of probability, both of plot connection and of mimesis, are appropriate to *Cligès,* can be left up to the individual reader to decide. It should be pointed out, however, that Chrétien also has used ambiguity as the basis of a scene of avowals: that between Fénice and Cligès. [135] Finally, the obvious must again be said: this passage bears not only on the relations among the characters in question, but on the reader's relation to the characters. The main function of the pun(s) is to place him in a position of understanding available to none of the characters in the scene: only the reader is fully aware of the meaning of Alexander's and Soredamors' paleness, only the Queen is confused.

The parallel to this scene in the second part of *Cligès* casts Thessala in the same role played by the Queen as the uncomprehending observer who assigns the appearance of illness to a physical cause rather than love:

> Thessala voit tainte et palie
> Celi* qu'Amors a en baillie,   *Fénice
> Si l'a a consoil aresniee:
> "Dex, fet ele, estes vos fesniee,
> Ma dolce dameisele chiere,
> Qui si avez tainte la chiere?
> Molt me mervoil que vos avez.
> Dites le moi, qui le savez,

---

[132] This is Foerster's text as printed by Paris in *Mélanges, loc. cit.*; where there are textual variations from the Micha edition, they will be noted. The passage is ll. 541-6 in the Micha edition.

[133] *Loc. cit.,* n. 1.

[134] This second reading is not possible in the Guiot copy used by Micha: *Et d'amors vient li max ques tient.* (544).

[135] *Supra,* pp. 79 ff.

> An quel leu cist max vos tient plus.
> Car se garir vos an doit nus,
> A moi vos an poez atandre,
> Car bien vos savrai santé randre.
> Je sai bien garir d'itropique,
> Si sai garir de l'arcetique,
> De quinancie et de cuerpous;
> Tant sai d'orines et de pous
> Que ja mar avroiz autre mire; ..."   (2971-87)

Again in these lines, Thessala is unaware of the irony of her words. It is only through our knowledge of the actual state of the characters' feelings—a knowledge not shared by the Queen or Thessala—that we perceive the incongruity between the Queen's analysis and Thessala's offer to cure Fénice of the symptoms of love, since she knows about dropsy, gout, angina or croup, asthma, since she knows so much about urine and the pulse... .

La "fausse mort"

By the time we come to its main embodiment, the episode of the *fausse mort,* we have become accustomed to seeing the action of the romance in terms of reality and illusion; so accustomed, in fact, that we merely assume the distinction unconsciously, and do not really see it any longer. Furthermore, we have become conditioned to a particular form of the distinction, that of the false deaths, by its several previous incarnations. In part, this frequency may be considered a preparation for what has been called "[*une*] *scène atroce et répugnante*"; it is also an indication of the universality of this theme in the world of *Cligès*.

Fénice introduces her proposal to "play dead" by citing false authority. She invokes St. Paul as recommending the worldly wisdom of *si non caste, tamen caute*: [136]

> "Qui chaste ne se vialt tenir,
> Sainz Pos a feire bien anseingne
> Si sagement que il n'an preingne
> Ne cri, ne blasme, ne reproche.
> Boen estoper fet male boche..."   (5266-70)

Paul, of course, said nothing of the sort, but recommended marriage for those unable to contain themselves. We may be permitted to doubt that a man with the (probably) clerical education of Chrétien would so blatantly confuse the Apostle's teaching in the First Epistle to the Corinthians (7, 8). The error, if such it is, must be attributed to Fénice, not the author. [137]

---

[136] Paris, *Mélanges...*, p. 302.

[137] Cf. *ibid.*, p. 292, n. 1; Paris makes this the occasion for a snide remark about Chrétien's morality. Rarely has the encounter of critic and literary work resulted in a greater mismatch than in Paris' lengthy essay on *Cligès*. Posi-

The ironic play between religion and Fénice's actions is continued throughout the episode. It had already been introduced, just before the description of Alis' dream of possessing Fénice:

> Or est l'empereres gabez.
> Molt ot evesques et abez
> Au lit seignier beneïr.
> Quant ore fu d'aler gesir
> L'empereres, si com il dut,
> La nuit avoec sa fame jut. (etc.) (3287-92)

The torture itself parallels a Christian martyrdom. [138] Even the word itself is not missing: the three doctors *Li feisoient sosfrir martire* (5941). [139] And later, as we have seen, Jehan refers to "dead" Fénice as *molt sainte chose*, a quality of which we are unlikely to be persuaded. [140]

The incongruity between religious values and Fénice's plot need hardly be emphasized. Without going as far as Gaston Paris, who indignantly condemned the girl for evading "*[le] devoir le plus strict du mariage*" [141] we may note that this undercurrent of comparison establishes, within the sympathy we experience for them, a certain distance between us and the attractive young pair. This distance, aesthetic more than moral, suggests that the parallelism between the episode of the false death and the Christian resurrection—the phoenix, after whom the heroine is named, was used as a symbol of Christ's resurrection— [142] is ironic; presumably at the expense of Fénice, rather than Christianity.

----

tivist more than rationalist, but rationalist far more than imaginative, Paris had no taste at all for the freewheeling intellectual fantasy and aesthetic playfulness in which Chrétien indulged himself and his audience never more than in *Cligès*. The illogicality of plot and mannerism of style Paris condemned in this romance are matched only by the banal absurdity of the encounter between two irreconcilable philosophical and literary attitudes.

Nevertheless, the very positivism which so radically falsified his judgment of the romance led Paris to note and refuse to forget or gloss over apparent contradictions in the narrative. With the exception of chronological negligence (on which see *Mélanges...*, p. 285), most of these contradictions are, from my point of view, not attributable to Chrétien's negligence or poverty of invention, but to a literary conception based on the functioning of incongruities. Cf. Frappier, *Cligès*, p. 58.

[138] See reference to Van Hamel, *supra*, p. 55, n. 68. Franz, "Die reflektierte Handlung...," p. 84; Frappier, *Cligès*, p. 57.

[139] Of course, this is an idiom which may mean no more than "to undergo great pain," as at l. 5461. The context, however, suggests the literal meaning as well.

[140] *Supra*, p. 33. Running parallel to this series of religious associations is the use of thoroughly common, everyday expressions such as *rost, greslie, al feu metre, rostir, graillier...*: Valeria Bertolucci, "Di nuovo su *Cligès* et *Tristan*," *Studi Francesi*, VI (1962), 401-13; p. 409.

[141] *Mélanges...*, p. 291.

[142] Robertson, "Chrétien's *Cligès* and the Ovidian Spirit," p. 40, n. 25; Micha, "Tristan et Cligès," p. 6, n. 2.

Chrétien stresses her trickery repeatedly:

> Quant Cligés antant le murmure*,   *of Fénice's
> A la cort vint grant aleüre,   "illness"
> Mes n'i ot joie ne deduit,
> Car triste et mat estoient tuit
> Por l'emperreriz qui se faint,
> Car li max dont ele se plaint
> Ne li grieve, ne ne se dialt. (5591-7)

Since we already know that the illness is feigned, the point of the passage is not information but interpretation. Chrétien goes further by displaying Fénice as shrewd in her trickery. She dramatizes her "illness" by having everyone cleared out of her room (5403-22). This leaves her in a quandary, since she certainly does not wish Cligès included in this exclusion, but, as a married woman, can hardly exclude everyone including her husband while admitting one young and attractive man. So the emperor and his nephew are both allowed to see her,

> Mes se l'empereres, ses sire,
> Ne vient a li, ne l'en chaut il. (5604 f.)

Cligès does come to her, and becomes part of the deception. After a brief moment, Fénice orders him out: so great is her illness that she will never rise healthy from her bed (5617-20). Again, Chrétien delights in the irony of deception:

> Cligés cui cist moz atalante
> S'an vet feisant chiere dolante,
> Qu'ainz si dolante ne veïstes.
> Molt puet estre par defors tristes,
> Mes ses cuers est si liez dedanz,
> Car a sa joie est atendanz. (5621-6)

And the scene closes with a return to Fénice's duplicity:

> L'empererriz, sanz mal qu'ele ait,
> Se plaint et malade se fait,
> Et l'empereres qui la croit
> De duel feire ne se recroit... (5627-30)

In these passages, Chrétien is not content with the usual sidewards wink with which he normally acknowledges the compact between himself and the reader: the point is driven home with such insistence that it is difficult to see how critics can have considered Fénice the incarnation of Chrétien's moral ideal. [143]

Thessala keeps busy in the meanwhile. She has found someone in the city who really is sick with the illness Fénice is feigning. She visits the patient often, assuring him (or her: the sex is unspecified) that she will cure him. In fact, she does nothing of the sort, but examines the patient's urine daily until she determines that he is beyond hope, and

---

[143] Eg., Paris, *Mélanges...*, p. 292, n. 1; cf. Frappier, *Cligès,* pp. 56-9.

that he will die that very day. That is the last we hear of this deluded patient; he is presumably left to die more peacefully than Fénice will live the next few hours, for all Thessala is interested in is urine. She steals a potful of it, takes it back to the palace, and passes it off as Fénice's to the emperor, inviting him to have it, but not Fénice, examined by his doctors (5652-76). They are properly duped and inform the emperor that his wife will not live beyond *none* (3 p.m.). Then, while Thessala gives Fénice the magic potion which removes all power of motion and speech, though not of hearing and feeling, the emperor, the palace retinue, and the entire populace of the city bemoan the passing of the empress with one of those *complaintes* against death which refers to Fénice as *la meillor chose et la plus sainte* (5728) as well as the Light God gave the world (5770 f.). [144]

At this point, enter the *troi fisicïen de Salerne,* three professionals, be it noted, of intelligence, integrity, and perseverance, who are thrown out of a palace window for their pains. Told that the "deceased" empress refuses to see any doctors, they immediately jump to the right conclusion: they remember the story of Solomon's wife, who tricked her husband by playing dead. [145] They hie themselves to the palace, take Fenice's pulse, and assure Alis, *Qui de duel s'afole et ocit* (5823), that his wife lives!, that they will return her to him alive, or he may kill them; alternatively, he may hang them (5830). [146] Over the objections of Cligès, Jehanz, and Thessala, they persuade the emperor to order the palace cleared for a proper examination of the patient—or an autopsy of the corpse.

Before turning to the gruesome details of the examination, let us' stress that the three excellent physicians from the greatest center of medical culture of their time are entirely correct in the diagnosis. Not only have they understood Fénice's "illness" before laying eyes on her, they have even traced it back to its literary source! If Chrétien calls them *li felon ribaut* (5919) and congratulates the ladies of the palace who toss them out of a window with *Einz mialz nel firent nules dames* (5966), he has made quite sure before presenting us with the scene of Fénice's "martyrdom" that we understand how right the three men are.

Their first attempt is to trick her (5860-77). When she does not respond, they threaten her, but with no greater success (5878-89). Then the torture starts, with a wealth of bloody detail which would have delighted the *divin Marquis*:

---

[144] *Supra,* p. 33.

[145] On this story, which has no biblical foundation, see Henri Hauvette, *La "Morte Vivante"* (Paris: Boivin, 1933), pp. 100-8; the essential paragraph is quoted by Frappier, *Cligès,* p. 44. On the XIIIth century *Marques de Rome,* which contains a version of Chrétien's source for *Cligès* and which Paris identifies with the *livre* of Beauvais Chrétien mentions in his prologue, see Paris, *Mélanges...,* pp. 308-313; he comments on the story of Solomon's wife, pp. 312-24. Briefer discussions of these two sources in Frappier, *Cligès,* pp. 43-6.

[146] Actually, only one of the doctors is speaking at this point, and only for himself.

Lors li donerent un assalt
Par mi le dos de lor corroies;
S'an perent contreval les roies,
Et tant li batent sa char tendre
Que il an font le sanc espandre.
Quant des corroies l'ont batue,
Tant que la char li ont ronpue
Et li sans contreval li cort
Qui par mi les plaies li sort,
N'en porent il ancor rien faire,
Ne sopir, ne parole traire,
N'ele ne se crosle, ne muet.
Lors dïent que il lor estuet
Feu et plonc querre, qu'il fondront,
Qu'es paumes gitier li voldront,
Einçois que parler ne la facent.
Feu et plonc quierent et porchacent,
Le feu alument et plonc fondent.
Ensi afolent et confondent
La dame li felon ribaut,
Qui le plonc tot boillant et chaut,
Si com il l'ont del feu osté,
Li ont anz es paumes colé.
N'encor ne lor est pas assez
De ce que li plons est passez
Par mi les paumes d'outre en outre,
Einz dïent li cuivert avoutre
Que, s'ele ne parole tost,
Or endroit la metront an rost,
Tant que ele iert tote greslie.
Cele se test, ne ne lor vie
Sa char a batre n'a malmetre. (5900-31)

A surprising passage to find in a romance said "courtly". One might almost suspect the author found some justified pleasure in this vivid ecphrasis. Nor is this possibility to be discarded completely: seen from the moral point of view, Fénice is hardly irreproachable, and might be said to deserve some kind of punishement. At least, her culpability to some extent justifies *a* punishment. But there is no denying that *this* punishment is extreme, though this does not hide the irony of the doctors who, correct in their diagnosis, nearly kill the patient in trying to make her talk. [147] Nevertheless, we cannot dismiss the problem by a simple-minded moralism similar to that of the Hollywood western which justifies punishment by audience expectation. If Chrétien dwells on a scene of horror out of keeping with the general tone of his romance, we can rightly expect and demand a literary accounting.

The idea of "tone" helps. One of the reasons this passage strikes us as extraordinary in the context of *Cligès* as a whole—aside from its subject matter—is the multiplicity of realistic detail which crowds

---

[147] Kellerman, *Aufbaustil und Weltbild...*, p. 73.

the description. [148] In spite of the fantastic potion which forms the narrative basis of the episode, there is no doubt of our being faced with an emphasis which presents these lines to our eyes most vividly. If the tone induced by the style is realistic, then we must for a moment think realistically about the character and her reactions. She hears and understands what is happening to her; from her reaction when the effect of the potion wears off, we learn that she feels it also (6184-96). What then is likely to be the reaction of a delicate and courtly young lady under such harsh treatment?

> Ensi afolent et confondent
> La dame li felon ribaut...
> . . . .
> Cele se test, ne ne lor vie
> Sa char a batre n'a malmetre.

Chrétien does not explain why she remains silent and does nothing to prevent them, but he does not need to: we know the simple answer is that she cannot, even if she wants to. Fénice, whipped until her skin breaks and the blood pours down her wounds, with boiling lead poured into and through her palms, is fully conscious of the treatment she is receiving, but can do nothing ... thanks to Thessala's potion. Not only is Fénice being punished for her deception: she cannot stop the punishment because of the plan devised according to her own cunning.

Fénice under torture is the trickster tricked, the comic version of tragic irony. Having devised a surreptitious plan of evading marriage and fidelity to Alis, she is trapped by the means of her deception into enduring—without recourse—a punishment as harsh as it is unexpected. Her attempt to circumvent social reality by the use of a magic illusion backfires with the ironically appropriate brutal reality of physical torture. We need discard neither our structural awareness that "she brought it on herself", nor our moral awareness that this is indeed extremely harsh punishment, to enjoy the dramatic and comic irony of the situation. Indeed, these two reservations tend to cancel each other out: one pits us against Fénice, the other ranges us in her defense, and with all aspects of our moral consciousness thus occupied, we are left to enjoy the paradoxical relationship of intention and outcome.

A number of the themes we have seen operating throughout Cligès come together here. To reach far back, into the first part of the romance, Fénice's torture parallels the tortures Alexander and Soredamors endured, each alone, during their lengthy monologues. Paradoxically, while the story of Cligès and Fénice is situated on a more sophisticated cultural level, the proportion of the parallel torture is inverted: the tortures of love experienced by the older couple were mental only, while Fénice's is brutally physical. At the same time, one trait is equal: the torture in each case is lonely, all the more in the

---

[148] I must admit to having noted the passage first merely as an example of realistic ecphrasis; but descriptive realism rarely exists for its own sake in Chrétien.

case of Fénice, as it is really impossible for her to speak and bring her torture to a halt. [149] This is also the most striking version of the false death episode, previously acted out by Alexander and Cligès. The three versions reveal an intentional gradation in complexity. Alexander, on the field of battle a straightforward warrior, puts on enemy armor to deceive the enemy; that his own side is also misled is unforeseen and, to him, accidental. Cligès, however, intentionally leaves behind his horse to deceive his own people, though no purpose is ascribed to this. In any case, he seems thoroughly to enjoy deception, as is further shown at the Oxford tournament. The false death of Fénice is the most complex, requiring the whole apparatus of the "witch" Thessala with her magic potion and other people's urine, two sets of physicians, and all the plans for the life following the exhumation. Its essential distinction, of course, is that in this case only, the false death backfires on its enactor.

This backfiring belongs to the paradoxical relation of intention and outcome, which is one aspect of the larger paradox of reality and illusion. An action based on an intention—*i.e.,* a reasonable, motivated action—is the projection of a particular view of what things will be like at a given time in the future. That this projection is often illusory, that the reality which in fact develops in place of this view contradicts it, lends not only spice to life but also structure to fiction. Fénice projected a vision of solitude and love with Cligès achieved without difficulty—social or other—by means of a magic potion. The reality was a false death which nearly became a real one.

A paradox not yet explored resides in the resonances of this episode. One set of resonances inheres in the suggestion that Fénice is like a saint undergoing martyrdom. However, *Cligès* is no Allegory: Fénice undergoes her martyrdom unwillingly, has stumbled into it for the sake of an illicit and carnal love, and can hardly be thought to represent a Christian virtue or model. If the scene of her torture and entombment constitute a kind of symbolic death and the stay in Jehan's tower a kind of resurrection, [150] it is as a saint and martyr of courtly love that she dies and is resurrected. [151] To what extent this represents Chrétien's attitude toward his heroine can best be seen in a discussion of the tower and the orchard.

---

[149] Cligès also undergoes a kind of torture, though mild by comparison to Fénice. Until she regains consciousness (after he has disinterred her, he believes her dead and holds himself responsible. Chrétien at one point suggests that Cligès may kill himself out of grief (6059-63), but Cligès himself does not broach the idea in his *complainte* (6154-81). It is overstating the case to speak of a *"suicide tenté"* in this context (Faith Lyons, "La fausse forte dans le *Cligès* de Chrétien de Troyes," in *Mélanges de linguistique et de littérature romanes offerts à Mario Roques,* 4 vols. (Paris: Didier, 1950), vol. I, pp. 167-77; p. 171.

The comparative mildness of Cligès' "punishment" accords with his role, which is secondary to that of Fénice; *supra,* pp. 73, 81.

[150] Van Hamel, "Cligès et Tristan," p. 478.

[151] The phrase "a saint and martyr of courtly love" is mine; it does not seem far removed from Frappier's discussion in *Cligès,* p. 55 f.

The Tower and the Orchard

This episode is crucial for the interpretation of *Cligès*. The narrative culmination of Cligès' and Fénice's efforts, it also represents the goal of their desires. The two lovers planned their evasion for the sake of what they intended to find there; Fénice suffered the tortures we have seen for its sake. Its importance is also clear from its uniqueness in the world of this romance: it is the only major episode in the second half for which there is no parallel in the first. This uniqueness also makes its interpretation more difficult, since there is no second term to which it can be compared. We will therefore approach it with care; the path leads through the cemetery where Fénice is buried.

She is buried in a sepulcher built by Jehan, who took charge of the interment. Now, he accompanies Cligès, in the middle of the night, for the disinterment. Thirty knights are on guard; angry at pulling guard duty, they have eaten, drunk, and fallen asleep (6084-7). [152] Nevertheless, Cligès faces certain difficulties: ten candles shed great light near the tomb (6082 f.), the cemetery is entirely surrounded by a high wall (6098 f.), and the gate is locked from the inside (6102 f.). At first, Cligès is stumped, but then *Amors li enorte et semont* (6107): he climbs up the wall. No details are given as to how he accomplishes this feat, at first so difficult as not even to have occurred to him, except for this line:

> Car molt estoit preuz et legiers... (6109)—

which does not really explain much. From the top of the wall, the rest is easy. Just within the wall is an orchard, one of whose many trees grows next to the wall, so that Cligès has no difficulty climbing down. He opens the gate for Jehan, extinguishes the candles, and then Jehan opens the tomb:

> La fosse et la sepolture oevre,
> Si que de rien ne la malmet. (6122 f.)

When Cligès has taken out the body of Fénice, Jehan closes the tomb again:

> ... Jehanz, au plus tost qu'il pot,
> A la sepolture reclose,
> Si qu'il ne pert a nule chose
> Que l'an i eüst atochié. (6130-3)

Then they quickly ride to the tower where, having unshrouded Fénice, Cligès, who knew nothing about Thessala's potion, bemoans the death

---

[152] Chrétien sometimes treats tertiary characters in the most cavalier manner! These knights have been "brought on" only to provide a temporary difficulty ... and to fall asleep. The same is true of the earlier group of knights who guarded Fénice's sepulture: Jehan was free to do whatever he wanted because Chrétien dismissed the knights in a faint! (6064-72). It is not adequate to agree that Chrétien was unconcerned, in *Cligès*, with mundane matters of plot probability. There is no need for the initial presence of either of these groups of knights: they serve only to fall asleep or faint, *i.e.*, to demonstrate the author's arbitrary freedom in the realm of unreality.

of his beloved. Gaston Paris found this ignorance of Cligès' "[*une*] *bien singulière invraisemblance*," [153] which it certainly is: it is not probable, in the customary, realistic way of things, that Cligès would have been left uninformed of such an essential element of the conspiracy.

Granted this improbability, we may ask whether it serves any function otherwise unattainable. The answer lies in Cligès' sorrow: he indulges, not entirely unexpectedly, in a *complainte* against Death: *Ha! fet il, Morz, com es vilainne, etc.* (6153 & ff.). Although the first few lines belong to the traditional topic, they lead him to a not unworthy insight into the plot of the romance:

> Or porroit an dire par droit,
> Quant morte estes par mon servise,
> Que je vos ai morte et ocise.
> Amie, don sui je la morz... (6164-7)

Nevertheless, the purely formal elements of the *complainte* are important too, for they place Cligès within the category of the other citizens of Constantinople we earlier saw grieving their "dead" mistress. Cligès too was fooled; since he was one of the conspirators, he was fooled as was Fénice, by backfire: the dramatic and comic ironies find another victim in Cligès, albeit not as greatly suffering a one as Fénice. [154]

As when she was being tormented by the Salernian physicians, she hears every word: *molt se travaille et esforce* to utter a word or give him a look of comfort (6148 ff.). Her heart nearly splits in twain for the grief she hears (6152 f.)—a remarkable degree of commiseration for one in her condition. Finally, when he has uttered his *mea culpa,* Fénice manages to breathe a sigh, to speak weakly and in a low tone:

> "Amis, amis, je ne sui pas
> Del tot morte, mes po an faut.
> De ma vie mes ne me chaut.
> Je me cuidai gaber et faindre,
> Mes or estuet a certes plaindre,
> Car la morz n'a soing de mon gap.
> Mervoille iert, se vive an eschap..." (6184-90),

which rounds out the toll of recognitions for the episode. In spite of her weakness, however, Fénice keeps her wits about her. When she asks for her *mestre,* who will cure her if any one can, Cligès is immediately ready to go off after Thessala. Chrétien does not specify the tone of voice in which Fénice prevents him:

> "Amis, einz i ira Jehanz." (6200)

When Thessala does arrive, Cligès greets her with extraordinary warmth, [155] perhaps because he is still very much aware of his respon-

---

[153] *Mélanges...*, p. 302 f.
[154] Cf. Faith Lyons, "La fausse mort..." p. 170.
[155]   ... "Bien soiez vos venue,
    Mestre, je vos aim tant et pris!" (6222 f.)

sibility for Fénice's plight. But the young lovers are quickly reassured: Fénice will be well within fifteen days ... and so she is, and so they spend fifteen months within the tower that Jehan built.

It is a beautiful and complex structure, whose isolation in a hidden place satisfies Fénice's requirements. She wanted a situation in which she would be "served" only by Cligès, in which she would find good whatever he did, for he would be lord of whatever *empire* they inhabited (5289-94). She had also wanted a situation in which everyone believed she had died (5300 f.)—for so her reputation would be unblemished. Obviously, the situation had to be one of utter isolation, and so it is. Only the two servants, Thessala and Jehan, know where the two are hidden, indeed, that Fénice is alive at all: for the world, she is dead and buried. Her plan, in spite of the temporary and painful interlude occasioned by the three doctors, is completely fulfilled.

The only thing Fénice had not foreseen was the comfort and magical beauty of the tower. Perhaps with the legend of Tristan and Iseut in mind, she had declared to Cligès that

> "Uns povres leus, oscurs et pales,
> M'iert plus clers que totes ces sales." (5295 f.)

In fact, it is a structure of several stories, with many rooms and chimneys, decorated with beautifully painted statues (5491-5). It has hidden rooms no man could find unless Jehan himself showed them (5508-15), and, most important, it is completely secure. Jehan leads Cligès by the hand to a door which is not only unrecognizable as such without prior knowledge, but also can be opened only in a secret manner (5522-47). Nothing is lacking, and we can only sympathize with Cligès who tells his serf that his *dameisele* will be happy there *Toz les jorz que ele vivra* (5503). We can also sympathize with Jehan's pride when he says that nothing required by a lady is lacking (5516 f.), though the tone of a slightly later description recalls nothing so much as a *concierge* displaying the amenities of a Parisian *pied-à-terre*:

> "An cest leu soit vostre repaires,
> Et vostre amie i soit reposte.
> Tex ostex est boens a tel oste,
> Qu'il i a chanbres, et estuves,
> Et eve chaude par les cuves,
> Qui vient par conduit desoz terre.
> Qui voldroit leu aesié querre
> Por s'amie metre et celer,
> Molt li covandroit loing aler,
> Einz qu'il trovast si convenable.
> Molt le tanroiz a delitable,
> Quant vos avroiz par tot esté." (5558-69)

Perhaps the fact that Jehan, Cligès' serf, is to be manumitted in return for his services has something to do with his eagerness.

But there is more to Jehan's ability to provide for any and all eventualities. When Cligès and Fénice have spent fifteen months indoors, an urge comes over her to see the sun and moon again. She has heard the nightingale sing one spring morning, and asks for an orchard. Which request is no sooner made than fulfilled by Jehanz:

> "Tot est apareillié et quis,
> Fet Jehanz, quanqu'ele comande.
> De ce qu'ele vialt et demande
> Est ceste torz bien aeisiee." (6290-3)

He need do nothing more than open a door ("I cannot tell what kind it was, nor say or depict the manner. None but Jehan could do it, nor could any one say, or did any one know, that a door or window was there, until the door was opened, so was it hidden and covered," adds Chrétien; 6298-6304), and Fénice beholds the shining sun, an orchard with a tall, trained fruit tree next to the wall for shade, and a meadow. "And the orchard was enclosed about by a high wall connecting to the tower, so that no thing entered there, except by the way of the tower. [156]

At this point, we exit quickly from this *locus amoenissimus,* this hidden paradise on earth, this magical creation of a single serf. For this unscalable wall just described is scaled less than thirty lines later, and with the greatest of ease:

> Tantost se vet au mur aerdre [Bertrand]
> Et fet tant que oltre s'an passe. (6360 f.)

And that's all. No further explanation, no details as to how the wall was rendered passable in a few lines. One can hardly avoid sympathizing with Gaston Paris' irritation and indignation: "Ici l'incohérence est vraiment par trop choquante: comment ce mur infranchissable devient-il tout à coup si facile à franchir? On ne peut mettre plus de négligence et d'étourderie dans la composition d'un récit." [157]

Perhaps. But we have seen before that Chrétien's apparent negligence may be purposeful. What is this place? The off-handed way in which Chrétien disclaims responsibility for knowing where doors and windows are located, for understanding how they are opened and closed, suggests that it is not entirely a real place; or that Chrétien is not, in a sense, its author. Everything is "laid on": whatever is desired is immediately provided, so quickly and easily that we are not sure whether the orchard was really there all the time—why did Jehan not

---

[156]   Et li vergiers ert clos antor
           De haut mur qui tient a la tor,
           Si que riens nule n'i montast,
           Se par la tor sus n'i entrast. (6333-6)

[157] *Mélanges...,* p. 305.

show it to Cligès when he first displayed the tower with such great praise?—or if Jehan did not in fact create it by magic when asked. This, is the first thing to note: Jehan, like Thessala, is a magician. [158] A magician gives us what we cannot have in reality. As Thessala provided magic potions for the deception of Alis and the "death" of Fénice, so Jehan, her opposite number with Cligès, provides the place to which they come after using Thessala's magic. Jehan has provided the ideal place, the ideal situation which the young couple could not have in real life: a way of living together, without Fénice enduring the *partage* she dreads, without tarnishing her reputation. Once in the *locus magicus,* every desire is fulfilled: doors open to unmentioned but imaginable places of pleasure. All that is required is the wish, the imagination; the "reality" is provided immediately. As befits both the *locus amoenus* and the *locus magicus* it is hidden, secret, isolated.[159] Only the magicians and their guests know of its existence: "Never was any man made by God in this place, except the two of us," says Jehan to Cligès when showing him the tower (5553-5). Our hidden wishes can be satisfied only in secret, far from the society of others, in the isolation of our wish and its object. High surrounding walls and unnoticeable doors and windows which can be opened only by the touch of the magician's fingers are the signs of the isolation which is his gift.

But Bertrand, led hither by the accident of a wandering sparrow-hawk, enters without difficulty. Why has magic not kept him out? He climbed the wall, and saw the couple in the shade of a tree.... A young man, on a high wall, difficult to scale, a tree growing just inside the wall, an orchard.... The episode of the *vergier* has no parallel in the first part of the romance but it does have a parallel within the second part. Bertrand climbs over the orchard wall to recognize Fénice, [160] just as Cligès climbed over the cemetery wall to rescue Fénice entombed

---

[158] Thessala
> ... savoit molt de nigromance.
> Por ce fu Thessala clamee
> Qu'ele fu de Tessalle nee,
> Ou sont feites les deablies,
> Anseigniees et establies.
> Les fames qui el païs sont
> Et charmes et charaies font. (2964-70)

Cf. also ll. 3014-8. On Thessala, see Robert-Léon Wagner, *"Sorcier" et "magicien", contribution à l'histoire du vocabulaire de la magie* (Paris: Droz, 1939), p. 69 f. I doubt, however, that Chrétien took Thessala seriously enough to warrant the affirmation that, in the passage just quoted, "[il] prend ainsi position sur la nature diabolique de la sorcellerie." (Wagner, *op. cit.,* p. 76).

[159] To the quotation in the following sentence, compare:
> Cligés voit la meison sostainne,
> Que nus n'i maint ne ne converse... (5496 f.).

[160] The emphasis is on Bertrand's recognition of Fénice, not of Cligès: ll. 6364-77.

in the sepulcher ... which also was built by Jehan. [161] And this orchard is guarded by a magic which, like the thirty knights guarding the sepulcher, went to sleep. [162]

The parallel coheres in more than just the narrative structure. Both places, the cemetery and the orchard which is a paradise on earth, are locations of false deaths. As Fénice was falsely entombed in the sepulcher, so was she falsely entombed in Jehan's tower for fifteen months. And as the first death was brought about by a magic drug, so was the second. A love lived or endured in isolation is always false for Chrétien. Alexander and Soredamors endured their emotions in isolation, [163] and were lectured for it by the Queen and ridiculed by Chrétien. We need go no further than his previous romance for a double portrait of an absolute *amour à deux*: Erec and Enide at the beginning, Maboagrain and Enide's cousin in the *Joie de la Cour* episode at the end, tell us clearly enough that love, for Chrétien, is possible and real only in a socialized setting. The love of two partners who isolate themselves from the world and other men is, however pleasurable, a living death for Chrétien.

"But Bertrand climbs over an unscalable wall!" Or perhaps, like the cemetery wall which also seemed unscalable to Cligès, it really isn't that difficult. Perhaps the "ideal situation", for which Cligès and Fénice plotted so carefully and suffered such torment, physical and mental, isn't really that difficult to achieve. Perhaps what had already become a myth in Chrétien's time, the great love overriding all convention and respect for social responsibilities—whether in the abandon and desperation of the Tristan legend, or the more elegant duplicity

---

[161] Jehanz opens the two in similar ways:

> Et Jehanz maintenant descuevre
> La fosse et la sepolture oevre,
> Si que de rien ne la malmet. (6121-3)

And in the tower:

> Jehanz, qui avoit feite l'uevre,
> L'uis del mur li desserre et oevre,
> Si ne le malmet, ne ne quasse. (5545-7)

[162] To my knowledge, the only previous attempt to interpret Bertrand's scaling of the unscalable wall is that of D.W. Robertson, in "The Doctrine of Charity in Medieval Literary Gardens: A Topical Approach through Symbolism and Allegory," *Speculum* XXVI (1951) 24-49. He sees Jehan's orchard as a Babylonian garden, its *ante* as symbolizing the tree of the vices, and Chrétien's purpose as showing "the foolishness of idolatrous cupidity" so as to implicitly "promote the opposite of cupidity, Charity." (p. 39 f.): "Thus the elaborate worldly wisdom of Jehan proves to no avail to the lovers as they lie in spiritual oblivion." (p. 39).

If Jehan is thought to be a magician, however, he is not likely to represent even an elaborate worldly wisdom. The dialectical (or ironic) opposition in my interpretation is between fantastic courtly ideals and common sense, the latter representing a common ground where ordinary secular thought and ordinary religious belief meet in agreement.

[163] I refer again to Frappier's perceptive comments on the dangers of a hidden, secret love: *Cligès*, p. 88. He applies them only to Alexander and Soredamors; they are equally valid for the second couple.

of the *Cligès* version—is not so great a challenge. After all, all it takes is a *pied-à-terre*.

That, I admit, is malicious. But Chrétien is also malicious, and we have seen his half-truths lead to a greater comprehension of larger truths. We do not intend to deal with "meanings" in the sense usually applied to works of literature: a more or less systematic relation of values found in the work. In terms of articulated values, *Cligès* is mainly negative: it ironizes at the expense of the *parvenu* to courtly values, and at the expense of a later generation which has made those courtly values entirely its own. But these values are the characters', not necessarily the author's. Speaking of style, Jean Frappier has pointed out that most of the preciosity for which *Cligès* has been criticized belongs to the characters rather than Chrétien: [164] the same is true of their ideas and their values. It is surely an error to confuse portrayal and endorsement, and on this basis to attribute the opinions and values of a character to his author. Achilles and Clytemnestra, Macbeth and Don Giovanni, Adolphe and Lafcadio, all claim and obtain our aesthetic sympathy without our moral approbation.

And so it is with doctrinal content and courtly values in Fénice's speeches. They have been taken to represent Chrétien's courtliness: while this is a theoretical possibility, it is a critical necessity first to see them as narrative materials which the author is free to use for his purposes, in the same manner as he disposes of description, monologue, dialogue, and all the other resources of his craft. Ideas in literature are to be judged as one of the many components within a complex system of relationships. As characters are judged according to their actions, so ideas are to be judged according to their bearing on and revelation of the character, and according to their effects.

Fénice demands three things. First, that she endure no *partage*:

> "Ja mes cors n'iert voir garçoniers,
> N'il n'i avra deus parçoniers.
> Qui a le cuer, cil a le cors,
> Toz les autres an met defors." (3121-4)

This is the absolute postulate: she will not share out her body between two men. Faced with the possibility that Alis will possess her, she will not accept another man:

> "Et quant il est de mon cors sire,
> S'il an fet chose que ne vuelle,
> N'est pas droiz c'un autre i acuelle." (3130-2)

Although she does not specifically say so, Fénice can only have Cligès in mind. [165] Second, granted that she will have only one man, she would prefer Cligès. Three, she wants Cligès without harming her reputation. These demands are perfect intellectual reflections of traits of character

---

164 *Cligès*, p. 87.
165 Cf. Van Hamel, "Cligès et Tristan," p. 467 f.

we have already observed in Fénice. In spite of the first impression of a simple, weak, and naïve young girl, we have seen her revealed as a strong-minded, independent, and confident young woman, quite certain of what she wants and how to obtain it. Without any of the self-doubt and hesitation of Soredamors, she knows her feelings and desires, and needs neither to protect herself against them nor to seek in herself to discover them. [166] She is certain not only of her being, but of her value as well. Finally, she is quite practical, especially with a magician at hand: one of her first thoughts is not to become the means by which Cligès loses his heritage (3148-53).

How does Fénice succeed with these demands? At first glance, the sum total of demand and success seems to run two to one in her favor. Although she does not manage the third demand—to keep her reputation—, she does manage to avoid any *partage* and also to be united with Cligès. However, this arithmetic overlooks the weight of the action. In order to satisfy only the first two demands, she could simply have accepted Cligès' suggestion that they escape to Arthur's court, thereby avoiding, incidentally, the bother and torture of her false death. Although the wish to keep her reputation intact is only tertiary in logical order, it seems as important to her as the first two demands, [167] and is in fact the primary determinant of all the later action. The ruse of the false death is entirely predicated on Fénice's concern with her reputation: since the goal is only temporarily achieved in the isolation of Jehan's tower, and since her reputation becomes a lesson for all later generations, embodied in the customs of the harem and the eunuch, as well as in the romance which ends on this smilingly admonitory note, the ruse of the false death is no more than a slightly qualified failure. [168]

And finally, as we have already seen, the alternative to the *partage* which Fénice envisions and does achieve for a time is as illusory as the means by which it is obtained. It is subject to the same charge of secrecy by which the Queen criticizes Alexander. The older couple endured the loneliness of hidden love because they were personally timid and socially inept. The younger pair willingly accept a furtive affair made possible only by the use of two magicians and their crafts, illusory as a practical alternative and in its essential idea: man does not exist outside of society.

"What could Fénice do, forced to marry a man she did not love, yet insistent on her integrity?" It is not the novelist's function to provide practical solutions to life's insoluble problems. He can describe and analyze the latter, or use them at greater remove in the realm of

---

[166] I take the scene in which Thessala explains to a "naive" Fénice that her malady is love to be light-hearted irony: Fénice seems quite aware that "it is Love" earlier, when she first sees Cligès and exchanges eyes and hearts with him (ll. 2773-8). She plays innocent here out of a combination of motives: modesty, and the need to obtain a pledge of secrecy from Thessala (3086 ff.).

[167] See her speech to Cligès, ll. 5173-5220.

[168] See Robertson, "Chrétien's *Cligès* and the Ovidian Spirit," p. 41.

fantasy. Chrétien actually does both, and goes one step farther: he points out the self-contradictory nature of one possible alternative. Fénice wants the pleasures of a great, asocial love, without the infelicities Iseut encountered. The ruse of the false death, the "courtly paganism beyond good and evil" she and Cligès enjoy in the tower and orchard are her alternative to the Tristan myth, not Chrétien's. [169] What does belong to Chrétien is the lesson that this alternative is self-contradictory, that the great passion of the Celtic lovers cannot be accommodated to a more elegant courtly life without incurring the same disadvantages which plagued Tristan and Iseut. Fénice's love is socially and morally adulterous, whatever the details of consummation. [170] Like Tristan and Iseut, she and Cligès incur such scandal as to become paradigmatic examples. As with most great characters of fiction and drama, comic as well as tragic, the essential conflict is not between the individual and the world, but in what the individual himself desires.

CONCLUSION

That is was possible to analyze irony in terms of classical grammar and rhetoric leads to the expected conclusion that a twelfth-century author with the literary sophistication and elegance of Chrétien de Troyes was well acquainted with such classical studies as were available in the schools of his time. Although the traditional school definitions exist at such an elementary and basic level that their applications can be quite varied, they provide nevertheless highly useful methods of literary analysis.

More interesting are the techniques of irony which Chrétien did not find in those text books, and which may be attributed to him—until and unless the study of his predecessors in narrative fiction proves otherwise. The essential step in this elaboration of an individual rhetoric (in the sense of the word that is synonymous with "literary structure") was noted briefly in our discussion of hyperbole. [171] Rhetorical exaggeration in classical oratory necessarily consisted of a disparity between the facts of the case discussed and the words chosen by the orator to present these facts in a manner favorable or unfa-

---

[169] "Cet idéalisme et ce paganisme mêlés situent l'amour courtois au delà du bien et du mal, dans un univers pourvu d'une autonomie morale." Frappier, *Cligès*, p. 57.

[170] On the position of the Church in the XIIth century toward unconsummated marriages such as Alis', see Kohler, *Ideal und Wirklichkeit...*, p. 162, n. 1. In the text of the same page, however, Kohler remarks: "Wenn Fenices Aufhebung einer (durch den Zaubertrank) nicht vollzogenen Ehe auch nach den Kirchenrecht des 12. Jahrhunderts möglich ist, so bleiben doch ihre Mittel im christlichen Sinne unmoralisch."

[171] *Supra,* p. 44 f.

vorable to his subject. This was necessarily so because the facts in most cases are likely to be unarguable data: it is their meaning which is in question. The writer of fiction is in a different position; he has the freedom to invent facts as well as to clothe them verbally. In the specific case of hyperbole, an example was cited in which the author gave no reason to doubt the adequacy of his description of certain love symptoms: it was these symptoms themselves which were ironically exaggerated. A further adaptation was noted in the discussion of *significatio per consequentiam.* [172] The rhetorical examples were based on a logical connection between a stated fact and its implications about the person concerned. Chrétien simply presented two facts about two characters—one calls a third *ami,* the other does not—and let the reader juxtapose these facts in order to draw a conclusion.

This principle of a suggested juxtaposition of two apparently independent narrative events is the link between the verbal ironies which were our concern at the beginning of this chapter and the parallelism which is the major principle of structural irony in *Cligès.* It is a principle with a wide variety of forms. On the largest scale, it juxtaposes the two parts of the romance, the apparently unrelated stories of Alexander and Cligès. At the other end of the scale are the brief notations in one part of the romance—sometimes as brief as a single word—which recall a more extensive narrative development in the other part. Thus, the mere statement that Cligès was *desafublez* was of no great import by itself; it gained meaning only when compared to Alexander's self-conscious removal of his coat before entering the King's palace. [173] While this provided an insight into Alexander's historical location at a protocourtly level, it also served to affirm Cligès' location in a fully courtly period. A more extensive parallel was found in the two scenes which elaborated the same narrative data in different ways: both Alexander and Cligès, as young men, wished to leave home for King Arthur's court, but went about satisfying their desire in ways which, when compared, revealed their different characters. [174] Further examination of these characters, especially as revealed in monologue and action, suggested a far-reaching parallelism between them which also affected their relations with their respective loves. Alexander was both the more interesting character of the first part of the romance and played the dominant role vis-à-vis Soredamors (though this dominance was strongly shaded by ironic paradox). The general parallel of the two couples indicated an inversion both of relative interest and dominance: in the second generation, the leading partner of the courtly pair was the lady, Fénice, while Cligès himself—ostensibly the hero—played second fiddle to her desires and principles. [175]

---

[172] *Supra,* p. 51 f.
[173] *Supra,* p. 64 f.
[174] *Supra,* pp. 66 ff.
[175] *Supra,* pp. 73, 80 f.

A particular case of irony is the use of traditional literary materials in a manner at variance with their inherent and assumed values. The first example of this was one of the best-known *topoi,* that of the world turned upside-down; associated with it was an equally traditional development of paradoxical love-imagery; both were presented as possible explanations for a character's behavior before being undercut by an earthier, more common-sensical explanation of a psychological and social order. [176] Another kind of traditional material is more than literary: the symbolism by which a person's name contains the essence of his character and being is both a part of primitive thought and frequent in the Middle Ages. [177] In a sense, this assumption is shared by Chrétien, but only in a restricted sense: he assumes this kind of thinking as a background for irony at his character's expense: since one of them is shown as believing in this kind of symbolic relation, that relation itself is touched by irony. [178] A third use of traditional material are the references to well-known literary personages: these are not mere displays of learning, but shed ironic light on the characters to whom they are compared. [179]

In addition to the materials of literary tradition, the formal structures of literature themselves can be used for ironic purposes. Techniques normally associated with the profound emotional impulses behind lyric and religious poetry can be transferred to battle descriptions and other literary situations where they are incongruous by reason of the subject or the character's intent. [180] The essential distinction between the literal and figurative levels of poetic speech can be disregarded or inverted in order to suggest ironic insights into the speakers. [181] This type of irony, which hinges on the essential structure of literature, can go no further than Chrétien has taken it when he plays with what is normally the basic assumption of (traditional) fiction: that a world is being elaborated, which while obviously bearing certain resemblances to that inhabited by the reader, is nevertheless endowed with an independent reality of its own. Most often, the author is a hidden power behind the articulated world of his fiction; when he comments directly to the reader, he tends to take on the *persona* of a narrator who may be quite distinct from the author; he tends to become a figure like Conrad's Marlowe. Chrétien's technique includes this kind of comment (e.g., the frequent references to his sources, or his disdain of repeating what the reader already knows), but goes much farther. At times, he operates like an intentionally inept stage-manager, bringing characters on stage only to have them faint or fall asleep with no valid reason but the stage-manager's whim. [182] More radically,

---

[176] *Supra,* pp. 61 ff.
[177] Frappier, *Perceval,* pp. 60-3.
[178] On Alexander, pp. 29, n. 11, and 66, n. 84; on Soredamors, p. 34; on Fénice, pp. 34, 54, 92; cf. p. 71, n. 95.
[179] *Supra,* pp. 55 ff.
[180] *Supra,* pp. 40 f., 60 f., 71 and n. 95.
[181] *Supra,* pp. 70-73, 76-78.
[182] *Supra,* p. 98, n. 152.

he will present an obstacle described as difficult which is in fact overcome with ease, [183] or present an obstacle described as impossible to
overcome, which is conquered with equal ease. [184]

These last examples touch especially closely on the function of all
the forms of irony discussed in this chapter. I have remarked several
times on the effect of aesthetic distance which Chrétien obtains from
the general artificiality of his romance as well as from particular
instances of this tone. At this point, the characterization of *Cligès* as
artificial, as a *romancier*'s romance, joins with the question of aesthetic
distance. We take pleasure not only from our superiority in regard
to the characters—a function of both verbal and structural irony—but
also in the metamorphoses Chrétien rings on the artifices of literature
itself. Though the matters of aesthetic distance and aesthetic pleasure
in the display of literary prowess are not identical, they serve the same
purpose in this case.

It is from this distance that the story of two successive generations
is to be observed. Alexander is presented almost as a *chanson de
geste* hero transplanted into the courtly world: this is reflected in
conscious attempts to follow proper modes of behavior. [185] In spite of
these attempts, the misjudgment and impulsiveness which were earlier
shown in his departure from Greece erupt again before the assembled
court when his desire for Soredamors comes into conflict with these
modes. [186] This character is also revealed in his immense monologue,
where simple, elemental drives pierce through the refined courtly language and imagery. [187] Soredamors' monologue shows a similar inability to cope with her feelings: it employs dialectical methods to
protest against the invasion of powerful emotions, a protest which
ironically continues to affirm what it would deny. The dialectic leads
to a resolve to act in a certain manner, but that resolution is never
acted on. [188]

By contrast, the monologue of the next generation shows no comparable inner conflict: its problem is how to satisfy a love which is
immediately accepted as fact and in courtly terms. Fénice knows that
she is in love from the first, and makes no attempt to disguise that
fact from herself. Her problem is not an inner one, but to ascertain
whether Cligès returns the same feelings. [189] In the scene of the
avowals, she takes advantage of an ambiguity in his words to lead
herself and Cligès to an open declaration of feelings. It is also in this
scene that Fénice, who had been pictured as a modest and shy young

---

[182] *Supra,* p. 98.
[184] *Supra,* pp. 101 ff. It will be noted that in both cases of this kind—the
tertiary characters, and the obstacles Cligès and Bertrand overcome—each occurrence is part of a pair, a parallelism. Is there a clearer way to indicate that no
error has been committed, that the "lapse" is quite intentional?
[185] *Supra,* pp. 64-7.
[186] *Supra,* pp. 68 ff.
[187] *Supra,* pp. 70-3.
[188] *Supra,* pp. 73-6.
[189] *Supra,* pp. 76-9.

maiden, who had imagined herself as Cligès' servant, becomes the leading actor for the remainder of the romance. Cligès, though his name is used to title the romance, though he seems to be its hero, is only concerned with the means of carrying out Fénice's determined course of action. [190]

It is a course of action in which culminates the development of a major theme. The narrative and thematic pivot of *Cligès* is the deluded "emperor" Alis, who prefers illusion to reality in politics (by contrast with Alexander) and receives illusion rather than reality in love (by contrast with Cligès). [191] The theme had already been the basis of extensive dramatic irony in the Alexander-Soredamors story: both allowed their illusory fears to hinder the reality of their mutual love. [192] The theme had also been used in a number of war and tournament episodes, with a major difference: Cligès, the fully courtly lover by comparison with his father, used deception willingly and even gratuitously while it had only been accidental (or directed only against enemies) in the story of Alexander. [193] These earlier appearances of the theme of illusion are only preparations for its major emergence as the basic means by which the courtly couple will attempt to fulfill their desire. Both the ruse of the false death and the existence of courtly love in an isolated tower depend on the conscious deception of others and the use of magic for that purpose. It is only in a world of magic fantasy that Fénice's dream of an exclusive and perfect love unencumbered by the demands of reality can exist. Both stages of the plot show that fantasy destroyed by reality. The ruse of the false death leads to the reversal by which the deceiver suffers helplessly the very real tortures of the three doctors who quickly perceive the essence of Fénice's plot. [194] The same is true of the lovers' life in the tower: in another affabulation of the ironic paradox between intention and outcome, their isolation—the condition of their love—is seen to lead to world-wide fame as an example of the deception lovers use: the means by which Fénice attempts to avoid the fate of Iseut leads her to the same fate. [195]

Chrétien accomplishes this by an interruption of his "contract" with the reader: he destroys the illusion basic to the fictional world he has created for us. [196] Ironically, this breaking of the fictional contract is both a natural outcome and a reaffirmation of another contract he has established more subtly throughout the romance. While displaying characters floundering in illusion, he has always let us know that their actions were based on illusions: we have always been privileged to know the reality withheld from the characters. The fantasy lives based on illusion were theirs, not that of readers placed at the same aesthetic

---

[190] *Supra,* pp. 79-81.
[191] *Supra,* pp. 82-5.
[192] *Supra,* pp. 85-7.
[193] *Supra,* pp. 87-91.
[194] *Supra,* pp. 97-7.
[195] *Supra,* pp. 98-106.
[196] *Supra,* pp. 101-4.

distance from the narrative enjoyed by the author. When Chrétien interrupts the fictional contract, he chooses to prefer reality over a fictional illusion, and shows this by affirming his freedom vis-à-vis that illusion. This interruption and affirmation are momentarily shocking, but they also reaffirm our own reality and freedom in regard to those same characters. The aesthetic distance from which we are to view the story is also a moral distance: both are preconditions to our own freedom.

Unfortunately, this kind of discussion does grave injustice to *Cligès*. It sometimes makes of a refreshing, genial and amusing romance a rather dour, doctrinal and moralistic treatise. Our experience of the characters is far from negative. We delight in their presence, their beauty and youth, their courage and wit; we marvel at their foolishness and ingenuity, and find their immorality charming. But in the "translation" from the state of incipient suggestion to precise formulation of their moral weaknesses, the latter grow disproportionately large until they begin to overshadow our primary aesthetic experience. Although *Cligès* is far from "negative", analyses of it tend to be. This is also due, in part, to the fact that Chrétien does not affirm an intellectual positive within the romance, either directly or by a fictional mouthpiece. [197] His beliefs, his own ideas on love and morality are nowhere stated. Nor will it do to attempt a deduction of positives by merely inverting the negatives: moral and psychological attitudes are not that simple.

It does seem to me, however—and this is entirely a personal, subjective impression—that a hint of what Chrétien found valuable in human behavior may be gleaned from the muted display of a quality rare in *Cligès* After Alexander has won his first *chevalerie,* he comes, as is is nightly habit, to the Queen's tent, wearing the shirt she gave him. She notices the golden hair, and suddenly remembers who made the shirt. She calls to Soredamors, who approaches and kneels before her. The two young people are so close they could touch, but they remain wordless and pale. The Queen compares this to their usual behavior with surprise:

> Bien aparçoit et voir li sanble
> Par les muances des colors
> Que ce sont accident d'amors;
> Mes ne lor an vialt feire angoisse,
> Ne fet sanblant qu'ele conoisse
> Rien nule de quanqu'ele voit. (1578-83)

---

[197] I agree with Frappier's opinion that the Queen, in her criticism of Alexander's mutism, represents Chrétien's opinion rather closely (*Cligès,* p. 88). We have seen that this criticism is relevant to the Cligès-Fénice episode as well (*supra,* p. 105). However, it is an indirect relevance, and this criticism is far from an *exposé* of the author's ideas on love and morality.

There is one other passage in which Chrétien speaks directly on a related matter: the short dissertation on whether two lovers can have the same heart. As we have seen, its interest was literary rather than doctrinal: *supra,* p. 79, n. 117.

But the most important indication of Chrétien's values is not so localized. It lies, I think, in our primary experience of the work itself. That we retain our sympathy for the characters while perceiving their weakness is profoundly meaningful. We need only think of Swift to recall how harsh and destructive a literary weapon irony can be against the characters who people a fictional world. Chrétien never uses it thus. Alexander and Soredamors, Fénice and Cligès, in their different ways, are foolish, weak, self-deluded in their desires and fears; yet we never experience them as "beyond the pale" of the author's acceptance or our own. His irony operates within a large range of sympathy, clear-sighted and analytical, but never destroyed by his perceptions. Perhaps that is the most important meaning of Chrétien's irony in *Cligès*.

CHAPTER II

PERCEVAL

In considering *Cligès,* it was possible to begin with certain elementary forms of irony which were analyzed for their own sake, outside the general structure of the romance as whole. As a result, we were able to approach the final climax of the narrative in its own terms and structure, but with a wealth of interpretative techniques elaborated on the basis of earlier parts of the text. This approach is impossible in the case of Chrétien's last romance. The fact that it is unfinished robs us of a goal towards which the narrative can be seen to lead and converge. Even within the fragment which has come down to us, the techniques of stylistic analysis which were so useful for *Cligès* lose some of their relevance. Though incongruity, and the aesthetic distance it establishes between reader and character, is still omnipresent and essential to the analysis of *Perceval,* its forms have changed. Irony is frequent, but most often it receives little of the stylistic emphasis which functioned as a kind of sign and indicator to the reader; it is usually perceptible only by juxtaposition either with the structural context or with general social ideals. [1] Furthermore, the incongruities in *Perceval* often obtain comic or even farcical effects rather than ironic tone: the structural principle of incongruity is the same, but its effect on the reader is different. [2] To some extent, this change from verbal to structural irony and comedy is part of Chrétien's general development as a writer: an excellent example midway between *Cligès* and *Perceval* is the first third of *Yvain,* where the two techniques are used in conjunction. [3] However, the emphasis on broader forms of incongruity in *Perceval* is also due to the character of its first hero: the stumblings of an ignorant *naïf* into society lend themselves to more elemental effects than those of stylistic irony.

---

[1] On the other hand, the techniques of material repetition and parallelism are even more important to the *Perceval.*

[2] The reader will recall our resolution not to deal with questions of literary theory, such as the difference between irony and comedy; see our Preface, *supra,* p. 11.

[3] The aspect of dramatic comedy in *Yvain* has been discussed by Walter Küchler, "Über den sentimentalen Gehalt der Haupthandlung in Chrestien's 'Erec' und 'Ivain'," *Zeitschrift für romanische Philologie,* XL (1919), 83-99; and Frappier, *Yvain,* pp. 86 ff.

Another problem is the relationship between the techniques of aesthetic distance and the structure of the romance. After *Cligès,* Chrétien returned to the heroic form we first see in *Erec et Enide.* Its pattern can be summarized as follows. The hero first appears in the context of his society, detaches himself from it for an initial adventure which leads to a first success about one third of the way into the story. This success proves short-lived: the hero is suddenly cast to the nadir of his existence, and must slowly prove and/or reconstitute himself as a knight through a series of increasingly heroic adventures which lead to eventual reintegration in society and marriage. [4] The purest example of this pattern is *Erec et Enide.* In *Yvain,* it is varied, with greater stress on the final reconciliation of the hero with his wife than with society as represented by King Arthur's court. The variation is even greater in *Perceval,* where the hero starts at a point outside of society; all but the last of his adventures described by Chrétien show him making his way toward that society. Nevertheless, as our commentary will indicate, there are important similarities in the structure of the Perceval section and the first part of *Yvain.*

This is a strong heroic pattern, so strong that most analyses of the *Perceval* have considered primarily the narrative action, relegating the generally acknowledged irony and comedy to the role of *hors d'œuvres* or *entremets,* that is, as occasionally amusing interludes which serve merely to make more palatable the serious concerns of the author. It is the thesis of this chapter that these techniques are intentionally used by Chrétien to provide a less than heroic view of both Perceval and Gauvain, and that they are essential to an understanding of his romance. Our method will be a continuous commentary on the text, with scrupulous attention to the order in which the author presents his material. [5] In part, this method is dictated by the fact that the romance is incomplete: it is all the more incumbent on the critic to follow what structure does exist rather than impose his own on the unfinished fragment. This will also respect one of the characteristics of comedy, which often depends for its effects on repetition.

This method presents two dangers. The first is that of extensive paraphrase of a story better told by its original author. Some of this is inevitable; it has been kept to a minimum. The second danger is inherent in the material, and has not been avoided: the commentary is as repetitious as the text, though—alas!—less amusing. I have felt bound to state the point made by Chrétien's comedy and irony, especially since they have been widely ignored by scholarship in spite of their frequency.

---

[4] See William S. Wood, "The Plot Structure in Four Romances of Chrestien de Troyes," *Studies in Philology,* L (1953), 1-15.

[5] Thanks to Frappier's perceptive outline and discussion of the Gauvain section, it will not be treated in as much detail as the first part of the romance (Frappier, *Le roman breton: Chrétien de Troyes, Perceval ou le Conte du Graal* [Paris: Centre de Documentation Universitaire, 1961], pp. 112-35). We will also tamper somewhat with the order of Gauvain's complexly interwoven adventures for the sake of brevity and convenience.

The Prologue

It has been said that the theme of the Prologue is the praise of *largesce*, [6] that it represents a fusion of *largesce* with Christian *caritas*, [7] and that it represents an opposition of knightly *largesce* with Christian charity as well as the superiority of the latter. [8] Though these formulations do not represent the full breadth of their authors' views, they serve to indicate that Chrétien's method of indirection has not always produced happy results. While an endless variety of interpretative possibilities may have been a goal of nineteenth century symbolism, the same attitude of critical freedom is misapplied to most of Chrétien's work. [9]

After naming himself and complimenting his audience by means of a proverb and its expansion, Chrétien states his theme: the comparison of Philip of Flanders with Alexander the Great (1-20). Philip is described: he dislikes gossip, loves justice, loyalty, and the Church, hates all *vilenie,* and is generous without ostentation, for he gives according to the injunction: do not let your left hand know what your right hand is doing (21-36). [10] The Biblical text is expounded in terms of an opposition between the vain glory which comes from false hypocrisy and Philip's behavior which comes from charity (37-56). The comparison is concluded to Philip's advantage (57-9), and Chrétien concludes the Prologue with a smiling allegorical request for his patron's generosity (60-8).

Even this cursory summary shows that Alexander gets short shrift. He is mentioned twice, both times in comparison with Philip (14, 58). The only direct description he receives is the following:

> ... il ot an lui amassez
> Toz les vices et toz les maus
> Don li cuens est mondes et saus. (18-20)

Nevertheless, he is present throughout as the implied contrast to Philip. If the latter is without hypocrisy and guile (30), this suggests these vices adhere to Alexander. Nor does the word *largesce,* so important in analyses of this passage, appear in the Prologue: only the adjective form *larges* is used, and then it is applied to Philip (28). It is equally applicable to Alexander however, who was renowned as the type of generosity itself. [11] Thus *largesce* itself cannot be in question here, since the two men being compared both possess this quality.

---

[6] Kellermann, *Aufbaustil und Weltbild...*, p. 186.
[7] Köhler, *Ideal und Wirklichkeit...*, p. 31.
[8] Frappier, *Perceval,* p. 21.
[9] However, cf. Reto R. Bezzola, *Le sens de l'aventure et de l'amour (Chrétien de Troyes)* (Paris: Editions de la Jeune Parque, 1947), pp. 1-10 and *passim*; cf. Jean Misrahi's review in *Romance Philology,* IV (1950-51), 348-361.
[10] *Matthew* 6, 3.
[11] He was already the standard of comparison in *Erec et Enide* (ll. 2213 f.; 6611 ff.); see also *supra,* p. 66, and note 84.

It is the motive for generosity which is being compared. The left hand, *selonc l'estoire,*

> Senefie la vainne gloire,
> Qui vient de fausse ypocrisie... (40 f.),

while

> ... li don sont de charité
> Que li bons cuens Phelipes done... (52 f.)

In both cases, one thing is seen as "coming" from another. False hypocrisy results in vain glory, while charity results in a hidden generosity without desire for what we would call "publicity." It is the manner and intent of the gift on which Chrétien focuses our attention in the largest part of the Prologue, but he is careful to leave the Queen of medieval virtues *hors de cause.* To some extent, this is probably a matter of tact, of not biting the hand that we may hope had often fed him, but it also avoids the implication of an antagonism between knightly generosity and a Christian ethic. They are related, not as antithetical choices, but as an action which may have various motives, one of these being charity.

To define this term is beyond our scope or capacity. It will be sufficient, for the moment, to note that Chrétien considers it in three ways in the Prologue. First, as something essential to God: *Deus est charité* (47). Secondly, as something bearing on the relationship between God and man:

> ... qui vit
> An charité, selonc l'escrit,
> Saint Pos le dit et je le lui,
> Il maint an Deu, et Deus an lui. (47-50) [12]

Third, as an impulse which results in generosity, charity has to do with the relationships among men:

> Donc sachoiz bien de verité
> Que li don sont de charité
> Que li bons cuens Phelipes done,
> Qu'onques nelui n'an areisone
> Fors son franc cuer, le deboneire,
> Qui li loe le bien a feire. (51-6)

It is this aspect of charity which is behind the first lines of the Prologue:

> Qui petit seme petit quiaut,
> Et qui auques recoillir viaut,
> An tel leu sa semance espande
> Que fruit a çant dobles li rande;
> Car an terre qui rien ne vaut,
> Bone semance i seche et faut. (1-6)

---

[12] As Hilka points out (note to l. 49), it is not Paul who says it but John, in his *First Letter* (4, 16).

The combination of the first line's traditional proverb with the reference to Christ's parable of the sower [13] suggests a process of increasingly fruitful exchange among men, profitable to each and Christian in ethical value. However, it is also a smiling allegorical request for the patronage Chrétien, at the end of the Prologue, claims to be quite certain of receiving. Having finished his demonstration that Philip is worth more than Alexander, our author concludes with a certain self-satisfaction:

> Donc avra bien sauve sa painne
> CRESTIIENS, qui antant et painne
> A rimoiier le meillor conte
> Par le comandemant le conte
> Qui soit contez an cort real:
> Ce est li contes del GRAAL,
> Don li cuens li bailla le livre,
> S'orroiz comant il s'an delivre. (61-8)

At the same time, the Prologue concludes with an example of the fruitful interchange which it suggested at the beginning. Philip gave Chrétien a book, Chrétien now gives the Count a romance, and expects a reward in turn.

Which of these three meanings of *charité* is most important to the romance can only be determined after the examination of the whole— or that whole which Chrétien completed. It is suggestive, however, that Tobler-Lommatzsch quote a passage from *Yvain* in which Chrétien uses the word, giving its meaning as *christliche Nächstenliebe*. [14] When the hermit saw the wild, naked hunter, he realized the man was not in his right mind. Out of fear, he jumped into his hut. Nevertheless,

> de son pain et de sa porrete
> *par charité* prist li boens hom,
> si li mist fors de sa meison
> desor une fenestre estroite... (*Yvain*, 2840-3)

Perceval and the Five Knights

The romance proper begins with a brief but lovely lyrical introduction which combines the themes of dawn and spring: [15]

---

[13] *Luke* 8, 8; *Matthew* 13, 8-23.
[14] Tobler-Lommatzsch, *Altfranzösisches Wörterbuch.*
[15] Frappier, *Perceval,* p. 35. Frappier quotes the following lines:
> Et maintenant li cuers del vantre
> Por le douz tans li resjoï
> Et por le chant que il oï
> Des oisiaus qui joie feisoient:
> Totes ces choses li pleisoient (86-90),
as revealing Perceval's aristocratic origin (*ibid.,* p. 37). Given the meaning of the last line quoted in my text (*Et tote riens de joie anflame...*), that interpretation seems overstressed: the boy reacts naturally, as would *tote riens.* As he notes, Chrétien leaves the vocation of his hero "à l'état purement instinctif," (*loc. cit.*), that is, undifferentiated from that of *tote riens,*
A comparison of this description with a similar one in *Yvain* indicates a

> Ce fu au tans qu'arbre florissent,
> Fuellent boschage, pré verdissent
> Et cil oisel an lor latin
> Doucemant chantent au matin
> Et tote riens de joie anflame... (69-73)

Shortly thereafter, a different sound invades the landscape, that of five knights

> De totes armes acesmez,
> Et mout grant noise demenoient
> Les armes de çaus qui venoient;
> Car sovant hurtoient as armes
> Li rain des chasnes et des charmes.
> Les lances as escuz hurtoient,
> Et tuit li hauberc fremilloient;
> Sonoit li fuz, sonoit li fers
> Et des escuz et des haubers. (102-10)

Two sounds, two kinds of music, we might say, two poles of human experience. The beauty of a burgeoning Nature where man is only→ an occasional observer; the crashing sounds of armored men, implying all that is original with man: production of useful objects, social organization, a knightly ethic and its role as the fulfillment of manhood. A sphere, not antagonistic to man, but basically indifferent to him; and the world man creates as his new, social nature.

These two poles of existence have been juxtaposed before in⟩ Chrétien's work. Perceval's meeting with the five knights has been compared with the encounter, in *Yvain*, of Calogrenant and the *vilain*, guardian of wild beasts. [16] In both cases, it is the meeting of two incongruous worlds that is portrayed, worlds nearly incomprehensible to each other but not hostile: both Perceval and the *vilain* eventually give their interlocutors the information requested. In both cases also, the inhabitants of the strange, asocial world are presented with ironic sympathy. There is no question of this in the case of Perceval, but the *vilain* is too easily taken as a mere exercise in grotesquerie. Surely it is crediting Chrétien with little profundity to ignore the implications of

---

"naturalistic" intention on Chrétien's part:
> doucemant li oisel chantoient
> si que molt bien s'antre' acordoient;
> et divers chanz chantoit chascuns;
> c'onques ce que chantoit li uns
> a l'autre chanter ne oï. (*Yvain*, 465-9)

The suggestion of a pathetic fallacy here turns the birds into imitators of polyphonic chant which was beginning to flourish at about this period (Théodore Gérold, *La musique au moyen âge*, in *CFMA*, vol. 73 [Paris: Champion, 1932], pp. 236-46); cf. Frappier, *Yvain*, p. 117.

[16] Hildegard Emmel, *Formprobleme des Artusromans und der Graldichtung. Die Bedeutung des Artuskreises für das Gefüge des Romans im 12. und 13. Jahrhundert in Frankreich, Deutschland und den Niederlanden* (Bern: Franck, 1951), p. 51; cf. Bezzola, *op. cit.*, p. 52 (on *Perceval*) and Köhler, *op. cit.*, pp. 70 and 82 (on *Yvain*).

literal truth in the *vilain*'s answer to Calogrenant's rather insulting
question:

> "Va, car me di
> Se tu es buene chose ou non!"
> Et il me dist: "Je sui uns hon. [17]

In fact, one critic has found this monstrous creature the most sympathetic secondary character in *Yvain*. [18] With both Perceval and the
vilain, though the creature untouched by the society Chrétien presents
as a norm is obviously incomplete from the viewpoint of that norm, he
is not antagonistic, however ugly or laughable.

The similarity between Perceval and the *vilain* has been remarked
from another point of view, that of literary tradition. Both are versions
of a type which became increasingly popular in the Middle Ages, that
of the "wild man". [19] Primitiveness was seen differently in this tradition than in modern thought. Where we often tend to consider the
"natural" elements in man as anterior and more essential to his being
than the restraining effects of civilization, the medieval tradition saw
the state of wildness rather as a fall from the normal human condition,
the result of psychological turmoil or a peculiar upbringing. What we
consider primitive and therefore essential was viewed as a lapse from
the essentially human: wildness "... implied everything that eluded
Christian norms and the established framework of Christian society,
referring to what was uncanny, unruly, raw, unpredictable, foreign,
uncultured and uncultivated." [20] Generously enough, the condition was
not considered irremediable. The removal of the original cause, combined with a process of acculturation, could allow the wild man to
resume his place in society without the burden of moral stigma.

---

[17] I am using Foerster's text here (ll. 328-30) rather than Roques':
> "Va, car me di
> se tu es boene chose ou non."
> Et il me dist qu'il ert uns hom. (326-8)

The main reason, I must admit, is my preference for the sharp antithesis of
Foerster's text. However it is also the *difficilior lectio* (a scribe would be more
likely to keep the grammatical unity of a line than interrupt it by direct quotation),
and more typical of Chrétien's usual style of rapid dialogue, which rarely uses
indirect discourse.
For *chose* as insulting when used for persons, see *Yvain,* ll. 1226, 4408.

[18] Mario Roques, Introduction to *Yvain,* p. xv. See Frappier's fine comments
on this dialogue, in *Yvain,* p. 73 f. Later, he notes that the description of the
vilain is also the only *"portrait en règle"* according to the rules of the *arts poétiques (ibid.,* pp. 1117-9; cf. Alice Mary Colby, "The Style of the Portraits in the
Works of Chrétien de Troyes," [unpublished Columbia Diss., 1962], pp. 163-194,
for a discussion of the independence of the vernacular poets *vis-à-vis* latin theory;
her analysis of the portrait of the Ugly Herdsman is on pp. 330-6); to put a
profoundly philosophical statement in the mouth of a ridiculous character is an
irony which can lead to extensive speculation.

[19] Richard Bernheimer, *Wild Men in the Middle Ages, A Study in Art, Sentiment, and Demonology* (Cambridge, Mass.: Harvard, 1952); this entire paragraph
is based on pp. 1-27 of this work.

[20] *Ibid.,* p. 19 f.

The *vilain* is merely the most unmistakable example of this type in Chrétien's works, as well as the most famous *exemplum* in medieval literature. [21] Yvain, naked and insane in the Hermit Episode after his expulsion from society, is an example of temporary degeneration. [22] The opposite process, that of the wild man slowly transformed into a knight, is shown by Perceval. [23] He is not, of course, insane at the beginning of the romance, but merely a *vaslet sauvage* (975), *qui petit fu senez* (281), *nices et bestïaus* (1299), and delightfully uncouth in the early scenes. Nor he is naked, only clothed in rude Welsh leather and linen. If Perceval is not the first of Chrétien's heroes to find himself in the wild forest and in the wild state, he is the first to start there. Others have started away from Arthur's court (Alexander and Cligès), and Erec, Yvain, Lancelot, and Gauvain (in the *Perceval*) have to leave the court for their adventures, but none of them has had his beginning marked by an initial definition of wildness and all that it entails in terms of asociality: ignorance of common objects, forms of behavior, conceptions of individuality and property, pity and sympathy, courtesy, and even of elemental religious beliefs and practices. All the things which are dependent on and defined by man's social life are, for Perceval, as much a wilderness as the grotesque *vilain* is to Calogrenant. Chrétien portrays him with sympathy and undimmed judgment.

His main technique in this portrayal is incongruity, ranging from irony to broad comedy. Perceval's first two reactions belong to the comedy of logical absurdity. Hearing the unknown racket of clashing armor among the trees, he is frightened, and immediately identifies the source of the noise as the most frightening thing he has heard of: devils. This leads to a second incongruity, as he prepares to deal with the devils with his javelin. His second reaction is to the actual sight of the knights. When they come out of the woods, he is struck by the beauty of their armor reflecting its colors to the sun, and swerves to the other extreme: they are angels, and here he will follow his mother's advice to kneel and adore them, especially their chief, more beautiful than the others, who must be God himself. And so it is that the five knights find kneeling before them in the prairie a wild youth saying his prayers and the credo. (100-58). [24]

---

[21] *Ibid.*, p. 27 f.

[22] *Ibid.*, p. 14.

[23] *Ibid.*, p. 21.

[24] Physical action becomes more and more important as Chrétien's comic talent develops. Yvain, led to meet Laudine, is so frightened as he enters the room that he retreats into the farthest corner, which unleashes Lunete's ridicule. She drags him forward by the arm, ridiculing him the while, and when she releases him, he falls to his knees and joins his hands (in prayer)—the same position Perceval is in. This can be a symbolic position: in Yvain's case, it has been interpreted as the one place where Chrétien uses the feudal terms by which the troubadours available to him express the love relationship (Tom Peete Cross and William A. Nitze, *Lancelot and Guenevere, A Study on the Origins of Courtly Love* [Chicago: University of Chicago, 1930], p. 97). In so far as symbolic meaning is present, however, it is part of the comedy of incongruity.

The youth is fortunate in that his first encounter with society brings
him into contact with a truly courteous knight and perspicacious
observer. [25] Nonetheless, the latter mistakes abnegation for fear, perhaps considering Perceval a peasant boy and serf afraid of a strange
knight. He tells his companions to remain behind:

> "Se nos alions tuit ansanble
> Vers lui, il avroit, ce me sanble,
> Si grant peor que il morroit,
> Ne respondre ne me porroit
> A rien que je li demandasse..." (163-7)

Indeed, though the knight will have some difficulty in obtaining the
answer he wants, this will not be caused by Perceval's fear but by
his earnestly egoistical curiosity,

> "Vaslez, n'aies peor."
> "Non ai je, par le Sauveor..." (171 f.),

assures him the youth, who immediately takes over direction of the
colloquy by a surprising turnabout:

> "Estes vos Deus?"—"Nenil, par foi."
> "Qui estes dons?"—"Chevaliers sui."
> "Ainz mes chevalier ne conui,"
> Fet li vaslez, "ne nul n'an vi
> N'onques mes parler n'an oï;
> Mes vos estes plus biaus que Deus... (174-9) [26]

The delightful absurdity of the last line quoted marks for the first time
a trait which will often be repeated, Perceval's insistence on retaining
whatever belongs to him—ideas, things, manners; in this case the
association of the knight with God—as well as some things which do
not belong to him.

---

[25] Frappier, *Perceval,* p. 37 f.

[26] Compare the similar exchange between Calogrenant and the *vilain.* After
the latter has explained his occupation, he asks:

> et tu me redevroies dire
> quiex hom tu ies, et que tu quiers.
> Je sui, fet il, uns chevaliers
> qui quier ce que trover ne puis;
> assez ai quis, et rien ne truis.
> —Et que voldroies tu trover?
> —Avanture, por esprover
> ma proesce et mon hardemant.
> Or te pri et quier et demant,
> se tu sez, que tu me consoille
> ou d'aventure ou de mervoille
> —A ce, fet il, faudras tu bien:
> d'aventure ne sai je rien,
> n'onques mes n'en oï parler. (*Yvain,* 356-69)

In both cases, the comedy faces the knight with an uncouth character and moves
technically by a turnabout.

Here starts the comedy of two trains of thought that continually collide, one of which is repeatedly derailed. [27] The knight approaches and asks Perceval if he has seen five other knights and three maidens, but

> Li vaslez a autres noveles
> Anquerre et demander antant... (186 f.)

He grabs the knight's lance, and inquires in the cajoling tone of a child asking something forbidden of its mother:

> "Biaus sire chiers,
> Vos qui avez non chevaliers,
> Que est ice que vos tenez?" (189-91)

With wry irony, the knight answers:

> "Or sui je mout bien assenez,"
> Fet li chevaliers, "ce m'est vis;
> Je cuidoie, biaus douz amis,
> Noveles aprandre de toi,
> Et tu les viaus savoir de moi.
> Jel te dirai: ce est ma lance." (192-7)

The name, of course, helps Perceval very little. With perfect logic, as before, he assimilates the new object to one he already knows, the javelin, and asks if the lance is used like the javelin, *i.e.,* if it is thrown. Told that he is a fool, that the lance is used to strike without being thrown, Perceval again reacts in a manner which, given his own experience and knowledge, is perfectly logical, yet absurd:

> "Donc vaut miauz li uns de cez trois
> Javeloz que vos veez ci;
> Car quanque je vuel an oci,
> Oisiaus et bestes a besoing,
> Et si les oci de tant loing
> Con l'an porroit un bozon treire*."   *shoot a bolt
> (202-7)

His only experience with weapons has been in hunting (we have seen him amuse himself at this before the knights arrived: 91-9), and he reduces the signs of the socialized world to the implements and values of the *Gaste Forez.*

---

[27] At first sight, this dialogue seems to belong to Henri Bergson's category of the *interférence des séries* (*Le rire, essai sur la signification du comique* [Paris: Presses Universitaires de France, 1947], pp. 73-8). However, since one of the series is repeatedly deflected, it rather resembles his description of a Punch and Judy show: "Quand le commissaire s'aventure sur la scène, il reçoit aussitôt, comme de juste, un coup de bâton qui l'assomme. Il se redresse, un second coup l'aplatit. Nouvelle récidive, nouveau châtiment. Sur le rythme uniforme du ressort qui se tend et se détend, le commissaire s'abat et se relève, tandis que le rire de l'auditoire va toujours grandissant." (*ibid.,* p. 53); cf. *infra,* p. 236 and n. 290.

After the lance, the same pattern of comedy is repeated for the shield and hauberk. Each time, the exchange begins with the knight's courteous question, which Perceval ignores completely in the literary equivalent of the dead-pan. Each time, with innocent insistence on his admiring and wide-eyed curiosity, Perceval shunts the dialogue over to his own interest. The second time, the knight repeats his frustrated protest that the boy is "changing the subject" (215-21); the third time, he resigns himself helplessly to the inevitable pattern. Omitting the protest, he explains that he is wearing a hauberk which is as heavy as iron—an ironic comparison, since that is precisely what it is made of. [28] But that is only the first step of the comic dialogue. Its function is to reveal Perceval's ignorance of the appurtenances the world of romance assigns to manhood. The next step goes farther. Perceval here "translates" these knightly appurtenances into the values of the hunting life he knows. As the javelin was better than the lance (an inversion of courtly values), so the hauberk is seen as a potential danger to Perceval's hunting:

> "Danz chevaliers, de teus haubers
> Gart Deus les biches et les cers;
> Que nul ocirre n'an porroie,
> Ne ja mes aprés ne corroie." (273-6) [29]

At this stage in the dialogue, it is not only at Perceval's factual ignorance that we laugh. The juxtaposition of the knightly lance with the hunting javelin, the transfer of the idea of armor to animals,

---

[28]   "Vaslez, c'est mes haubers,
S'est aussi pesanz come fers."
"De fer est il?"—"Ce voiz tu bien." (263-5)
This is another example of irony using literary forms as its basis (see *supra*, p. 108 f.). A simile is assumed to bring together two different entities; this assumption is a normal "contract" between writer and reader. When something is compared to itself, the implication is that it is different from itself, which our surprised realization denies: *tropus per contrarium quod conatur ostendens.*

[29] Lucien Foulet ("Sire, Messire," *Romania*, LXXI [1950], 1-40, 180-221) has found that *dan* is an older form than *sire* (p. 2), sometimes used for merchants (p. 7), and frequently carrying a pejorative tone (p. 8). He specifically points to Perceval's use of it in adressing the Red Knight (ll. 1091 and 1097 in the Hilka edition) as a "*dan* ironique" (p. 12); I would add that the same characterization is valid here. The question is, however, who is the object of the irony? In the mouth of a person cognizant of contemporary linguistic fashions, such usage is intentional irony at the expense of the person addressed. But Perceval and his mother have been living in the *Gaste Forez* since he was two years old (458). The fact that Chrétien did not use *dan* until the *Perceval,* where it is still used without ironic intent as well (*loc. cit.,* p. 11), suggests that it was acceptable in certain circumstances, but old-fashioned and therefore subject to ironic use. The change in linguistic level presumably occurred during Perceval's youth in the forest; it was still acceptable when his mother, noble and proud of it, arrived there. The lady, unaware of changing linguistic fashions, has given her old-fashioned ways to her son. That he uses it without consciousness of its dated character may cause the knight a momentary wince, but it reflects far more on Perceval himself.

represent a kind of mental process that occurs quite normally. It is a spontaneous bypassing (usually) of socially learned categories. The normal reaction when this occurs is to consider it a funny quirk of the mind, and either leave it unmentioned or express it as a joke. Perceval takes it quite seriously, however. It is not ignorance *per se* which is the source of comedy, but the serious expression of something we are taught by socialization to consider lightly. It is his lack of socialization, the absence of patterns of thought considered to be normal, that gives rise to this humor.

This second step is missing in the dialogue about the shield. In its place, there is a brief conference between the knight and his companions. The latter impatiently ride up to learn the cause of the delay. Told that the boy never answers *a droit* (239), one of them explains:

> "Sire, sachiez bien antreset
> Que Galois sont tuit par nature
> Plus fol que bestes an pasture:
> Cist est aussi come une beste;
> Fos est qui delez lui s'areste,
> S'a la muse ne viaut muser
> Et le tans an folie user."

To which the knight who has been speaking to Perceval answers:

> "Ne sai," fet il, "se Deus me voie,
> Einz que soie mis a la voie,
> Quanque il voldra li dirai,
> Ja autremant n'an partirai." (242-52)

Though this is a "discrete antithesis" between the courtly tact and kindness of the knight and the short-sightedness of his companions, [30] this should not blind us to the grain of truth in the short-sighted view. A few lines later on, Chrétien himself calls Perceval *cil qui petit fu senez* (281), [31] and is often as uncomplimentary. The most frequent tag for Perceval is *nice,* whose range of meaning includes "ignorant, foolish, simple, innocent." [32]

These two aspects of Perceval—the inherent kernel of something better than his words reveal, and the ludicrousness they do reveal—are not contradictory. In fact, the difference between them resembles the distinction elaborated in the Prologue. There, a distinction was made between act and motive. Here, we have two views of the same character: it is a quality of lively energy, youthful self-confidence, and intense concentration on what has aroused his curiosity that appear through Perceval's comic disrespect, egotism, and self-absorption. Both views of the character arise out of the comedy; the formulation that

---

[30] Frappier, *Perceval,* p. 37 f.

[31] Cf. l. 394: *A guise d'ome mal sené.*

[32] Ll. 681, 701 (*nicemant*), 1365. He is also called *sot* (1365), *fol* (1173), and *sauvage* (975); in these references, it is the author speaking: other characters within the romance often repeat these adjectives and add others. This emphasis by verbal frequency extends up to and including the Gornemant episode.

the episode has a comic effect *but* that its essential basis is earnestly serious is both ungrateful and superficial. [33] It is the comedy which is the source both of our understanding of Perceval and our sympathy for him.

This same identity of comic and serious communication can be seen in Perceval's capstone question. Having taugt te Wels lad to recognize lance, shield, and hauberk, the patient knight asks his question again:

> "Vaslez, se Damedeus t'aït,
> Se tu me sez dire noveles
> Des chevaliers et des puceles?"
> Et cil qui petit fu senez
> Li dist: "Fustes vos einsi nez?" (278-82)

It is a comic line, of course, [34] but it also leads to the information that the speaker was knighted only five days ago, and by King Arthur. He is, then, the civilized analogue of Perceval, the image of what Perceval might be at this moment had he received the education, training, and socialization to which his noble lineage entitle him. The encounter with the newly dubbed knight goes further than merely juxtaposing the *vaslez sauvage* to a representative of a more normal social order: it brings him face to face with a counterpart of himself. As in a dyptich, Chrétien places the two portraits, drawn entirely in conversation, of the same figure: the youth who has inherited his normal social role, and the youth relegated to an upbringing in a wilderness aefined by its withdrawal from the normal social structure. [35] The full distance of the incongruity between them is measured by Perceval's comic:

> "Fustes vos einsi nez?"

At the end of the Five Knights Episode occurs a section of eighteen lines which are funny enough in themselves, but whose authenticity

---

[33] Kellermann, *Aufbaustil und Weltbild...*, p. 131.

[34] "Being born that way" seems also to suggest beauty or fitness. Later in the *Perceval*, Chrétien writes: "... onques si biaus Chevaliers ne fu nez de fame..." (1864 f.). Another occurrence of this association is in the *Lancelot*, though this seems decidedly ironic. Chrétien has described Lancelot's arming and impressive appearance, mounted and in full knightly panoply, before commenting:

> ... il ne vos fust mie avis
> qu'anprunté n'acreü l'eüst;
> einz deïssiez, tant vos pleüst,
> qu'il fu ensi nez et creüz;
> de ce voldroie estre creüz. (*Lancelot*, 2672-6)

[35] The *Gaste Forez* is not a wasteland in any physical or agricultural sense. As we have seen, springtime brings its usual burgeoning of greenery and birds; harrowers are working over land plowed for oats (307-10); see Paul Imbs, "Perceval et le Graal chez Chrétien de Troyes," *Bulletin de la Société Académique du Bas-Rhin*, LXXII-LXXIV (1950-52), 37-79; p. 46, n. 17. I recoil from explaining the prase in terms of "symbolic meaning", an explanation rather overdone in Chrétien scholarship. It is unnecessary in any case, since the meaning of the *Gaste Forez* is clearly defined in the actions and character of Perceval.

has been questioned. [36] Before leaving, the knight asks the Welsh boy's name, and must ask it three times, as he is answered first by *biaus filz,* then *biaus frere,* and finally *biaus sire.* Asked if he has any other name beside these, Perceval replies:

> "Sire, je non,
> Ne onques certes plus n'an oi."
> "Si m'aït Deus, mervoilles oi,
> Les greignors que j'oïsse mes
> Ne me cuit que j'oie ja mes." (356-60)

Though pleasant enough, this comedy is featherweight by comparison to the preceding scene. It is anti-climactic both in intensity of the comic and in revelation of character and situation. It is also unique in Chrétien's works in laying a heavy stress on the audience's ignorance of the hero's name: our author normally makes no reference to his withholding of names. [37]

Perceval's Mother

After that brilliant chapter of exposition through comedy, Chrétien shifts to a more somber tonality which paradoxically provides the explanation for the comedy. Perceval's mother, *la veve dame* (74), tells a story of the gradual loss of position, wealth, two other sons, and finally her husband, concluding with four lines that reveal her fearful apprehension and retreat into a complete isolation of herself and her last remaining son:

> "Et je ai vie mout amere
> Soferte puis que il fu morz.
> Vos estiiez toz li conforz
> Que je avoie et toz li biens..." (482-5)

---

[36] Ll. 353-60. Noting that only two mss. contain this passage (including B.N. 794), Hilka comments: "Diese 18 Verse, die auch in Prosa fehlen, sind, wie Baist zuletzt empfahl, aus einem endgültigen kritischen Text zu eliminieren..." (note to these lines).

Unfortunately, Alexandre Micha has not dealt with this specific question in *La tradition manuscrite des romans de Chrétien de Troyes* (Paris: Droz, 1939).

[37] Stylistic considerations are not the most reliable basis for textual criticism; an editor may wish to consider them, however.

These lines may be considered a preparation for Perceval's return to his mother a few lines later:

> Cort contre lui et si le claimme
> 'Biaus filz, biaus filz' plus de cant foiz... (373 f.)

She further addresses him in the same manner six times in the following speeches (ll. 374, 388, 396, 408 [*Biaus douz filz*], 413, 418). This already represents an unusually heavy emphasis for Chrétien.

However, the passage in question may have been interpolated with this in mind, and, more important, to provide some explanation for the perplexing auto-divination of Perceval's name.

The question is not of great importance at this point; it does have bearing on the interpretation of Perceval's divination of his name; see below, pp. 177-81.

Her pessimism and rejection of the world, *i.e.*, the society of which knighthood is the determining factor, appears even as she proudly remembers her lineage:

> "Es Isles de mer n'ot lignage
> Meillor del mien an mon aage;
> Mes li meillor sont decheü,
> S'est bien an plusors leus seü,
> Que les mescheances avienent
> As prodomes qui se maintienent
> A grant enor et an proesce.
> Mauvestiez, honte ne peresce
> Ne chiet pas, car ele ne puet;
> Mes les bons decheoir estuet." (425-34)

The isolation she has imposed on herself and her son is the expression of a general withdrawal from a world which seems to her ridden through with sorrow and evil. It also has the specific intention of preserving her sole surviving son from the fate which overtook his brothers and father: the former died *as armes* (475), and *Del duel des filz mourut li pere* (481). Though Perceval should have been a knight (412),

> "... de chevalerie
> Vos cuidoie si bien garder
> Que ja n'an oïssiez parler
> Ne que ja nul n'an veïssiez." (408-11)

Small wonder then, that she faints at hearing him utter the word *Chevalier* (402): the suddenly discovered goal of his desires means only pain and sorrow to her. [38] A knight is the instrument of death. When Perceval, incongruously recalling the earlier comedy, says that he saw those angels of which she had told him, she replies, with bitter irony:

> "Tu as veü, si con je croi,
> Les anges don les janz se plaingnent,
> Qui ocient quanqu'il ataingnent." (398-400)

Her life, and the deaths of sons and husband, are evidence to her of the evil of knighthood, an evil she seeks to escape and dispel from her son's future by a complete rejection of a world whose center is knighthood. The alternative she has chosen is isolation in a wilderness defined by the absence of mankind.

Chrétien's moving portrait of the mother is both an explanation of the previous episode with the five knights and an ironic juxtaposition to the world represented by those knights. While this scene explains Perceval's ignorance and total lack of social awareness, it also presents an inversion of the knightly world's values. Against prowess, adventure, and the life ruled by a social ethic, it erects defenses of withdrawal, solitude, and primitiveness. It is meant to give Perceval one virtue in particular, innocence. It was in order to avoid death that

---

[38] Emmel, *Formprobleme...*, p. 54.

the mother retreated to the *Gaste Forez,* both the possibility of her son being killed [39] and the possibility of his learning to kill as a knight. Her success is undoubted, if innocence is equated with laughable ignorance. [40] But it is laughable only in the first scene. Here, its other side is revealed, turning to a harsh rudeness when son addresses mother with *"Teisiez, mere!"* (390). After the long story of her losses and sorrows, his only reaction is:

> "A mangier," fet il, "me donez!
> Ne sai de quoi m'areisonez..." (491 f.)

These words spring from the same character, the same innocence and ignorance which were the subject of the comedy with lance, shield, and hauberk.

From the mother's point of view, the events of this episode are pathetic. From the reader's point of view, they are sadly ironic. As Perceval rides off to rejoin the world she rejected, his mother falls in a faint. Just a stone's throw away, Perceval sees her fall ... *Et cil ceingle de la reorte* (626). It is perfectly correct to note that there is not the least feeling of pity or charity in his heart, [41] but this absence of humane feelings is part of his innocence and ignorance, themselves results of the mother's withdrawal to the *Gaste Forez.* Perceval's behavior is a result of her choice: it is this choice of isolation from society which results in her abandonment *au chief del pont.* [42]

The first chapter of this romance has presented a series of dyptichs: the sound of birds, the sound of armor; the sound of armor, the sight of armor; the brilliance of knighthood, the flat ignorance of Perceval; the brilliance of knighthood, knighthood's cost in death and sorrow; sorrow leading to a willful search for innocence, innocence shown as ignorance and brutal rudeness. Each of these terms is related to the next ironically and dialectically: ironically, in that each is shown to bear values other than it seems to possess at first; dialectically, in their contradictory linkages which lead to further links in the chain. The minimal conclusion to be drawn is that experience in this romance is likely to be ambiguous, and that incongruity is likely to recur.

This is certainly true of the rules which Perceval's mother provided to regulate his behavior. They are simple—perhaps she was suiting the lesson to the student—but this simplicity, as the course of the

---

[39] When she thinks of his going to Arthur's court for armor, she expects him to be unable to fight and defend himself (516-22).

[40] "Tout ce que sa mère aura obtenu, c'est de rendre son fils irrespectueux, sensuel et exigeant jusqu'à la brutalité, insensible à la douleur d'autrui..." Imbs, "Perceval et le Graal...", p. 45.

[41] Frappier, *Perceval,* p. 38.

[42] The importance of accepting Chrétien's method of objective presentation (which Frappier refers to as "impressionist": *Perceval,* p. 31), *i.e.,* of revealing things only as they are revealed to his hero, is indicated by this scene. If we add here our knowledge that his mother is to die as a result of his lack of feeling, this turns into a tragedy with Perceval as antagonist for whom sympathy would be difficult, at least.

narrative will show, is treacherous. The first rule is to help ladies in need. To this is appended the permission to kiss ladies if they consent, but a prohibition of the *soreplus*; if she offers a ring or purse as a gift, they may be accepted. Secondly, do not wait too long before asking a companion's name,

> "Car par le non conoist l'an l'ome" (562)

Associate with *prodomes* and follow their advice. Third, go to church and minster to pray our Lord that he give you honor in this world and help you behave so that you come to a good end (527-72). [43]

The last recommendation leads to two questions:

> "Mere," fet il, "que est iglise?" (573)

When this has been explained, the next is:

> "Et mostiers quoi?"... (577)

The questions, again, are comic, and of the same order as those about the lance, shield and hauberk, but they reveal another aspect of the *Gaste Forez*. If it is essentially defined as a place away from society, this includes the absence of religious structures, the places of worship and the sacraments. Religion is a function of society, and exists only in the context of a society. [44] It is as part of his isolation that Perceval is ignorant of churches, and it is part of his approach to society that he be told what churches are.

He is also given some instruction in Christian belief. It is both brief and simple. God is described as the Creator; the mystery of the Host is referred to but hardly explained; the same is true of the Harrowing of Hell; and the Passion is sketched as if the mother were recalling some striking frescoes she saw, years ago, before coming to the *Gaste Forez*. [45] This is the entirety of Perceval's religious

---

[43]
> "Alez proiier nostre Seignor,
> Qu'an ceste siecle vos doint enor
> Et si vos i doint contenir
> Qu'a bone fin puissiez venir." (569-72)

These lines should dispel the false antithesis that has been drawn between the mother's religion as spiritual and Gornemant's as worldly: David C. Fowler, *Prowess and Charity in the "Perceval" of Chrétien de Troyes*, in *University of Washington Publications in Language and Literature*, Vol. XIV (Seattle: University of Washington, 1959), p. 18 f.

[44] The hermits in *Yvain* and *Perceval* are the only exceptions to the social character of religion in Chrétien's work. Even in the latter case, the hermit is not a solitary: he has a chapel provided with a priest and a young cleric, to which people come for confession on Good Friday.

[45] A church is
> "Uns leus ou an fet ie servise
> Celui qui ciel et terre fist
> Et homes et bestes i mist." (574-6)

A minster is:
> "Une meison bele et saintisme
> Et de cors sainz et de tresors,

training. It is meaningful by its suggestiveness to a person with some knowledge of Christianity, but what can they possibly mean to Perceval? His response reveals little comprehension:

> "Donc irai je mout volantiers
> As iglises et as mostiers
> Fet li vaslez, "d'ore anavant:
> Einsi le vos met an covant." (595-9)

Chrétien stresses *d'ore anavant* by its disjunction from what it modifies: it is only henceforth that Perceval will go to church, he has not done so before. Perceval himself reduces religious duty to the level of any task demanded by a parent: "I promise I'll do it."

The Tent

Perceval's compliance with these rules is soon demonstrated: his first sally into the world beyond the wilderness provides him with an opportunity to use those dealing with ladies and churches. The episode begins

> Au main, au chant des oiselez... (635)

A pretty line which would go unnoticed except for the previous appearance of birds: these are courtly. Perceval arrives at a lovely meadow in which stands a marvelous tent of green, red, and gold, on top of which is perched a gilded eagle. It is probably the same eagle that so frequently appears atop courtly tents. [46] Here, it is further associated with the sun,

> Qui mout luisoit clers et vermauz,
> Si reluisoient tuit li pré
> De l'anluminemant del tré. (646-8)

> S'i sacrefie l'an le cors
> Jesucrist, la prophete sainte,
> Cui giu firent honte mainte:
> Traïz fu et jugiez a tort,
> Si sofri angoisse de mort
> Por les homes et por les fames;
> Qu'an anfer aloient les ames
> Quant eles partoient des cors,
> Et il les an gita puis fors.
> Cil fu a l'estache liiez,
> Batuz et puis crocefiiez
> Et porta corone d'espines.
> Por oïr messes et matines
> Et por cele Seignor aorer
> Vos lo gié au mostier aler." (578-94)

[46] For example, the fairy's tent in *Lanval*, whose right flap was worth more than all the wealth of Semiramis or Octavian, was also topped by a golden eagle: *Les lais de Marie de France*, ed. Jeanne Lods, in *CFMA*, Vol. 87 (Paris: Champion, 1959); 80-90. See Hilka's note to l. 644 for further references.

This refulgence is not only a heightened description of nature, but a characteristic sign of the presence of courtly love. [47] The setting, then, is one of those privileged locations which is usually the scene of particularly intense and meaningful events, especially those associated with the *avanture* of courtly love.

Perceval, seeing the tent, exclaims:

> "Deus! or voi je vostre meison.
> Or feroie je mesprison,
> Se aorer ne vos aloie.
> Voir dist ma mere tote voie,
> Qui me dist que mostiers estoit
> La plus bele chose qui soit,
> Et me dist que ja ne trovasse
> Mostier qu'aorer n'i alasse." (655-62)

The comic process is the same as with the knights who were devils, angels, and God, that of misidentifying what he has never seen before, and of misidentifying in a manner which radically transgresses learned social distinctions. [48] This humor is continued by an incongruity which is also a radical reduction in the level of associations. His mother had urged Perceval to pray for guidance in action and honor in this world. He substitutes another reason:

> "Je l'irai proiier, par ma foi,
> Qu'il me doint ancui a mangier,
> Que j'an avroie grant mestier." (664-6) [49]

He enters the tent on his horse, and Chrétien records no sign of surprise on his part when he discovers a sleeping girl in the "house of God". She awakens when his horse stumbles, to find herself face to

---

[47] When Cligès and Fénice first meet, the sun itself is somewhat dimmed, but

> ... uns rais de lor biauté issoit,
> Don li palés resplandissoit
> Tot autresi con li solauz
> Qui nest molt clers et molt vermauz. (*Cligès,* 2717-20)

[48] "Er bezieht eben alles auf seine eigene dürftige Erfahrung." (Kellermann, *Aufbaustil und Weltbild...,* p. 141). It is not even his own experience, of course, only hearsay.

[49] Fowler finds irony in this scene, particularly in "... the fact that he intends to pray to God for food," without realizing that God provides a different kind of food, *i.e.,* the Host (*Prowess and Charity...,* p. 14). The scene strikes me as more comic than ironic, but that can be a matter of different readers' reactions. However, there is no basis for an irony of physical vs. spiritual food here. Perceval may mistake the tent for a minster; the reader does not, and has no reason for associating the Host with the tent. Since Chrétien has not referred to the Host, there is no reason to think of it unless we come to the romance with the predisposition of reading it in specifically religious and sacramental terms.

face with a wild youth dressed in the coarse clothes of a Welshman,
who politely addresses her:

(a)	"Pucele, je vos salu,
(b)	Si con ma mere le m'aprist:
(b)	Ma mere m'anseigna et dist
(a)	Que les puceles saluasse,
(c)	An quel que leu que jes trovasse." (682-6)

Explaining one's greeting as "a lesson my mother taught me" is itself
destructive of politeness—formality accomplished with the ease of the
natural. The point is stressed with a double repetition of *ma mere*,
a triple repetition of *m'aprist, m'anseigna,* and *dist*. But this is only
a build-up toward the last line. The first four lines are structured
chiasmically (two series: [a] *Pucele*—[b] *mere*—[b] *mere*—[a] *puce-
les*; [a] *salu*—[b] *aprist*—[b] *anseigna et dist*—[a] *saluasse*), which
rounds them off as a completed entity. This sets off the last line,
which is "free" of the closed structure, and underlines its emphasis.
There is really nothing wrong with greeting young ladies wherever
one finds them, but to state this everyday assumption with such grandiose universality is perhaps a sign of innocent pomposity and in-
ordinate self-satisfaction?

The same automatism recurs a few lines later, but with a new
complexity. In the preceding passage, Perceval's foolishness is not
in following his mother's perfectly good advice, but in explaining that
he is doing so. Now, however, his *niceté* misinterprets that advice.
She had permitted him to kiss a maiden *S'ele le vos ... consant* (547).
When the Tent Maiden urges him to leave before her *ami* returns, the
mother's permission is turned into a command:

> "Einz vos beiserai, par mon chief,"
> Fet li vaslez, "cui qu'il soit grief;
> Que ma mere le m'anseigna." (693-5)

The girl's reaction is: "Not if I can help it!" [50] and she adds that her
friend will kill the youth if he finds him. But *Li vaslez avoit les braz
jors* (700), a simple declarative statement which leads to a consequence
both incongruous and appropriate: [51]

> Si l'anbrace mout nicemant,
> Car il nel sot feire autremant. (701 f.)

Perceval's mother, it may be recalled, had forbidden the *soreplus*
even if a kiss was granted. Chrétien plays with visual suggestions of
this "remainder":

> Mist la soz lui tote estandue,
> Et cele s'est mout desfandue
> Et deganchi quanqu'ele pot;
> Mes desfanse mestier n'i ot... (703-6)

---

[50]   "Je, voir, ne te beisera ja,"
                 Fet la pucele, "que je puisse." (696 f.)
[51] A comic adaptation, then, of *significatio per consequentiam*; cf. the next
footnote.

The physical positions are fearfully suggestive. Has Perceval forgotten the prohibition, as he misinterpreted the conditional permission of a kiss?

> Que li vaslez an un randon
> La beisa, volsist ele ou non,
> Vint foiz, si con li contes dit... (707-9)

Though Perceval does not, in fact, transgress the prohibition, he compensates by emphasis on the first step, and Chrétien underlines the incongruity with a mock-serious scholarly reference to his source. [52]

Perceval continues kissing the girl until he catches sight of a ring on her finger. Again, the automatism of invoking his mother goes into effect, and his own words underline the repetition:

> "Ancor" fet il, "me dist ma mere
> Qu'an vostre doi l'anel preïsse..." (712 f.)

In addition to repeated automatism and repeated misinterpretation, a further absurdity arises here as Perceval's mother is granted prophetic precision: she told me to take *your* ring. His acquisitive eagerness overwhelms the distinction between general rules and particular cases as he perverts one of those rules, intended to help him get along in polite, courtly society, into a sanction for theft.

But Perceval is nothing if not a courteous thief. Considering his visit to the "House of God" finished, he bids the damsel farewell with what he intends as a courteous compliment:

> "Pucele, bien aiiez:
> Or m'an irai je bien paiiez,
> Et mout meillor beisier vos fet
> Que chanberiere que il et
> An tote la meison ma mere;
> Que n'avez pas la boche amere." (723-8)

The maiden, not flattered, weeps and begs him to return the ring: she will be mistreated for the loss, and he will lose his life for it. But,

> Li vaslez an son cuer ne met
> Rien nule de ce que il ot... (734 f.)

He hears, but doesn't listen. The same thing was noted when his mother recited the sorrows of their family:

> Li vaslez antant mout petit
> A ce que sa mere li dit. (489 f.)

---

[52] The structure of this build-up can be described in terms of *significatio* with a slight change: it leaves more in expectation than is contained in the outcome. The anticlimatic conclusion can be seen as a modified *significatio per abscisionem*. Strictly speaking, this is a suggestive breaking off; what we have here is an underfulfillment of expectations aroused by the suggestiveness of the build-up. The only importance of this point is to show the identity of ironic and comic structures.

and it will be noted again later. It suggests an egotism typical of childhood, and especially of the kind of solitary childhood which was Perceval's.

This is equally true of the next occurence, though we may think of adolescence rather than childhood when Chrétien explains Perceval's inattention as an effect of hunger:

> Li vaslez an son cuer ne met
> Rien nule de ce que il ot,
> Mes de ce que geüné ot
> Moroit de fain a male fin. (734-7)

Like any adolescent, he is always hungry.[53] Fortunately, he finds a keg of wine, a silver cup, and three mutton pies in the tent, and plunges right in. In another parody of politeness, the thief invites the weeping hostess to have some, and even commends the food:

> "Venez mangier, il* sont mout buen   *the mutton pies
> Assez avra chascuns del suen,
> Si an remandra uns antiers." (753-5)

Chrétien stresses the boy's repeated disregard for the other person: she weeps in spite of his repeated urging to eat, and weeps and twists her hands (756-60). And he ate as much as he pleased, and drank until he had enough, and covered up what was left over. He then takes his leave, reassuring the girl that he will repay her for the ring before he dies, with a polite formula of leave-taking:

> "Je m'an vois a vostre congié." (772)

The girl's response reveals this as a blatant inaccuracy:

> Et cele plore et dit que ja
> A Deu ne le comandera..." (773 f.)

This is also the same principle of taking a purely social formula literally which we have seen Chrétien use before.[54]

Eleven lines after Perceval's departure, the girl's *ami* returns, and there ensues a scene in both senses of the word. There is little comedy in it, though the sharply etched portrait of suspicious jealousy can be considered generally ironic both by comparison to our knowledge of what did not happen and the ideals of courtliness. We are led step by step to the knight's full flowering of suspicion, as each partial explanation by the girl is transformed into a sign of her infidelity: the tracks of the visitor's horse, the missing food and wine, the stolen ring, and finally, the admitted kiss. When the last is revealed, his jealousy explodes into a tirade of accusation, for he assumes that one thing leads to another. He further goes on to describe her punishment. They will ride on together without rest until he is avenged, and he dwells on her likely discomforts: her horse will receive no care, and if it dies,

---

[53] *Supra*, p. 128.
[54] *Supra*, pp. 46 f., 49.

she will follow him on foot; her clothes will never be changed, but she will follow him on foot and naked until he has taken the offender's head (813-32). Lest we take all this too seriously, however, Chrétien adds one line which suggests a note of incongruity. After all this passion,

Atant s'assist et si manja. (833)

So far, each reference to food has cast ridicule on the eater. [55]

From the reader's point of view, the entire scene is dramatic irony, since we know that the knight's jealousy is entirely unfounded. Furthermore, this little scene is a departure from Chrétien's usual technique of delayed explanation or consequence: what is here predicted is retold later when Perceval meets the same damsel after the encounter with his cousin. The fact that we may remember this prediction lessens the effect of the later scene. Chrétien, then, is making a point by this shift. He is showing us, once again, that the event at which we laugh also has a serious side: it was comic in the performance, but its result will be grievous. This is the same dyptich technique we found in the Five Knights episode juxtaposed with that of Perceval's mother. As in that case, the technique is used to reveal the ambiguity of experience and action.

The knight's jealousy also continues the theme of erotic suggestiveness begun in Chrétien's description of the position in which Perceval placed the maiden in order to kiss her, surely an unnecessary manœuver for the purpose. This aspect of the scene suggests Perceval's ignorance of sexual matters, and prepares us for the similarly anticlimactic episode with Blanchflor.

The entire Tent Episode also forms a pendant to that of the Five Knights. The first displayed to Perceval the masculine, warrior-side of chivalry; the second its feminine aspect of courtliness, delicacy, and a gentler beauty than that of the armor flashing in the sun.

Perceval at Arthur's Court

While the jealous knight rages, Perceval rides on until he meets a charcoal burner driving an ass before him, from whom he inquires the way to Carduel. Why a charcoal burner, driving an ass? There is no precise or certain answer. [56] Knights are more frequently helped on

---

[55] *Supra,* pp. 128, 134.

[56] See, however, Rita Lejeune, "La date du *Conte du Graal* de Chrétien de Troyes," *Le Moyen Age,* LX (1954), 51-79, where she places this meeting among a series of parallels between Perceval and the young Philippe-Auguste of the years 1178-81, whose preceptor was Philip of Flanders, to whom the present romance is dedicated. A number of the parallels are striking, and I see no reason to reject the possibility that Chrétien was consciously referring to certain aspects of the young prince's life in *Perceval.* However, this in itself does not provide an interpretation of the literary structure, intent, and meaning of the romance. A source—whether it is a literary text, the oral recital of a *jongleur,* or actual contemporary event—provides the artist with material; what the artist does with that material is an entirely different matter.

their way by various ladies, but there is a series of exceptions to this: the *vilain,* guardian of savage beasts in *Yvain*; the dwarf of the cart in *Lancelot*; and more recently, Perceval himself in the Five Knights Episode. Each of these figures is associated with a humiliation or inconvenience for the knight involved. [57] So also, Perceval's encounter with the *charbonier* prefigures his failure to obtain knighthood at Arthur's court. The encounter also provides us with information preparing us for Arthur's condition at Carduel, and with a reiteration of Perceval's inability to learn and listen. Arthur, says the charcoal burner, is both happy and doleful. When Perceval asks the reason for this, we learn his happiness is due to a great victory, his sorrow to the dispersal from the court of his companions. In spite of the fact that he himself requested this explanation,

> Li vaslez ne prise un denier
> Les noveles au charbonier... (859 f.)

This is the third time Chrétien states this trait of his hero.

Perceval rides on until he comes to a fine castle, out of whose gate comes a knight in red armor carrying a gold cup:

> "Par foi,
> Cez* demanderai je le roi: *the arms and armor
> S'il les me done, bel m'an iert,
> Et dahez et qui autres quiert!" (875-8)

That the knight might object does not occur to Perceval; the person under the armor has no more reality to him than a mannequin. He sees the brightly colored armor, and wants it ... period. What is more, he says so to the knight. When the latter asks where he is going, Perceval answers:

> "Je vuel", fet il, "a cort aler
> Au roi cez armes demander." (885 f.)

What is ridiculous here is not the desire itself, but its direct expression. To want another's possession is not, after all, infrequent. But to express this desire openly, without awareness of a social transgression, and to the face of the man whose possession is in question, represents an extraordinary lack of socialization. The only way to meet such naïveté and presumption without descending to its level is to ignore its absurdity with irony. The Red Knight answers:

> "Vaslez", fet il, "tu feras bien..." (887)

He adds an outrageous message to the King, to whom he refers as the *mauvés roi* (889): unless a defender is sent out to challenge his claim,

---

[57] The *Yvain* parallel seems the closest. In spite of Calogrenant's discomfort when he first sees the *vilain* and the ironic juxtaposition which does not leave him untouched, the main humiliations are delayed: his disastrous encounter with Esclados, and the subsequent humiliation of telling the story of that humiliation to his fellows.

Arthur will hold his land as a fief from the Red Knight. How outrageous this is is indicated by the knight's conclusion:

> "Et a cez ansaingnes t'an croie
> Que devant lui pris or androit
> Atot le vin dont il bevoit
> Ceste cope que je an port." (894-7)

No one would believe such effrontery on the face of it: some evidence of serious intent must be shown, therefore the *ansaingnes*. Anyone would be struck by the enormity of the challenge, anyone, that is, except Perceval:

> Or quiere autrui qui li recort;
> Que cil n'i a mot antandu... (899 f.)

For the fourth time, Perceval hears without understanding: he wants the armor, and nothing else can pierce his attention.

Perceval's first sight of the *roi qui les chevaliers fet* (333) [58] is strange and disconcerting: looking for the "greatest king who ever was or will be," [59] he finds a silent figure, entirely withdrawn into its own meditation. [60] At first, in fact, he cannot distinguish the great King from the others seated at the table: a squire must point him out: "*Amis, veez le la!*" (921), which hardly sounds complimentary. Perceval, still mounted as in the tent of the preceding episode, advances toward the silent figure,

> Sel salua si come il sot. (923)—

as well, at least, as he could. But the King was absorbed. ... Again the youth addresses him, with the same lack of response. Our *vaslez sauvage* is not entirely blameworthy when he reflects:

> "Par foi", dist li vaslez adonques
> "Cist rois ne fist chevalier onques.
> Quant l'an n'an puet parole treire,
> Comant porroit chevalier feire?" (927-30)

This self-absorption is as contrary to the basic courtesy of true knighthood as Perceval's completely unreflective self-absorption. Yet Arthur's withdrawal of attention is a state to which Chrétien repeatedly draws our attention:

> ... li rois Artus s'ert assis
> Au chief d'une table pansis... (907 f.)
> ....
> ... [il] fu pansis et muz. (911)
> ....

---

[58] Almost the same formula at l. 494: Perceval would go *Au roi qui fet les chevaliers.*

[59]   ... le meillor roi del mont
Qui onques fust ne ja mes soit. (*Cligès,* 304 f.)

[60] Emmel, *Formprobleme...,* p. 55.

Li rois pansa et ne dist mot. (924)
....
Li rois panse et mot ne li sone. (926)

This is surely more stress than is needed merely to communicate Arthur's mental state. We are being presented with a contrast and encounter between two kinds of thoughtlessness, very different in character and origin, certainly, but equally reprehensible from the point of view of social courtesy, and equally comic. The two forms of thoughtlessness meet when a disgusted Perceval turns his horse around to leave ... and "breaks the spell" by knocking off Arthur's cap.

Chrétien had already exercised his comic talents at the expense of the pensive state in an earlier romance. After Lancelot and Gauvain separate, one heading for the Sword Bridge, the other for the Water Bridge, the hero allows himself to become fully absorbed in thoughts of love. As in Arthur's case, Chrétien uses the word *panser* in various forms during the scene. [61] While Lancelot rides on, abandoned to his thoughts, the horse takes control, choosing the best road in a brief inversion of the master-servant relationship, until he spies a ford. Being thirsty, the horse heads for the water. But the ford is guarded by a knight, who twice warns the approaching Lancelot to turn back. Lancelot hears none of this, the thirsty horse continues toward the water, and the spell is broken only when the guarding knight charges Lancelot at a gallop, knocking him off his horse so that he falls stretched out into the water as lance and shield fly off his neck:

> Quant cil sant l'eve, si tressaut;
> toz estormiz an estant saut,
> ausi come cil qui s'esvoille,
> s'ot, et si voit, et se mervoille
> qui puet estre qui l'a feru. (*Lancelot*, 767-71) [62]

The effect is less obvious in the Arthur passage, for several reasons. The comic means are grosser in the Lancelot episode, including movement, a number of "properties", and a more direct preparation for the comic climax. By comparison, the only object of importance is Arthur's cap, and the only movement that of Perceval's horse. There is also a question of focus of attention: whereas we have been following Lancelot, and the other knight has just come into view, it is Perceval (who plays the other knight's role in the comic pattern) to whom we direct our main attention. The Lancelot episode is farcical; the Perceval parallel is suggestive only. This is probably also because the ridicule in this scene is to be distributed evenly: Perceval is as clumsy as the Red Knight was outrageous in pouring wine over the Queen:

---

[61] *Lancelot*, 711, 714, 723, 737, 745; the adjective form *pansif* is absent from this list.

[62] "Le rappel de Lancelot à la conscience de la réalité par sa chute inattendue ... est vraiment plus comique que touchant." Roques, Introduction to the edition of the *Lancelot*, p. xxxi.

he brought his horse too close to the King, *A guise d'ome mal sené* (934). However, we are accustomed to seeing Perceval as inept in society: it is Arthur who suffers most in this scene. It has been noted before that he has become more senile since the *Yvain*, [63] and that except for *Cligès*, he "is not only a figure-head, a static monarch, but a *roi fainéant* whose weakness the poet mentions again and again, and not without humor." [64] He is, in fact, the butt of at least a suggestion of comedy.

Capless, Arthur makes his excuses: his anger at the Red Knight's challenge and at the humiliation undergone by the Queen, who has now retreated to her room in great grief and anger *ou ele s'ocit* (965). All this means absolutely nothing to Perceval. For the fifth time, he disregards what he hears:

> Li vaslez ne prise une cive
> Quanque li rois li dit et conte;
> Ne de son duel ne de la honte
> La reïne ne li chaut il.
> "Feites moi chevalier", fet il,
> "Sire rois, car aler m'an vuel." (968-73)

Again, Perceval displays a total disregard for the condition of those about him: face to face with sorrow and humiliation, his uninterruptable obsession with becoming a knight can only urge the King to hurry up with the job.

It is at this point that the description of Perceval occurs which has been cited as evidence of essential nobility which cannot but shine through his foolish naiveté: [65]

> Cler et riant furent li oel
> An la teste au vaslet sauvage.
> Nus qui le voit nel tient a sage;
> Mes trestuit cil qui le veoient,
> Por bel et por jant le tenoient. (974-8)

This is a striking description, of course, but it is difficult to find nobility in it. The only word which might suggest this quality is *jant*. Foerster's *Wörterbuch* gives three kinds of meanings. [66] The first refers to personal beauty, more or less the same meaning as *bel*. The second

---

[63] Kellermann, *Aufbaustil und Weltbild...*, p. 150.

[64] William A. Nitze, "The Character of Gauvain in the Romances of Chrétien de Troyes," *Modern Philology*, L (1953), 219-25; p. 222.

[65] Frappier, *Perceval*, p. 42.

[66] Wendelin Foerster, *Kristian von Troyes, Wörterbuch zu seinen sämtlichen Werken* (Halle: Niemeyer, 1914). The meanings given are: "schön, hübsch, zart, anmutig, artig, stattlich." The adjective *jantis* can mean "noble", but that, of course, is another word: it is the one Arthur later uses to describe Perceval (1. 1013). For *jant*, compare both Godefroy and Tobler-Lommatzsch (under *gent*), neither of whom gives "nobility". Von Wartburg (*Französisches Etymologisches Wörterbuch*) does record *gent=né d'une famille noble*, but provides only two references against many for the more usual meanings.

group refers to social qualities: tender, charming, gracious, polite.
These are, to say the least, inappropriate to the character we know, and
can be assigned to *jant* here only ironically. The third meaning refers
to a personal quality, but one which is defined in terms of its effect
on others: splendid, imposing. This seems to me the likeliest meaning
of *jant* in this context: it is neither merely repetitious of *bel*, nor contradictory to everything we know of Perceval's character and actions.
Furthermore, this meaning fits into the form of the description, which is
based on the contrast between the inner, mental being of the youth and
his external, physical appearance. The latter is emphasized in the
first two lines. With a slight change, the first line could have been
grammatically independent of the second: *Cler et riant furent si oel*;
the antecedent is obvious since Perceval has just spoken. The addition
of the second line brings a further stress on the physical (*An la teste...*),
another on his inconsiderate wildness (*... au vaslet sauvage*), and above
all, a striking oxymoronic rhyme: *sauvage/sage*. No one finds him
sage, but all are struck by his appearance: there is no reason why the
vaslez sauvage should not seem imposing, especially since he is on
horseback and everyone else is seated at table.

Perceval also remained mounted when he entered the tent in the
preceding episode. In fact, he has been off his horse only once since
leaving home (as far as we know), and that was to embrace the tent-
maiden and eat her food. The reason for this persistence is revealed
as Arthur invites him to dismount, assuring him that the horse will
be well looked after. Perceval answers:

> "Ja n'estoient pas desçandu
> Cil que j'ancontrai an la lande,
> Et vos volez que je desçande?
> Ja, par mon chief, n'i desçandrai;
> Mes feites tost, si m'an irai." (986-90)

That King Arthur should be a better guide to knightly deportment than
the newly dubbed man on horseback he saw the previous day does
not occur to Perceval—and we have seen he has some justification for
this. Nevertheless, what is involved is a matter of social propriety, for
which Arthur would normally be accepted as adequate authority. It is
not clear whether Perceval intends to remain mounted more or less
permanently, or if it is his judgment that he cannot be knighted otherwise. In spite of the repeated discourtesy of the last line, the King
is still willing to accede to Perceval's demand. But being knighted is
not enough in itself:

> "Foi que je doi le Criator,"
> Fet li vaslez, "biaus sire rois,
> Ne serai chevaliers des mois
> Se chevaliers vermauz ne sui.
> Donez moi les armes celui
> Que j'ancontrai defors la porte,
> Qui vostre cope d'or an porte." (994-9)

At this point enters Keu the Seneschal, wounded and angry at what he hears, with another example of Chrétien's new mode of irony:

> "Amis, vos avez droit:
> Alez li tolir or androit
> Les armes, car eles sont voz.
> Ne feïstes mie que soz
> Quant voz por ce venistes ci." (1003-7)

There are no stylistic variations from the norm in the speech to indicate its ironic intent: no figurative usage, a thoroughly normal vocabulary and sentence structure. [67] We find it ironic only if we agree with Keu on judging Perceval's desire absurd; if we do agree with Keu at this point, we will be confirmed by Arthur's long, reproachful lecture to him. [68]

Arthur's speech, however, is largely beside the point. His first words are not unlike those of Guenièvre in a similar situation, though somewhat milder: [69]

> "Keu", fet li rois, "por Deu merci!
> Trop dites volantiers enui,
> Si ne vos chaut onques a cui.
> A prodomes est ce trop lez vices. (1008-11)

He continues with a plain, straightforward analysis of Perceval's character and a guess at his biography, and incidentally reveals the basis of the Perceval section:

> "Por ce, se li vaslez est nices,
> S'est il, espoir, mout jantis hon;
> Et se ce li vient d'aprison
> Qu'il a esté a vilain mestre,
> Ancor puet preuz et sages estre." (1012-6) [70]

---

[67] Keu's words will have the effect of making Perceval believe he has been granted the red amor by Arthur (ll. 1083-5): he has taken the seneschal's words literally. Emmel has drawn attention to Keu's role as an incentive to knightly achievement (*Formprobleme...*, p. 24 f.), and has noted that the function is performed by his sarcasm. This is also true, of course, of Keu's speech to Yvain, which is an excellent example of Chrétien's older form of irony: it is it is full of the forms of *significatio* and *paroemia* (*Yvain*, 590-611). In *Perceval*, this style is used only by Keu in his sarcastic speeches against Gauvain: see below, pp. 194 ff.

[68] This scene is "explicated" later in the romance, when Arthur describes it to Gauvain. He summarizes Keu's words, and adds:

> "Cil* qui ne sot le gap antandre   *Perceval
> Cuida que il* voir li deïst   *Keu
> S'ala aprés et si l'ocist*..."   *The Red Knight
>
> (4120-2)

[69] See Guenièvre's speech to Keu, *Yvain*, 86 ff.

[70] Since Arthur recognizes that Perceval is *nice*, *jantis* refers to his birth, not a moral quality, and the last line must be taken to refer to the future.

Immediately after this, however, Arthur divagates. The remainder and longest part of his speech betrays the promise of the beginning as he lectures Keu on the evils of making promises one cannot fulfill, and lectures at length. [71]   In so doing, he is addressing himself to Keu's grant of the armor. This grant was ironic, and Arthur is addressing himself to the literal meaning of the words, not their real intent. Strangely enough, Arthur reacts to Keu's words in the same way as Perceval, who will tell the Red Knight his armor has been granted to the youth by the King. [72] Yet, as his first remarks to Keu prove, Arthur was perfectly aware of the latter's intent. Perhaps this is an example of Arthur's senility. Or it may be the mark of too great courtesy, as when we accept a *faux-pas* as a perfectly normal statement in order to save the speaker from embarrassment.

In any case, Arthur's divagation loses him Perceval. Chrétien informs us of this in a parenthetical phrase:

> Einsi li rois a Keu parloit
> Et li vaslez, qui s'an aloit... (1033 f.) [73]

He has taken Keu's words literally, and is going out to claim "his" armor. On the way, however, he sees a young girl,

> Bele et jante, si la salue,
> Et ele lui et si li rist
> Et an riant itant li dist:
> "Vaslez, se tu viz par aage,
> Je pans et croi an mon corage
> Qu'an trestot le monde n'avra,

---

[71]
> "Vilenie est d'autrui gaber
> Et de prometre sanz doner;
> Prodon ne se doit antremetre
> De rien nule a autrui prometre
> Que doner ne li puisse ou vuelle,
> Que le maugré celui n'acuelle
> Qui sanz prometre est ses amis
> Et, des que il li a promis,
> Si bee a la promesse avoir.
> Et par ce si poëz savoir
> Qu'assez vandroit il miauz veer
> A home que feire beer;
> Et qui le voir dire an voldroit,
> Lui meïsmes gabe et deçoit
> Qui fet promesse et ne la sout,
> Car le cuer son ami se tout." (1017-32)

Hilka quite properly notes that "dieser moralisierende Exkurs ... nicht recht in den Zusammenhang passt," but does so on the basis that Keu did not actually promise the armor! He continues by explaining the lecture as Chrétien's desire to teach a moral lesson, and to display his clerical learning by adapting a passage from the *Disciplina clericalis*, which he quotes (note to l. 1018). The irrelevance is not the author's but the character's.

[72] *Supra,* p. 141, n. 67.

[73] Hilka prints a period after *parloit,* for which I can see no necessity.

> N'il n'iert, ne l'an ne l'i savra
> Nul meillor chevalier de toi:
> Einsi le pans et cuit et croi." (1036-44)

Perhaps Chrétien intended to show this prophecy fulfilled in the parts of the *Perceval* he did not write. At the moment, however, it is paradoxical. So far, Perceval has shown himself to be a thoroughgoing fool: our awareness of this has been interrupted only by others' foolishness. He has behaved abominably with his mother, the tent damsel, and the King. Still unknighted, and untested, he has shown little promise so far except in the direction of unintentional comedy. This paradoxical intent is also evident in the verbal structure of the passage, as well as by the girl's laughter: apparently, she had not seen anything so funny in over six years. [74] Her speech uses several suggestive techniques. She begins with a qualifying clause: *se tu viz par aage*. If we recall that this youth has no weapon but for a single javelin, no armor, no training in knighthood, and that he intends to obtain the armor of a full-fledged knight who has challenged King Arthur, this qualification may give us pause. [75] If the young girl's thought seems extravagant, its expression certainly is. Reduced to its essential message, it reads: *Je pans qu'an trestot le monde n'avra meillor chevalier de toi*—eleven words, as against the thirty-one she actually uses. [76] We have seen occasions where the introductory phrase of indirect discourse received three repetitions; [77] here, it receives five. An equally inconspicuous word, the copulative verb, is similarly expanded: *n'avra, N'il n'iert, ne l'an ne li savra*.

Such expansion is stylistically suspicious, but it can be as characteristic of prophecy as of irony. Since Keu becomes incensed at her words, he believes she means them literally. The irony is addressed by the author to the audience through the unknowing character. [78] But that the statement is ironic seems inevitable given the context of Perceval's past actions. That she is supported only by the court fool is another indication; and even Arthur, who has greeted Perceval sympathetically, will find it difficult to believe Yonet's report that the Welsh lad won back his cup from the Red Knight. [79]

---

[74] That she was under a *geis* in Chrétien's source is perfectly possible; that she is under a *geis* in *Perceval* is to be demonstrated.

[75] He will win, of course, but that is still in the future. For the time being, we can enjoy the freedom of laughing in error.

[76] Counting contractions as single words, by charity.

[77] *Supra*, p. 59.

[78] Cf. *supra*, p. 51.

[79] Ll. 1207 ff.; *infra*, p. 146. Gustave Cohen considers the verbal repetitions in this passage an example of "le défaut de la cheville-synonyme." (*Un grand romancier d'amour et d'aventure au XIIe siècle, Chrétien de Troyes et son œuvre*, 2nd ed. [Paris: Rodstein, 1948], p. 490).

The Red Knight

The comedy of this episode develops some earlier themes, but in a broader, more obviously comic vein. Arthur's challenger, expecting *Chevalerie et avanture* (1075), gets instead the uncouth young Welshman he had used as bearer of his challenge. [80] Their battle is first on the verbal level, and its basic principle recalls the encounter with the chief knight of the first episode: it is a variation of Bergson's *interférence des séries*. [81] When Perceval had approached within earshot of the Red Knight,

> Si li cria: "Metez les jus
> Les armes, ne les portez plus;
> Que li rois Artus le vos mande."
> Et li chevaliers li demande:
> "Vaslez, ose nus ça venir
> Por le droit le roi maintenir?
> Se nus i vient, nel celer pas."
> "Comant, deable, est ce or gas,
> Danz chevaliers, que vos me feites
> Qu'ancor n'avez *mes* armes treites?
> Ostez les tost, jel vos comant!"
> "Vaslez", fet il, "je te demant
> Se nus vient ça de par le roi
> Qui conbatre se vuelle a moi."
> "Danz chevaliers, car ostez tost
> Les armes, que je nes vos ost,
> Que plus ne les vos soferroie.
> Bien sachoiz que je vos ferroie,
> Se plus parler m'an feisiiez." (1083-1101)

The source of Perceval's belief that Arthur has granted him the armor has already been noted. That Perceval disregards Arthur's disassociation from Keu's "grant" in his long reproach to the latter, and that Perceval seems to identify Keu with Arthur, suggest the intensity of his desire. This intensity remains totally unacknowledged, for the Red Knight has his own *idée fixe*: the *vaslez* is nothing but an instrument for him, a messenger of no importance in himself. Perceval's

---

[80] The Red Knight was "expecting a challenger from the court and not the youth..." William A. Nitze, *Perceval and the Holy Grail: An Essay on the Romance of Chrétien de Troyes*, in *University of California Publications in Modern Philology*, Vol. XXVIII (Berkeley and Los Angeles: University of California Press, 1949), p. 293.

[81] In the Five Knights episode, one of the series continually gave way before the other; here, both are repeatedly affirmed in total disregard of each other. Noting the variety of forms in which this technique occurs, Bergson gives a general definition: "Une situation est toujours comique quand elle appartient en même temps à deux séries d'événements absolument indépendantes, et qu'elle peut s'interpréter à la fois dans deux sens tout différents." (*Le rire*, p. 73 f.) Here, we really have two situations, completely independent of each other, and interfering with each other: there is not even a common element which can be interpreted in different ways, since the Red Knight does not even recognize Perceval's claim to the armor.

second speech increases the intensity: the armor has become *mes armes,* and it is not Arthur any more who commands, but Perceval himself (*jel vos comant*). It also includes the comic opposition of the first line's indignation ("What the devil, are you kidding?) to the merely formal politeness of *Danz chevaliers,* an appellation itself ironic. [82] The knight's second speech is a mock-patient reaffirmation of his own insistent concern, again denying the existence of Perceval in his own right: that the youth might be dangerous never occurs to him. Perceval's indignation rises: in spite of the superficial (but ironic) politeness with which he starts, his threat to strike the knight is spoken from the assumed position of a superior (*plus ne les vos soferroie*) who may be annoyed beyond endurance (*Se plus parler m'an feisiiez*). [83]

The verbal comedy ends as the angered knight swings his lance with both hands across Perceval's shoulders, knocking him down to the neck of the horse. The youth responds in the only way he knows, with the only means available to him: he throws his javelin through the knight's eye and into his brains. In this manner was Arthur's land defended and Guenièvre's humiliation repaid: in so far as Arthur's court represents the locus and epitome of courtly knighthood, it is ironically defended by the antithesis of its own values.

Perceval now has what he wanted, the knight's bright armor. Or almost: the lance and shield give him no trouble, but he cannot figure out the straps by with the helmet is tied to the dead man's head, nor can he pull the sword from its scabbard. As for the scabbard itself, he can only start pulling at it repeatedly. At this point, Yonet, the squire from Arthur's court who has followed Perceval, bursts out laughing: "What are you doing?"—"I don't know: I thought your king gave me these arms, but I'll have carved this dead man in slices before I can bear any of the arms, for they stick so to the body that the inside and the outside are all one, so it seems to me, they stick together so." [84] The comedy here is merely a mechanical one: the youth's ignorance of the world goes so far that he cannot cope with the buckles and straps of helmet and scabbard. To this is added the psychological touch as he seems to blame Arthur for his frustration. The same naiveté is the

---

[88] *Supra,* p. 123, n. 29.

[83] Another use of comic inversion of roles: cf. *supra,* p. 138.

[84]　　　 "Ice que est", fet il, "amis?
　　　　　Que feites vos?"—"Je ne sai quoi:
　　　　　Je cuidoie de vostre roi
　　　　　Qu'il m'eüst cez armes donees,
　　　　　Mes einz avrai par charbonees
　　　　　Trestot esbraoné le mort
　　　　　Que nule des armes an port;
　　　　　Qu'eles se tienent si au cors
　　　　　Que ce dedanz et ce defors
　　　　　Est trestot un, si con moi sanble,
　　　　　Qu'eles se tienent si ansanble." (1132-42)
One of Perceval's sympathetic qualities is that he is as direct in expressing his own frustration as in causing others'.

basis of Perceval's refusal to exchange the *bons dras* his mother made for the soft, thin shirt of the knight, though this comes closer to the purely social values of dress and fashion he does not know. Chrétien comments on this, repeating what has by now becomes a leit-motif:

> Mout griés chose est de fol aprandre... (1173) [85]

This is the last statement of the thought in the romance, but the idea will be embodied in action later.

Yonet helps Perceval on with the armor, and is charged with delivering a message to the young girl whom Keu slapped for her prophecy: he will avenge her before he dies. [86] Yonet agrees to bear the message, and it is him we follow back to the court for a recapitulation of Perceval's "victory" as seen by a witness. It is turned to comedy. Yonet enters with the cup, saying it is being sent back by the "knight" who was here. [87] Arthur has no idea who is meant. When Yonet explains it was the *vaslez* who just left, Arthur cannot believe his ears:

> "Diz tu donc del vaslet galois
> Qui me demanda" fet li rois,
> "Les armes de sinople taintes
> Au chevalier qui hontes maintes
> M'a feites selon son pooir?" (1219-23)

Assured that it was indeed the same, Arthur asks whether the knight liked Perceval so much as to give him the cup! [88] Yonet's retelling of the brief combat is the cue for further reproaches to Keu for having caused Arthur the loss of a knight who has served him so well—the King is apparently not concerned with the fact that Perceval's manner of fighting is hardly knightly. Nevertheless, the scene ends with his worried prediction that the untrained youth will soon be killed or wounded by some *vassal,*

> "Tant est nices et bestïaus
> Tost avra fez ses anvïaus." (1299 f.)

---

[85] Cf. *supra*, pp. 133 f., 136, 137, 139.

[86] Perceval embellishes this vow with wordplay of a popular flavor:
"Li* *cuit* je si bien metre *cuire*   *Keu
Que por vangiee se tandra." (1202 f.)

[87]   "Sire, or feites joie;
Que vostre cope vos ranvoie
Vostre chevaliers qui ci fu."
"De quel chevalier me diz tu?"
Fet li rois, qui an sa grant ire
Estoit ancore. "Enon Deu, sire,"
Fet Yonez, "del vaslet di
Qui or androit parti de ci." (1211-8)

[88] "E ma cope comant ot il?
Aimme le tant ou prise cil
Qu'il li et de son gré randue?" (1225-7)

This closes the first series of Perceval's adventures, endured under the sole aegis of his mother's advice and rules. Since leaving home, he has had his first experience with a courtly lady, with Arthur's court, and "knightly" combat. In one way, he has obtained what he wanted: a kiss, food, red armor. But from the viewpoint of his overriding desire, that of becoming a knight, each of these "successes" is a failure. He has obtained none of the rewards a knight might have from an encounter with a courtly lady, the *donoi* which is the equivalent of flirtation, [89] or the ultimate satisfaction of the *soreplus*. The same is true of the second adventure: even though he has been of service to Arthur and now wears the red armor, he has not been knighted. He is quite sure that this armor makes him a knight; he will soon be disabused. [90] He will also have an opportunity to try himself in the same two situations, with a courtly lady, with battle against knights. His successes will again be mixed.

Gornemant de Goort

Perceval's basic training in the knightly part of chivalry is preceded by a precise description of Gornemant's castle—[91] a precision which

---

[89] Frappier, *Le roman breton: Les origines...*, p. 99.

[90] Frappier, *Perceval*, p. 44. It is not quite exact to state that "le Simple réussit, à cause de son inconscience même, là où les habiles étaient impuissants." (Jean Fourquet, "Le rapport entre l'œuvre et la source chez Chrétien de Troyes et le problème des sources bretonnes," *Romance Philology*, IX (1955), 298-312; p. 308). Perceval is able to fight the Red Knight because all of Arthur's other heroes are either away from the court (one point of the *charbonnier's* speech; *supra*, p. 136) or wounded like Keu. Their absence and physical incapacity have been arranged by the author precisely in order to allow Perceval his first opportunity. This is probably the reason for Keu's anger: he is always eager for battle, even when outmatched (*Yvain, Lancelot*), but he cannot claim this battle because of his wound. Instead, he must see the honor fall to an uncouth provincial youth.

It is also difficult to see how Perceval's innocence or unawareness help him succeed. Do training in knighthood and awareness of danger later impede him?—Chrétien does not have either a romantic or a mystical view of innocence. His entire effort in the Perceval section is to depict its hazards and risibility.

[91]
      Anmi le chastel an estant
      Ot une tor et fort et grant;
      Une barbacane mout fort
      Avoit tornee vers le gort,
      Qui a la mer se conbatoit,
      Et la mers au pié li batoit.
      A quatre parties del mur,
      Don li quarrel estoit dur,
      Avoit quatre basses torneles,
      Qui mout estoient forz et beles.
      Li chastiaus fu mout bien seanz
      Et bien aesiez par dedanz;
      Devant le chastelet reont
      Ot sor l'eve drecié un pont
      De pierre et d'arainne et de chauz;
      Li ponz estoit et forz et hauz,

will be used for comic effect later. [92]   Our attention is called to it by
a suggestive introduction.   It is situated on the slope of a cliff across
the river which Perceval has been following and which flows into
a bay:

> Si con l'eve aloit au regort,
> Torna li vaslez a senestre
> Et vit les torz des chastel nestre;
> Qu'avis li fu qu'eles neissoient
> Et que fors del chastel issoient. (1324-8)

The description is from the rider's point of view: as he follows the
curving path, the changing perspectives from which he sees the castle
impart the illusion of movement so that the towers seem to be growing
out of the mass of the structure.

The meeting with Gornemant starts on a familiar note.   Perceval
greets the older man and explains:

> "Sir, ce m'anseigna ma mere." (1363)

Gornemant replies courteously, but "places" the youth immediately:

> "Deus beneïe toi, biaus frere!"
> Fet li prodon, qui nice sot
> Au parler le conut et sot... (1364-6)

Learning that the youth has just come from Arthur's court, he inquires
what he did there.   Gornemant betrays his surprise at hearing Perceval
(still in Welsh clothes under his armor) claim to have been knighted
by the King, but quickly catches himself:

> "Chevalier? Se Deus bien me doint,
> Ne cuidoie qu'ore an cest point
> D'itel chose ii sovenist:
> D'el cuidoie qu'il li tenist
> Au roi que de chevalier feire." (1371-5)

The polite interrogation continues.   Who gave you these arms?—The
King—*Dona*? *Comant*? (1379).   And the youth tells the older man just
how the King "gave" him the arms. [93]   Throughout the exchange,
Gornemant courteously hides his amazement at the strange youth and

---

> Abatailliez trestot antor;
> Qu'anmi le pont ot une tor
> Et devant un pont torneïz,
> Qui estoit fez et establiz
> A ce que sa droiture aporte:
> Le jor ert ponz, et la nuit porte. (1328-50)

The reason for the long and precise description, as well as the striking introduction, is to fix it in the reader's mind for later (comic) use.

[92] *Infra,* p. 164.

[93] Perceval here is in the same position as Calogrenant telling of his ill-
fated adventure in court.   The major difference is that Calogrenant is perfectly
aware how foolish he looks, whereas Perceval has no inkling of this.   In this
case, the reader shares a viewpoint with Gornemant which excludes Perceval.

the extraordinary story which reveals his ignorance and misunderstanding of what has happened to him. As courteously, he restrains what must be amusement while Perceval explains what he can do with his war-horse: run uphill and down just as he did with the hunter at his mother's. As for the armor, he can put it on and take if off, just as Yonet showed him. What's more, he bears it so lightly that he hardly notices the armor! [94]—The effect of the conversation is remarkable. Gornemant is all courteous restraint, Perceval's answers are as straight-forward as they are naïve, and the contrast between the youth's self-assurance in his knighthood and the lack of knighthood it betrays to Gornemant's unexpressed standards is one of the most subtle examples of Chrétien's juxtaposition of two disparate worlds of awareness.

The same intellectual incongruity, in which the reader shares Gornemant's awareness as against Perceval's simplicity, continues when the latter is asked what need has brought him: his answer fits into the other main source of comic effect in the romance, that of automatism:

> "Sire, ma mere m'anseigna
> Que vers les prodomes alasse
> Et que a aus me conseillasse,
> Si creüsse ce qu'il diroient;
> Que preu i ont cil qui les croient. " (1402-6)

There are lessons which Perceval retains all too well and thoroughly. Gornemant, who has heard him refer to his mother four times by now, answers with private irony:

> "Biaus frere,
> Beneoite soit vostre mere,
> Que ele vos conseilla bien!" (1407-9)

Again, there are no stylistic effects; only the context provides the basis for the ironic intent. Nevertheless, Gornemant shows himself a shrewd instructor: rather than express his irritation at the constant reference to his pupil's former teacher, he associates himself with her. He asks and receives a boon from Perceval, that he believe *Le consoil vostre mere et moi* (1417).

---

[94]   Et li prodon li redemande
    Qu'il set feire de son cheval.
    "Jel cor bien amont et aval
    Tot autresi con je coroie
    Le chaceor quant je l'avoie
    An la meison ma mere pris."
    "Et de voz armes, biaus amis,
    Me redites: qu'an savez feire?"
    "Jes sai bien vestir et retreire
    Si con li vaslez m'an arma,
    Qui devant moi an desarma
    Celui que je avoie mort;
    Et si legieremant les port
    Que eles ne me grievent rien." (1384-97)

This combination of shrewdness and consideration continues during the actual instruction. Gornemant both encourages and spurs the student on to further effort when the latter asks if he is doing well:

> "Amis, si le cuer i avez",
> Fet li prodon, "mout an savroiz,
> Ja mar cusançon an avroiz." (1502-4)

For Gornemant, three things are required to learn anything: effort, desire, and practice. [95] He absolves Perceval from blame for not knowing what he has never learned, [96] and Chrétien explains his progress as a result of his inborn nature. [97] In spite of this, however, Perceval, though talented for knighthood, lacks the necessary practice. Gornemant reflects that he would have been well taught *if* he had spent his whole life at it. [98] The conditional is important: according to Gornemant, Perceval "has promise," but he needs practice. Quite a bit of practice, in fact, since the courteous *prodon* will offer the trainee his hospitality for a month or even a year to teach him what he needs to know (1570-8).

One day's *us* does not the flower of chivalry make, as the continuation of Perceval's lesson reveals. After Gornemant's laudatory reflections, he asks what Perceval would do if a knight struck him?—I'd strike him back.—And if your lance shattered?

> "Aprés ce n'i avroit il plus,
> Mes qu'as poinz li corroie sus." (1515 f.)

Even now, Perceval can still reduce a knightly encounter to a barnyard brawl. Even now, however, Gornemant is still patient enough to explain the next step: You would use the sword. Putting his hand to the weapon,

> "Amis", fet il, "an ceste guise
> Vos desfandroiz, s'an vos assaut."
> "De ce", fet il, "se Deus me saut,
> Ne set nus tant come je faz,
> Qu'as borriaus et as talevaz
> Chiés ma mere an apris assez
> Tant que sovant an fui lassez." (1528-34)

---

[95] « Il covient a toz les mestiers
Et painne et cuer et us avoir. » (1466 f.)

[96] « Et quant vos onques nel feïstes
Ne autrui feire nel veïstes,
Se vos feire ne le savez,
Honte ne blasme n'i avez. » (1469-72)

[97] Car il li venoit de nature,
Et quant nature li aprant
Et li cuers del tot i antant,
Ne li puet estre riens grevainne
La ou nature et cuers se painne. (1480-4)

[98] ... se il fust tot son aage
D'armes penez et antremis,
S'an fust il assez bien apris. (1488-90)

Again, knighthood is incongruously reduced in a misidentification which is both functional and social. A *talevaz* is a wooden shield for protection against arrows, [99] used primarily by foot-soldiers, not knights.[100] *Borel* is generally defined as a kind of pillow; [101] in this context, it may refer to a stuffed bag used in arms practice. [102] Thus, the climactic encounter in knightly combat is associated with the games and practice the *vaslet sauvage* learned from the serving-men of his mother's house in the *Gaste Forez,* and the whole is concluded with a pitiable expression of the weariness such efforts brought to the child.

There is a limit to the patience of the most patient teacher. This latest recurrence of automatism ends the day's lesson as far as Gornemant is concerned:

> "Donc alons hui mes a l'ostel.." (1535)

But Gornemant cannot escape so easily. As the older knight and his young pupil head toward the castle side by side, he is pursued further:

> *"Sire, ma mere m'anseigna*
> Qu'avuec home n'alasse ja
> Ne conpeignie o lui n'eüsse
> Granmant que son non ne seüsse;
> *Et s'ele m'anseigna savoir,*
> Je vuel le vostre non savoir." (1541-6) [103]

"Gornemanz de Goort ai non" (1548), Perceval is told, and so the two continue to the castle. Gornemant does not ask his guest's name here. When they first met, after Gornemant's privately ironic blessing of Perceval's mother, he had asked:

> "Mes volez vos plus dire rien?"
> "Oïl."—"Et quoi?"—"Tant et non mes
> Que vos me herbergiez hui mes." (1410-2)

The request was granted of course, but was this what Gornemant had expected? The small exchange "Yes."—"What?", may indicate a small turn of suspense to which Perceval's answer is a surprising outcome. Was it not an occasion for Perceval, who had already referred to his mother several times, to introduce himself? Was Chrétien here teasing his audience with one of the questions on their minds, the name of the hero? To return to the present scene, isn't the complement of

---

[99] Von Wartburg, *FEW.*

[100] See also the examples in Godefroy, *Dictionnaire de l'ancienne langue française....*

[101] Tobler-Lommatzsch (*AW*), under *borrel,* and Meyer-Lübke (*Romanisches etymologisches Wörterbuch*), under *bourrel.*

[102] I owe this suggestion to Professor Lawton P.G. Peckham.

[103] If the last two lines quoted are read as a conditional construction, this is an important indication of Perceval's willing submission to Gornemant's judgment.

asking someone's name the statement of one's own? [104]   As it is, Perceval will have been educated and knighted by a man who doesn't even know his name.

After dinner, when Gornemant invites the youth to remain with him for a month or a year (1570-8), Perceval declines in the first sign of charity he has shown: [105] he wishes to return to his mother whom he saw faint as he left,

"Si ne sai s'ele est vive ou morte." (1586)

Instead, Perceval will leave the following morning. At that time, Gornemant knights the *vaslet* and also provides him with further advice: this will again be misinterpreted, simplified, and misapplied, as was the mother's advice. Both his mother and his knightly instructor offer Perceval no more than guides for practical behavior, perfectly valid in themselves, but which assume a context of social awareness to give them relevance which Perceval lacks totally. It is this lack which results in the comic processes characteristic of the *vaslet sauvage*. When he is knighted the following morning, according to the forms of an ancient ceremony, [106] he has received basic instruction in the manipulation of the tools of his *mestier,* but he is clearly not yet a knight even in the limited sense of the word represented by Gornemant. [107] When the latter wishes to clothe him in the delicate silks appropriate to a knight, Perceval at first refuses to doff the Welsh garments he still wears. It is only by invoking his earlier promise to follow his

---

[104] The suggestion must be made hesitantly. The contrast would be to what people did in normal social life, not to literary forms. Gauvain's custom is to give his name when asked, but not before. Given his highly self-conscious courtliness, this may be accounted for by a social modesty: to announce his identity of his own volition would be the equivalent of saying "I am Gauvain, and you know that means Gauvain the Great." If this interpretation is accepted, it implies that the norm was to introduce oneself without extraordinary reticence or fuss, at least for those whose reputation as heroes was not as widespread as Gauvain's.

[105] Frappier, *Perceval,* p. 45; he adds that this charity is "en accord avec les sentiments naturels." (*loc. cit.*). It is not a mystical or even specifically religious feeling, but concern for another human being—the first time Perceval has shown such concern.

[106] *La costume soloit teus estre...* (1626) implies a superannuated form.

[107] Marc Bloch found Gornemant's actual instruction to be disappointingly meager after his proud declaration that he has given Perceval

La plus haute ordre avuec l'espee
Que Deus et feite et comandee:
C'est l'ordre de chevalerie,
Qui doit estre sanz vilenie... (1635-8)

(*La Société féodale,* 2 vols. [Paris: Michel, 1949], Vol. II: *Les classes et le gouvernement des hommes,* p. 56). Though Bloch was concerned, at this point, with the relationship between religion and knighthood, it is obvious that the passage does not represent a philosophical justification of knighthood but one knight's normal human pride in his calling and profession. Cf. Sidney Painter, *French Chivalry, Chivalric Ideas and Practices in Mediaeval France* (Baltimore: Johns Hopkins, 1940), who considers the *Perceval* a compromise between Chrétien's supposed desire "to please his aged and pious patron" and the author's "courtly past and his grasp of human realities..." (p. 168).

teacher's advice that Gornemant effects even this superficial change. And when Gornemant advises the youth to go to church, the response is another repetition of the automatism "what my mother told me" (1672 ff.). Gornemant's teaching has not worked an essential change in Perceval: some new practical guides to behavior have been imparted under a new authority, no more. [108]

Gornemant's rules are of two sorts: three that govern the behavior of any knight, two that are addressed more to Perceval's personal behavior. The first group consists of showing mercy to a defeated opponent (1640-7), helping men and women who find themselves without protection (1656-62), and going to church (1667-70). Only the first, the rule of mercy, represents a new element here. The last two repeat advice Perceval had already received from his mother. [109] When Perceval remarks on this, Gornemant is irritated and provides a further, personal, guide:

> "Or nel dites ja mes, biaus frere",
> Fet li prodon, "que vostre mere
> Vos et apris ne anseigné.
> De ce mie ne vos blasme gié,
> Se vos l'avez dit jusque ci;
> Mes des or mes, vostre merci,
> Vos pri que vos an chastiiez.
> Et se vos plus le disiiez,
> A folie le tandroit l'an:
> Por ce vos pri gardez vos an!" (1675-84)

The last three lines show clearly that this is a matter of social propriety; people would consider it *folie* if a knight were to continue defining himself in terms of his mother's advice. Instead, Perceval may refer to Gornemant:

> "Li vavasors, ce poëz dire,
> Qui vostre esperon vos chauça,
> Le vos aprist et anseigna." (1686-8)

Gornemant does not even intend to cure Perceval of automatism, but merely to substitute the aegis under which it functions. The last rule, that of silence, is also advice on personal behavior seen from a view-

---

[108] According to Fowler (*Prowess and Charity*...), "the main purpose of the whole interlude is to give the hero his chivalric education, and ... to strip him of the surviving traces of his mother's influence..." (p. 17 f.); at the end of the episode, Perceval is "recreated in the image of his tutor" (p. 18 f.). Besides the evidence already cited, Perceval's encounters with Anguingeron and Clamadeu also show that there are important aspects of knighthood which Perceval has not learned from Gornemant (see below, pp. 163 ff.). On Fowler's contrast between Gornemant's religion and that of his mother, see *supra*, p. 129, n. 43.

Chrétien is an unusually subtle portrayer of character. It is inappropriate to approach this romance with antinomies which, however perceptive and useful in elucidating a given episode, become constrictive when applied to even the first part of the *Perceval*.

[109] *Supra*, p. 129 f. In the second rule, Gornemant has added men among those to be protected.

point of social propriety. Gornemant here does not invoke the danger that people would consider too much talking *folie*; instead, the specter of *vilenie* is raised:

> "Nus ne puet estre trop parliers
> Que sovant tel chose ne die
> Qu'an li atort a vilenie..." (1650-2)

Again, it is the thought of a possible social effect which is invoked to correct a fault. [110]

Gornemant's lessons are perfectly valid, but they represent goals restricted to the observance of ordinary social norms appropriate to the knightly class. They differ from the mother's instructions only in their affirmation of a more masculine attitude toward self-definition and in their emphasis on greater social awareness. The latter emphasis is particularly revealed by the element which the three *new* rules share. To show mercy for a defeated opponent, to cease referring continually to his mother, to cease speaking too much, these three rules represent restraints Perceval will have to impose on propensities which have been amply demonstrated in earlier action: the killing of the Red Knight, the references to "mother," the equally continual naive expression of things normally repressed by social mores, these have been etched in our memory by ample comedy. To restrain these, as Gornemant recommends, means to accept social limitations on the individual impulses which, in Perceval's case, are close to primitiveness. To some extent, Perceval has already begun to accept the necessity of such limitations in submitting to Gornemant's authority. The entire episode, cast in the form of teaching and learning, is the first step in the socialization of the *vaslet sauvage*. [111]

---

[110] Both Kellermann and Nitze consider this advice as pertaining to the knightly virtues, the former specifying it as an aspect of *prudentia* (*Aufbaustil und Weltbild...*, p. 178; Nitze, *Perceval and the Holy Grail...*, p. 294). In so far as this and Gornemant's other rules are seen as part of a general knightly ethos, they seem rather to emphasize how distant Perceval is, at this point, from adhering to that ethos.

[111] For similar comments, see Nitze, *op. cit.*, p. 301 f., where he notes that the plot is "a study in adolescence" (his comparison of Perceval to Hamlet and mention of the Œdipus complex, however, do not seem particularly relevant); Frappier, *Perceval*, p. 31 f.; and Antoinette Fierz-Monnier, *Initiation und Wandlung; Zur Geschichte des altfranzösischen Romans im zwölften Jahrhundert von Chrétien de Troyes zu Renaut de Beaujeu* (Zürich: Schwarzenbach, 1951), pp. 63-83. The last work is a thesis heavily indebted to Bezzola, the author's thesis director. As is true of Bezzola, Fierz-Monnier's methodology is sometimes dubious (on Bezzola, see Jean Misrahi's review of *Le sens de l'aventure...* in *Romance Philology*, IV [1950-1951], 348-61): she confuses humor at a character's expense with a humorous character (p. 69 f.); mixes up Guinganbresil and the King of Escavalon (pp. 70, 72, *etc.*); baldly states that "In Belrepeire ... begegnet Perceval erstmals der Frau," a meeting she characterizes as being on the level of a *natürliche Erotik* without commenting on the Tent episode (p. 66); and dismisses Gauvain's killing of a knight without challenge as offending "nur die soziale Konvention" (p. 68). Nevertheless her emphasis on Perceval's psychological development is close to mine, and I have found her comments helpful.

Nevertheless, it is only a first step, and one which can lead Perceval to errors as real, if not as egregious, as those of his past.

Blancheflor and Belrepeire

Perceval sets out from Gornemant de Goort's, and Chrétien suggests that we are heading further from the courtly region towards a more elemental one:

> Si se met es forez soutainnes,
> Que assez miauz qu'as terres plainnes
> Es forez se reconoissoit... (1703-5)

This suggestion is reinforced by the realistic description of the devastation wreaked on the town of Belrepeire by war. Though the castle is *fort et bien seant* (1707)

> ... fors des murs n'avoit neant
> Fors mer et eve et terre gaste. (1708 f.)

The bridge to the fortified town is so weak it can hardly support horse and rider; when the visitor's knocking and calling at the locked outer door are finally answered, it is not by a soldier or guard, but *Une pucele meigre et pale* (1724), who warns him he will not be grateful for the requested hospitality; the men at arms who accompany him into the town bear great axes, but show marked effects of hunger and night-long vigils. Within the castle walls, the marks of devastation are equally evident: the streets are desolate, the houses caved in, and only *nonains esbaies* and *moines esgarez* (1758 f.) remain in the religious establishments; these are bare of decoration or tapestries, and their roofs have fallen in; the mills do not grind, nor the ovens bake, and nothing is sold anywhere... (1710-70). The description is extensive and emphatic: the town is the opposite of what it should be, and in need of a knight to carry out Gornemant's advice to help the unprotected.

The descriptive inversion prefigures another inversion, this one comic, in Perceval's behavior. In spite of the devastation, he is greeted hospitably by a beautiful and richly dressed young lady accompanied by two *prodomes*. The trio lead their guest to a large, elegant room, where Perceval is seated next to his hostess on a samite-covered bed. Groups of knights enter after them,

> ... et mot ne distrent,
> Et virent celui qui se sist
> Delez lor dame, et mot ne dist... (1854-6)

for he remembered Gornemant's *chasti*. The knight advised discretion in speech, Perceval remains absolutely silent. And so the handsome young pair sits wordless before the company's amazed speculations:

> "Deus!" fet chascuns, "mout me mervoil
> Se cist chevaliers est muiaus.
> Granz diaus seroit; qu'onques si biaus
> Chevaliers ne fu nez de fame:

> Mout avient bien delez ma dame,
> Et ma dame aussi delez lui,
> S'il ne fussent muël andui... (1862-8)

the change in outer garment has left the youth inside unchanged. The psychological process by which Perceval has misinterpreted Gornemant's advice is reductive, as were his misidentification of the knightly weapons in the first episode and that of the tent in the second; it is an oversimplification, the same process by which he turned his mother's permission to obtain a kiss and a ring into an order to take them.

Though the psychological process is the same, the effect on the reader is different. One reason is the admiration of the attendant knights at Belrepeire, and the simple fact that Perceval, now dressed in proper knightly clothing, is seated as an honored guest, next to a beautiful young lady. More important, however, is the change in the expression of the same principle. In earlier episodes, Perceval's simplicity expressed itself in comically absurd action; here, it expresses itself in the absence of action. The same psychological principle—an oversimplifying reduction—is displayed in opposite ways: the chattering assault on the Tent Maiden, the silent disregard of Blancheflor. Perceval has not changed internally: he has learned restraint. It also can be dangerous.

But the evening scene is merely the introduction to the major irony of the episode. Though he may not speak to his hostess for a while, he will spend the night in bed with her. It is not the first time, of course, that he has lain close to a damsel. This is his first adventure since leaving Gornemant; so also, in his first adventure after leaving his mother's home, he encountered the Tent Maiden. One of the techniques Chrétien used on that occasion was the ambiguity of physical position, suggesting that a more drastic demand was to be made on the damsel than a mere kiss. He uses the same technique in describing the "relations" of Perceval and Blancheflor.

The young knight is bedded luxuriously, with beautiful linen, expensive coverings, and a pillow for his head. He had all the ease and delight possible in bed,

> Fors que solemant le deduit
> De pucele, se lui pleüst,
> Ou de dame, se lui leüst... (1938-40)

The parenthetical subjunctive clauses—"if it had pleased him, if it had been allowed him"—are indirect indication that he is innocent, at least of sexual pleasure. This is stated baldly in the following lines:

> Mes il n'an savoit nule rien,
> N'il n'i pansoit ne po ne bien,
> Si s'andormi auques par tans,
> Qu'il n'estoit de rien an espans. (1941-4)

Blancheflor, however, cannot sleep for the conflict that rages in her:

> Mout se trestorne et mout tressaut,
> Mout se degiete et se demainne. (1950 f.)

The situation, and even the vocabulary of the last quotation, are reminiscent of a much earlier situation. Alexander and Soredamors were also near each other and unable to sleep, and yet prevented from communicating: she out of modesty, he, not unlike Perceval, out of a lack of social graces. The differences. however, are greater. The earlier couple loved each other, even without any declaration; there has been no hint of such emotion in this case. Perceval, as far as the reader can tell, has no inkling of that emotion. As for Blancheflor, it is not love that brings her to her guest's room in the middle of the night, but the demands of an immediate political and military reality: the devastating siege, the approaching defeat and the surrenders it would entail, to Anguingeron militarily, to Clamadeu physically. [112] And so Blancheflor

> ... s'est an avanture mise
> Come hardie et corageuse... (1954 f.) [113]

The entire scene is bathed in delicate but unmistakable erotic suggestiveness. Blancheflor is wearing nothing but a short mantle of scarlet silk over her chemise, but we are assured that *ce n'est mie por oiseuse* (1956). However, this raises the question just what "foolishness" she might commit? Trembling and weeping, she kneels at Perceval's bedside, bent over the sleeping man. She is, after all, only a modest young maiden:

> N'a hardemant que plus an face. (1970)

Plus? Just how much more was she thinking of? But she only weeps, until he is awakened by her tears on his face to see the girl kneeling by him. Now we learn that she was holding him *Par le col anbracié estroit* (1976):

> Et tant de corteisie fist
> Que antre ses bras la reprist
> Maintenant et vers lui la trest. (1977-9)

The pivot word here is *corteisie*: how much and what kind of *corteisie* can we expect of Perceval? Courtliness in Gauvain's sense, whose reputation in relations with the fairer sex was well established? [114] Courtly in the sense of consideration for another's sorrow? On is he to be courtly ironically, *i.e.,* in a manner opposite to whatever we mean by *corteisie*? [115]

---

[112] In this respect, Blancheflor resembles Laudine, on whom see Frappier, *Chrétien de Troyes,* p. 160.

[113] These lines betray no hint of moral disapproval for her action on Chrétien's part.

[114] See William A. Nitze, "The Character of Gauvain...," pp. 219-25; for Gauvain's reputation before Chrétien's romances, see Frappier's "Le personnage de Gauvain dans la *Première continuation de Perceval (Conte du Graal)*", *Romance Philology,* XI (1958), 331-44; p. 332 f.

[115] This entire passage is a kind of *significatio,* different from the rhetorical figure in being only suggestive without leading to a definite meaning.

In answer to her host's question (for the roles of host and guest have now been inverted) as to the purpose of her visit, Blancheflor begs him not to hold her *vil* (1984) for having come *pres que nue* (1986), assuring him that

> "N'i pansai je onques folie
> Ne mauvestié ne vilenie.... (1987 f.)

For the reader, informed by a description which occurred while Perceval was sleeping, this is still ambiguous. It may color the reader's attitude toward the long speech (1982-2037) which moves from apology to grief to a hint of suicide; a detailed and precise outline of her plight; a return to the threat of suicide, including a description of the fine knife she keeps in a jeweled chest and which she will use for the purpose; and which concludes on a most disingenuous note:

> "Itant a dire vos avoie.
> Or me remetrai a la voie,
> Si voe leisserai reposer." (2035-7)

Perceval responds with surprising tenderness, but Chrétien interposes a note of psychological realism which also provides an aesthetic distance from this delightful pair:

> Par tans se porra aloser
> Li chevaliers, se feire l'ose;
> Qu'onques cele por autre chose
> Ne vint plorer desor sa face,
> Que que ele antandant li face,
> Fors por ce qu'ele li meïst
> An corage qu'il anpreïst
> La bataille, s'il l'ose anprandre,
> Por sa terre et por li desfandre. (2038-46)

Did Chrétien fear that pity for the distraught Blancheflor and sympathy for Perceval's new-found tenderness might lead the reader to too easy an acceptance of the characters at their own valuation? In any case, this author's comment, in his own *persona,* has the effect of drawing the reader away from the pair much as dramatic irony did in *Cligès.* As a result, we see the gentleness, even the kindliness of Perceval's words as the effect of psychological manipulation, as a rising to the bait:

> "Amie chiere,
> Feites enuit mes bele chiere;
> Confortez vos, ne plorez plus
> Et traiez vos vers moi ceisus,
> S'ostez les lermes de voz iauz.
> Deus, se lui plest, vos fera miauz
> Demain que vos ne m'avez dit." (2047-53)

That we understand this to be a result of trickery does not deny its inherent value. Awakened in the middle of the night, Perceval reacts with an immediate human understanding and sympathy which happens to be in accord with advice he has been given, [116] but which does not seem caused by that advice. He comforts a helpless woman without, as far as Chrétien tells us, any reflection on whether or not this is knightly. A comparison with the Tent Maiden episode shows how appropriate this revelation of a new aspect of the hero is to the situation. In the earlier meeting with a damsel, Perceval was struck by the imposing beauty of the tent; but the damsel's first words were urgent recommendations to leave at once. Here, the dismal condition of Belrepeire and Blancheflor's appeals to his courage, pity, and masculine superiority find their mark—with the help, of course, of surprise and trickery. [117]

Perceval's new tenderness does not replace his earlier naïveté and foolishness, it is associated with them. He concludes his comforting words with an invitation which returns to erotic suggestiveness:

> "Lez moi vos couchiez an cest lit;
> Qu'il est assez lez a oés nos;
> Hui mes ne me leisseroiz vos." (2054-6)

His entire speech (the last two quotations together), coming from another man, might be part of a seduction. That is a sophistication from which Perceval remains far distant. His reaction is appropriate to his character, *i.e.*, it is the reaction of a child. As a child wanting comfort goes to its parents' bed, so Perceval, wanting to comfort Blancheflor, invites her to his bed, assuring her it is wide enough for them both! Chrétien concludes the scene with a brief flight of lyricism whose inner ironies are slight but which benefits from the momentum of ambiguities still in the reader's mind: [118]

> Et cil la beisoit,
> Qui an ses braz la tenoit prise,
> Si l'a soz le covertor mise
> Tot soavet et tot a eise;
> Et cele suefre qu'il la beise,
> Ne ne cuit pas qu'il li enuit.
> Einsi jurent tote la nuit,
> Li uns lez l'autre, boche a boche,
> Jusqu'au main que li jorz aproche.
> Tant li fist la nuit de solaz
> Que boche a boche, braz a braz,
> Dormirent tant qu'il ajorna. (2058-69)

Chrétien has continued the technique of erotic suggestiveness and ambiguity. He does not tell us whether Perceval remains as innocent

---

[116] Both his mother's and Gornemant's, to help unprotected ladies; *supra*, pp. 129, 153.

[117] This is not the first time Perceval shows this kind of feeling: compare his wish to return to his mother, *supra*, p. 152. However, that was a memory which had percolated in his mind for several days. Here, the reaction is immediate, direct, face to face with another person.

[118] On the ironization of lyricism, see above, pp. 60 f.

11

as when he went to bed, but raises the question in our mind. It is a question which can be answered only in terms of what we know of the character. Nothing the author has shown of this character indicates a basic change in his essential *niceté*. The irony is not just that Perceval remains innocent, but that he is unaware of having a choice between innocence and consummation. He is tricked into tenderness, and remains innocent through ignorance. [119]

The paradox obviously reflects on Perceval ironically. Irony, like youth, *se pose en s'opposant*. Whether it is considered on the simple

---

[119] Chrétien de Troyes was no prude. He enjoyed the humor known as Gallic, especially in the *Lancelot* (perhaps in reaction to an overall assignment he found distasteful). Lancelot does not notice that he has wounded his fingers in pulling aside the bars of Guenièvre's room until he is leaving. He is not angry about the damage, for he would rather have lost both arms than not have gone into the room,

> mes s'il se fust aillors quassez
> et si laidemant anpiriez,
> molt an fust dolant et iriez. (*Lancelot*, 4734-6)

Earlier, when told that the golden hairs left between the teeth of a comb he has found in the forest are the queen's, he remarked:

> "Par foi,
> assez sont reines et roi..." (*Lancelot*, 1419 f.)

See also my comments on the pleasures of the "first night" (Alis and Fénice) in *Cligès, supra*, p. 84 f.

That Chrétien never portrays the acts of love itself is due, as he himself explains, to propriety (which, of course, does not affect Gallic humor!). Having united Guenièvre and Lancelot in bed, he refers to the *joie* and *mervoille* they shared:

> tel c'onques ancor sa paroille
> ne fu oïe ne seüe;
> mes toz jorz iert par moi teüe,
> qu'an conte ne doit estre dite.
> Des joies fu la plus eslite
> et la plus delitable cele
> que li contes nos test et cele. (*Lancelot*, 4678-84)

I do not think this principle of propriety can be used in favor of the argument that Perceval and Blancheflor do enjoy sexual congress. Chrétien, as we have just seen, does not hesitate to state this directly: he only says he will not describe it. Secondly, this would put Blancheflor in the position of having prostituted herself for gain: it seems impossible that this would be considered by anyone acquainted with Chrétien's heroines and his attitude toward them. Whatever morality might say, there is a world of difference in literature between a heroine taking such a chance, and having her actually succeed. Finally, were the consummation reached, what has been erotic suggestiveness would be open to the charge of prurience. This also seems out of character with everything we know of Chrétien as a writer.

Similar opinions on Perceval's "chastity" have been held by Albert Pauphilet (*Le legs du moyen âge, Etudes de littérature médiévale* [Melun : Librairie d'Argences, 1949], p. 171), Cohen (*Un grand romancier d'amour...*, pp. 460-62), and Frappier (*Perceval...*, pp. 48 ff.). Frappier also notes that his innocence is in accord with the mother's lesson which permits a kiss but not the *soreplus*; he adds: "... il n'est pas sûr que Perceval ait compris de quoi il s'agissait..." (*ibid.*, p. 49, n. 2). This would add a further irony that Perceval adheres to advice without realizing it; compare Cligès being tricked to his own advantage, *supra*, p. 41 f.

verbal level of the trope or on the more complex level of an extended narrative development, irony at least suggests a value which may remain unspoken, but which is nonetheless present *per contrarium.* In earlier episodes, the mainsprings of irony (and comedy) were ignorance of wordly matters and the proper forms of social intercourse, against which were played the crudeness of the *vaslet sauvage,* his automatism and behavior by precept. In the scene with Blancheflor, however, a new term comes to the fore as the implied contrast to form the incongruence of his behavior. It is not only by comparison to social assumptions that his persistent innocence is risible, but by comparison to nature. To spell out the obvious, it is the way of nature for man to know woman. [120] The entire play of ambiguity, from the first hint in the word *oiseuse* to the final "lyrical" passage, is based on the reader's normal expectation that Perceval will, or might. behave in the normal male fashion, just as Blancheflor's approach—tears, her sad story, a certain deshabille—is based on the general predictability of masculine reaction. The teasing of both heroine and author imply a fundamental "naturalism", a robust good sense which has too often been slighted in Chrétien scholarship. [121]

At the same time, this naturalistic standard is associated with socialization: Perceval cannot behave naturally precisely because he is too natural, too much a *naïf.* [122] This social side of the paradox is further developed as Blancheflor, still not certain of having a champion, meets her knight again the following morning, this time in public. In an apparently benign and courteous speech, which ostensibly will allow the guest to depart with a clear conscience, she inserts two oblique remarks referring to the previous night. She expects him to leave, she says, without delay, and claims that this causes her no concern:

> "Que ne seroie pas cortoise,
> S'il m'an pesoit de nule rien;
> *Que point d'eise ne point de bien*
> *Ne vos avomes ceanz fet.*
> Mes je prie Deu que il vos et
> Apareillié meillor ostel,
> Ou plus et pain et vin et sel
> *Et autre bien* que an cestui." (2088-95)

Perceval rises to the occasion, snaps at the bait, and adds puerility to innocence. He asks a recompense if he succeeds against her

---

[120] The controversy which has surrounded this episode is evidence to the point: no one can accept the hero's innocence without some explanation.

[121] "... Chrétien is a poet, with flights into the mystery and wonder of life. Yet, at heart, he is a bourgeois or cleric with his feet on the ground and a strong ironic sense." Nitze, *Perceval and the Holy Grail...,* p. 287. For the retrospective reader, it is also ironic that Perceval actually obtains as much as will Gauvain, without the latter's courtliness; see below, p. 215, and n. 253.

[122] The same convergence of the "natural" and the "social" was found in the discussion of the "wild man"; *supra,* p. 119 f.

assailant. Having muffed the opportunity to make love to Blancheflor that night, he asks her the following morning to grant him her *druerie*— a term whose ambiguities are adequately translated by the English "intimacy". [123]

Blancheflor answers cleverly (*par cointise*: 2107) with a feigned modesty that depreciates the value of the requested reward, and urges him to the fight by contraries, *i.e.*, by saying he is neither strong nor old enough to take on so strong and great a knight as Anguingueron.

> Tel plet li a cele basti
> Qu'ele li blasme, et si le viaut;
> Mes sovant avient que l'an siaut
> Escondire sa volanté
> Quant an voit bien antalanté
> Home de feire son talent
> Por ce que miauz l'an atalant.
> Aussi fet ele come sage,
> Qu'ele li a mis an corage
> Ce qu'ele li blasme mout fort. (2128-37) [124]

Her ruse works, of course—or rather, the accumulation of ruses. The lines immediately following the above passage are bare of ornamentation, but constitute a fine *significatio per consequentiam*:

> Et cil dit que l'an li aport
> Ses armes.   (2138 f.)

So ends the first part of Perceval's stay at Belrepeire, that concerned with his relations with the gentler sex. He has revealed a potential of direct warmth, tenderness, and pity for a helpless but resourceful woman—he has revealed an aspect of what religion calls charity. This feeling does not replace his ingenuousness, but is associated with it, and has the immediate effect of leaving him open to the manipulations of a young woman as shrewd as she is charming and vibrant. [125]

---

[123] The word frequently has carnal meaning: Raphael Levy, "The Motivation of *Perceval* and the Authorship of *Philomena*," *Publications of the Modern Languages Association*, LXXI (1956), 853-62; p. 857. In the *Perceval* itself, however, *druerie* and *drue* are used in contexts where they can have no carnal meaning: ll. 5418, 9014.

Levy's suggestion that, though Perceval and Blancheflor remain chaste on the first evening, they compensate for their omission later during his stay at Belrepeire, has no textual basis: Chrétien describes their later relationship in the same kind of terms he used for the first night.

[124] The same idea is expressed in *Lancelot*:

> "... qui blasme, bien le savez,
> son voloir a home n'a fame,
> plus en art et plus en anflame." (1758-60)

The same (unintentional) effect is obtained by Keu's sarcasm to Yvain (*Yvain*, 590 ff.).

[125] Blancheflor combines traits of Laudine (the helpless, responsible *châtelaine*) and Lunete (the manipulator of others), though without Lunete's delight in this process.

Perceval's first knightly battle pits him against Anguingueron, seneschal to Clamadeu. He wins, of course, but the achievement, as usual, is immediately qualified. The two begin on horseback, as knights should, and shatter their lances. The seneschal is wounded and falls to the ground,

> Et li vaslez a pié desçant,
> Qu'il ne set a cheval requerre.. (2224 f.)

In fact, it was precisely at this point of knightly combat that Gornemant, helpless before a foolish remark of his pupil's, gave up the day's lessons. [126] Nevertheless, the youth engages his opponent in the passage at swords until the latter falls before the fierce attack and asks for mercy. Perceval remembers Gornemant's advice on this subject, but it is difficult to put into practice:

> Et li vaslez dit qu'il n'i a
> De la merci ne tant ne quant,
> Si li sovint il neporquant
> Del prodome qui li aprist
> Qu'a son esciant n'oceïst
> Chevalier, des que il l'eüst
> Conquis et au desore an fust. (2236-42)

As the ensuing dialogue makes clear, Perceval's inner conflict is caused by his misunderstanding of the nature of "mercy", and is resolved by a further lesson in chivalry delivered by the conquered knight lying on the ground and arguing for his very life. Anguingueron explains to the young man that he is, in fact, a very good knight, but not so good that people would believe he had killed the seneschal by his own arms alone. On the other hand, if Perceval spares him, Anguingueron will bear witness to the fact and increase his honor:

> "Et garde, se tu as seignor
> Qui t'et bien ne servise fet
> Don le guerredon eü n'et,
> Anvoie m'i, et j'i irai
> De par toi et si li dirai
> Comant tu m'as d'armes conquis,
> Et si me randrai a lui pris
> Por feire quanque buen li iert." (2260-7)

Anguingueron has just explained the profitable rationale behind showing mercy and the manner in which this is done—details Gornemant had not explained, which he assumed the young knight would know, but which Perceval has had to learn on the field of battle from a vanquished foe. Again, as with the mother's precepts, as with Gornemant's advice to speak with discretion, the intent of a lesson has been lost because of Perceval's ignorance of his society's assumptions. When he rejects the seneschal's plea for mercy, he is apparently under the impression that it would mean letting his opponent go scot free. Once

---

[126] *Supra,* p. 150 f.

he understands that it is merely an attenuated form of victory which will bring him further profit, he recognizes a good proposition:

> "Dahez et" fet il, "qui miauz quiert!" (2268)

However, all is not settled yet: there is still room for *contretemps*. The victor first proposes to send his opponent to what is, for Perceval, the obvious place: the castle from which he came, *A la bele qui est m'amie...* (2271). Anguingueron answers that Perceval might just as well kill him on the spot, for Blancheflor surely would. He not only besieged her castle, starved her people, and killed or imprisoned most of her men, he also killed her father. Perceval's next choice is to send him

> A un chastel a un prodome,
> Et le non au seignor li nome,
> N'an tot le monde n'a maçon
> Qui miauz devisast la façon
> Del chastel qu'il li devisa:
> L'eve et le pont mout li prisa
> Et les torneles et la tor
> Et les forz murs qui sont antor,
> Tant que cil antant bien et set
> Que el leu ou l'an plus le het
> Le viaut anvoiier an prison. (2293-2303)

This is the humor of misplaced memory. Perceval was so struck by his first sight of Gornemant's castle—which Chrétien described at length— [127] that he recalls each detail perfectly. What he has forgotten, or finds irrelevant, is a fact he learned from Blancheflor the previous evening, namely that Gornemant is her uncle (1896-1901) and therefore the brother of her father ... whom Anguingeron killed, as he just told Perceval. The quality of this mercy also would be strained for the seneschal: he refuses again. It is only on the third try—as we retreat one episode in Perceval's biography with each attempt—that he hits on the right name: he will send Anguingueron to Arthur's court, a destination the seneschal finds more to his taste.

One function of the center of Arthurian society is revealed by this episode. One reason that Arthur's court is the normal destination of vanquished knights is that it is a place where both victim and victor can be certain that mercy will be meaningful: the victim is assured of his safety, the victor of avoiding the embarrassing *contretemps* Perceval has just experienced (without any indication of awareness that it is embarrassing). The situation does not occur in any other romance of Chrétien's. The victors know where to send their defeated opponents, and it is only the ignorant and inexperienced Perceval who has two offers of mercy refused before thinking of Arthur's court.

The Clamadeu episode is largely a doublet of the Anguingueron sequence of events. The siege of Belrepeire is elaborated with questions

---

[127] *Supra*, p. 147, n. 91.

of tactics, the figure of a bad counselor, and a brief but strikingly described attack and retreat. Perceval fights and overwhelms master as readily as seneschal, and goes through the same routine of wanting to send his conquered opponent first to Blancheflor, then to Gornemant, with the same results we have just seen, until he thinks of Arthur again. Perceval is a slow learner: though the leit-motif has not been heard for a long time, it is still valid. [128] The Clamadeu sequence is also enlivened by the pleasant scene in which a merchant ship arrives laden with victuals, and everyone in the castle joyfully eats to the full again—scenes which again stress a descriptive realism, although in a more agreeable vein than Perceval's first ride through the town.

The most problematic aspect of this section has to do with Blancheflor. It has been said that her coquetry here turns ot true love, [129] and it must be admitted that Chrétien does not state the contrary. When she leads Perceval to his room, it is

> Por reposer et aesier.
> De l'acoler et del beisier
> Ne li fet ele nul dangier:
> An leu del boivre et de mangier
> Joënt et beisent et acolent
> Et deboneiremant parolent. (2357-62)

After the arrival of the merchant ship:

> Or se puet li vaslez deduire
> Delez s'amie tot a eise:
> Cele l'acole, et il la beise,
> Si fet li uns de l'autre joie. (2574-7)

In neither case does Chrétien suggest any after-thought or ulterior motive. The same is true of Blancheflor's entreaties not to fight Clamadeu. The latter's challenge arrives:

> Quant la pucele ot ceste chose
> Qui a son ami est nonciee,
> Mout est dolante et correciee... (2600-2)

When Perceval accepts the challenge,

> Lors anforce mout et angraingne
> Li diaus que la pucele an fet;
> Mes ja por duel que ele an et
> Ne remanra neant, ce cuit. (2606-9)

In fact, one would say that throughout these domestic scenes, Chrétien is at pains to present an external objective view of what occurs and is said. But can we forget Blancheflor's earlier manipulation?

In the passage immediately following her prayer to Perceval not to fight Clamadeu (2625-9), Chrétien writes:

---

[128] Cf. *supra*, p. 146.
[129] Frappier, *Perceval*, p. 51.

Mes tot ce ne valut neant,
Et si *fu ce mervoille estrange*
Que il avoit an la *losange*
Grant douçor qu'ele li feisoit;
Car a chascun mot le beisoit
Si doucemant et si soef
Que ele li metoit la clef
D'amor an la serre del cuer,
N'onques ne pot estre a nul fuer
Que ele l'an poïst retreire
Que la bataille n'alast feire,
Einz a ses armes demandees.   (2630-41) [130]

Whatever Blancheflor's unrevealed thoughts, her behavior and its effects are exactly those of the previous day.   Whether she really wishes him to abstain from battle, or whether she is using the same devious psychology as before, the effect is to urge Perceval to go out and fight.   This identity of pattern casts some doubt on the phrase *mervoille estrange*.   Neither the pleasure Perceval took in her attentions nor his reaction to them can seem marvelous strange to the reader who recalls the same attentions, the same effect, before Perceval fought Anguin-gueron.   The very word for these attentions, *la losange,* is at least suspicious in its ambiguity: meaning attentiveness as well as flattery, it raises the question of its present sense. [131]

Finally, there is the rather precious-seeming metaphor Chrétien uses to describe the psychological effect of these attentions, that of "putting the key of love in the lock of his heart."   In truth, it is a metaphor which has called a large amount of criticism down on Chrétien for its preciosity. [132]   This criticism, however, assumes the metaphor is meant to express the emotion of love: as such, it would be a surprising throwback to the style of *Cligès* and exceptional in the more spare style of *Perceval*.   This assumption is not necessarily induced by the text.   The lines which immediately follow this metaphor state that Blancheflor cannot prevent the youth who loves her so greatly from going into battle.   According to this interpretation.   Chrétien would first indicate the growth of true love in Perceval's heart, and then immediately show that this love gives Blancheflor no power over his actions. [133]

---

[130] Hilka prints a semi-colon after *estrange,* which seems unnecessary.

[131] See *Lancelot,* 6, 8, 15, for *losange*=flattery; *Lancelot* 3213, *Yvain* 5419, for *losange*=attentiveness.   Godefroy gives only equivalents of flattery; Tobler-Lommatzsch includes *Freundlichkeit* among the meanings.

[132] "Chrétien jars the sensitive reader by his mannered (*courtois*) treatment of Blancheflor's love." (Nitze, *Perceval and the Holy Grail*..., p. 304); cf. Cohen, *Un grand romancier d'amour*..., p. 491.   Frappier thinks better of it: *Cligès,* p. 80.

[133] "Comme par une ironie du destin ou du romancier, c'est à partir du moment où Blanchefleur est vraiment amoureuse que diminue le pouvoir qu'elle exerçait sur Perceval; en réalité ce changement est dû au développement logique du caractère du héros." Frappier, *Perceval,* p. 51.

Let us return to the metaphor. The key controls a lock, and whatever is locked in. The person in possession of the key controls the door and whatever is on the other side of the door. Blancheflor has the key to Perceval's heart, *i.e.,* the source of his energy and commitment. By this key, she has control over his actions. From this interpretation of the metaphor, we might paraphrase the last lines of the passage as follows: "She made up to him so skillfully that she ruled him completely, so that she could never have dissuaded him from fighting by mere words, and indeed he called for his weapons."

This interpretation seems indicated by the description of Perceval's departure from Belrepeire. He is first shown as enjoying life with his *amie, la bele* (2912). Then he remembers his mother, her faint, and his desire to see her again, and this desire is greater than anything else. But one thing restrains him:

> Congié prandre a s'amie n'ose... (2922)

So well has she inserted the controlling key into his heart that this young *enragé* whom nothing could formerly restrain—mother-love, pity or compassion, respect for an admired older man—does not even dare ask leave to see his mother. The *vaslez sauvage* has fallen victim, not to the Red Knight, Anguingueron or Clamadeu, but to the *losange* of a girl named Blancheflor. She is, however, a kindly and considerate victor; above all, she is cognizant of the author's plot requirements. Perceval is allowed to leave on the basis of a promise to return to Belrepeire. If his mother is alive, he will make her a nun in Belrepeire; if not, she will be buried there; in any case, he will return. [134]

The Fisher King

This episode falls into three sections: a psychological introduction, the mysterious procession, and a comic conclusion. The introduction is brief. Perceval meets the Fisher King and follows his directions to his castle. He is shown as still subject to violent reactions when faced with even momentary frustration. He is quite polite when speaking to the Fisher King, who informs him that there is no crossing point to the river within twenty leagues, but offers hospitality for the knight: his castle stands in a nearby valley, and can be seen from the top of a nearby boulder. Following his directions, Perceval climbs up, and is not only disappointed but incensed not to see the castle immediately:

---

[134] Is Blancheflor in love with Perceval? There is no reason to affirm or deny the possibility strenuously. Chrétien's texte hovers ambiguously about the two poles of love and self-interest; presumably, the ambiguity was to be resolved at the end of the romance. What can be said with some certainty is that he saw no inherent contradiction between love and self-interest. On the contrary, the two motives join to persuade Laudine to marry Yvain.

This may have been Chrétien's manner of correcting both the notion of an overwhelming romantic love which disregards practical considerations—as in the adulterous troubadour tradition, the Tristan legend, and the attempt of Fénice and Cligès—and the historical reality in which personal emotions were overwhelmed by the practical advantages accruing from political marriages.

"Que sui je venuz querre?
La musardie et la bricoingne.
Deus li doint hui male vergoingne
Celui qui ça m'a anvoiié,
Si m'a il or bien avoiié
Que il me dist que je verroie
Meison quant ça amont seroie!
Peschiere, qui ce me deïs,
Trop grant desleauté feïs,
Se tu le me deïs por mal!" (3040-9)

Just then, however, he catches sight of a tower: [135]

Lors vit devant lui an un val
Le chief d'une tor qui parut;
L'an ne trovast jusqu'a Barut

---

[135] Mario Roques considered the castle and everything that happened in it to be a vision; "Pour l'Introduction à l'édition du *Roman de Perceval* de Chrétien de Troyes," *Romania*, LXXXI (1960), 1-36; p. 21 f. However, the description of the castle's appearance to Perceval's eyes is very similar to the appearance of Gornemant's castle to Perceval, except that the visionary quality is far stronger in the latter case; *supra*, p. 147, n. 91.

Later, Perceval's cousin will say that there is no lodging to be found within 25 leagues (3469-73); this is qualified, however, by the phrase *ce tesmoingne l'an* (3469): "that's what people say." It should be noticed that she does not say there is no habitation within that distance: her comment refers only to lodging (*uns osteus*: 3472). When Perceval contradicts her, explaining that he found very fine lodging indeed for the night within shouting distance, she immediately understands he means the Fisher King's castle. A little later, describing the latter's vicarious pleasure in his men's hunting, she adds:

"Por ce li plest a converser
An cest repeire ci elués;
Qu'an tot le mont a oés son oés
Ne puet trover meillor repeire,
Et s'i a fet tel meison feire
Come il covient a riche roi." (3529-33)

This certainly sounds like the description of a perfectly physical and material habitation.

The apparent contradiction between the cousin's two statements can be resolved by reasonable conjecture: she did not consider the Fisher King's castle a likely place to obtain lodging. Perhaps she did not know he was at this residence (the fact that he had it built after being wounded may imply other residences); perhaps it is not his custom to receive knights for overnight lodging.

Kellermann, dealing with the same question, views the sudden appearance of the castle from a psychological viewpoint, and explains it as a sensory description told from Perceval's point of view: it shows his strong reaction to the apparently false information of the Fisher King (*Aufbaustil und Weltbild...*, p. 208).

The existence of the Fisher King's castle presents no great problem. It is there, as many other strange things are there in Chrétien's romances, because the author put it there. Since he does not distinguish its mode of existence from the rest of his literary world any more than he distinguishes, for example, the garden of the Joie de la Cour, Jehan's tower and orchard, the Château de Pesme Aventure, or the Kingdom of Gorre, there is no reason to doubt that the castle of the Fisher King stands on ground as firm as any of these.

On the literary function of this description, see the following footnote.

> Si bele ne si bien assise:
> Quarree fu de pierre bise,
> S'avoit deus torneles antor.
> La sale fu devant la tor,
> Et les loges devant la sale. (3050-7) [136]

As soon as he sees the object he was seeking, his anger is dissipated as quickly as it came:

> Li vaslez cele part avale
> Et dit que bien avoiié l'a
> Cil qui l'avoit anvoiié la,
> Si se loe del pescheor
> Ne l'apele mes tricheor
> Ne desleal ne mançongier,
> Des que il trueve ou herbergier. (3058-64)

Chrétien underlines the exactness of the turnabout in his own commentary (*Si se loe del pescheor, etc.*), and reduces the entire emotional upheaval in the last line quoted which juxtaposes the emotions to their absurdly simple and everyday cause, the question of finding lodging. [137] Whatever overlay of knighthood his successes in war and "love" have given him, Perceval is still the violent and volatile youth we met at the beginning of the romance. Although they are not as crudely expressed to others, the same emotions still move him.

Nevertheless, conscious since his meeting with Gornemant of social rules and limitations, Perceval attempts politeness of behavior when he enters the castle. His host apologizes for being unable to rise in greeting his guest:

---

[136] This recalls the description of Gornemant's castle (*supra*, p. 147 f.) which was later used for comic purpose in the encounter with Anguingueron (*supra*, p. 164). The pattern of repetition of this visual theme is similar to the use of music (birdsong and clashing armor) in the Five Knights and Tent Episodes. In the former, the sounds of birdsong and clashing armor suggested two worlds which were contrasted in the actions of the characters; in the Tent episode, the representative of one of those worlds stumbled into the other, with comic effects.

Here, the pattern of repetition is slightly different. The first repetition of the theme (with Anguingueron) signaled the comedy of misunderstood advice (therefore a parallel with the Tent episode); now, the theme signals the return of another rule (that of discretion), but one whose affabulation suggests tragic rather than comic effects. In both cases, Chrétien uses a descriptive theme to signal the relevance of episodes to each other, to suggest a relationship of simultaneous identity and difference.

[137] The rich rhymes associated with anger (*anvoiié/avoiié*) are enriched and inverted in the description of the anger's dissipation (*avoiié l'a/anvoiié l'a*). However, the absence of stylistic convergence at this point makes it difficult to determine whether or not this was intentional. If it is considered intentional, it suggests an assimilation of the psychological turn-about to the kind of mechanical rigidity Bergson considered a source of laughter: "Est comique tout arrangement d'actes et d'événements qui nous donne, insérées l'une dans l'autre, l'illusion de la vie et la sensation nette d'un agencement mécanique." (*Le rire...*, p. 53).

> "Amis, ne vos soit grief,
> Se ancontre vos ne me lief;
> Que je n'an sui pas aeisiez." (3107-9)

Although we are ignorant of the nature of the Fisher King's disability, it is clearly the occasion for concern, perhaps even the expression of sympathy and a hope for the return of good health. Perceval attempts but does not quite achieve this kind of politeness:

> "Por Deu, sire, or vos an teisiez,"
> Fet il, "qu'il ne me grieve point
> Se Deus joie et santé me doint." (3110-2)

Perceval's attempt to be polite, to reassure his host that no offense is taken at the omission of the normal greeting, comes out quite differently than intended: the host's ill health is disregarded, and the wish for good health turned back upon Perceval himself. Again, his attempt at knightly courtesy is derailed by an essential, childish egotism and lack of social practice.

His host is not only a man of great courtesy, but of sympathy and commiseration. Himself infirm, he sorrows for his guest:

> Li prodon tant por lui se grieve
> Que tant come il puet se sozlieve... (3113 f.)

Why so great a sorrow as to urge him to rise *tant come il puet,* a painful movement from what we have just learned? The only answer in the text lies in Perceval's words, which are pitiable indeed. The conflict between intention and accomplishment, which has given rise to so much comedy up to now, begins to be seen from a more serious point of view. But this suggestive glimpse is quickly succeeded by a brief exchange of polite conversation. The Fisher King invites his guest to sit next to him and inquires from where he traveled that day. When Perceval tells him he left Belrepeire that morning, his host exclaims: "That's a long day's journey. You must have left before dawn!"—"Not at all, it was already six a.m., I assure you!" [138]

The transition from the psychological introduction to the mysterious procession is performed by a passage which combines psychology and mystery. A *vaslez* enters from the front door, bearing a sword brought to the Fisher King by his niece. The weapon and its value are described at length, after which the host gives it to Perceval with these words:

> "Biaus sire, ceste espee
> Vos fu jugiee et destinee,
> Et je vuel mout que vos l'aiiez;
> Mes ceigniez la, si la traiiez." (3167-70)

---

[138]   "Si m'aït Deus", fet li prodon,
"Trop grant jornee avez hui feite:
Vos meüstes, einz que la gueite
Eüst hui main l'aube cornee."
"Einz estoit ja prime sonee "
Fet li vaslez, "jel vos afi." (3124-9)

Here, irony mingles with mystery. Though no one else in the world of this romance has known the identity of the still nameless young man since he left home, this invalid does, with no more formal introduction to the hero than we have received. Much has been made of Perceval's failure to ask a later question, [139] but from the psychological view point, there is a more obvious and immediate question Perceval should ask, one which concerns himself. Not only his identity but even his destiny are known to his host: surely this should bring forth the question: "Who, me? How do you know who I am?" [140]—For the reader, another irony is that this suggestion of a great destiny associated with the gift of the magnificent sword comes immediately after a renewed demonstration of Perceval's unformed personality.

The sword is only the first object brought to our attention. This is a scene of objects, inciting our curiosity by their aura of opulent mystery, but the scene is not to be defined by these objects or even their mystery. The objects are one pole of the tension, the psychological reaction of Perceval the other pole. As Chrétien describes the passage of each object, he turns to the observing guest and notes his reaction. First the lance passes by: Perceval's curiosity and silence are recorded. A *graal* and a *tailleor* are carried through the room: Perceval's curiosity and silence are recorded. The meal is served and described, the *graal* is brought through again: again, Perceval's curiosity and silence are recorded. Finally, dessert and liqueurs are served: this time, it is merely noted that Perceval marvelled about all he had not learned (3334 f.). Our attention alternates between the objects and Perceval. If we consider only the lance, grail and *tailleor* (leaving aside the foodstuffs), we find an approximate equality in the number of lines devoted to these objects and to Perceval. [141] This is all the more striking in view of the fact that Perceval's reaction, each time, is the same. Each time, we are told of his curiosity, his wish to inquire, his silence, and the explanation of that silence: he restrains himself because he remembers Gornemant's injunction not to speak too much. The second time, Chrétien remarks in his own *persona* that one can be as foolish by too much silence as by too much speech. [142] The third time, he adds that Perceval plans to ask about these things in the morning, and so has postponed the matter.

---

[139] This is due, of course, to the fact that Perceval's cousin and the Ugly Damsel are concerned only with the later question. Only the reader, along with the Fisher King, is privy to this earlier, foreshadowing failure to ask a question.

[140] Frappier has noted that the Fisher King somehow manages to return to the castle before Perceval arrives there (*Perceval*, p. 54): this also might have given rise to a curious inquiry on Perceval's part.

[141] Objects: 51 lines; Perceval: 43 lines. The descriptions of Perceval's reaction refer to the objects, of course, but the question is the focus of our attention.

[142]
> ... [je] criem que il* n'i et domage   *Perceval
> Por ce que j'ai oï retreire
> Qu'ausi bien se puet an trop teire
> Con trop parler a la foiiee. (3248-51)

The structural pivot of the scene is Perceval and his reaction. [143] The objects exist to set him a problem and a test. [144] They are functions and their function is mystery and the arousal of curiosity. However, it is not only Perceval's curiosity that is aroused, but the reader's as well. As readers, however, we cannot satisfy that curiosity ourselves: we are entirely dependent on Perceval. It is only his questions, if he asked them, that could solve the mystery for us as well as for him. As our curiosity is aroused by the repeated procession, as we, the readers, desire more intensely to learn the identity and meaning of those objects, we may become irritated with our surrogate in the world of the romance, whose incongruous application of an irrelevant rule of social propriety frustrates our curiosity. At this point, our desire for knowledge comes into conflict with the literary function of these objects. They can function only if they are mysterious that is, if we do not know what they signify. [145]

---

[143] Cf. Kellermann, *Aufbaustil und Weltbild...*, pp. 205-7.

[144] "Quant au Graal, dans la scène du château, il n'a pas d'autre fonction apparente que d'inciter Perceval à poser une question: où on le porte, ce qu'on en sert, ou qui on en sert." Fourquet, "L'œuvre et la source...," p. 306. "Rappelons ... l'optique propre de Chrétien, qui voit le graal en fonction de Perceval." Imbs, "Perceval et le graal...," p. 52.

[145] Literary mystery functions by an unfulfilled suggestion of recognition: the object seems vaguely familiar and incites a desire for fuller recognition. Thus, it is not the elaboration of possible identifications but the attempt to impose definite identifications and meanings which seems to me contrary to Chrétien's intention: "C'est volontairement, en artiste très conscient, que selon nous Chrétien a laissé subsister autour du graal un halo d'incertitude..." (Frappier, "Le Graal et l'Hostie [Conte del Graal, v. 6413-6431]," in *Les romans du Graal aux XIIe et XIIIe siècles,* in *Colloques Internationaux du Centre National de la Recherche Scientifique,* III, Strasbourg, 29 mars - 3 avril 1954 [Paris: Editions du CNRS, 1956], pp. 63-78; p. 68). I would extend this statement to the other objects as well. I would also be hesitant to define the grail even as vaguely as Frappier does, "comme un objet-symbole, ambigu entre le paganisme et le christianisme...." (*loc. cit.*); see also *Perceval,* pp. 83-111): while this may describe its genesis in the author's mind, is it as such that it functions in the romance?

This dualism is reflected in Frappier's interpretation of the scene as presenting Perceval with an implicit choice between wordly and spiritual values (*Perceval,* p. 58). What remains implicit for Frappier is quite explicit for Fowler: "We see two kinds of food, physical and spiritual, repeatedly offered to the young knight, and along with this Chrétien builds an atmosphere of mounting tension in one of the most remarkable passages of the medieval poetic description (3213 ff.), so that the charged silence of the hall seems to be shattered by the unspoken imperative: *choose! choose!*" (*Prowess and Charity...,* p. 33).

This is striking literary interpretation, but it is irrelevant to the scene in question. The hall does not resound with "choose!", and though there is certainly tension, it is not a tension between different kinds of foods. We do not "see" two kinds of food, nor is there any way during this scene that we can guess that two kinds of food are available. The only food we "see" in the Fisher King's castle is the usual kind of victuals, meat, groceries, cakes, and wine, sumptuously presented.

It is only in the Hermit Episode that we learn the content of the grail: a host. The reader has no way of knowing this during the scene in the castle. Does

If the objects are mysterious, the opposite is true of Perceval. Chrétien repeats three times that the reason for his silence is his observance of what he construes as Gornemant's lesson of silence. It has been suggested that Chrétien's irony at the expense of the *chastoiements* is only a nuance. [146] Were this the only occasion on which such irony has been displayed, this judgment would undoubtedly impose itself, but the inefficacy of perfectly sound precepts acted on by an essential and unalterable naïveté has been the subject of so much structural comedy and irony in this romance that it can hardly be relegated to a "nuance". It was in the belief that he was acting out his mother's precepts that Perceval invaded the "tent-church", kissed the maiden twenty times, and stole her ring; that he so self-assuredly rode into Arthur's court to demand the Red Knight's armor; it was in the belief that he had received Arthur's grant of that armor that he killed the Red Knight; it was in the belief that he was following Gornemant's instructions that he remained silent the first evening with Blancheflor, and it was the incomplete understanding of his tutor's lesson of mercy which brought him the confusion of having his mercy rejected by Anguingueron and Clamadeu. One of these, in fact, is the analogue to his silence in the Fisher King's castle: the silence with Blancheflor. That the same principle of behavior is here presented for the first time without a comic affabulation does not change its psychological identity. [147] The reminders of Perceval's essential character at the beginning of this episode point in the same direction: Perceval is still reacting, albeit with more restraint, according to the same psychological principles he has displayed throughout this romance.

As we have seen, it is only since Gornemant's lessons that he obeys any restraint at all. [148] But the circumscription of human nature's "wildness" must be cautious. Already in the Blancheflor episode, Per-

---

Perceval? Much has been made of the interpretation of one line, *Le graal trestot descovert* (3301). On one side, it is interpreted as meaning that the grail was without a lid and that its content was therefore visible to Perceval (Fowler, *op. cit.*, p. 71, n. 25, where he gives further references for this interpretation); Frappier, on the other hand, interprets the phrase as meaning that the grail itself was uncovered and perfectly visible (*Perceval*, p. 91, and n. 1, for further references to his more detailed discussions).

The question, however, is irrelevant to the analysis of this scene. Had Chrétien intended to present his hero with a choice between two kinds of food, or between earthly and spiritual values, he would certainly have given us more basis for discerning this intention than a two-word adjectival phrase which is immediately followed and superseded by Perceval's curiosity as to who is served with the grail, and by his decision to wait until the following morning to ask about it—matters of greater importance to Chrétien. The tension here, repeatedly emphasized by the author, is whether or not his hero will ask about what he sees.

[146] Frappier, *Perceval,* p. 59.

[147] Though it may color our view of the scene: since this psychological principle has continually been associated with comedy previously, it is difficult to erase that association in our minds.

[148] *Supra,* p. 154 f.

ceval's veering from no restraint at all to extreme restraint was ludicrous. Here we sense that his silence is not appropriate (not only by comparison to natural behavior, but also because of Chrétien's stress on his silence), but we learn only much later of the dire effects of his silence. For the moment, it is merely one more sign of social ineptness. As in the Blancheflor episode, his error is, ironically, the result of Perceval's attempt to behave properly and according to rule. It is his self-conscious attempt to adhere to a misformed idea of propriety that defeats his desire for propriety. [149]

A further irony, more pathetic this time, is suggested by his juxtaposition to the Fisher King, a host of "exquisite courtesy." [150] Perceval is not what he is by choice or stupidity: he is marked by an upbringing in the *Gaste Forez,* a place to which he was condemned by the tragic family history whose burden he continues to bear. Emerging from the *Gaste Forez* into a world of men formed according to patterns of behavior which have become their very natures, Perceval remains the raw material of knighthood without the inner definition which constitutes manhood. The rules which he attempts to use consciously represent patterns of behavior which have become as good as innate for those who should be his fellows, those whose equal he is by birth. The world of normal social behavior remains a group of external rules to be consciously remembered and followed even to the extent of denying those natural impulses acceptable to society such as curiosity.... Perceval, like the Fisher King next to whom he is seated, is infirm. Perhaps that is the meaning of his host's great sorrow: pity.

But this is only a glimpse which depends on a consideration of the entire romance as well as the physical juxtaposition next to the Fisher King. [151] The tone of the episode moves from mystery to conclude on a note of gustatory comedy. If Chrétien avoids spiritual food in this scene, he makes up for this lack in the wealth of mouth-watering but purely physical nourishment described and consumed. Dinner starts with a haunch of deer accompanied by hot pepper condiments served on slices of bread, amply washed down by wines and juices which are continually replenished. After the main course, dessert is served: dates, nuts, figs, cloves, pomegranates. It is a large and sumptuous feast, and it is hardly surprising to find that it is followed by a fair range of medicinal preparations to assure proper digestion:

> Et leituaires an la fin
> Et gingenbrat alixandrin
> Et pliris aromaticon,
> Resontif et stomaticon. (3327-30) [152]

---

[149] Frappier seems to me to over-emphasize Perceval's self-satisfaction at this point; *Perceval*, p. 58.

[150] *Loc. cit.*

[151] This is not the first time, however, that such a juxtaposition of Perceval with another man is suggestive: see *supra*, pp. 125 and 138.

[152] For details on these various preparations, see Hilka's note to these lines.

The combination of rich, learned rhymes with visceral subject matter is a technique Chrétien has used before with ironic intent. [153] But these are not the end of the meal. In addition to all the wine that accompanied the meal itself, liqueur is served at the end:

> Apres si burent de maint boivre:
> Pimant, ou n'ot ne miel ne poivre, [154]
> Et bon moré et cler sirop.
> De tot ce se mervoille trop
> Li vaslez, qui ne l'ot apris. (3331-5)

The following morning, no one is about to assist the guest in arising: the contrast to the courteous welcome of the previous evening is unmistakable. However, it is not the intentional discourtesy or Perceval's reaction to it that Chrétien stresses, but the sheer difficulty of getting out of bed:

> ... il ne vit leanz nelui
> Quant il garda anviron lui,
> Si l'estut par lui seul lever.
> Que que il li deüst grever,
> Des qu'il voit que feire l'estuet,
> Si se lieve, que miauz ne puet... (3359-64)

Has the *vaslet sauvage* from the *Gaste Forez* been so cosseted that not being assisted out of bed is so grievous? Or are his difficulties a result of the evening's unaccustomed imbibing?.... It will be a difficult day for our hero, and it starts appropriately. He finds no one in the castle, and rides out to ask about the lance and grail he saw the previous evening. The drawbridge is down, but as he rides across, he feels it being raised,

> Et li chevaus fist un grant saut,
> Que, s'il n'eüst si bien sailli,
> Anbedui fussent maubailli
> Li chevaus et cil qui sus iere. (3406-9)

This is the courtly equivalent of farce's kick in the pants. [155] He turns around and calls to the invisible person who has raised the draw-bridge: he wants to ask a question. Ironically, when he is ready to ask the

---

[153] When Thessala, not knowing what ails Fénice, recommends her services, she does so with words of the same category:

> "Je sai bien garir d'itropique,
> Si sai garir de l'acertique,
> De quinancie et de cuerpous;
> Tant sai d'orines et de pous
> Que ja mar avroiz autre mire." (*Cligès*, 2983-7)

Cf. *supra*, p. 90 f.

[154] Without honey or pepper: straight liquor then, good and potent enough not to require additives.

[155] Compare Yvain's narrow escape from the sliding, sharp-edged portcullis which comes crashing down to cut his horse in half *a res del dos* (*Yvain*, p. 950).

question, he receives no answer. "Il ne soupçonne même pas qu'il vient de subir une humiliation." [156]

The Sorrowing Cousin

The pattern of the romance up to this point has been to provide Perceval with the basis for action in others' advice, first his mother's, then Gornemant's. Moving from these bases, the hero seems to make progress in the world but the reader's evaluation of this apparent progress is modified by irony and comedy. The pattern of action which develops from the two bases is similar. In each segment, Perceval has encountered first a lady (Tent Damsel, Blancheflor), then a king (Arthur, Fisher King). The third step in each segment is also similar: it includes the death of a knight, a death caused by Perceval. In the case of the Red Knight, Perceval was directly responsible for his death. In the second segment, he first meets a maiden weeping over a dead knight, then we learn that this death is the indirect result of Perceval's behavior with the Tent Damsel. The structure of the two segments is similar then: advice which leads to foolish behavior first with a lady, then a king; then, the confrontation with death.

There is a major difference between the last step in the two segments, however. The killing of the Red Knight was the direct narrative sequel to the Arthur scene which preceded it. The death of the cousin's *ami* is not the sequel to any episode within the Gornemant segment, but a long-delayed result of the previous segment; in fact it has developed from the first adventure of Perceval under the aegis of his mother's advice. In the Orguelleus de la Lande episode, Perceval is also confronted with the result of his own past actions. Both episodes, then, are less part of the structure of Perceval's progress through narrative action than a turning towards past action. In each case, however, the consciousness in terms of which the past is viewed is another character's: the cousin and the Orguelleus. For much of these two episodes, Perceval is the observer of an unfriendly view of his own actions—an ironic situation *par excellence*. Irony here is no longer commentary on narrative action: it is the basis of the literary structure itself.

Following fresh tracks which he thinks will lead him to the inhabitants of the deserted castle, Perceval comes upon a maiden weeping and grieving over a dead knight. He overhears her *complainte,* and then inquires who killed the knight. Her answer is brief, [157] but it leads, rather surprisingly, to a long description of the fine condition of his horse. In spite of her grief, she dwells on this in great detail: considering that there is no hostel nearby, she marvels at the animal's full flanks, his brushed hair, the indices that he has been washed and combed, and fed with hay and oats. If this sequence of speeches seems inconsistent from the psychological veiwpoint, this has the effect of

---

[156] Frappier, *Perceval,* p. 59.
[157]   "Biaus sire, uns chevaliers l'ocist"
    Fet la pucele, "hui cest matin..." (3464 f.)

drawing our attention to them as literary structure. The two speeches are juxtaposed as contrasting panels: the grief of the girl, Perceval's well-being. [158]

The matter of his hostel leads to Perceval's retelling of the previous episode, after which the maiden submits him to a point-by-point questioning on the events he witnessed the previous night. When he admits not asking about the bleeding lance, nor whither the procession went, her comments show that she considers this a mistake, but not one she becomes terribly excited about:

> "Si m'aït Deus, or sachiez donques
> Que vos avez esploitié mal." (3554 f.)
> ....
> "Si m'aït Deus, de tant vaut pis." (3571)

It is only after the young knight reveals his name and she recognizes him as her cousin, that his failure enrages her and that she inveighs against him violently:

> "Tes nons est changiez, biaus amis."
> "Comant?"—"Percevaus li cheitis!
> Ha! Percevaus maleüreus,
> Con fus or mesavantureus
> Quant tu tot ce n'as demandé!" (3581-5)

But it is the revelation of the hero's name itself which is the most puzzling aspect of this episode. Not only is this the first time in the course of the romance that his name is mentioned—this retardation of information is a general technique of Chrétien's not restricted to names—[159] but the manner of its revelation is, at the very least, extraordinary. When the sorrowing maiden asks the knight's name, Chrétien gives it in his own words:

> Et cil qui son non ne savoit
> Devine et dit que il avoit
> Percevaus li Galois a non,
> N'il ne set s'il dit voir ou non;
> Mes il dist voir, et si nel sot. (3573-7)

On the face of it, one must agree with Jean Fourquet's comment that to guess one's name without ever having heard it is absurd: [160] one's name is precisely what one learns from others' usage, especially one's parents. For the moment we may call Chrétien's statement paradoxical.

The most interesting attempt to explain this crux derives from Bezzola's view that this sudden "revelation" is symbolic of Perceval's

---

[158] The description of his horse is also to be contrasted to the Tent Damsel's horse in the next episode (*infra*, p. 182): this is another of those descriptive pivots Chrétien uses (*supra*, p. 169, n. 136).

[159] See Kellermann, *Aufbaustil und Weltbild...*, ch. iv: "Retardatio, Wunder und Doppelsinn als Erwecker der kompositionellen Spannung," pp. 60-83.

[160] *Wolfram d'Eschenbach et le Conte del Graal* (Paris: 1938), p. 43; quoted by Frappier, *Perceval*, p. 61, n. 4.

self-recognition: the dismay of his failure at the Fisher King's castle leads him to "plunge into the abyss of his own existence and to guess its meaning in guessing his name." [161] Frappier continues this line of thought by pointing to other "symbolic" uses of names in Chrétien's works: Enide is first named on the day of her marriage, and Soredamors discovers and finds justification of her *destinée amoureuse* in her name, the Blonde of Love. Frappier also cites Perceval's mother's advice ("Le non sachiez a la personne; Car par le non conoist l'an l'ome."; 561 f.) as an example of the medieval symbolic thinking in which the name corresponds to the person's moral reality and essence. [162]

The example of Enide is the most convincing. On the day of her marriage, she undergoes a radical change, from being the daughter of a poor and peripheral *vavassor* to a *dame* admitted to and admired by the entire Arthurian court. But *Erec et Enide* is Chrétien's first work, *Perceval* is last. The former is characterized by a thoroughgoing acceptance of a fashionable and heroic ideology of chivalry, in spite of Chrétien's refusal to accept an adulterous courtliness from the Provençal tradition. But there is a radical change in the relationship of the author to his material in the following romance, *Cligès,* a change which is retained in the subsequent romances, though in a subtler manner. Quite specifically, we have seen that the "symbolic" value of Soredamors' name, as well as that of other names in *Cligès,* was used ironically by Chrétien. [163] Their symbolic values are not meanings which Chrétien is at pains to indicate: symbolism, in these cases, is material for irony. It is rather an assumption on the basis of which he writes than the purpose of the literary process.

The basis of the "symbolic" interpretation, however, is not a meaning to be assigned to the name itself, as in the case of Soredamors: [164] it is rather the act of divination itself which is considered important:

> Le jeune homme, consterné de sa faillite au château du graal, se plonge dans l'abîme de sa propre existence et en devine le sens en devinant son nom. Ce nom, c'est lui, comme 'le neuf était Béatrice'. Par son nom, Perceval le Gallois, il entrevoit pour la première fois le fond de sa personnalité. [165]

---

[161] *Le sens de l'aventure et de l'amour...,* p. 56.

[162] *Perceval,* pp. 60-63.

[163] *Supra,* p. 108 and n. 178.

[164] Chrétien does use "meaningful" names in *Perceval,* of course, such as Blancheflor, the Orguelleus de la Lande, and the Orguelleuse de Logres. Their "symbolic" power, however, is minimal: they are rather allegorical on a very low level of allegory, and designate an obvious trait in the characters: pride, or beauty.

[165] Bezzola, *op. cit., loc. cit.,* Paul Imbs does suggest a value for the name itself: "...*Perceval le Gallois* dit assez bien la double nature du héros: en tant que *Gallois,* il est nice; *Perceval* traduit sa nature impétueuse et prime-sautière." ("Perceval et le Graal...," p. 53, n. 4). While this is not inappropriate, I would consider his *niceté* allied with his impulsiveness against the process of socialization; and therefore the name, as interpreted by Imbs, would hardly cover the essential tension in the character.

If it is the act of onomastic divination which is crucial, it must be considered in its narrative context. If this "symbolic" interpretation is juxtaposed to the text and context, it becomes untenable. Bezzola's interpretation posits Perceval's realization of his failure at the Fisher King's castle as the cause of the "divination". Chrétien conceives the relationship differently. Up to the point that Perceval "learns" his name, as I have pointed out, [166] the conversation with his cousin is rapid and catechetical. Her comments on his failure are restrained, no more than vague and as yet unjustified comments which, by themselves, are unlikely to plunge anyone into the "abyss of his existence". Before the knight states his name, the cousin sees him merely as a stranger about whose success or failure she is only moderately concerned. It is only *after* he states his name (at line 3575) that she flies into a rage and reveals the nature and extent of his failure; in fact, it is only after identifying himself that Perceval learns he has failed in any real sense. Thus for Chrétien, it is not Perceval's discovery of his failure that leads to his onomastic divination, but the revelation of his name that leads to his learning of his failure. Had Chrétien—or even any journeyman writer— wished to establish the causal relationship Bezzola describes, he could hardly have indicated it in a more obfuscating way. [167]

Let us return to the text. If Chrétien had merely written:

> Et cil qui son non ne savoit
> Devine et dit que il avoit
> Percevaus li Galois a non... (3573-5),

it would be possible to read this as a profound intuition or even a miracle. But Chrétien does not leave it at that. He comments on the "discovery", not to stress its profundity or miraculous nature, but its absurdity:

> N'il ne set s'il dit voir ou non;
> Mes il dist voir, et si nel sot. (3576 f.) [168]

The truth of Perceval's "discovery" is born out by his cousin, who thereupon recognizes him. The effect of Chrétien's stress then is to emphasize Perceval's ignorance, which is truly amazing in this circumstance. Or is it another kind of ignorance Chrétien is pointing to? Throughout the entire romance, Perceval is shown as reacting almost entirely to external stimuli—the basis of the *chastoiement* comedy. The reverse of the coin is that he does not act unless a stimulus is

---

[166] *Supra*, p. 177.

[167] As for the mother's words to Perceval, they seem to me to bear a very simple meaning in agreement with the context of down-to-earth precepts of which they form a part: *par le non conoist l'an l'ome* means no more than "you will know whether a man is noble or not, and to what level of nobility he belongs, by his name"—an interpretation in agreement also with the mother's pride in her own nobility.

[168] The stress is especially strong, since these two lines essentially repeat the sense of *"cil qui son non ne savoit"* (3573).

present. [169] The stimulus for Perceval's statement of his name has been lacking up to now: before the encounter with his cousin, no one has asked his name. [170] There have been occasions where an introduction of himself might have been in order, as with Gornemant de Goort. [171] To introduce himself without being asked directly to do so might have indicated a social presence of mind out of character with what we have seen repeatedly of that character. In this interpretation, Chrétien's "explanation" and its stylistic stress, appears as one more among the many ironies by which Perceval's social ineptness has been revealed. [172]

Frappier has warned that this kind of interpretation would be unsatisfactory "in the circumstances." [173] To a large extent, however, the "circumstances" are those of an interpretation which insists on symbolism as a prime mode of communication in the romance, at the expense of a more literal and psychological analysis. [174] There is a parallel to this paradoxical revelation of the hero's name in the immediate context. It is again the revelation of a character's name, and one which Frappier has noted as being presented with an *humour à froid*. [175] Perceval's cousin explains that the Fisher King's infirmity prevents him from hunting, and adds:

> ... quant il se viaut deporter
> Ou d'aucun deduit antremetre,

---

[169] There are three major exceptions to this: Perceval's desire to be a knight—an assumption of the whole romance; his memory of his mother's faint and desire to return to her; and his reaction to Blancheflor at night—a reaction well colored by irony.

[170] This assumes that ll. 343-60 are, as Baist and Hilka thought, an interpolation: see above, p. 125 f. and nn. 36 and 37.

[171] *Supra*, p. 151 f.

[172] As noted, this interpretation is based on the assumption that an earlier passage is an interpolation. If ll. 343-60 are retained, I would consider this another example of Chrétien's occasionally willful disregard of his fictional premises. We have seen how Cligès and Bertrand both overcome seemingly impossible obstacles (*supra*, pp. 101 ff.), and how minor narrative details are quite intentionally stage-managed to demonstrate their artificiality (*supra*, p. 98, n. 152; Chrétien will use the same technique again shortly: *infra*, pp. 188-193). The purpose here would be dual: the knight must be identified to satisfy the necessities of the plot. In doing so, Chrétien again stresses the distance of the *Gaste Forez* from normal society: a boy can grow up without even a name.

[173] "... parler d'un trait d'humour, de la galéjade d'un auteur pince-sans-rire ne serait pas du tout satisfaisant dans la circonstance..." (*Perceval*, p. 61).

[174] In a general context, Frappier has written that: "La symbolique [qui] appartenait à l'"outillage mental" du Moyen Age ... est restrainte chez lui [*i.e.*, Chrétien] par le goût de la vérité psychologique—il est surtout un peintre de caractères—et par une tournure d'esprit qui l'inclinait aux explications positives. Il n'était ni Dante ni l'auteur de la *Queste del Saint Graal.*" (*Chrétien de Troyes*, p. 21). But in discussing the revelation of Perceval's name, it is precisely Dante to whom he refers (*Perceval*, p. 62, n. 4). In fact, his analysis of Perceval's progress is basically symbolic. Referring to "la composition symbolique de l'œuvre," he states that "chaque épisode est une image synthétique d'une étape de l'existence humaine." (*Ibid.*, p. 67).

[175] *Perceval*, p. 95.

> Si se fet an une nef metre
> Et vet peschant a l'ameçon;
> Por ce li rois Peschierre a non." (3516-20)

It is a whimsical baptism, and one which, prefiguring the Perceval parallel by less than fifty lines, cannot but affect our reading of the latter. The purpose of the parallelism would seem to be to recall the similarities and contrasts between the Fisher King and Perceval which were noted previously. [176] In this particular context, the contrast is similar to that established between Perceval and his cousin: [177] Perceval, healthily seated on a sleek horse, as against the infirm Fisher King whose only sport is fishing.

If the paradox of Perceval's onomastic divination can be resolved as an irony at the expense of his *niceté,* this is not true of another paradox in this episode. After the cousin's first explosion of bitter anger at his failure and the explanation of the good that would have resulted if he had asked the question, she adds:

> "Por le pechié, ce saches tu,
> De ta mere t'est avenu;
> Qu'ele est morte de duel de toi." (3593-5)

The matter quickly drops out of sight. She identifies herself as his cousin, and equates his failure to ask the proper question with her sorrow for the dead knight and for the death of Perceval's mother. When Perceval has an opportunity to speak again, he does not refer to the matter either. Therefore, the suggestion of a relationship between his disregard of his mother's faint and his failure at the castle of the Fisher King is merely a passing glance at an idea which will be taken up again later. We will postpone considering this idea until it returns in the Hermit Episode. [178] For the moment, we may simply note how strange and paradoxical it is. Chrétien's repeated ironies and comic developments at the expense of Perceval's basic *niceté* and at his attempts to correct it have accustomed us to seeing his actions as caused by simple psychological principles. The introduction of the notion of sin here is perfectly appropriate to the occasion on which Perceval learns that he caused his mother's death by disregarding her faint. What seems to have no connection with the romance up to now is the notion that this sin caused his silence in the castle of the Fisher King.

It is all the more strange since we are immediately returned to the operation of familiar psychological principles. Faced with his cousin grieving over her dead knight, Perceval invites her to accompany him in words that are "violent, almost insulting": [179]

> "Que cist* ne vos vaudra mes rien   *the dead knight
> Qui ci gist morz, jel vos plevis:

---

[176] *Supra,* p. 174.
[177] *Supra,* p. 176 f.
[178] *Infra,* pp. 226 ff.
[179] Frappier, *Perceval,* p. 63.

'Les morz as morz, les vis as vis.'
Alons an moi et vos ansanble.
De vos grant folie me sanble
Que ci sole gueitiez cest mort..." (3628-33)

The use of a popular proverb is hardly ironically intended by the
speaker, but Chrétien's intention in putting it in Perceval's mouth is clear:
the harsh lack of awareness of another's grief, or the inability to deal
with it, the words that though perhaps uttered with a kindly intention
leave his lips with a brutality destructive of whatever kindliness may
have been intended—the situation and results are familiar: they were
last seen at the beginning of the Fisher King Episode. Perceval the
mal sené, nice et bestïaus, the Perceval of the beginning has not been
remade into a new man.

The Orguelleus de la Lande

Leaving his cousin grieving over her dead knight, Perceval rides
until he finds ... another grieving lady. Before we overhear her *complainte,* however, we are given a dual portrait of decrepitude. First the
horse: [180] it is so skinny it shivers as if sick, its ears hang low, it has
nothing to offer the waiting dogs but leather and entrails, for nothing
but skin is left on its bones. The lady who rides this nag is in just
as sorry a state. Though she would have been elegant and beautiful in
better circumstances, her dress is everywhere torn, and her breasts
protrude through the tears. The flesh which peers through among the
knots and coarse sewing which hold the rags together is cracked and
burned from heat, dryness, and frost. Her tears flow down to her
knees, and as Perceval approaches, she draws her clothing together,
only to make it open in a hundred places as she closes one.... The
point of the dyptich is obvious: the lady has been reduced to the level
of the animal she rides. [181] It also recalls—by opposites—the description of Perceval's well-fed and groomed mount at the beginning of the
previous episode. Like his cousin, this damsel also is weeping; he is
responsible for both their sorrows. Both episodes represent a shock
for the hero as he learns the harsh results his "innocent" actions have
had. One major difference between them is that there was nothing he
could do to remedy his cousin's grief. Here, he will be able to resolve
a conflict.

As soon as she has finished her *complainte,* Perceval rides up to
the lady and addresses her: "Bele, Deus vos saut!" (3778). Considering
her condition, being addressed as *Bele* amounts to a cruel irony; as she

---

[180] In fact, we are not even aware of the rider until the description of the
horse is complete:

Percevaus la santele va
Toz uns esclos tant qu'il trova
Un palefroi et megre et las... etc. (3691-3)

[181] There is no moral value in this degeneration: it is entirely a matter of
the lady's situation.

says: "[je] n'i ai mie droit" (3784). Once again, Perceval's attempt to
be polite has miscarried; not understanding why his polite greeting is
rejected, he blushes with shame and disclaims ever having seen or
harmed her:

> "Si as", fet ele, "que je sui
> Tant cheitive et tant ai d'enui
> Que nus ne me doit saluer;
> D'angoisse me covient suer
> Quant nus m'areste ne esgarde." (3791-5) [182]

Perceval excuses himself; such was not his intention. But he does not
take the hint. Instead, he persists in speaking to her, insisting on her
appearance and asking for her sad story:

> "... des que je vos oi veüe
> Si antreprise et povre et nue,
> Ja mes joie an mon cuer n'eüsse,
> Se la verité n'an seüsse
> Queus avanture vos demainne
> An tel dolor et an tel painne." (3801-6)

Perceval's interview with his cousin does seem to have taught him to
follow his curiosity ... but again, he does so in the wrong circumstances.

What was a hint before is now explicitly stated: she urges him to
leave in terms ambiguous enough to be taken either as a plea for her
modesty or a warning for his safety. [183] Perceval takes the speech
entirely as a warning of imminent danger and disregards her situation:

> "Ice" fet il, "vuel je savoir
> Por quel peor, por quel menace
> Je fuirai quant nus ne me chace." (3812-4)

We learn that her knight, the Orguelleus de la Lande, fights anyone
who stops to talk to her, and has in fact just killed a man (the knight
over whom Perceval's cousin was weeping):

> "Mes il conte einçois a chascun
> Por quoi il m'a an tel vilté
> Et mise an tel cheitiveté." (3828-30)

---

[182] The lady is unlikely to recognize Perceval. When she saw him previously,
he was still in Welsh garb; now he is knightly armor. At the most, Chrétien
may be teasing the reader with ambiguity. Cf. Paul Salmon, "Ignorance and
Awareness of Identity in Hartmann and Wolfram. An element of Dramatic
Irony," *Beiträge zur Geschichte der deutschen Sprache und Literatur*, LXXXII
(1960), 95-115; p. 105. In spite of Salmon's careful analysis of parallel scenes
in Chrétien and the German authors who used his stories, his article is without
value for Chrétien studies: he totally disregards the place of a given scene
within Chrétien's romance, and therefore has no comprehension of Chrétien's
intention in that scene.

[183]   "Ha! sire", fet ele, "merci!
> Teisiez vos et fuiiez de ci,
> Si me leissiez an pes ester.
> Pechiez vos fet ci arester;
> Mes fuiiez, si feroiz savoir." (3807-11)

Sure enough, as soon as she finishes these lines, out rides the Orguelleus

> ... come une foudre
> Par le sablon et par la poudre... (3833 f.),

shouting a grandiloquent speech of threats ... ending on a bump:

> "Voir, mar i arestas
> Tu qui lez la pucele estas!
> Saches que ta fins est venue
> Por ce que tu l'as retenue
> Ne arestee un tot seul pas.
> Mes je ne t'occiroie pas
> Tant que je t'eüsse retret
> Por quel chose et por quel mesfet
> Je la faz vivre a si grant honte;
> Mes ore antant, s'orras le conte." (3835-44)

Enough strange adventures have intervened since Perceval's first adventure outside the *Gaste Forez* to excuse any reader who has not recognized the couple up to this point. On the other hand, the lady's *complainte* indicated clearly enough that her condition was forced on her by a knight for a fault she did not commit. This, together with the description of her condition and the horse's, might suggest to the retentive reader the plan outlined by the Orguelleus: that her horse would not eat or be cared for, and her clothes not changed, until he wreaked his revenge on the *vaslet galois*. [184] Perhaps it is best to conclude that the author is indulging in the not unfamiliar pastime of teasing the reader.

In any case, there is no doubt that both we and Perceval recognize who is meant when the knight speaks of the *vaslez galois* (3850) six lines after he begins the tale of the damsel he had left unguarded in a tent. From here to the end of the speech some forty lines later, as the knight pungently describes and comments on a scene he did not see, the situation is one of dramatic irony. The irony cuts both ways: the knight's jealous rage makes him ridiculous, especially since we know it is without foundation. But he was already subjected to this irony when he returned to the tent. Perceval, who endures the tirade wordlessly, is also ridiculed here. The Orguelleus says that he does not care whether the kiss was given or stolen; the important thing is what followed the kiss:

> "Oïl, ce ne crerroit ja nus
> Qu'il la beisast sanz feire plus;
> Que l'une l'autre chose atret:
> Qui beise fame, et plus n'i fet,
> Des qu'il sont seul a seul andui,
> Dons cuit je qu'il remaint au lui.
> Fame qui sa boche abandone
> Le soreplus de legier done..." etc. (3857-64)

---

184 *Supra*, p. 134 f.

It is not enough to note that this reads like much medieval anti-feminist literature, [185] or that jealousy is not courtly. As when a movie camera is focused on the listener rather than the speaker, so our attention here should also be on Perceval. He is being ridiculed, though the Orguelleus is unaware of this, and ridiculed more deeply than the Orguelleus could realize even if he knew that his listener is the *vaslet galois*. Though the effect of the episode as a whole may be to impart to Perceval a sense of responsibility for his acts and the idea that his rights are limited by those of others, [186] the immediate effect of the Orguelleus' speech is more likely to suggest to Perceval that in the eyes of others, his behavior with the Tent Maiden can appear ludicrous because incomplete. But more important than the Tent Maiden may be the memory of Blancheflor; was there then something other than kisses and caresses that might have been appropriate when she spent the night in bed with him? [187] If the thought does not occur to Perceval, it may well occur to the reader.

The Orguelleus is not only passionately jealous, he also has an excellent memory. Not only did the intruder take a ring from her finger besides "everything else",

> Mes ainz but et manja assez
> D'un fort vin et de trois pastez
> Que je me feisoie estoiier..." (3881-3)

There is nothing inherently absurd about an exact memory, but the recall of infinitesimal and unimportant detail in the course of such passion is as ridiculous as it is true to life. The knight, however, is coming to the end of his tirade. His *amie*, as Perceval can see, has received a *cortois loiier* (3884) for her fault. She will remain as ill-clothed and badly mounted until he finds the man who "forced" her,

> "Et mort et la teste tranchiee." (3898)

Perceval is now in the situation in which Gauvain will find himself more than once: he is told that his interlocutor has sworn to kill him, but the latter does not know he is speaking to his intended victim. Perceval, it must be said, does not come off badly in his answer. He starts with irony (the girl has done her *penitance* [3902], ironic since she committed no sin), identifies himself as the one who kissed her, took the ring by force (but did nothing else), and corrects the Orguelleus on one further matter:

> "Et si manjai, je vos afi,
> Des trois pastez un et demi
> Et del vin bui tant con je vos:
> De ce ne fis je pas que fos." (3907-10) [188]

---

185 Hilka, note to l. 3860.
186 Frappier, *Perceval*, p. 64.
187 The theme will be continued later: see below, pp. 188 ff.
188 Food in this romance is almost always the sign of someone's ridicule; *supra*, pp. 135 and n. 55, 174 f.

This identification results in battle, which quickly leads to the Orguelleus' plea for mercy. Perceval has made progress indeed, for he now dispenses a justice as poetic as it is moral:

> "Je n'avrai ja merci de toi
> Jusque tu l'aies de t'amie..." (3938 f.)

He has also learned how to deal with his victims. He does not first attempt to send the Orguelleus back to his cousin, whose knight he killed: he will go to Arthur's court. Nevertheless, Chrétien affirms the permanence of his hero's character by portraying him as still consciously ruling his behavior according to Gornemant's precepts:

> Et cil qui n'onques n'oblia
> Le prodome, qui li pria
> Que ja chevalier n'oceïst
> Puis que merci li requeïst... (3933-6),

sends the Orguelleus and his *amie* to Arthur's court.

Arthur's Court

Perceval and the courtly pair separate in the forest, and it is the latter we follow as they make their way to Arthur's court. Their submission increases the honor both of the King and of the knight, Perceval. The Orguelleus, of course, is not the first to fulfill this function. Yonet, after the Red Knight Episode; Anguingueron and Clamadeu, after being beaten on the field of battle; all have come to the court with the same effect. The repeated reports of the unknown knight in red armor and his victories have endowed him with a martial reputation which is the wonder and admiration of the court. Who can this knight be, asks Gauvain (in his first appearance in the romance), who conquered a knight as good as the Orguelleus? (4088-90). Though no one knows his identity—Arthur must answer Gauvain's question with the helpless paradox: I don't know him, but I saw him— [189] his actual arrival in court is preceded by the elaboration of a *persona* based entirely on his martial exploits.

Without denying the importance or value of these, it must be emphasized that the court knows only one aspect of Perceval's person: the most successful one. The court is unaware of his failure at the castle of the Fisher King; it has not been privy to the slow process of development by which this knight has obtained at least a "presence" oi knighthood, nor to the comedies to which his observance of Gornemant's precepts have led. It has not been privileged to see even his martial actions through the author's style of indirection and comedy. The court is informed only of the most flattering selection of facts: the reader sees more deeply into the hero's mind and emotions.

---

[189]   "Biaus niés, je ne le conois mie",
          Fet li rois, "et si l'ai veü..." (4096 f.)

This does not mean that Perceval would not be accepted by the court if it knew him better. Arthur's court is not interested in character. It includes, after all, those "deux importuns, deux échantillons d'une chevalerie imparfaite, Sagremor, la brusquerie irascible et la brutalité, Keu, la vantardise et l'éternelle envie." [190] It has also been shown in earlier romances to be, not so much the goal of Chrétien's heroes, as a circle which accepts him with imperfections and which he must leave to expiate an error and, perhaps, to prove himself. When Erec and Yvain return to the court after their lacks have been exposed and after their series of personal adventures, it is also only after they have surpassed certain dangers of the courtliness associated with Arthur in extraordinary adventures. Erec vanquishes the danger of an asocial, solitary love, not only in his own life, but in the dangerously magic circle of the Joie de la Cour orchard. Yvain, after a series of adventures in which his rescues of helpless ladies would certainly suffice to rehabilitate him at the level he occupied at court before the arrival of Laudine's messenger, achieves the liberation of hundreds of maidens enslaved at the Château de Pesme Aventure in an episode whose realism—a trait not notably associated with Arthur's court—is markedly emphasized. Furthermore, in the case of Yvain, the return to Arthur's court is not the conclusion of the tale. The hero's personal *avanture* must find its own outcome away from that court in the reality of Yvain's relationship to his wife. [191]

Arthur's court is not so much a final goal as the representative of social norms which, considering the behavior of Sagremor and Keu, as well as the early acceptance of flawed knights such as Erec and Yvain, are not terribly stringent. Within Chrétien's fictional world, it performs the function of ratifying, not the extraordinary hero, though it admires and embraces him, but that level of social acceptability without which society could not survive.

This judgment, as any social judgment of the sort, is superficial. This is not meant pejoratively, but simply in the sense that the court is concerned with external matters: the functioning of a man, not his inner being; his capability and reputation as a knight, not the morality of his knighthood; [192] his politeness, not the state of his character or soul. [193] Its acceptance ratifies normative standards which are fairly elastic, not greatness of achievement or inner development.

---

[190] Frappier, *Perceval,* p. 71; the context is Perceval's combat with these two.

[191] In this connection, see Emmel's remarks on the establishment of a sphere different from Arthur's court but whose challenges reach beyond that court: *Formprobleme...,* p. 38 f.

[192] Arthur was not concerned about the manner in which the Red Knight was killed, only the fact that his enemy was destroyed, his wife avenged, and his cup returned. He even wished to retain the *vaslet galois* at court; *supra,* p. 146.

[193] Considering Keu's manners, even politeness is not so necessary. That he is retained at court (and even highly valued by Arthur in the *Lancelot*) in spite of resentment at his manners and sarcasm is further evidence that the Arthurian court represents less an ideal than a social norm.

It is therefore not paradoxical to say that Perceval can obtain acceptance, recognition, even admiration from the court and still carry within himself the essential wildness of his beginnings. Chrétien has dwelt on this inner permanence throughout the romance, especially when the glory of knightly victory might lend the progress of the hero too high a gloss.

Is this view of Perceval and the court reflected in the episode which ends in what we may ironically refer to as his courtly apotheosis? I think the note of delightful superficiality is struck very quickly, with the summer advent of snow. Frappier has pointed out that this is no blunder on Chrétien's part, that he is perfectly aware of its abnormality, and points to the author's attempt to parry objections by the quietly humorous explanation:

> Au matin ot mout bien negié;
> Que froide estoit *mout* la contree. (4162 f.),

with its *mout* strongly marked by "la coupe du vers," [194] and, we may add, by the fact that it is a repetition. I would only quarrel with the idea that Chrétien wished to "parry objections," which seems to imply helplessness before given source materials. Of course, Chrétien wanted to work in the little episode of blood-drops on the snow, but it seems to me that he uses the meteorological absurdity as a kind of off-hand wink to the reader which we have seen before. He stresses the absurdity of what he states as a fact with a straight face, by surrounding the given "fact" with incongruities. It would not have been difficult, for example, to write a few lines on a sudden and unusual drop in temperature during the night, accompanied by a few snow flurries, to attenuate the "fact" of snow. But Chrétien's intention is not to reconcile his story with a naturalistic mimesis: on the contrary, he underlines his refusal to do so and thereby suggests we watch the scene with an eye to further wit and incongruity. Bertrand climbed an unscalable wall without difficulty; snow has fallen three or four weeks after Pentecost ... just after the description of the court packing up its tents: we may observe a scene rich in suggestive ambiguities.

Into the snow-covered field, early one summer morning, where Arthur's court is camped, rides our hero looking for *avanture et chevalerie* (4167). But before arriving at the tents, Perceval catches sight of a flight of wild geese blinded by the snow. He hears them too, for they are calling loudly: a falcon is pursuing them. The falcon attacks one goose which has become separated from the flock, strikes her so that she falls to the ground ... and then flies off, leaving his prey on the snow. A trained falcon, taught to leave its prey for its master? Chrétien does not say so. Instead, he explains in a manner as absurd as his explanation of the summer snow, that it was too early in the morning!

> Mes trop fu main, si s'an parti... (4182)

---

[194] *Perceval*, p. 68.

An odd bird indeed: not too early to find and attack a prey, but too early for further action... It is also too early to understand the point Chrétien is making; we will return to it. By the time Perceval arrives at the spot where the goose fell, she has already flown off: the falcon's attack was not only without issue, it was also ineffectual. The goose was slightly wounded on the neck, no more, shed three drops of blood on the snow, and flew off again.

Perceval falls into a trance at the sight, a trance Chrétien explains by a pretty allegory in the form of three variations on the theme of the colors red and white which recall Blancheflor's face:

> ... li sans et la nois ansanble
> La fresche color li resanble
> Qui ert an la face s'amie,
> Si panse tant que il s'oblie;
>
> Qu'autresi estoit an son vis
> Li vermauz sor le blanc assis
> Con cez trois gotes de sanc furent
> Qui sor la blanche noif parurent.
>
> An l'esgarder que il feisoit
> Li ert avis, tant li pleisoit,
> Qu'il veïst la color novele
> De la face s'amie bele. (4199-4210)

The main technique is the interweaving of verbal and motif repetitions: *sans, vermauz, sanc*; *nois, blanc, blanche noif*; *color, color novele*; *face s'amie, an son vis, face s'amie bele*; *li resanble, Si panse tant que il s'oblie, A l'esgarder*. It is a lovely lyric passage ... but we have seen Chrétien use such markedly lyric techniques with ironic intent. That this scene opened with two paradoxes may indicate another such intent.

This is reminiscent, of course, of the troubadour theme of the *amor de lonh*: Perceval is thinking of a distant damsel. It has also been suggested that there is a specific allegorical relationship between the goose and Blancheflor. [195] This is certainly in keeping with the situation and the context: when has the sight of a free-flying bird not filled a yearning man with thoughts of reunion? If this is so, however, the allegory must be completed: it will not do to assign a particular role to the goose who flies away, and disregard the falcon. If the victim is Blancheflor, the falcon, who slightly wounds the goose in the neck but leaves before doing her real damage, is Perceval, who left a tempting, seductive, and perhaps willing Blancheflor without doing her any damage either.

This would explain Chrétien's curiously ambiguous choice of words in describing the departure of the falcon:

> Mes trop fu main, si s'an parti,
> Qu'il ne s'i vost *liier* ne *joindre*. (4182 f.)

---

[195] Frappier, *Perceval*, p. 70 and n. 3. Frappier speaks of a "symbol", though the relationship is one to one and quite definite; I prefer "allegory" in such cases.

As Isidore might ask, *quomodo liier, quomodo joindre*? Nor is the suggestion isolated:

> Si l'a si ferue et hurtee
> Que contre terre l'abati. (4180 f.)
> ....
> La jante n'ot mal ne dolor,
> Qui contre terre la tenist.. (4190 f.)

As for the time of the morning, it too has meaning in the allegory. It was too early in Perceval's development for him to realize and take advantage of the opportunity offered.

Chrétien does not say that Perceval is thinking of anything other than Blancheflor's face in looking at the drops of blood on the snow. He supplies a fleeting hint of allegory and some suggestive vocabulary reminiscent of the erotic suggestiveness he has used in earlier episodes: those of the Tent Maiden, the night with Blancheflor, and the two commentaries of the Orguelleus de la Lande, where the suggestiveness of recounted events was forced to a "natural" though false conclusion. Not surprisingly, the similarity of technique in these episodes parallels their narrative function. In each case, the hero has been seen in a situation related to love, but from a different point of view: a girl to whom he is not attracted, another to whose charming wiles he succumbs, and a jealous lover unable to believe in the existence of such innocence in another man. While the identity of theme and similarity of technique seem to me undeniable, a difficulty arises as to their purpose at this point: is Chrétien suggesting that in addition to thinking about Blancheflor's face, Perceval is also evaluating his actions (and lack of action) with her? I find no evidence to this point in the text. What can be asserted confidently is that whether Perceval is aware of his past history or not at this moment, it should be present in the reader's mind as an ironic juxtaposition to the troubadour theme of *amor de lonh*.

The extensive ramifications of this *sanblance* (4198) occupy Perceval the early morning long:

> Percevaus sor les gotes muse,
> Tote la matinee i use... (4211 f.),

immobile, still on his horse, leaning on his lance. He has, in fact, fallen into a familiar state: he is *pansif*. In various forms, the word is used eleven times in this scene. [196] To the rest of the world, however, he seems merely to be asleep:

> Tot la matinee i use,
> Tant que fors des tantes issirent
> Escuiier, qui muser le virent,
> Si cuiderent qu'il *someillast*. (4212-5)

---

[196] Ll. 4202, 4262, 4356, 4361, 4363, 4367, 4425, 4430, 4446, 4447, 4458.

Sagremor the Unruly is up early, and asks the squires why they are standing in front of the King's tent so early:

> "Sire", font il, "fors de cest ost
> Avons veü un chevalier
> Qui *somoille* sor son destrier." (4224-6)

Straightaway, Sagremor runs to the King and wakes him with the words:

> "Sire", fet il, "la fors *somoille*
> Uns chevaliers an cele lande." (4232 f.)

This little scene (4213-35) has two main functions. The first is narrative: Sagremor obtains permission to bring back the "sleeping" knight, which leads to the first combat. The second is to contrast two views of Perceval. In his own terms (those Chrétien uses to describe him), he is absorbed in ethereal thought; to the outside world, he is asleep. [197] At first, this reductive view seems to be an irony at the expense of Sagremor and the squires.

It also cuts the other way. The Sagremor by-play also brings in Arthur, who is literally asleep. Arthur and his sleep are immediately juxtaposed to Perceval and his trance: The squires saw Perceval,

> Si cuiderent qu'il someillast.
> Einçois que li rois s'esveillast,
> Qui ancor dormoit an son tré... (4215-8),

Sagremor came up. That Arthur is literally asleep, or merely in a near-somnolent state, is not infrequent: that is how he first appears in this romance. [198] That Perceval now finds himself in a similar state does indicate a progress in his education, of a sort, but it leaves him open to new forms of irony and comedy. The state of inattention to the surrounding world may be admirable in the mystic united with the object of his contemplation, but it is also one of the basic situations of comedy. Arthur was at least tinged with irony in his first encounter with Perceval. In a closer parallel, Lancelot, also absorbed in thoughts of love, came to an unmistakably comic and wet end. Now Perceval is discovered in the same state, and two other knights play the same role he played *vis-à-vis* Arthur in the earlier scene. One after the other, Sagremor and Keu come to disturb the knight in his *panser*. Not being heroes of the romance, they are less fortunate than he and suffer discomfiture.

Not only the basic assumption, but the technique of the scene strongly resembles the *Lancelot* parallel. Lancelot was addressed repeatedly by the knight guarding the river; so Perceval is addressed

---

[197] Cf. the similar juxtaposition of different registers of meaning and value in the scene of Fénice's "martyrdom", *supra*, p. 92 and n. 140.

[198] *Supra*, p. 137 f. Cf. the beginning of Yvain, where Arthur, seduced by Guenièvre, breaks with the traditional observance of Pentecost: he remained so long with the Queen *Qu'il s'oblia et andormi* (*Yvain*, 52).

repeatedly by the two knights. The warnings were unheeded by Lancelot; so Perceval disregards, or does not hear, the summons of the two knights. The major difference is that Lancelot did not "wake up" until his opponent knocked him into the river. Perceval is spared this indignity—he comes to each time, just as Sagremor and Keu rush at him with their lances—but this only makes him subject to a different form of humor. Lancelot, once off his horse and in the water, realizes that something has happened to him; the awakening is comic, but it is an awakening. Perceval, though momentarily conscious enough to defend himself, plunges right back into his abstraction without a word or glance for the fallen knights, returning to the same spot and the same position. After Sagremor has been disposed of—his horse returns riderless toward the tents, just in time to greet those whose were getting up—it is Keu's turn:

> Armez est et monte et va s'an
> A celui qui tant antandoit
> As trois gotes qu'il esgardoit,
> Qu'il n'avoit d'autre chose soing. (4290-3)

The automatism is stressed even more after Keu's defeat. The seneschal's collar-bone is dislocated and his right arm broken. His horse, like Sagremor's, returns to the tents without a rider, the court finds Keu in a faint and believes him dead.

> Lors comença uns diaus si forz
> Que sor lui firent tuit et totes.
> Et Percevaus sor les trois gotes
> Se rapoia desor sa lance... (4326-9)

And again later, when Gauvain takes his turn, he finds Perceval in the same position:

> [Gauvain] vint au chevalier tot droit,
> Qui sor sa lance ert apoiiez,
> N'ancor n'estoit pas enuiiez
> De son pansé, que mout li plot. (4422-5)

The basic pattern is clear: absorption, interruption, disposal of the interruption with minimal attention (Perceval remains totally unaware of the identity of his opponents), and the automatic return to absorption. The mechanical quality of this pattern is underlined by another repeated pattern beyond Perceval's focus of attention of which he remains totally unaware: the horse of the wounded knight returns to the tents without its rider, and the court's reaction is given: Keu's sarcasm when Sagremor's mount returns alone, the court's sorrow when Keu is dismounted and wounded. To all this, Perceval pays no attention whatever: he is not even aware any of it is happening. [199]

It is generally said that Gauvain succeeds where others failed because of his great courtesy to the pensive knight. Chrétien also

---

[199] See the quotation from Bergson, *supra,* p. 122, n. 27.

presents another cause. The automatism is determined by an external cause, and can be broken only by the removal of that external cause:

> Et neporquant li solauz ot
> Deus des gotes del sanc remises,
> Qui sor la noif furent assise,
> Et la tierce aloit remetant;

(and Chrétien adds with mock seriousness:)

> Por ce ne pansoit mie tant
> Li chevaliers come il ot fet. (4426-31)

The automatism is complete: Perceval remains fixed in his abstraction until its external cause is removed. Were the sky clouded, and the sun less strong, who knows but that Gauvain might have suffered the fate of the first two messengers? [200]

After the summer snow, after the falcon which leaves its prey because it is too early in the morning, this is the third mock-serious explanation in the scene. Surely these signposts planted by the author around Perceval's distraction indicate the attitude he wishes to communicate to the reader. That the hero is plunged in the "conceptions les plus éthérées de l'amour courtois," [201] *soit!,* but this does not necessarily force us to plunge in after him. These signposts as well as our knowledge of the author's attitude toward the state of distraction, place the reader at an aesthetic distance which precludes identification with the hero or acceptance of his values, and demands instead observation and judgment while suggesting laughter.

Perceval is not the only source of entertainment in this episode. That antithetical pair, Keu and Gauvain, also provide amusement. When Sagremor's horse returns without its master, Keu

> S'an gabe et dit au roi: "Biaus sire,
> Veez con Sagremors revient!
> Par le frain le chevalier tient,
> Si l'an amainne maugre suen." (4276-9) [202]

The *gab* angers the King, and he tells Keu to pit himself against the knight in the field:

> ... et si verromes
> Con vos le feroiz miauz de lui." (4282 f.)

The seneschal answers with mock submission:

> "Sire", fet Keus, "mout liez an sui
> Quant il vos plest que je i aille..." (4284 f.),

---

[200] In view of the last passage quoted, to say that Perceval here goes beyond the realm of sensory appearances (Frappier, *Perceval,* p. 70), while literally true (he is thinking of a person not physically present), is misleading if it suggests freedom from the world of the senses.

[201] *Ibid.,* p. 69.

[202] The first sentence is *ironia;* the second is a combination of *ironia* and *significatio per consequentiam.*

thus turning the tables on Arthur, who earlier had taken Keu at the literal meaning of his words. [203] When Keu, defeated and disabled, returns to court, he hears Gauvain expostulate with the King: the knights who tried to force Perceval *de son panser* were wrong, and he offers to bring him back by force of words (4350-69).

Keu's answer proves that, if Chrétien has generally moved away from the formulaic ironies described in the school-books of his time, he is still capable of using them amply:

... "Ha! mes sire Gauvain Vos l'an amanroiz par la main Le chevalier, mes bien li poist.	ironia, significatio per consequentiam & exsuperationem;
Il iert bien fet, se il vos loist Et la baillie vos remaint.	s. per consequentiam;
Einsi an avez vos pris maint: Quant li chevaliers est lassez	s. per consequentiam;
F, il a fet d'armes assez, Lors doit prodon le don requerre Que l'an li lest aler conquerre.	ironia, s. per consequentiam;
Gauvains, çant dahez et mes cos, Se vos estes mie si fos Que l'an ne puist a vos aprandre!	asteismos;
Bien savez vos paroles vandre, Qui mout sont beles et polies.	s. per similitudinem;
Granz orguiauz et granz felenies Et grant enui li diroiz ja.	ironia, s. per consequentiam;
Maudahez et qui le cuida Et qui le cuide que j'i soie!	sarcasmos;
Certes, an un bliaut de soie Porroiz ceste besoingne feire; Ja ne vos i covandra treire Espee ne lance brisier.	s. per consequentiam;
De ce vos poëz vos prisier	ironia;
Que, se la langue ne vos faut Por dire: "Sire, Deus vos saut Et il vos doint joie et santé!" Fera il vostre volanté.	s. per consequentiam;
N'an di rien por vos anseignier; Mes bien le savroiz apleignier Si come an aplaingne le chat,	s. per similitudinem;
Si dira l'an: "Or se conbat Mes sire Gauvains fieremant."	ironia, s. per consequentiam;

(4371-4403)

It is a masterpiece of its kind, but it was not composed only for its own sake: it presents Gauvain with the necessity of answering. On the one hand, some defense or self-assertiveness is required; on the other,

---

[203] *Supra*, p. 142.

Gauvain's courtesy cannot allow him to indulge in sarcasm as harsh as Keu's. His first words are a mildly complaining understatement:

> "Ha! sire Keus, plus belemant"
> Fet il, "le me poïssiez dire.

This is followed by admirable psychological perception which also contains an *ad hominem* argument:

> "Cuidiez vos or vangier vostre ire
> Et vostre mautalant a moi?"

His courteous mildness next clothes the irony of a disdainfully suggested comparison:

> "Je l'an amanrai, par ma foi,
> Se j'onques puis, biaus douz amis,   ironia
> Ja n'an avrai le braz maumis,
> Et sanz chenole desloiier,   s. per consequentiam
> Que je n'aim mie tel loiier."   s. per similitudinem
>
> (4404-12)

Throughout, of course, Gauvain has remained superficially polite ("sire Keu," "biaus douz amis") and appropriately modest ("Se j'onques puis"); he has also not denied the essence of Keu's accusation, that he prefers using words to fighting with arms.

In this answer, courtesy serves to adapt disparagement to Gauvain's literary personality. Both are continued as he addresses Perceval, but the courtesy is addressed to his interlocutor, the disparagement refers to others; that they are not present permits him to use stronger words than he did directly to Keu. Not only does Gauvain compliment Perceval on his *panser*—it was not *vilain* at all, but *mout cortois et douz* (4458 f.)—, he harshly criticizes those who disturbed the pensive knights as *fos et estouz* (4460), thus adding insult to their substantial injuries. When the time comes, Gauvain raises the question of Perceval's accompanying him to court with politic caution:

> "Mes or desir mout et covoit
> A savoir que vos voldroiz feire.
> Au roi, s'il ne vos doit despleire,
> Vos manroie mout volantiers." (4462-5)

Keu, however unpleasant, was not entirely wrong in his suggestion that Gauvain is expert in "selling" *paroles beles et polies*. His manners and speech are courteous, no doubt, but also insinuatingly flattering. They are also effective. Perceval accedes to Gauvain's invitation:

> "Par foi,
> Donc irai je, car il est droiz,
> Volantiers la ou vos voldroiz,
> Et mout m'an ferai or plus cointes
> De ce que je sui vostre acointes." (4496-4500)

After his mother, after Gornemant de Goort, Perceval has found a third instructor, this time in the field of manners and fine speech.

Cointe has such meanings as "courtly, educated, proper;" it can also connote "affected, frivolous". [204] Linker, in his translation, has straddled the ambiguity in exemplary fashion: "... I shall now act much more agreeable because I am your acquaintance." [205]

Chrétien gives Keu one last opportunity to reaffirm his view of Gauvain. As Arthur's nephew and Perceval walk toward the tents, the seneschal bitterly and ironically addresses the King:

> "Ore an a le pris et l'enor
> Mes sire Gauvains, vostre niés.
> Mout fu or perilleuse et griés
> La bataille, se je ne mant;
> Que tot ausi heitieemant
> S'an retorne come il i mut,
> Qu'onques d'autrui cop n'i recut,
> N'autres de lui cop n'i santi;
> Neïs de mot nel desmanti,
> S'est droiz que los et pris an et
> Et que l'an die qu'il a fet
> Ce don nos autre ne poïmes
> Venir a chief, et s'i meïmes
> Toz noz pooirs et noz esforz." (4518-31)

There is something both pitiable and ridiculous about this speech. Nevertheless, Keu is quite right on the matter of Gauvain's painless victory which required neither battle nor verbal contradiction. In a society in which prowess at arms was still a major virtue, [206] this is not a consideration without weight. That Keu is wrong-headed and malicious should not lead us to the conclusion that his sarcastic speeches contain no truth at all. Chrétien invites us to think on this:

> Einsi dist Keus, fust a droiz ou torz,
> Sa volanté si come il siaut. (4532 f.)

Our opinion of Gauvain is important at this point not for his sake—there will be ample opportunity later for the author to demonstrate what Gauvain is made of—but in relation to Perceval. He has now learned the externals of knighthood, how to fight according to the rules, and how to restrain his impulses so as to be at least acceptable socially. The next stage, in Chrétien's fictional world, is to become not just a knight, but a courtly knight. One pattern which can be imitated is that of Gauvain, the embodiment of certain aspects of courtliness. Another pattern might be such a knight as Yvain who, at the end of his adventures, is both the equal of Gauvain and quite different from

---

[204] Godefroy includes "bien soignié, élégant, coquet;" as a substantive, *cointe* can mean "un beau, un élégant tout plein de lui-même.... Dans un sens défavorable, syn. de malicieux."

[205] *The Story of the Grail,* p. 94.

[206] Kellermann considers *fortitudo* still the major virtue in Arthurian society (*Aufbaustil und Weltbild...,* pp. 170-2); see also Painter, *French Chivalry...,* p. 29.

him. [207] But it is Gauvain Perceval has met, and it is Gauvain he seems set on imitating. Chrétien criticizes neither the choice nor the person directly: he merely suggests a doubt as to Gauvain's character and value.

Before arriving at court with Perceval and his new mentor, we should note that it is during their conversation that our hero learns he has fulfilled his vow to avenge *la pucele qui rist,* and who was slapped for her prophecy by Keu. This vow has been kept constantly in our minds throughout the story as the conquering hero sent one messenger after another to court to reiterate his pledge. Yonet, Anguingueron, Clamadeu, and the Orguelleus de la Lande, have all performed this role. Each of these was the occasion for a double exposition of the vow: [208] first Perceval gave the messenger the oath, then the knight reported it in court. Thus, the vow has been repeated seven times since Perceval's first visit to Arthur's court. In addition, the vow was stressed by associated developments such as the King's repeated criticism of Keu, the fool's prophecy, and Clamadeu's visit to the *pucele* herself. I can think of no other event in Chrétien's work which receives so continuous and emphatic a build-up.

Yet the actual fulfillment of the oath is anti-climactic. Perceval disposes of Keu without being aware of it. When Gauvain informs him that he has beaten and wounded the seneschal, the revelation is commented on matter-of-factly:

> "Donc ai je bien" fet il, "vangiee
> La pucele que il feri." (4476 f.)

This remark is not even written for its own sake: it is the clue by which Gauvain recognizes his interlocutor as the knight Arthur has been searching for. The suppression of a major reaction here is not a postponement for a more impressive display in the court itself: Perceval meets the maiden, embraces her, and thanks her in the space of seven lines (4596-4603). Nor can this anti-climax be attributed to the mere fact that Perceval and Keu, when they fight, do not know each other's identity. Chrétien was able to use a similar lack of recognition at the end of *Yvain* as a means of intensifying and dramatizing the battle. The difference is that Perceval is not only unaware of his opponent's identity: he is not interested in the opponent or the battle itself. His abstraction is far more interesting to him than the identity of his attacker(s), and he loses part of his triumph because of that distraction.

---

[207] See Frappier's fine pages on "La Chevalerie," *Yvain,* pp. 99-106. The only reservation I would have on his treatment is the tendency to idealize the hero, especially in religious terms: he is called "presque un saint de la chevalerie" (p. 101), and even compared to "une sorte de Messie, non pas céleste mais terrestre..." (p. 104).

[208] Except for Anguingueron: we are only told he delivered the message, but do not hear it delivered: ll. 2759 ff.

It is not only this particular triumph that is denied Perceval. His acceptance at court is described briefly and almost meagerly. From the viewpoint of stylistic emphasis, its high point is the speech by which Gauvain introduces the newly clothed hero:

> "Sire, sire, je vos amain"
> Fet messire Gauvains au roi,
> "Celui que vos, si con je croi,
> Veïssiez mout tres volantiers,
> Passé a quinze jors antiers:
> C'est cil don vos tant parliiez,
> C'est cil que querant aliiez.
> Je le vos bail, veez le ci." (4546-4558)

A short speech, but packed with a rhetoric whose accompanying gestures are as obvious as they are grandiose: the repeated title of the first line; the full, disjunctive line of suspense, instead of the usual *fet il*, ponderous with the two titles flanking Gauvain's name; the note of humility ("as I believe"); the double and synonymous emphasis of *mout tres*; the parallelistic structures marked beginning (*C'est cil...*) and end (the rich rhymes in *-liiez*); and the final gesture of the arm, as the speaker steps aside to reveal the subject of his brief oration; the whole rhetorical ... and pompous! Pomposity is the last of Chrétien's faults; the quality is entirely Gauvain's. The speech serves at least as much to characterize Gauvain as to introduce Perceval.

In addition, there are Arthur's welcoming speech (of refreshing directness after Gauvain's), in which he congratulates Perceval for having fulfilled the prophecies of the maiden and fool; the arrival of the Queen, and an exchange between her and Perceval in which he reveals a sudden adeptness in courtly compliments (Gauvain's influence works quickly); and the brief greeting with the *pucele qui rist*. The whole, from the introduction to Arthur up to the arrival of the Hideous Damsel, occupies no more than seventy lines. [209]

To any reader who recalls the sumptuous literary descriptions of the celebrations in honor of Erec and Yvain at the same point in their respective stories, this meagerness is surprising. It is not just a matter of counting lines. Though the more than 140 lines in which Chrétien described the *Yvain* parallel are double the length of the present scene, this is a very crude yardstick. It is the content of the scenes that matters. In *Yvain*, Arthur's entire court is greeted with an extensive display of hospitality: the streets are decorated with silken hangings, covered by rugs, and shaded by curtains; church bells, horns, and trumpets sound; where young girls greet him, they are accompanied by flutes, fiddles, and drums; Laudine, regally dressed, greets the King, and Gauvain, the sun, *s'acointe* with Lunete, the moon, who tells him the story of Yvain's "conquest" of Laudine. And the others of the two courts follow the example of the sun and the moon by enjoying the

---

[209] Ll. 4541-4611.

pleasures of the *donoi* .. etc. (*Yvain*, 2331-2477). The *joie* is general, and the reader is made to share it. [210]

The contrast with *Perceval* is striking. Though the hero is greeted by the King, Queen, and the *pucele qui rist,* the rest of the court is not in evidence. Only when the Hideous Damsel is to be introduced does Chrétien refer to others, and then only as a contrast to the arrival of the ugly creature. [211] The crowds, essential to any royal celebration, are marked by their absence; they can only be imagined by recourse to some phrase such as: "c'est toute la cour qui l'accueille par la voix de la reine..."—[212] a subterfuge unnecessary in earlier romances. Thus, not only does Perceval flub what should have been a great personal triumph; he is also denied the kind of royal festivities which attended his predecessors' triumphs.

It is fitting that Perceval's acceptance at court be conducted with restraint, especially from the point of view of the reader. As was pointed out at the beginning of this section, the reader is all too familiar with the hero's character to be persuaded by an impressive celebration that Perceval has really "arrived". [213] But there is another side to this

---

[210] It may be objected that it is Yvain who offers the celebration to the King, not the other way around; but we know that the gift reflects on the giver as well, and that it is Yvain who has just come to the end of his first round of adventures triumphantly.

[211]   Granz fu la joie que li rois
            Fist de Perceval le Galois
            Et la reïne et *li baron,*
            Qui l'an mainnent a Carlion;
            Que la nuit retorné i sont,
            Et tote nuit grant joie font,
            Et l'andemain autel refirent
            Jusqu'au tierz jor que il i virent
            Une dameisele qui vint... (4603-11)

There is a radical literary difference between saying that something happened, and describing it.

[212] Frappier, *Perceval*, p. 71. It is possible, of course, to consider the entire episode symbolic—a mode in which the writer is absolved of the necessity of showing his meaning in the actions of his characters, which in turn must be psychologically justified. One can point, for instance, to the fact that Perceval here accepts new, courtly clothing from Gauvain without a moment's hesitation (4537-45), and contrast this to his refusal to wear the Red Knight's clothes and his recalcitrance to accept Gornemant's clothing. The fact of wearing clothes at certain times, if presented alone, might be symbolic (but cf. *supra,* p. 88 f., where the "symbolism" of Cligès' different suits of armor is the source of irony) or allegorical. But in each of these cases, it is not the clothing itself which is important, but Perceval's attitude toward the clothing and the grounds on which he decides whether or not to wear it. These attitudes and decisions are based on his previous experience, and easily traceable to it. They undoubtedly indicate his state of mind at the moment, but this is a presumption for any act of any character in a psychologically-based narrative. Perceval's attitudes, decisions, and acts are perfectly explicable in terms of character and plot development. His story, and Chrétien's romances from *Cligès* on are "symbolic" only in the sense that all writing is symbolic, from the *Iliad* to the current *anti-roman.*

[213] *Supra,* p. 186 f.

knowledge that the reader shares with the author. Perceval is a marked man. He has already broken a pledge to a lady (to return to Belrepeire), and has also failed in a mysterious test. Given the dynamics of Chrétien's romances, Perceval has been living on borrowed time since the encounter with his cousin. [214] From that point on, where he learned of his failure in the Fisher King's castle, and had the opportunity to return to Blancheflor according to his promise, his progress has been ironic. It is appropriate that the Hideous Damsel's first words to him hold up the ironic duality of Fortune and of his actions:

> "Ha! Percevaus, Fortune est chauve
> Derriers et devant chevelue.
> Maudahez et qui te salue
> Et qui nule bien t'ore ne prie!
> Que tu ne la retenis mie
> Fortune quant tu l'ancontras!" (4646-51)

These words are the introduction to her speech, but they also function retrospectively. They represent a summation of the tension which has been building since the cousin's revelation of failure. The expectation of reversal has also been intensified by two episodes which have shown the evil effects of Perceval's earlier actions: the meeting with his cousin and the Orguelleus de la Lande. These two responsibilities for evil effects on others, added to the broken pledge and the failed test, represent a burden of guilt and failure a knight cannot absorb with impunity. That he seems to progress superficially nonetheless is a structural irony which continues earlier techniques, and which serves to build a tension finally dissolved by the vituperations of the Hideous Damsel and the resultant dispersal of the knights at court, including Perceval. [215]

This brings us to a difficult question: the structural relationship of the two parts of this unfinished romance. After a subtly structured section of nearly five thousand lines in which our attention has been almost exclusively centered on the slow, comically painful socialization of the wild Perceval—a process not yet completed—, Chrétien abandons the hero to whom we have become attached to follow with nearly equal exclusiveness the adventures of Gauvain. The only exception to this new focus is a single, brief episode, ensconced between two of

---

[214] From the structural viewpoint, this is a major difference between *Yvain* and *Perceval*. In the former, the hero breaks his promise to return only after the great Arthurian celebration; here, his breach of promise precedes this peripety. In *Yvain*, Laudine's messenger arrives a mere 66 lines after the parting of the couple. In *Perceval*, four episodes intervene between the parting and the arrival of the messenger (the Fisher King, Perceval's cousin, the Orguelleus de la Lande, and Arthur's court). Of course, the Hideous Damsel castigates Perceval for his failure at the Fisher King's, not for the broken promise; that still leaves an interval of three episodes between the stated cause of the peripety and its occurrence.

[215] Thus, one result of the change noted in the preceding footnote is to lessen the effect of shock which accompanies the peripeties of *Erec* and *Yvain*. Chrétien's development seems in part to have been toward a greater psychological realism.

Gauvain's adventures. A reunion of the two heroes? Not at all: the shift of attention here is absolute. We see Perceval speaking first to another knight and then to a hermit in an episode whose relevance seems at first sight entirely restricted to the story of Perceval. Because of this, a critic who otherwise follows Chrétien's narrative order treats the Hermit Episode immediately after the Hideous Maiden episode. [216] As a result, an even stronger emphasis develops on the duality of the romance. This, together with a disproportionate emphasis on the Fisher King episode, has made it almost impossible to see the two sections as functional elements of a whole which, if it cannot be called integral by reason of its incompleteness, is far from a mere juxtaposition of two stories with occasional but vague relationships.

A similar duality was problematic in *Cligès*. There also a romance was divided into two apparently discrete sections with different heroes and hardly any connection in terms of plot. The unity of the earlier romance was found not in the preference of one hero over the other, but in a consideration of the parts as two panels depicting different embodiments of the same idea, that of courtliness. The two embodiments were not presented from the viewpoint of one or the other—though the Cligès section represented a more complete version of courtliness than was available to the previous generation of Alexander—but from a viewpoint which, finally, was external to them both. I suggest that the same is true of the incomplete *Perceval*. Though it is too early to compare Chrétien's intentions in the two sections, two links between them can be made out. The first is narrative: the Hideous Damsel starts a general dispersal of the knights at court, including both Perceval and Gauvain. Her importance, however, is reduced by the fact that Gauvain's purpose is soon changed by the arrival of Guinganbresil. Another link, both narrative and intellectual, is more important for the interpretation of the romance. The basic structure of the Perceval section is the comedy based on the *chastoiements* and Perceval's attempts to carry them out. Having learned to restrain his wildness, he is ready to advance to a further stage, that of courtly behavior. At this point, he meets Gauvain, the exemplum of a certain type of courtly knighthood, and is so impressed by the great knight's politeness (or flattery) that he determines to accept him as the model and pattern for further imitation. In a sense, then, the Gauvain section represents a third, potential stage in Perceval's socialization. Instead of seeing Perceval actually imitating Gauvain, however, we see the latter engage in a series of adventures. Thus, it is not the attempt

---

[216] Frappier, *Perceval,* pp. 75-82. Scholars have gone further. Ernst Hoepffner considered the Perceval and Gauvain sections independent fragments joined by an editor after Chrétien's death (in his review of Fourquet's *Wolfram d'Eschenbach et le Conte del Graal, Romania,* LXV [1939], 397-413; p. 412). Phillipe-August Becker denied the Gauvain section to Chrétien entirely ("Von den Erzählern neben und nach Chrestien de Troyes," *Zeitschrift für romanische Philologie,* LV [1935], 385-455; pp. 400-16). Becker is followed by Nitze (*Perceval and the Holy Grail...,* p. 290, n. 2), and apparently by Imbs ("Perceval et le Graal..."), who disregard the Gauvain section entirely.

of the *vaslet sauvage* to carry out a new pattern of behavior that is the subject of the new section, but the pattern itself. The subject is no longer the fumbling imitation of certain social values, but those values themselves. It is the implications of a certain kind of courtliness (which Perceval wished to imitate) that Chrétien works out in narrative terms by following Gauvain's adventures. [217]

Nevertheless, the differences between the two sections are not to be underestimated. As Kellermann pointed out, the difference in "spiritual" worlds between the two sections is reflected in the literary techniques used to portray those worlds. [218] Even the methods of structuring the sections differ: while the Perceval section consists of discrete, successive episodes, much of the Gauvain section depends on

---

[217] It is inconsistent to consider Gauvain the type of courtliness itself, and then claim that the comic adventures to which he is subjected do not undermine the courtly basis of the action, as does Kellermann (*Aufbaustil und Weltbild...*, p. 150, n. 1; cf. Köhler, *Ideal und Wirklichkeit...*, p. 182).

Why not accomplish this by retaining the same hero? To lead Perceval through Gauvain's adventures—or another series of adventures like them—would certainly give rise to ample comedy, but it would be of the same sort as already exists in the Perceval section. Specifically, the comedy would be at Perceval's expense, and would leave the values in terms of which he would be risible untouched. Since there is no discrepancy between Gauvain's abilities and his values, it is the values themselves that come into play.

To a limited extent, this structural interpretation is closer to that of critics like Pauphilet (*Le legs du moyen âge...*, p. 202) and Micha ("Le *Perceval* de Chrétien de Troyes," in *Lumière du Graal...*, p. 127) who see Gauvain as the fulfillment of a pattern sought after by Perceval, than to Frappier's, who considers that Perceval has already reached Gauvain's level and that he is destined for a far higher kind of achievement than Gauvain, while the latter is merely ridiculed in his adventures. Frappier's interpretation is based on what seems to me too high an evaluation of the level Perceval has attained. As such, it implies a profound miscalculation on the author's part. If, in fact, Perceval is already at Gauvain's level, what is the purpose of exploring that level farther? Where is the narrative tension of seeing Gauvain operate on a level already achieved by Perceval? It is as if Erec were again to be faced with the count of Limors after having succeeded in the Joie de la Cour episode. If the principle of the gradation of adventures has any meaning, it is that the narrative succession leads to adventures on a more demanding level, and that the values of each level are somehow "higher" or more difficult to attain than those of the preceding level.

It would be an oversimplification, however, to assume that Chrétien used a single, vertical, and exclusive scale of values for the scaffolding of his romances. This is Perceval's view in fixing on Gauvain as the next model of behavior, not necessarily the author's. If Perceval was to progress beyond the point he reaches in the unfinished romance, nothing proves that he must first become another Gauvain—especially since Chrétien's effort in the Gauvain section is to reveal the latter's inadequacies—and then attain a level better than Gauvain's. It is more likely that Perceval has approached the mode of behavior represented by Gauvain as closely as he ever would, and that his future progress, if any, was to be in a different direction: see below, pp. 257 ff.

[218] "Im Percevalroman haben wir eine Doppelheit der geistigen Welt vor uns, der eine Doppelheit in der Romantechnik entspricht." Kellermann, *Aufbaustil und Weltbild...*, p. 15.

an intertwining of adventures. [219] The two series of adventures are related by the technique of parallelism Chrétien first developed in *Cligès*. There, the technique was primarily thematic: a given situation would be repeated, with the two heroes reacting in ways both similar and different. The same technique is used in *Perceval,* and another is added: this is the technique which has already been noted several times within the Perceval section, that of the descriptive pivot which functions as a signal that the two episodes identified by the pivot are relevant to each other. [220]

The Maiden with Narrow Sleeves

After the Hideous Damsel has addressed Perceval, she turns to Arthur and the court in general to suggest two adventures. The first is to go jousting at the Chastel Orguelleus, where five hundred and sixty-six famous knights are ready to do battle. This seems to be a general offer which can accommodate a large number of Arthur's knights, but the second adventure is fitted for the one knight *qui voldroit le pris avoir De tot le mont* (4701 f.): it is to rescue a damsel seated on the peak of Montescleire. Gauvain jumps to his feet to claim the latter adventure, which is suitable to two of his propensities: love of reputation and association with the fair sex. As he is arming himself, Guinganbresil enters the hall to accuse Gauvain of having killed his lord without challenge:

> Honte et reproche et blasme i as,
> Si t'an apel de traïson... (4762 f.)

Gauvain, *toz honteus* (4767), denies the accusation but accepts the challenge, though not before his brother urges him not io shame his lineage and offers to fight in his stead. Gauvain proudly refuses this, and agrees to meet Guinganbresil before the King of Escavalon in forty days. Guinganbresil leaves, and Gauvain returns to the business of arming himself. All the court turn well-wishers: whoever had a good shield, lance, helmet or sword offers it to him,

> ... mes ne li plot
> Qu'il an portast rien de l'autrui... (4802 f.)

As he leaves (with seven squires, seven horses, and two shields!) the court is invaded by grief, particularly on the part of the ladies:

> ... n'i ot dame si senee
> Qui por lui grant duel ne demaint... (4810 f.)

A number of important traits are touched on in this brief scene. The most general one is his pride: he refuses to accept the offer of

---

[219] *Ibid.,* p. 21. This results from the character of the heroes. The principle of discrete episodes is more suited to revealing a partial development in Perceval. Gauvain, as Frappier has said, is a static hero (*Perceval,* p. 114): his permanence lends itself to the function of unifying the intertwined episodes.
[220] *Supra,* pp. 118, 147 f., n. 91, 164, 169, n. 136, 177, n. 158, 182.

any weapon, as he also refuses to allow his brother to defend their *lignage*. [221] Another is his association with the fair sex, shown both by his choice of adventure (that which combines honor with the deliverance of a damsel, as opposed to that which offers honor alone) and the grief of even the "most sensible" ladies of the court. A third point is his even greater care for reputation: when that is attacked, even an adventure leading to the "greatest glory in the world" as well as a damsel in distress immediately drops out of sight. Finally there is the matter of Guinganbresil's accusation. Gauvain denies it, and there is no reason to doubt his good faith; but the same situation will recur later. Another knight will accuse him of ill-treatment, Gauvain will deny this, only to be forced to recognize the truth of the accusation. [222] At the moment. however, there is no more than the accusation that Gauvain has been guilty of the same impropriety as Perceval, who also killed the Red Knight without challenge.

But the world associated with Gauvain is quite different from Perceval's world. As he leaves Arthur's court, the first thing to cross his line of vision is a troupe of knights going to a courtly tournament. One of the squires explains that the troupe belongs to Meliant de Liz. The latter fell in love with the daughter of Tiebaut de Tintaguel, the man who brought up Meliant. The daughter, however, was a courtly lady: she refused his love until he should be made a knight. When this was accomplished, she temporized further until he should demonstrate his love by prowess in jousting. She urged him, in fact, to tourney against Tiebaut, her own father and his tutor, to which he agreed. It is a curious tale, told by a squire without comment. Nor does Chrétien himself comment on it. Only Gauvain, told that Meliant will tourney against Tiebaut, exclaims:

> "Deus!" fet mes sire Gauvain lors,
> Don ne fu Melianz de Liz
> An la meison Tiebaut norriz?" (4838-40)

Gauvain's sentiment does him justice. The young lady's courtliness has pitted her father against her putative lover—as if Perceval were to tourney against Gornemant de Goort for Blancheflor!

Interestingly enough, the girl explained (or sweetened?) her temporizing by a not unfamiliar idea:

> "... les choses qu'an a an bades
> Ne sont si douces ne si sade
> Come celes que l'an conpere." (4861-3)

It is interesting because this is an idea which received its fullest elaboration by Gauvain himself, albeit in another romance of Chrétien's. When he is urging Yvain to leave Laudine—for the purpose of tourneying—Gauvain propounds the courtly and epicurean theory that

---

[221] Compare Gauvain's dismissal of a squire who, after informing him of a nearby tournament, is bold enough to urge him to join it (4879-81; *infra*, p. 205); and his refusal of supplies from Tiebaut de Tintaguel (5318-30).

[222] In the Greoreas episode: ll. 7085-7140.

love becomes more pleasurable when delayed. [223] The idea is more appropriate to the tension of the troubadour version of courtly love than to the love between husband and wife Chrétien posited as both the norm and the goal for Erec and Yvain. [224] On both occasions that this idea is expressed in Chrétien's works, it is in connection with the disruption of familial ties: Gauvain persuades Yvain to leave his wife, with nearly disastrous results, and two close relationships are threatened in the present case.

As the squire concludes his tale, he urges Gauvain to join the tournament ... and thereby trespasses on Gauvain's sense of propriety. The squire is patronizingly dismissed:

> "Frere, va t'an
> Siu ton seignor, si feras san,
> Si leisse ester ce que tu diz." (4879-81)

Nevertheless, Gauvain hies himself to Tintaguel. [225] Finding all the entrances to the city barred, he assembles his seven horses around an oak from which he also hangs his two shields. The tree is right in the lee of the castle tower. From that vantage point, the ladies assembled to watch the tournament also observe him. The wealth of his accoutrement gives rise at first to wonder—what will he do with so many harnesses, horses, and two shields:

> "Ainz chevaliers ne fu veüz
> Qui portast deus escuz ansamble..." (4976 f.)

—and then, as the tournament continues and Gauvain remains below out of the fray, to sarcasm and disdain:

> "Deus!" fet l'une des dameiseles,
> "Cil chevaliers desoz cel charme
> Que atant il que il ne s'arme?"
> Une autre plus desmesuree
> Redist: "Il a la pes juree." (5054-8)

The first remark ("What is he waiting for?"), though it suggests some impatience, is neutral. The second indirectly accuses him of cowardice

---

[223]   "mervoille est comant en a cure
de l'eisse qui toz jorz li dure.
Bien a donc cist ou delaier
et plus est dolz a essaier
uns petiz biens, quant il delaie,
c'uns granz, qui tot ades l'essaie.
Joie d'amors qui vient a tart
sanble la vert busche qui art,
qui dedanz rant plus grant chalor
et plus se tient en sa valor,
quant plus demore a alumer." (*Yvain,* 2515-25)
"Gauvain, l'épicurien courtois, s'est fait un art de vivre..." (Frappier, *Yvain,* p. 72).

[224] See the analysis of Bertran de Born's "Quan vei la laudeta mover" in Jackson, *The Literature of the Middle Ages,* pp. 246-51.

[225] On the remainder of this episode, compare Frappier's commentary, which brings out many of the same points (*Perceval,* pp. 115-8).

by ironically offering an excuse: he is bound by an oath to keep the peace. [226] The third goes much farther: while the sarcasm of the preceding remark at least allowed Gauvain the status of a knight bound even by a fictitious oath, the third lady denies that status and reduces him to the level of a merchant leading horses for sale:

> Et une autre redist aprés:
> "Marcheanz est; nel dites mes
> Qu'il doie a tornoiier antandre:
> Toz cez chevaus mainne il a vandre." (5059-62)

That the final effect of such a remark is an irony at Gauvain's expense is indubitable: it is problematic, however, whether this is intended as irony by the speaker. Kellermann thought that the lady actually mistook the largely appareled Gauvain for a merchant. [227] Frappier, considering these remarks in general to be mockeries, [228] implies thereby that the ladies are quite aware that the man by the oak tree is in fact a knight, but mock him for not daring to take part in the tournament. The latter seems more likely to be correct, especially since Chrétien himself refers to all of these remarks as *ranposnes* (5092) : raillery, mockery, jeering, all of which imply an awareness of what one is doing.

But the ironic degradation of Gauvain goes one step farther. The suggestion of cowardice and social demotion to the merchant class is not enough:

> "Einz est changierre" fet la quarte,
> "Il n'a talant que il departe
> As povres chevaliers ancui
> Cel avoir qu'il mainne avuec lui.
> Ne cuidiez pas que je vos mante:
> C'est monoie et veisselemante
> An cez forriaus et an cez males." (5063-9)

Poor Gauvain hears all these *ranposnes* clearly (5091 f.),

> S'an a grant honte et grant enui... (5094)

Why should this pattern of knighthood endure such mockery? Why does he not take part in the tournament? He is accused of treason, and must defend himself and all his lineage according to his *covant*; so he thinks, *si a reison,* comments Chrétien (5095). But that meeting will not take place for another forty days?

---

[226] It should be noted that the only indication that this is in fact intended ironically is Chrétien's comment on the speaker, that she is more *desmesuree* than the previous one.

[227] *Aufbaustil und Weltbild...,* p. 167. Kellermann also gives the basis for the irony here. He notes that wealth and freedom from the need of earning a livelihood are assumptions of the *höfischen Menschentum*: "Denn Verhaftetsein im Beruflich-Materiellen und wahre 'hautesce' schliessen sich aus." (*Ibid., loc. cit.*)

[228] *Perceval,* p. 117.

> ... por ce qu'il ert an redot
> Qu'il ne fust afolez ne pris,
> Ne s'est del tornoi antremis,
> Et s'an a il mout grant talant... (5102-5)

This is a perfectly reasonable calculation, but such reasonable calculations are somewhat out of character for a knight, at least as Chrétien has portrayed the figure of the knight before. Yvain, with only a few hours left before his defense of Lunete—to which he is also bound by a *covant*—does not hesitate to battle the giant Harpin de la Montagne that very morning. [229] It is not fear of personal harm which restrains Gauvain, as the last line makes clear. But the possibility of being wounded or taken prisoner—a possibility no other knight Chrétien has described considers before battle—becomes very real to him when the honor and reputation of a *covant* are at stake. Thus, the demands of his form of courtliness and his care for reputation have led Gauvain, during his first day away from court, to suffer the paradoxical situation of hearing himself dishonored and mocked in order to save his honor and reputation.

The means by which this humiliation occurs are also due to his own character and action. When he left Arthur's court, he refused to accept the offered weapons and equipment of others. Instead, Chrétien briefly noted,

> Set escuiiers mainne avuec lui
> Et set destriers et deus escuz. (4804 f.)

Not only pride, but a conspicuous display of his self-regard, is characteristic of Gauvain. It is this display, as well as the incongruity between the extraordinary number of weapons and their non-use, which makes him subject to their mockery.

But Gauvain finds a defender among the ladies, a very young and fashionable little girl who is the younger sister of Meliant de Liz' lady-love. Her precise age is never given, but she is young enough to be carried home late at night in her father's arms (5429 f.). Her sartorial concerns are indicated by her name, *la pucele as manches petites* (4989). The fashion was for sleeves worn very tight as far as the wrist. [230] She exaggerates this by omitting the usual puffed cuffs and tightening the sleeves so much they seem "written" or "painted" on her arms:

> ... si cointemant se vestoit
> De manches qu'apelee estoit
> La Pucele as Manches Petites,
> Qu'anz es bras les avoit escrites. (4987-90)

As might be expected, she is also a coquette, though a naive one. Explaining to her father the quarrel with her older sister, she tells him of a *covant* by which, if Gauvain does not beat Meliant de Liz,

---

[229] *Yvain*, 3797 ff.
[230] Baist's comment, quoted by Hilka, note to line 4990; and Frappier, *Perceval*, p. 116, n. 1.

> "Les treces jusqu'au haterel
> Andeus tranchier me leisseroie,
> Don mout anpiriee seroie..." (5404-6)

She is also a shrewd little girl, though the first evidence of this
shrewdness is incongruous. When her companions in the tower call
the knight below a merchant or money-changer, she observes that this
is improbable:

> "Cuidiez vos que marcheanz port
> Si grosses lances con cist porte?" (5072 f.)

Of course, if her companions were being consciously ironic, her
shrewdness is misplaced: she is taking their figurative words literally.
She can also turn her shrewdness to spiteful uses and calculated taunts.
After Gauvain has beaten Meliant, she tells her sister:

> "Suer, or poëz veoir
> Dan Meliant de Liz gisant,
> Que vos aliiez si prisant.
> Qui set si doit a droit prisier:
> Ore i pert ce que je dis ier,
> Or voit an bien, se Deus me saut,
> Que il i a tel qui miauz vaut." (5532-8)

Lest we take this as mere childish naïveté, Chrétien adds:

> Tot einsi cele a esciant
> Va sa seror contraliant
> Si qu'ele la giete del san... (5539-41)

And when this drives the older sister to threaten to give her such a
slap it will knock her off her feet, [231] the younger one retreats with
sweet hypocrisy:

> "Avoi! suer, de Deu vos sovaingne..." (5546)

This vivid portrait, more likely to be the product of observation
than literary tradition, [232] is worthy of being set next to that of Lunete
as one of Chrétien's brightest, most enjoyable creations. Gauvain, it
seems, was delighted by her also: it is for her sake that he puts into
escrow all his concern for honor, reputation, and lineage, as he accepts
her "service" in the tournament. He has received the hospitality of a
vavassor in Tintaguel. In the evening, he explains his reasons for
abstaining from the tournament, and receives his host's understanding
approval. [233] Later, he repeats his explanation to the lord of Tintaguel,

---

231   "Je t'irai tel bufe doner
       Que n'avras pié qui te sostaingne." (5544 f.)
232 A modern psychologist would speak of sibling rivalry.
233   Li vavassors mout l'an prisa
       Et dist que bon gré l'an savoit:
       Se il por ce leissié l'avoit
       Le tornoi, il ot fet reison. (5200-3)

Tiebaut, and again finds his action approved. [234] Gauvain, then, has obtained explicit confirmation of the values for the sake of which he endured shame and dishonor from two sound and serious men ... and then abandons these values for the flattering pleasure of being the first knight who ever bore arms for the little girl. She rushes into the room where the three men are speaking, embraces the still unnamed knight by the leg, and makes her plea:

> "... a vos de ma seror me clain,
> Cui je n'ai chiere ne ne l'ain,
> Que por vos m'a hui fet grant honte." (5345-7)

Gauvain is unable to make anything of this. Tiebaut, the girl's embarrassed father who had already taken his leave, asks her what she wants from the knight and tells him to pay no attention to her:

> "Anfes est, nice chose et fole." (5358)

There is, at times, a spirit of contradiction in Gauvain. "I would be too *vilain* if I did not do her will. Tell me,

> Mes anfes douz et deboneire,

what justice could I do you about your sister, and how?" (5360-5). The rest is just a matter of child's play. In spite of her father's protestations, Gauvain insists on becoming the little girl's champion *une piece* (5381).

Gauvain has endured the humiliations of the ladies in the tower. Does his victory in the tournament against Meliant de Liz provide reparation? Gauvain presumably thinks so, but Chrétien may be of a different opinion. It was the custom for a knight to wear a token of his lady's in a tournament. [235] Her father reminds the *pucele as manches petites* of this and urges her to send Gauvain *aucune druërie, ou manche ou guinple* (5418 f.). Like Gauvain, the little girl is trapped by her own characteristic; her sleeves are too small:

> "Espoir se je li anveoie,
> Il ne la priseroit ja rien." (5424 f.)

Her father kindly takes care of the matter. He has a sleeve made to order out of scarlet material, *Une manche mout longue et lee* (5453), which his daughter presents to her knight the following morning, who apparently wears it proudly.

The extent to which Gauvain is being ridiculed, however, appears only when we accept Chrétien's structural hints and bring the technique of parallelism into operation. It has been noted before that the slapping of the *pucele as manches petites* recalls the slap Keu gave the

[234]   "Acheison eüstes leal"
      Fet li sire, "sanz nule faille..." (5312 f.)
[235] Hilka, note to 5418.

prophetic *pucele* in Arthur's court. [236] In both cases, the harsh treatment is the result of a girl's perception of knighthood in a man who
seems absurdly distant from that calling to others who see him. There
is a difference, however. In the case of Perceval, discerning the poten-
tiality of knighthood beneath the Welsh clothes and rude behavior of
the *valet sauvage* was truly extraordinary, even while it stressed the
absurdity of his manner and dress. With Gauvain, the perception
consists in the courage of believing the obvious: the man under the
castle tower has all the accoutrements of a knight, but it is difficult to
accept these indices of knighthood since his behavior is so unlike that
of a knight. What at first appears to be a compliment to the little girl's
perception and an affirmation of Gauvain's essential qualities turns
out to stress his unknightly behavior. [237]

But the *pucele qui rist* was not the only one in the first section of
the romance to "discover knighthood." This was the subject of the
opening scene of the romance in which Perceval first saw knights.
There is a certain similarity between Tiebaut's younger daughter and
the Perceval of that episode, where he also appears at his youngest.
Chrétien even uses familiar words to describe the two: *la pucele as
manches petites* is called [*une*] *nice chose et fole* (5358); later, it is
said that *mout fu sinple* (5420). [238] This parallelism suggests that
Gauvain is to be equated with the five knights who Perceval thought
were angels, and the little girl's admiration for the exemplum of
chivalry with the boy's adoration. This similarity of childish admi-
rations lays even more stress on the basic irony of the episode. If the
pucele as manches petites partly resembles the Perceval of the opening
scene, Gauvain's championship of her is seen as not only ill-advised
from the viewpoint of his personal honor but ludicrous in terms of
knightly service. Gauvain here commits the psychological error so
frequent in Perceval's early adventures, that of misidentification—a
basic technique of comedy. As Perceval kneels to pray to knights he
believes are angels, or mistakes a courtly tent for a minster, so Gauvain misidentifies the little girl with tight sleeves, charming and foolish,
shrewd and spiteful, as the object of courtly service.

The misidentification also turns the episode into a parody of the
courtly *dame* and courtly service. It is only the first of such parodies
we will find in the Gauvain section. Its first aspect is the simple
reduction in size: the courtly lady to whom Gauvain swears undying
allegiance (5650-2) is dwarfed to the dimensions of a child carried in

---

[236] Köhler, "Zur Discussion über die Einheit von Chrestiens *Contes del
Graal*," *Zeitschrift für romanische Philologie*, LXXV (1959), 523-39; p. 537; and
Frappier, *Perceval*, p. 116.

[237] If our interpretation of the ladies' mockery as quite conscious is correct,
and the little girl's rebuttal is seen as an error in the level of linguistic usage,
her perception is reduced in value even farther.

[238] Compare to the vocabulary applied to Perceval; *supra*, pp. 120, 124
and n. 32. Here, however, there is no stress by frequency comparable to that
in the Perceval section: the lines quoted in the text are the only uses of such
vocabulary I have found.

her father's arms. [239] The second is more serious. Surprising as it may seem for one of his reputation, this episode is the only one in which Gauvain fights in defense of a maiden or her honor in the *Perceval*. [240] It is then a parallel also to Perceval's defense of Blancheflor, and suggests an equation between the little girl's slap and Blancheflor's situation ... a suggestion made only to be unacceptable. Blancheflor was not only concerned with her personal honor; indeed, she was willing to risk sullying that honor for the sake of her responsibilities as a feudal lord. [241] By comparison, Gauvain rides to the defense of the injured party in a grievous case of sibling rivalry ... Perceval and Gauvain undertake the "same" adventure, but the values of their undertakings are quite different.

The Sister of the King of Escavalon

The episode proper is preceded by a brief and puzzling interlude. After spending the night in a religious house, Gauvain is attracted by some animals at the edge of the forest. He takes his best horse and a lance *mout roide et fort* (5657) to hunt one of the animals, a white doe. He pursues her through many twists and turns, overtakes her near a briar patch,

> ... et si li mist
> Sor le col la lance an travers. (5678 f.)

He has missed his aim. The doe jumps off, Gauvain continues his pursuit and might have caught the doe if his horse had not lost a shoe and begun to limp. He is forced to abandon the hunt, and cannot ride the horse until it has been reshod (5653-5702).

This interlude has seemed so enigmatic that one of the most serious students of Chrétien's literary technique thought it had no function at all, and served merely as an introduction to the following episode. [242] An introduction, however, presumably has some relevance to what is introduced. Right after this failed hunt, Gauvain meets the King of Escavalon ... who is going hunting. Unfortunately, we are never told how successful the King was, so that no comparison is possible. Another suggestion is that the doe's whiteness indicates its magical and other-worldly character: Gauvain's failure in this chase would foreshadow his inability to succeed in the adventure of the Other World. [243]

---

[239] The basis of this parody is a primitive one: we find it humorous on the same basis as we laugh at the dwarfs in a circus.

[240] Gauvain does defend the sister of the King of Escavalon, of course, but that is a battle into which he is forced in self-defense, not for the sake of honor.

The caution must be admitted that this is true only within the fragmentary state of the romance. However, the indication, at the end of the fragment, that Gauvain is about to fight before Arthur's court, suggests that his cycle of adventures was nearly over.

[241] *Supra*, p. 157 and n. 112.

[242] Kellermann, *Aufbaustil und Weltbild...*, p. 65.

[243] Frappier, *Perceval*, p. 119.

However, the following episode is, in part, remarkably of *this* world:
the realism of the description of Escavalon is almost unequalled in this
romance. A third suggestion is that Gauvain's difficulty with the horse
is a familiar epic warning. [244] This would at least suggest that the
approaching episode is fated to turn out badly for its hero, as indeed
it does.

This last approach can be extended one step forward, or backward
rather, by noting a similar stumbling of Perceval's horse in the Tent
Maiden Episode. [245] It is unnecessary to review in detail the extensive
comic and ironic aspects of that episode: it will suffice to recall that
it hinged on the encounter of the hero with a maiden in a particularly
courtly setting. The situation of Gauvain with the sister of the King
of Escavalon is an obvious parallel. Although Perceval obtained what
he wanted on first seeing the tent—food—, he made a fool of himself
in the process, especially in the context of a courtly setting. The
contrast here is clear: Gauvain, as we will see, has a way with the
ladies, a courtly way to which his companion of the moment succumbs
in short order. His polite and glib words earn him the kisses and
caresses of the *donoi*. On this score, the contrast favors Gauvain.
However, this success is short-lived: Gauvain's approaches are interrupted, and by the end of the episode, he has endured humiliation and
ridicule comparable to Perceval's, and by the same standard of courtliness.

A more precise interpretation and parallel are also possible. At the
beginning of the interlude, Gauvain is riding a paifrey, a light riding
horse. On seeing the doe, he exchanges this for his best horse, presumably a war horse. [246] As we have seen, he also takes a strong,
heavy lance. Thus, Gauvain starts on the pursuit of a doe which will
take him down a turning, twisting trail among briar patches, mounted
on a heavy horse more suited to war and tournaments, with a weapon
also more suited to martial pursuit than to the hunt. The lance, of
course, is not a weapon that is thrown. Therefore, Gauvain is forced
to attack the doe directly:

> .. si li mist
> Sor le col la lance an travers. (5678 f.)

A lighter horse might have taken the turns and twists without throwing
a shoe; a more appropriate hunting weapon might have been more

---

[244] Fowler, *Prowess and Charity*..., p. 51.
[245] *Supra,* p. 131 f.
[246]   Yonet dit que il s'arest,
             Qui un de ses chevaus menoit,
             Tot le meillor, et si tenoit
             Une lance mout roide et fort.
             La lance dit qu'il li aport
             Et que son cheval li restraingne,
             Celui qu'il mainne an destre, et praingne
             Son palefroi et si li maint. (5664-71)

successful, especially since the hunter was close enough to touch the deer on its neck with the lance.

Gauvain is a self-conscious literary character. Aware that the white doe may lead to a special adventure, he dresses, as it were, in a manner he deems appropriate to his role, disregarding the demands of the particular adventure at hand. It is his *persona* he brings to the adventure, the *persona* of Gauvain the great knight, mounted on his best war horse, armed with a heavy war or tourneying lance, both thoroughly inappropriate to the job of hunting down a fleeing deer. In this interlude, pride goeth before a stumble. [247]

There is a precise parallel in the Perceval section. It is as a hunter that we first see Perceval, a literary character (at that point) with no self-consciousness whatever. His manner of hunting is instructive: he is mounted on a *chaceor* (78, 92), and his weapons are three javelins (79, 96)—weapons to be thrown. In this respect, Perceval's quite unconscious correctness (he didn't know what a lance was, and probably had never seen a war-horse either) leads him to appropriate behavior, while Gauvain fails. [248] There is more, however. Perceval's lack of awareness led to the brilliant comedy of the misidentification of objects: the knightly lance and hauberk were reduced to the utilitarianism of the hunter. Though the Gauvain parallel is not elaborated comically, he proceeds quite consciously by exactly the same process, though in reverse: riding a war-horse and using a lance are an attempt to raise the level of the hunt to that of knightly exploit. In both cases, the error is the disregard of categories that can be regarded as social and, in so far as any society supposes its categories to be inevitable, natural as well. Again Perceval and Gauvain are shown to follow the same pattern: the *vaslet sauvage* and the greatest Arthurian knight make the same mistakes, in different ways.

Gauvain resumes his journey and soon meets a group of people on a hunting excursion. Among them is a young man, handsomer than the rest, who, without any introductions being exchanged, invites Gauvain to spend the night at his castle:

> "J'ai une seror mout cortoise,
> Qui de vos grant joie fera." (5724 f.)

He turns to one of his companions:

> "Alez, je vos anvoi
> Biaus conpainz, avuec cest seignor,

---

[247] The hunt of a white animal is frequently associated with a love adventure (see Bezzola, *Le sens de l'aventure...*, p. 94 f.), though the association is too vague at the end of the twelfth century to speak of a symbol: Erec enters on the adventure in which he will win Enide precisely because he does not partake in the hunt of the white doe. Nevertheless, insofar as Chrétien intentionally suggests this association here, he is ironic: Gauvain will fail in the love adventure as he fails in the hunt.

[248] Chrétien did not mention Perceval's success, if any. The description was rather that of playful practice (95-100).

> Si le menez *a ma seror.*
> Saluez la premieremant,
> Puis li dites que je li mant
> Par l'amor et par la grant foi
> Qui doit estre antre li et moi,
> S'ele onques ama chevalier,
> Qu'ele aint cestui et taingne chier
> Et qu'ele autant face de lui
> Con de *moi qui ses frere sui:*
> Tel solaz et tel conpeignie
> Li face que ne li griet mie..." *etc.* (5728-40)

The underlined phrases are only the verbal surfacing of the basis of
the dramatic irony in this speech and situation, noteworthy since they
are repetitive. To the reader, aware of Gauvain's identity, this seems
like very strange advice to give one's sister. But of course, the young
knight is ignorant of this identity. Otherwise, his invitation to the
wandering knight would more likely be to a duel than for hospitable
purposes: as we learn later, the young knight is the King of Escavalon,
whose father Gauvain has been accused of killing. This dramatic
irony will be fully exploited later in the episode. At this point, it is
the ambiguity of *amor* which is the focus of irony in the context of
our knowledge of Gauvain's identity. The twelfth century used *amor*
and *amitié* interchangeably, either bearing either or both meanings. [249]
The young host is offering his guest the friendship of hospitality; our
knowledge of Gauvain's identity makes us aware that the word's other
meaning is also relevant.

The ambiguity of the situation, though not the ambiguity of vocabulary, is continued when Gauvain's guide brings him to the sister:

> "Amie bele,
> Vostre frere saluz vos mande
> Et de cest seignor vos comande
> Qu'il soit enorez et serviz,
> Si nel feites mie a anviz,
> Mes trestot ausi de buen cuer
> Con se vos estiiez sa suer
> Et con s'il estoit vostre frere.
> Or gardez ne soiiez avere
> De tote sa volanté feire,
> Mes large et franche et deboneire." (5792-5802)

As the guide takes his leave to return to the hunt, the young lady
expresses her delighted gratitude for the *bel conpeignon* her brother
has so lovingly "lent" her (5808 f.). She invites him to sit by her and
promises to be hospitable because he is so *bel et jant,* and because her
brother asks her to do so. The two are left alone: *mes sire Gauvains*

---

[249] Frappier, *Yvain,* p. 97 f.

does not complain of being left alone with the maiden, and she was so well brought up that she has no fear of being left alone with him. [250]

The situation clearly fits into the series of situations with erotic potential which Chrétien has used previously in the *Perceval*, but he does not exploit it with erotically suggestive vocabulary. The author probably restrains himself here because the characters themselves are indulging in that kind of conversation:

> D'amors parolent anbedui;
> Car s'il d'autre chose parlassent,
> De grant oiseuse se meslassent.
> Mes sire Gauvains la requiert
> D'amors et prie et dit qu'il iert
> Ses chevaliers tote sa vie. (5824-9) [251]

As we are apparently being led toward a natural conclusion, the shift in the meaning of *amors* is complete. When an inconsiderate *vavassor* enters the room,

> Si les trova antrebeisant
> Et mout grant joie antrefeisant. (5835 f.)

Gauvain has nearly reached that *soreplus* which Chrétien, assuming a sense of the natural sequence of events in the reader, expects us to expect. But in fact, Gauvain does not achieve that final goal here or anywhere else in this romance. [252] For one reason or another, he never passes beyond the earlier, incomplete stage of the *donoi*, the flirtation with its verbal exchange of loves and, as here, kisses and caresses. The "love" Gauvain enjoys remains a formalized social pass-time with no satisfaction other than the pride of another unconsummated conquest. [253]

---

[250]
> "Et mes sire Gauvains remaint,
> Qui de ce mie ne se plaint
> Qu'il est seus avuec la pucele,
> Qui mout estoit cortoise et bele,
> Et tant estoit bien afeitiee
> Que pas ne cuide estre agueitiee
> De ce que ele est sole o lui. (5817-23)

[251] As Frappier points out, this is the same pledge Gauvain made to the *pucele as manches petites* (5692-10; *Perceval*, p. 119).

[252] Nor, as far as we know, in any of Chrétien's other romances. The closest he comes is with Lunete in the *Yvain*, but the status of their relationship is left indefinite by the author (*Yvain*, 2395 ff.).

[253] I find no trace, anywhere in this romance or in any of Chrétien's other works in which Gauvain appears, of the "rasch und heftig entflammte sinnliche Leidenschaft" attributed to him by Köhler (*Ideal und Wirklichkeit...*, p. 182). On the contrary, it seems to me that part of Chrétien's irony is to portray Gauvain as playing the role of the "courtly lover" up to the hilt without ever obtaining a satisfaction Chrétien considers normal, and perhaps even finding a greater satisfaction in playing that role so fully than he would from its fulfillment. It is an irony directed not only to the character of Gauvain, but also to the idea of *amor purus*, on which see Jackson, *The Literature of the Middle Ages*, p. 97.

The *vavassor* does more than interrupt Gauvain's amorous efforts, however far the latter intended to pursue them. Recognizing the guest, he turns on the hostess with a violent anti-feminist tirade which concludes:

> "Mes tu es fame, bien le voi;
> Que cil qui la siet delez toi
> Ocist ton pere, et tu le beises.
> Quant fame puet avoir de ses eises,
> Del soreplus petit li chaut." (5861-5) [254]

Once again Gauvain is caught between two themes which reflect two aspects of his character: knightly prowess and adventure, which leave him subject to such accusations, and his involvement with women. The lady, in this case, faints dead away, but is revived thanks to his ministrations. She points out that he has put her life in danger, and then provides him with weapons for their mutual defense, since he had left his own weapons outside (5787). Chrétien does not stress this, but Gauvain, who normally insists on not using anyone else's weapons, here has no choice in the matter. What is more, the substitute for his own shield is rather unexpected. No shield is available, but Gauvain proves himself a quick thinker and a gallant improviser:

> ... fist escu d'un eschequier
> Et dist: "Amie, je ne quier
> Que vos m'ailliez autre escu querre." (5893-5)

Knocking the chess-pieces to the floor—they are of ivory, ten times the usual size, and will figure again shortly—he takes his post at the entrance to the tower, armed with the great sword Escalibor and a chess board. [255]

In the meanwhile, the *vavassor* has gone out to arouse the townspeople against the murderer of their former king.[256] Gauvain, after having

---

[254] Köhler quotes the last two lines as evidence of Chrétien's recognition that courtly love has become inadequate to regulate behavior (*Ideal und Wirklichkeit*..., p. 182 f.). However, this is the *vavassor* speaking, not Chrétien, and it is poor critical method to use a character's opinion as the author's unless there is good reason to consider him the author's spokesman.

In general, however, it was a suggestion of the *Cligès* chapter that Chrétien considered at least certain aspects of courtliness inadequate as early as *Cligès*.

[255] No explanation is given in the text of how Gauvain came to be in possession of the sword traditionally associated with Arthur: see Hilka's note to l. 5902, and Nitze, "The Guinganbresil Episode in Chrétien's *Perceval*," *Romania*, LXXII (1951), 373-80; p. 375 & n. 1. The only point I can see to its introduction here is a dual incongruity, first with Gauvain's general principle of not using anyone else's possession, and second with the absurdly juxtaposed chess-board shield.

[256] The townspeople also come in for irony, some of it friendly, some of it harsh. The *vavassor* speaks to various

> ... borjois a foison
> Qui pas n'avoient pris poison,
> Qu'il estoient et gros et gras. (5909-11)

The assortment of weapons used by the *vilain*—a mixture of real weapons and

been trapped in a scene not inappropriate to drawing room comedy, is trapped again, this time in a situation which could fit into a swash-buckling adventure tale: in both cases, in love and in battle, the event is turned to his humiliation. His post is to guard the door of the tower, a situation which may stir heroic associations in our minds but did not in Chrétien's. The townspeople attack, armed with a motley and farcical assortment of weapons which includes a door, a winnow, and a pitch-fork (5936-45). Against these, the great Gauvain takes his stand in the door:

> ... mout lor a bien desfandu
> Li portiers qui dedanz estoit... (5988 f.)

He "pays" the first so well the others are frightened:

> Nus si hardiz avant ne vient
> Qui le portier tant ne redot... (5996 f.)

Even when they do attack, however, the location—a low and narrow door—is such that one good man can hold them off:

> Por vilains desarmez porfandre
> Jusqu'es danz et escerveler
> N'i covenoit mie apeler
> Meillor portier qu'il i avoit. (6024-7) [257]

The irony is progressively increased. The first designation of the hero as "doorman" reflects little more than an amused comment on the location of the action. The first repetition induces a doubt that more is intended, a doubt fully justified by the last repetition which defines Gauvain's unheroic victory: of course it isn't difficult for a trained and expe-rienced knight in his position to bar passage to a rabble of ill-equipped and frightened vilain. [258]

The exploit is even less heroic when seen in the context of the lady's actions. After a long speech of self-justification which opens with full-throated curses at the rabble she faces—quite a different view

---

farm implements—is also part of the fun.
The harsh irony is entirely the lady's, who rages at the

> ... vilenaille,
> Chien anragié, pute servaille,
> Quel deable vos ont mandez?" etc. (5955-7)

The difference in tone and implication between Chrétien's good-humored joking and the lady's violent outburst is obvious: the latter should not be attributed to the author, especially since it is a function of her role as a courtly lady whose supposedly secret love has just been publicly discovered. As Frappier comments: "Qu'est devenu le beau secret des amours courtoises?" (Perceval, p. 120).

[257] The word desarmez must be taken in the sense of "without armor", not "without weapons"; compare ll. 5936-45, and Foerster's Wörterbuch, under desarmer.

[258] Stanton de V. Hoffman considers that "Gawain", even here, "carries courtesy and courtly manners to their perfection..." ("The Structure of the Conte del Graal," Romanic Review, LII [1961] 81-98, p. 97).

of the lady whom we have previously seen only as a noble and susceptible maiden—she brings aid to Gauvain *come hardie* (5953), playing the role of artillery support:

> La dameisele les eschas
> Qui jurent sor le pavemant,
> Lor rue mout irieemant,
> Si s'est estrainte et escorciee
> Et jure come correciee
> Qu'ele les fera toz destruire,
> S'ele onques puet, ainz qu'ele muire. (6000-5)

Her speech and behavior may not seem the acme of courtliness, but her action is highly effective: most of the townspeople flee before the rain of giant chessmen.

The episode which began in the privacy of the boudoir ends in farcical public shambles. On the point of another courtly conquest, enjoying a delicate tête-à-tête which is his reputation's due, Gauvain is suddenly interrupted by a *vavassor* who recognizes and accuses him of being the killer of the father of the lady receiving his advances. He then must undertake to defend himself and the lady, not against the knightly opponent who would constitute a proper adversary, but a rabble of enraged *vilain* who force him to use the protection of a narrow door, while the lady is metamorphosed into a furiously swearing virago hurling, besides her words, the nearest available missiles, the pieces of the chess set whose board Gauvain is using as a shield.

It would be wrong, however, to limit the bearing of this comedy to the humiliation of the characters involved. Gauvain and the sister of the King of Escavalon represent the conventions of a literary ethic and a mode of life codified by that ethic. The situation in which they were discovered was typical of that mode: the knight and lady, sitting by each other's side, exchanging vows of love and social compliments—this is half the *raison d'être* of the characters, the mode, the ethic. It is not only a couple which is under fire, but the conventional ethic according to which they were acting.

This becomes even clearer when the common elements of this episode and its parallel from the Perceval section are juxtaposed. Like Gauvain's, Perceval's knightly combat was preceded by a peaceful social scene. He also sat next to a lady with whom he was to have a certain relationship, Blancheflor. At this level, the comparison turns to the advantage of Gauvain's polish as against Perceval's mutism which was a wonder to the onlookers and an embarrassment to the hostess. Strangely enough, though, the outcome is the same: neither enjoys the *soreplus* which might have been his. Gauvain's sophistication in speech and manners wins him no greater laurels than Perceval lost through boorish ignorance.

In the second element of both episodes—achievement in knightly prowess—Perceval actually comes off better. Although he was still subject to the comedy of not understanding the concept of mercy and of being unable at first to use it properly after it has been explained to him, he did, at least, do battle with knights against whom he won his first knightly honors.

These two elements refer only to the success and failure of the characters themselves. It is the third element of the two episodes which expands their significance beyond that level. Both are marked by a feature not found elsewhere in this romance, and infrequent in Chrétien's other works. This element is the realistic description of the towns in which the action takes place. A modern Belgian scholar found Escavalon so convincingly portrayed that he felt immediately "at home". [259] While these realistic descriptions are noteworthy in themselves, they also function as "descriptive pivots" and provide a perspective by which to evaluate the episodes they identify as parallels. First, they are antithetical descriptions: Belrepeire is a devastated town without supplies, Escavalon is a prosperous city full of commerce. The antithesis works down to the details. There is nothing outside the walls of Belrepeire *Fors mer et eve et terre gaste* (1709); Gauvain finds animals to hunt and a troop of hunters. The streets of Belrepeire are desolate: *ome ne fame n'i avoit* (1755); Escavalon is *Pueplee de mout bele gent* (5759). In Belrepeire, there is no bread *Ne rien nule qui fust a vandre Don l'an poïst un denier prandre* (1769 f.); Chrétien richly describes the *divers mestiers* (5764) and *totes marcheandises* of which Escavalon is full for over twenty lines (5760-82). The *pucele* who greets Perceval at Belrepeire is *meigre et pale,* and the four men-at-arms who escort him to the castle show signs of hunger and vigils (1745-8); the people of Escavalon, as we have seen, are big and fat (5909-11).

Perceval finds a besieged town at the point of falling to a harsh enemy, a town which desperately needs his help. Gauvain comes to a prosperous city *ou de mort le heent tuit* (5750). Perceval is the savior of Belrepeire. Gauvain brings dismayed shame on its lady, embarrassment to her brother who at first does not know how to deal with a guest who is his mortal enemy, and causes a popular uprising which is quelled with difficulty. The ridicule Perceval endures is a function of his lack of courtliness and ignorance of knightly behavior. Gauvain's misfortune is caused precisely by his great courtliness: he does not identify himself, and he is successful with the lady.

Gauvain's difficulties arise because he is so courtly, so conscious of his courtliness and the conventions of his role. A knight takes part in tournaments, and so Gauvain risks his reputation; a knight cham-

---

[259] "Le sujet est traité avec un réalisme si précis et dans des termes si peu ambigus que, dès la première lecture, je me suis senti en Belgique. Le poète semble avoir trouvé spirituel de travestir l'épisode à la mode de chez nous." Maurice Wilmotte, *Le poème du Graal et ses auteurs* (Paris: Droz, 1930), p. 99. The description is quoted by Anthime Fourrier as an example of Chrétien's "don remarquable d'observation, [d'] observation aiguë, vivante et pittoresque." (*Le courant réaliste dans le roman courtois en France au moyen âge,* 2 vols. [Paris: Nizet, 1960], vol. I, *Les débuts* [XIIᵉ siècle], p. 116; the passage is quoted on p. 118).

pions ladies, and so Gauvain champions the honor of a little girl; a
courtly knight makes love to maidens, and so Gauvain, the most
courtly of Chrétien's heroes in the most courtly situation, makes love
to the daughter of a former victim only to be surprised, reviled, and
attacked. It is courtliness, then, and its conventions, that are in
question, especially since they are contrasted to an undoubted reality.
Perceval, for all his ludicrousness, served the demands of the reality in
which he found himself. Gauvain's adherence to the conventions of
courtliness sets him against a reality which has no use for him, and
which turns a dangerous face towards him. When this happens, he
becomes as ridiculous as the uncourtly Perceval: he cannot help but
play the role of a doorman and shield himself with a chessboard
precisely because he observes so perfectly the conventions of an ethic
which makes this situation ludicrous.

The Hermit Episode

The contradictory relationship between courtliness and reality is
further emphasized by the insertion of the Hermit Episode after the
Escavalon adventure. The change of affective registers extends to the
stylistic contrast: Chrétien's normal mode of brilliant visualization and
concreteness of description is almost completely absent from this
episode. [260] It is spare in language and event, as befits the mental state
of the hero, Perceval.

The location of the episode is important. In keeping with the
general spareness of style, there is no description of the area, but one
word is dropped; Perceval was going through a *desert* when he met
the group of three knights and five ladies (6219). An empty, vapid
space, then, appropriate to the state of Perceval's mind. But this is
not merely geography reflecting the mental state of a character: it is
a specific location of existence, the abode of a hermit to whom a group
of people wend their way on bare feet in the penitence of Good Friday.
We are far from the normal region of the knightly world: [261] to say
as much in the context of Chrétien's romances is to say that we are
in a region apart from society. As we have seen, this was also true
of the *Gaste Forez* of Perceval's childhood. [262]

Is there any further evidence of this similarity? Not directly in the
Perceval, but in the *Yvain.* There also, the hero comes into contact
with a hermit who showed him charity. It was immediately after the
messenger from Laudine found and denounced him that Yvain abandoned society for fear that he would go mad before his fellow *barons*
(*Yvain,* 2798). At first, just after he had heard the maiden's denunciation, *sans et parole* failed him (2777). His anguish grew so great
that whatever he saw was painful, and whatever he heard anguished

---

[260] Kellermann, *Aufbaustil und Weltbild*..., p. 214.
[261] Emmel, *Formprobleme*..., p. 65.
[262] *Ibid., loc. cit.*; and *supra,* pp. 118 ff.

him (2783-5). He wanted to flee alone *en si salvage terre* that no one could find him or know anything about him (2786-90):

> Ne het tant rien con lui meïsme,
> ne ne set a cui se confort
> de lui qui soi meïsme a mort. (2792-4)

When he leaves the court, and is far from the tents and pavilions,

> Lors li monte uns torbeillons
> el chief, si grant que il forsane;
> si se dessire et se depane
> et fuit par chans et par arees... (2806-9)

Wandering alone and naked, he tries to steal a bow and arrow from a boy,

> por qant mes ne li sovenoit
> de rien que onques eüst feite. (2824 f.)

He hunts wild beasts in the forest and eats them raw. And he remained so long in the woods *com hom forsenez et salvage* (2830) that he came to a hermit's meager hut.

Perceval does not go as far in his alienation as Yvain—for a simple and appropriate reason, as we shall see. But he also loses his memory:

> Percevaus, ce conte l'estoire,
> A si perdue la memoire
> Que de Deu ne li sovient mes. (6217-9) [263]

he also hates himself:

> "S'an ai puis eü si grant duel
> Que morz eüsse esté mon vuel..." (6381 f.);

he also remains far from society: his only contact was to send sixty vanquished knights to Arthur (6233-5). The essential identity between the states of mind of Perceval and Yvain, the centering of both episodes around the figure of the charitable hermit, and the similar placement (in the heroes' careers) of the two episodes immediately after the heroes' respective denunciations by female messengers, justifies the identity of location of the two episodes.

As we have seen, the asocial location of madness brought about by suffering—the downfall of the individual from all social norms—is precisely the *Gaste Forez*, the place of desolation defined by its alienation from society. The hero's alienation is more strikingly portrayed in the *Yvain*: nakedness and feeding on raw meat are obvious indices of his fall absent in Perceval. One reason for this lack is the spare descriptive tone required by this episode as a contrast to the surrounding courtly world of Gauvain. More basic is the fact that Perceval, though perhaps as alienated as Yvain, does not go mad nor lose the sense of his identity, even though he has experienced the same

---

public denunciation at Arthur's court as Yvain. The explanation of this
is fairly simple. Yvain was an Arthurian knight to whom the messenger's denunciation was a complete reversal: to be expelled from
the only social context he knew was to lose his very manhood. Perceval, however, never really became an Arthurian knight, in spite of the
external progress which was so impressive to the court. When the
Hideous Damsel denounces him, she is merely repeating something he
has already learned from his cousin, and his expulsion is merely the
return to a state of being he left only a short time before making his
way to the court. To be outside of society, to live in alienation from
one's fellow men, is after all a condition Perceval knows better than
that which he is forced to leave. Above all, there is the fact, of which
the reader was continually reminded during the entire Perceval section,
that his "progress" affected externals only. The lessons he has learned
and put into practice with increasing success represent only restraints
imposed on impulses which were still functioning: Perceval still carries
his essential wildness with him.

Like Yvain, Perceval in the Hermit Episode is at the nadir of his
existence. For both, the Hermit Episode is the bottom of the *abisme*
(*Yvain*, 2791), a place where their resurgence begins, thanks to the
charity of the hermit.

This is indicated also by the structure of the episode. Perceval
hears about religion from two characters, one of the penitent knights
and the hermit. Surprisingly, the instruction of the penitent knight is
more profound than that of the hermit. From the knight, Perceval hears
of the Passion of Christ; a reference to original sin; the paradox of
the God-Man; the Virgin's conception by the Holy Ghost; the Harrowing
of Hell; and the paradox that great good came from the Jews' cruci-
fixion of Christ (6269-96). This is not theology, [264] though it is the
material of theology: the central mysteries of the Christian religion.
If one may be allowed the word in such a context, these are also the
clichés of Christianity, the content of the catechism. Although the
matters touched on include the most profound mysteries of Christianity,
they are also the beliefs central to that religion, and as such equally
the property of the theologian and the peasant. [265]

By comparison, the hermit's teaching is far less ambitious. (1) Go to
the minster daily and hear out the service completely:

---

[264] Kellerman considered these formulations to be "kein Ausdruck naiver
Volksfrömmigkeit, sondern theologische Formulierungen," (*Aufbaustil und Weltbild...*, p. 197).

[265] The most thorough and recent study of Chrétien's "literary religion" is
that of Paul Imbs, "L'élément religieux dans le *Conte del Graal* de Chrétien
de Troyes," in *Les romans du Graal...*, pp. 31-53. "Cette religion est une
religion de prière, d'adoration, d'amour de Dieu ... La religion de Chrétien est
essentiellement théocentrique ... Mais l'accent est mis sur Jésus-Christ ... La chris-
tologie de Chrétien de Troyes est très simple, très traditionnelle, mais avec une
note paulinienne qui met l'accent sur le péché." (*loc. cit.*, p. 46). Pauphilet had
already noted that "il n'y a rien là qui dépasse l'endoctrinement le plus familier
et le plus banal." (*Le legs du moyen âge...*, p. 201).

> "Se ce te vient a volanté,
> Ancor porras monter an pris,
> S'avras enor et paradis." (6456-8)

Like Perceval's mother, like Gornemant, the hermit urges attendance at church on the basis of advancement in this world as well as the next. (2) Love God, your neighbor, and the priest:

> "Deu croi, Deu aimme, Deu aore,
> Buen home et buene fame enore,
> Contre le provoire te lieve;
> C'est uns servises qui po grieve,
> Et Deus l'aimme por verité
> Por ce qu'il vient d'umilité." (6459-64)

The first line of this passage is sometimes quoted alone; in context, it clearly reflects the injunction to love God and neighbor, with the addition of the priest. Since all three come from humility, the last three lines may be read as modifying all three injunctions. [266] (3) Help ladies—*pucele, veve dame, orfeline: Aïe lor, si feras bien* (6469).

Except for the special mention of the respect due to the priest, there is nothing in this teaching which was not already offered Perceval by his mother and Gornemant de Goort. [267] In so far as actual religious teaching is concerned, the hermit is merely repeating the lessons Perceval failed to learn from his previous teachers, not presenting a new aspect of religion. Why this contrast between the lessons of the knight and the hermit? Simply, I think, because the hermit, Perceval's uncle, is aware of the character and limited mentality of his nephew. Undeceived by the knightly armor, he offers simple spiritual food to one who is still a simpleton. This is indicated when the hermit reveals their familial relationship in the middle of a long speech which treats, in addition, of Perceval's mother's death, the sin Perceval then incurred, the fact that this sin caused his silence at the castle of the Fisher King, the mercy God has shown Perceval on account of his mother's prayer for him, the fact that the grail contained a Host which fed the father of the Fisher King who has not left that room for fifteen years, and that he (the hermit) will now give Perceval a penitence. Of all this, touching on so many mysteries, Perceval retains only one thing:

---

[266] Imbs seems to restrict the humility to the respect for the priest (*loc. cit.*, p. 47).

[267] *Supra*, pp. 128 ff., 153 f. The hermit also adds a prayer containing many names of God (6481-8). Kellermann considers this a trait of primitive religion with an eastern source (*Aufbaustil und Weltbild...*, p. 203), Frappier considers it "le secret d'un lignage privilégié, et l'un de ces alliages légèrement ésotériques, dont la littérature du Graal fournit maint exemple, entre la religion et la chevalerie." (*Perceval*, p. 80). However, Spitzer, in his review of Kellermann's book, pointed out that the names of God are also mentioned in the *chansons de geste,* including the *Roland,* and that this should be considered a trait of popular religion (*Modern Language Notes,* LV [1940], 222-6; p. 225; see also below, p. 229 f.).

"Biaus oncles, einsi le vuel gié"
Fet Percevaus, "mout de buen cuer.
Quant ma mere fu vostre suer,
Bien me devez neveu clamer
Et je vos oncle et miauz amer." (6434-8)

Structurally and psychologically, this is the same relationship between
mystery and its focus we saw in the Fisher King episode. Perceval is
presented with the sight or sound of strangeness, the mysterious
cortege of objects, the paradoxical relationships of apparently unrelated
events, and the hint of a religious value in a previous event ... but the
only item to which he reacts is the revelation of the familial tie, the
simplest, most basic, and in moral terms, the least significant of relationships. The hermit's reaction, tinged with a "gentle irony", [268] takes
note of this reaction:

"Voirs est, biaus niés; mes or antant..." (6439)

and proceeds to offer Perceval the simple practical lessons we have
seen. These are not unimportant, but the contrast between the religious
mysteries recounted by the penitent knight and the literary mysteries
revealed by the hermit on one hand, and the single, childish reaction
of Perceval on the other, demonstrates that he is still Perceval, the
vaslet nice of the beginning *qui petit fu senez.*

In no way does this invalidate the sincerity or meaning of his
repentance and penitence. [269] In spite of the weight of its theological
tradition, Christianity is also a pastoral religion serving the poor, meek,
uncomprehending but faithful masses whose submission to the teaching
of the Church is as valuable and effective for individual salvation as
that of the more educated. Perceval the *nice* can feel repentance,
undergo penitence, and receive communion as well as a doctor of
divinity. But that he experiences these religious feelings does not in
itself indicate a change in intellectual status. On the contrary, every
aspect of literary analysis converges to show that he is undergoing a
fundamental experience which brings him back to the minimal level of
humanity, not to a stage beyond the common run of man, or knighthood.
The bareness of style, the structure of the episode, the structural and
thematic comparison of this text with another romance, all point in
this direction: Perceval's religious experience on Good Friday is the
first step, but only the first, toward a return to the existence of a man
in his normal, social context.

---

[268] The phrase and perception are those of a critic whose stress on the
religious aspect of the romance has frequently been noted: Mr. Fowler, in
Prowess and Charity..., p. 57. He also feels that Perceval "absorbs everything
that is said..." in this scene (*loc. cit.*). Fowler's error throughout his book is
to consider that Perceval's mental and moral level is determined by what he is
told, rather than by what he says and does.

[269] Compare the manner in which Chrétien showed Perceval's new tenderness
in Belrepeire, *supra,* p. 158 f.

That the religious content of this scene has received a disproportionate attention reveals more about the different places of religion in the Middle Ages and in our time than about the text. Neither the hermit's teaching nor Perceval's religious experience here is anything other than what should have been normal. Basic religious concepts were established, objective realities for a medieval writer, [270] materials which he could assume rather than subjects of extraordinary literary value. [271] This is clearest in one of the cruces of *Perceval* studies, that of the Holy Grail. It should be noted first of all, that that expression does not occur in Chrétien: *tant sainte chose est li graaus* (6425) is the closest that noun and adjective come in *Perceval*; it is also the only occasion they are linked at all. The context makes it clear that this linking as being presented as a surprising conjunction. The hermit tells Perceval that the grail serves someone he believes to be the father of the Fisher King. But, he warns,

> "... ne cuidiez pas que il et
> Luz ne lamproies ne saumon..." (6420 f.)

i.e., do not think that the grail contains these fish with which it is more commonly associated.

> "D'une sole oiste li sainz hon,
> Que l'an an cest graal li porte,
> Sa vie sostient et conforte;
> Tant sainte chose est li graaus,
> Et il est si esperitaus
> Qu'a sa vie plus ne covient
> Que l'oiste qui el graal vient." (6422-8)

The intent of the explanation is to present an extraordinary juxtaposition, one which may be considered either paradoxical or mysterious according to the reader's temperament. We are told first of a container, then told that it does not bear its usual content: instead of the fish which might have been expected, it contains a single Host. [272] This is not all: not only do we hear of an unexpected Host in the grail, we

---

[270] Kellermann, *Aufbaustil und Weltbild...*, p. 122 f.

[271] *Ibid.*, p. 194: here, Kellermann is making this point about the opening scene with the five knights, and finds a completely different kind of piety in the Hermit Episode. Admitting that the intermediate stages of Perceval's supposed progress are portrayed with little concreteness, he explains that the narrative techniques of the time were inadequate to the purpose (*loc. cit.*).

This disregards entirely Chrétien's wide range of techniques for showing inner change and development: direct psychological analysis, as in the *Cligès* and *Yvain* monologues; a combination of the latter with objectively reported conversation, as in Laudine's slow acceptance of the idea of marrying Yvain; a completely objective gradation of externally reported actions, as in the adventures which follow the turning point in both *Erec* and *Yvain*. To say that Chrétien was unable to reveal his character's inner life is to discard one of his most extraordinary technical achievements.

[272] "Ce qui nous semble révélateur, c'est le désaccord entre contenant et contenu: le récipient est nommé d'un terme TECHNIQUE du service de table...; cela n'appelle nullement une hostie comme contenu." Fourquet, "L'œuvre et la source...," p. 307.

learn that a man—whom we have not seen or heard of before this speech —lives entirely from the sustenance of the Host carried in the grail.

It has been noted that the expression *tant sainte chose* is unusual in Chrétien's works. In fact, the only parallel usage occurs in *Cligès,* where *mout sainte chose* is used by Jehan (who knows that Fénice is faking death) of Fénice's supposed corpse.[273] The *Cligès* usage was ironic. The same obviously cannot be said of the *Perceval* phrase, but the two do share the characteristic of incongruity. The passage of the hermit's speech can also be compared to the scene of the cortege in the Fisher King's castle: both present extraordinary events which remain unexplained, because their common function is to contrast the simplicity of Perceval's reaction with a mystery or paradox which should elicit a response cognizant of their unusual quality. The literary means employed by the two scenes are very different. The procession of objects in the Fisher King episode is mysterious, suggestive of hidden preparations and destinations, richly described itself but also incomplete by reference to areas of the castle and its life undisclosed but implied by the strange movements. By contrast, the reflection of that episode in the hermit's "explanation" is bare, declarative in form, but paradoxical in its simplicity. Both mystery and paradox, however, are too far beyond the reach of Perceval's mind: unable to deal with them in his own terms, he refers one to a social rule which he misapplies, and ignores the other.

From this point of view, the hermit episode continues the principles of character portrayal and literary technique of the Perceval section. Nevertheless, it is an unusual episode in the romance and, indeed, in Chrétien's writings as a whole. Part of its effect is due to the contrast in affective and stylistic registers between it and the surrounding Gauvain world. However, this does not account for its exceptional position in these courtly romances: it is the only time in Chrétien's work that the story of a knight is seen from a religious viewpoint. Its narrative value is limited: Perceval's abnegation, as has been said, is merely a first step, essential but minimal, back to the full life of man in society. There is also the matter of the family relationships which

---

[273] Imbs, "L'élément religieux dans le *Conte del Graal*...," p. 42. This is part of a section on "Le vocabulaire religieux de Chrétien et le Graal," pp. 36-44, which contains a useful collection of materials, unfortunately partly unrefined. Imbs stresses the religious character of the *Cligès* phrase quoted above by associating it with the *sainteire* in which Fénice is to be buried, ignoring the ironic intent of the phrase as well as of the entire episode. Similarly, he cites the use of *saintime* and *sainte* in Chrétien's allegorical developments during the duel between Yvain and Gauvain at the end of the *Yvain* (6044, 6046) as examples of *religious* uses of these words, disregarding the obvious paradoxical intent of the allegory (those united by "holy friendship" are fighting each other ferociously), its subtler paradoxical reflection on the whole romance (was Gauvain really acting as a friend in urging Yvain to leave Laudine?), and the thoroughly non-religious character of the allegory, which deals with friendship under the name of *amor*. The technique of crude word-count is of limited usefulness in stylistic analysis, and particularly misleading in a writer for whom irony is a basic mode of writing.

bind the hero, the hermit, the Fisher King, and the latter's father—information which was meant, perhaps, to become functional when Perceval returned to the center of attention. The specifically religious aspect of the episode, however, does not function sequentially but reflectively: it is not so much part of the narrative as a manner of looking at the entire sequence of events which includes it as a (minor) part. As Chrétien earlier used another encounter with another inhabitant of the *Gaste Forez*—the *vilain*, guardian of wild beasts in *Yvain*—to suggest a view of courtly knighthood from a position outside the courtly world, so here, in the meeting of another imperfect knight with an inhabitant of the same region, we are also placed in a location and point of view outside the scene of the *Perceval*'s major actions. In *Yvain*, the encounter was only ironically subversive: the *vilain*, a parody of horrendousness, is no more than a comic figure before he simple-mindedly drops a remark which implies a universal philosophical attitude toward mankind whose full meaning he can hardly comprehend. By contrast, the hermit is kind, understanding, humane, and commiserating where rebukes might have been expected. Above all he is religious, and markedly so: his presence in a chapel turns the *desert* into a location which can no longer be defined only by its distance from society. Although it is still outside the circle of courtliness, it is suddenly invested with an authority of moral and religious interpretation which was completely absent in both the *vilain* and hermit scenes of *Yvain*.

It is with this in mind that I would suggest an interpretation of the hermit's "explanation" of Perceval's silence. Telling his nephew that his mother died on account of his departure, he adds:

> "Por le pechié que tu an as
> T'avint que tu ne demandas
> De la lance ne del graal,
> Si t'an sont avenu maint mal,
> Ne n'eüsses pas tant duré,
> S'ele ne t'eüst comandé
> A Damedeu, ce saches tu." (6399-6405)

It should be noted first of all that the statement does not link only Perceval's silence with the causative sin, but *maint mal* as well: whatever we find misadventurous in the romance—the harsh treatment of the Tent Maiden, the killing of the Red Knight, Perceval's various rudenesses and crudities—all of these are to be linked with that "original sin". If the statement is to be taken literally, it must also be taken as a whole, and the entire psychological structure of the romance disregarded: it is all a result of Perceval's first lack of compassion. The sequence of instructors and their misapplied lessons—the mother, Yonet, Gornemant de Goort, Anguingueron and Clamadeu—all these are so much narrative dissembling until the author leads us to the one, single cause of the action, a theological *Schuldautomatismus*. [274]

---

[274] Kellermann, *Aufbaustil und Weltbild...*, p. 109.

Furthermore, if we take the last three lines as exclusive truth, we must also conclude that Perceval's courage and strength had nothing to do with his successes against the Red Knight, Anguingueron, Clamadeu, the Orguelleus de la Lande, Sagremor le Desreez, and Keu the seneschal.

Considering the generally acknowledged excellence of Chrétien's literary psychology, it seems unlikely that many readers would accept such conclusions. They not only disregard the structure of the romance, they also belie our literary experience of the character: rarely has such a convincing portrait been painted of youth's energy, equally charming and destructive, as it comes into contact and conflict with the limitations society imposes on each individual, and its slow, painful, and hesitant taming by masculine guidance and feminine coquetterie. To equate the hermit's interpretation with a total analysis of the romance is a reduction most readers will find unacceptable.

But this antinomy between the structure and the hermit's words is not a necessary one. Chrétien does not present us with an either/or situation in which we must choose one interpretation as against the other. No more than Catholic doctrine conceives of the theory of original sin as destructive of free will, need we replace the carefully elaborated psychological structure of the narrative by a single, simple theological statement. I have said that the religious element of this episode functions primarily as a reflection on the rest of the narrative. That Perceval's sin in ignoring his mother's plight caused *maint mal,* including his silence with the Fisher King, is a religious interpretation and evaluation of his story, not a substitute for it. The hermit, looking at this story, finds that it contains a wrong which has a religious value, and tries to impart that idea to a simpleton in a simple manner, by phrasing it in immediately apprehensible words. The hermit is not the author, any more than the other characters who have advised Perceval are equatable with Chrétien. They present a particular view of Perceval and his actions which, if not exclusively correct, provides one more aspect of the hero. This aspect, in the present scene, is religious, but it is only one aspect of the romance, not its entirety or even, perhaps, its main intention. [275]

---

[275] This interpretation owes something to Frappier's analysis. He finds three levels of meaning in the romance. The first is that of the *apprentissage du nice.* The second, primarily moral, is "celui de la personnalité, de la conscience que prend le héros de sa responsabilité et de sa liberté intérieure." The third, "d'abord caché, puis entrevu, puis dominant, est religieux et mystique: le péché commis contre sa mère est la cause profonde du silence de Perceval; déserté par la grâce, longtemps fermé au repentir, il est sauvé spirituellement le jour du vendredi saint." (*Perceval,* p. 81 f.; see also *Chrétien de Troyes,* p. 185 f.). The essential notion I owe Frappier is that "ces sens se superposent et se complètent, *ils ne se contredisent pas.*" (*Perceval,* p. 82; my emphasis).

I find his second level dubious: as Frappier himself has pointed out, Perceval is not a character who analyzes himself (*ibid.,* pp. 70, 79), a prerequisite, I should think, for the discovery of moral responsibility and inner freedom. However, it is the basic conception of «three levels of meaning" which seems to me most inappropriate: it verges on considering *Perceval* an allegory. It also results

To the modern reader, this religious element may seem an intrusion into the world of courtly romance. I would suggest that it was felt as such by the original audience as well, but in a different way. The modern reader, once accustomed to the elaboration of a world of fantasy in these romances, accepts this as a literary assumption, a "contract" between himself and the author. When religion intrudes in more than its normal and quite frequent ceremonial function, [276] it is as a totally foreign and strange interruption which breaks this contract. For the medieval reader, however, this interruption is not strange and by no means foreign: it is rather a return to a point of view more mundane and familiar to him than to many modern readers. It is part of his own world which suddenly intrudes into the fantasy world which is Gauvain's habitat, a world where ethical values are most frequently cast in religious terms. The hermit's teachings of loving God and neighbor and respecting the clergy are more likely to have struck the medieval audience as a memory of last Sunday's sermon than a call to theological or mystical speculation.

The introduction of elementary Christian values and beliefs in the Hermit Episode is an invitation to reflect on the narrative of which it is a part in more basic and fundamental terms than the values and beliefs which operate as purposes and goals for the characters of the narrative. These terms are indubitably religious, but they invoke religion at a fundamental level where it fuses with daily, practical ethics and morality. The simplicity of these terms, as well as the restrained tone of the episode, recall an earlier passage of the romance: its Prologue. As we saw, Chrétien there treated charity from three points of view. Charity is God himself—a statement which may be mystical, or theological, or merely a cliché of religious writing, but which is irrelevant to the action and words of the romance itself. Charity is also part of the relationship between God and man: "He who abides in love abides in God, and God abides in him." [277] Finally, charity is seen as bearing on the relationship of man and man; this was expressed in the Prologue as a properly motivated generosity. [278]

The word charity does not occur in the Hermit Episode, but its last two aspects are reflected in the central lesson of humility given Perceval by the hermit in lines already quoted:

> "Deu croi, Deu aimme, Deu aore,
> Buen home et buene fame enore,

in the distinction in which the supposedly religious and mystical level provides a more "profound" cause of Perceval's silence than does the literary structure of the work: as we have seen, the latter is considered to add no more than a "nuance" to this profound meaning (*supra*, p. 173). In this manner, what Chrétien elaborates by literary means becomes less important that what he supposedly suggests "symbolically".

In addition, this interpretation makes the Gauvain section irrelevant (since neither of the two "higher" levels has any function there) as well as anticlimactic.

[276] Imbs, "L'élément religieux dans le *Conte del Graal...*," p. 44 f.
[277] 1 *John*, 4, 16.
[278] *Supra*, pp. 115 ff.

> Contre le provoire te lieve;
> C'est uns servise qui po grieve,
> Et Deus l'aimme por verité
> Por ce qu'il vient d'umilité." (6459-64)

The first two lines of this passage contain the lesson of charity as it applies to any Christian, peasant, knight, or emperor: ignoring the theological question of the nature of God, they repeat the fundamental Christian law of love of God and fellow men. These two lines also contain the essence of the hermit's entire religious teaching. Going daily to services and hearing out the service completely—his first injunction—is an expression of love for God. His third lesson, bringing help to women, is the embodiment of the love of neighbor appropriate to the knight of the romance. From the purely religious point of view, the statement of this dual commandement is as trite as it is profound. Whatever is problematic is disregarded in its prescriptive tone. Its bland absoluteness is slightly fleshed out by the other specifics of church attendance and knightly succour, but, as we have seen, these are equally trite in the world of this romance, since this advice has been given to Perceval before.

The lesson of charity becomes valuable only as a commentary on the action of the romance, a commentary equally valid and obvious. To say that Perceval lacked charity in regards to his mother, the Tent Maiden, the Red Knight, the Fisher King, and his cousin in the forest—this does not reveal the "profound meaning" of the romance, it merely represents an obvious moral interpretation of Perceval's actual relationships with other characters in the romance. It is equally true and obvious to say that Perceval lacked charity in his relationship to God by not fulfilling the Christian duty of going to church. In each of the personal relationships mentioned, his egoism and social ignorance prevent or impede a recognition of the rights of other people, or even of their existence as anything but obstacles to Perceval's desires. Little wonder that, with such alienation from those physically present to him, Perceval does not recognize the existence of the unseen God. In both cases, Perceval's behavior is determined by a simple psychology, by his *niceté*. When, in the early sections, Chrétien's irony suggests a judgment, it is usually in terms of Perceval's own goals of knighthood and courtliness. The function of the Hermit Episode is to recall the suggestion of the Prologue, that there is another set of terms and values which are relevant to his behavior, the values of a daily morality stated in fundamental Christian terms. These values, reflected in the word "charity", are precisely those embodied by that other hermit, the wordless character in *Yvain* who, though frightened by the sudden appearance of a naked madman outside his little hut, gave him of his own meager nourishment:

> de son pain et de sa porrete
> par charité prist li boens hom,
> si li mist fors de sa meison
> desor une fenestre estroite... (*Yvain,* 2840-3)

Greoreas, the Orguelleuse de Logres.

Gauvain's first encounter after the Hermit Episode reveals the connection between the concept of charity and Gauvain's fantasy world. He finds a maiden weeping over a wounded knight

> Qui le vis avoit depecié
> Et ot une plaie mout grief
> D'une espee parmi le chief,
> Et d'andeus parz parmi les flans
> Li coroit a randon li sans.
> Li chevaliers pasmez se fu
> Sovant del mal qu'il ot eü,
> Tant qu'an la fin se reposa. (6552-9)

Over the maiden's protests, Gauvain awakens the knight in order to ask *des afeires de ceste terre* (6570). The knight warns Gauvain not to continue into Galvoie: he himself is the only man to have returned alive from the encounter with the knight who guards its frontier. The effect, of course, is to encourage Gauvain all the more. [279] He leaves the wounded man and his maiden, enters Galvoie, meets the Orguelleuse de Logres—of whom more anon—and returns without difficulty to the wounded knight. The weeping maiden speaks to Gauvain:

> "Biaus sire chiers,
> Or cuit je que cist chevaliers
> Est morz, qu'il n'ot mes ne antant." (6919-21)

Gauvain takes the man's pulse and temperature: He is alive, I assure you, and I have brought an herb to alleviate part of his pain. And so it is: the man is saved by Gauvain's ministrations.

From the narrative viewpoint, this episode with Greoreas (the wounded knight) is of secondary importance. It leads to the meeting with the Orguelleuse, but is by no means essential for that purpose. It also leads to two comic scenes (the fights with the Red Squire and Greoreas' nephew), neither of which is essential to the general structure; in addition, the structure of this episode is not necessary to bring about the two comic scenes. It is probable, then, that this episode makes a point of its own.

The basic structure is that of a sequential dyptich: first Gauvain meets a wounded knight, and leaves him; he attends to the knight on his return. At that time, Chrétien reveals that Gauvain is particularly knowledgeable in medical matters:

> ... mes sire Gauvains savoit
> Plus que nus hom de garir plaie... (6910 f.)

---

[279] In this respect, Gauvain's psychology is similar to Perceval, who also was urged on to do something by contraries: *supra,* p. 161 f. The Orguelleuse de Logres will intentionally manipulate Gauvain as Blancheflor did Perceval: *infra,* pp. 238 ff.

He expertly discerns the appropriate herb and picks it on the way back. After his examination of Greoreas, he addresses the maiden with the assurance of a professionnal:

> "Cist chevaliers," fet il, "pucele
> Est vis, tote an soiiez certainne,
> Qu'il a buen pos et buene alainne;
> Et se il n'a plaie mortel,
> Je li aport une herbe tel
> Qui mout, ce cuit, li eidera
> Et les dolors li ostera
> De ses plaies une partie
> Tantost come il l'avra santie..." (6926-34) [280]

Gauvain continues with a detailed exposition on the qualities of the herb, and then binds the wound with a borrowed wimple as bandage.

The question raised by the two-part structure is: if Gauvain is so adept in medicine, why did he not make use of this knowledge when he first saw the wounded man? Surely it would have been the simplest and most immediate kind of reaction to attend to a man who is at least grievously wounded as soon as he found him. When Greoreas responds to Gauvain's care and comes to, he is still not certain that he will survive:

> "Deus li mire
> Qui la parole m'a randue;
> Que mout ai grant peor eüe
> De morir sanz confession.
> Li diable a procession
> M'ame estoient ja venu querre." (6964-9)

He requests that he be brought to a nearby *chapelain* (6972) for confession and communion: he will not fear death after taking communion and making his confession. The speech, not very long (6964-83), is almost entirely religious in thought and vocabulary: devils, a chaplain, and his sins are referred to, as well as communion (twice) and confession (four times). This stress on the last rites suggests that it was not only a man's life Gauvain endangered by his thirst for adventure and quest for reputation, but his salvation as well. [281] In the first adventure after the Hermit Episode, Gauvain is shown to have lacked in charity.

---

[280] Note the pompous effect obtained by the disjunctions in the first two lines: Gauvain (represented by *fet il*) stands between the knight and the maiden. His essential message ("Est vis") is squeezed in between his introduction and the comforting phrase ("tote an soiiez certainne", which suggests his own certainty in diagnosis as well), before coming to the expansive conclusion of the third line; cf. *supra*, p. 198.

[281] When Gauvain rejects Greoreas' advice not to wander into Galvoie, the latter states his motive clearly:

> "Vos i iroiz, que mout volez
> Vostre pris croistre et alever." (6626 f.)

Perceval also met a weeping maiden. His cousin's knight was dead, but there was still a form of charity appropriate to the situation: to help with his burial. Instead, he urged her ot leave the dead to themselves and accompany him. As is usual in these parallels, the motives for the similar actions differ. Gauvain's is clear: pride in reputation as the epitome of courtly knighthood. Perceval's may have been an inability to express pity, or, as Frappier has suggested, a repression of possible repentance. [282] In any case, whatever the motives, the result is the same: Perceval and Gauvain, with all their differences, commit the same act.

Chrétien faced a particularly difficult technical problem at this point. On the one hand, he wished to indicate the validity of the perspective given in the Hermit Episode to the Gauvain section: his second hero was to be seem from the same point of view as his first. But Gauvain was to remain the hero for at least two thousand lines more, and the reader's sympathy could not be alienated. A similar problem existed in the Perceval section. To have revealed the death of Perceval's mother when she fell as Perceval rode away would have destroyed the reader's sympathy. [283] Instead, Chrétien showed his lack of compassion but delayed the revelation of its effect. Here, the possibility of Greoreas' death is suggested, but he does not die: his delayed succour preserves him to bring humiliation on Gauvain.

At the same time that Chrétien wished to show the relevance of a certain point of view, he also had to return from the spare style of the Hermit Episode to the tone of fantasy characteristic of the Gauvain section. Both the moral and aesthetic problems are faced and solved by the resources of style in a passage that starts some sixty lines after the Hermit Episode. When Gauvain first rides up to the maiden, he asks a question which, if harmless, seems besides the point and not particularly kindly in tone:

> "Bele, que vos est vis
> Del chevalier que vos tenez?" (6562 f.)

Her answer tells him he has asked the obvious:

> "*Veoir poëz*
> Qu'an ses plaies a grant peril;
> Que de la menor morroit il." (6564-6)

So far, however, we are merely at the level of a certain lack of sympathy, a coldness Gauvain has demonstrated before. [284]

His next request displays both politeness and a surprising heartlessness:

> "Ma douce amie,
> Esveilliez le, ne vos poist mie;

---

[282] *Perceval*, p. 63.
[283] *Supra*, p. 128, n. 42.
[284] See Emmel's comments on Gauvain's role in his relationship to Yvain (*Formprobleme...*, pp. 30 f., 33 f.).

> Que noveles li vuel anquerre
> Des afeires de ceste terre." (6567-70)

Ma bele amie, ne vos poist mie, these are marks of the courtesy associated with Gauvain, but they are sharply incongruous with the content of his request. [285] There is nothing ironic in the demand for information itself: it is the context which determines the irony. Gauvain wishes to disturb a man who appears to be mortally wounded for the sake of general travel information, and reveals thereby an egoism as deep as Perceval's. The conjunction of politeness and egoism stresses the extent of the latter and reveals the superficiality of the former.

The maiden naturally refuses: she would rather let herself be cut to pieces than wake him. What is the reaction now of the paragon of courtly knighthood?

> "Et je l'esveillerai, par foi",
> Fet mes sire Gauvains, "mon vuel." (6580 f.) [286]

At this point, lack of sympathy and heartlessness turn to an almost brutal lack of charity... or they would, if the point were not both stressed and evaded by a brief passage which shifts the narrative into the sphere of fantasy even as it climaxes Gauvains's heartlessness:

> Lors torne* devers l'arestuel   *Gauvain
> De sa lance et si l'an adoise
> A l'esperon; ne pas n'an poise
> Au chevalier, s'il l'esveilla,
> Car si soavet li crolla
> L'esperon que mal ne li fist,
> Einçois l'an mercia et dist :
> "Sire, cinc çanz merciz vos rant
> Quant vos si deboneiremant
> Boté et esveillié m'avez
> Que de neant n'an sui grevez." (6582-92)

This is a master ironist's *gageure*. Within the shadow of the Hermit Episode, Chrétien effects a transition which both makes his moral point and disguises its sting. Once Gauvain's lack of charity has been shown, it is disregarded not only by the author but the victim as well: Greoreas' effusive gratitude for not having been harmed by Gauvain's inconsiderate act returns us to a plane of courtly fantasy in which manners are more important than action and its moral value. The passage is a transition which achieves more than merely to serve as a

---

[285] Compare the politeness of Gauvain's answer to Keu, above p. 194 f.

[286] The expression *mon vuel,* set off at the end of the line by disjunction, is reminiscent of a similar characterization of Alexander; see *supra,* p. 66.

At about this point, the reader may also come to feel that the distinguished designation which continually accompanies the present hero—*mes sire Gauvain*—is weighed with irony (on the particularly close relationship between this appellation and Gauvain, see Foulet, "Sire, messire...", p. 21.

bridge between two sequences of events: it joins two narrative worlds aesthetically and morally. [287]

The transition continues as Chrétien shifts from suggestiveness and moral relevance to pure farce. We left Greoreas expressing a wish to see a nearby chaplain. For this, he will need a horse, and asks for the *roncin* of an approaching squire. This is the red-haired squire, who is described in one of the traditional "inverted portraits".[288] Not only the squire but his mount as well are exceedingly repulsive: Gauvain would prefer to give Greoreas seven chargers, if he had them there, than the *roncin*. Nevertheless, approach the squire he must, and courteously tries to start a conversation by asking where he is going. *Cil qui n'estoit pas deboneire* (7123) tells him it's none of his business, to which Gauvain answers by a satisfying blow of the hand which has the weight of the metal-covered arm behind it. [289] The results of this blow are pure farce. The Red Squire is knocked out of the saddle,

---

[287] One may also speculate about the words used by Chrétien and Greoreas. *Adoisier* is normal usage for "touching delicately"; *croller* and *boter*, however, are ambiguous. Though both can be used in the sense of "nudging", they frequently have stronger meanings such as "shaking" or "pushing". If they are taken in the stronger sense, the modifiers *soavet* and *deboneiremant* form oxymorons and are ironic.

That is a linguistic question. Another is factual, but equally difficult to resolve. A lance, after all, was not a child's plastic toy. It was long enough to allow Perceval to lean on it while still mounted. It was made of strong wood to avoid shattering in the clash of combat. It had a metal head and leather or metal hand-guard. Though specific information on twelfth century lances is hard to find (see Francis Grose, *Military Antiquities Respecting a History of the English Army from the Conquest to the Present Time,* 2 vols., [Picadilly: Stockdale, 1812], vol. I, p. 277; and Léon Gautier, *La chevalerie,* [Paris: Delgrave, 1884], p. 709, note), we do know that Gauvain's lances are particularly large (see the comment of the *pucele as manches petites,* ll. 5072 f.). We may wonder whether a knight, even Gauvain, could so precisely control his lance, especially with the heavier end hanging down. If this consideration is thought relevant, the entire description of Gauvain's act is ironic.

[288]
Ses chevos ot meslez et ros,
Roides et contremont dreciez
Come pors qui est hericiez,
Et les sorcius ot autretés;
Que tot le vis et tot le nés
Li covroient jusqu'as grenons
Que il avoit tortiz et lons;
Boche ot fandue et barbe lee,
Forchiee et puis recercelee,
Et cort le col et le piz haut. (6988-97)

Kellermann allowed the descriptions of ugliness as the only purely comic figures Chrétien painted (*Aufbaustil und Weltbild...,* p. 130); see also Mario Roques, "Pour l'Introduction à l'édition du *Roman de Perceval* de Chrétien de Troyes," p. 12, n. 1.

[289]
... il le fiert de la paume overte
A ce qu'il ot le braz armé
Et del ferir grant volanté... (7020-2)

Linker translates *A ce qu'il ot le braz armé* by "while he had his arm ready." (*The Story of the Grail,* p. 144).

> Et quant il relever se cuide,
> Si rechancele et rechiet jus
> Et se pasme set foiz ou plus
> An mains de terre, sanz nul gap,
> Ne tient une lance de sap.
> Et quant il se fu relevez,
> Si dist: "Vassaus, feru m'avez. (7024-30)

The gigantic blow, the staggering, falling, rising, falling again of the victim in less space than a lance takes up—*sanz nul gap!*— and the victim's first comment, sheepish or resentful, as he hesitatingly finds his feet again: "You hit me!" ... the viewer of early Chaplin films recognizes the pattern immediately. [290]

Enjoyable as farce, it is also functional in larger terms. It locates the action at the level of low comedy where Gauvain's courteous apology is ludicrously out of place. He first admits his "guilt":

> "Voire" fet il, "feru t'ai gié,

minimizes it:

> Mes ne t'ai gueires domagié;

apologizes for it:

> Et si me poise tote voie
> Quant t'ai feru, se Deus me voie;

and excuses it:

> Mes tu deïs grant musardie." (7031-5)

If adherence to the highest standards of courtliness is an admirable principle in the abstract, a particular situation may reveal it in a comically absurd light. Even this adherence is dubious, however, since Gauvain was responsible for the whole farce with his blow.

This broad comedy also is part of the larger parallelistic scheme. Both heroes of the romance meet a Red Man whom they fight in scenes that include broad humor and are associated with death or grievous suffering. Perceval, of course, killed the Red Knight, while Gauvain only mauls his red opponent about a bit: the real parallel to the Red Knight's death is Greoreas, whom Gauvain almost let die by negligence. The motives in the two scenes are identical: both Perceval and Gauvain want something which belongs to their opponent: armor, a horse, and both use force to obtain it, with some excuse. The differences are

---

[290] Or the viewer of a Punch and Judy show. I take the liberty of quoting again a passage already used: "Quand le commissaire s'aventure sur la scène, il reçoit aussitôt comme de juste, un coup de bâton qui l'assomme. Il se redresse, un second coup l'aplatit. Nouvelle récidive, nouveau châtiment. Sur le rythme uniforme du ressort qui se tend et se détend, le commissaire s'abat et se relève, tandis que le rire de l'auditoire va toujours grandissant." (*supra*, p. 122, n. 27). Gauvain is distinguished from Punch in that his first blow was powerful enough to insure the succession of falls and risings: one blow, and the Red Squire contains within himself both principles of external cause and reaction.

important also. The most obvious one is that Greoreas survives, while the Red Knight died; though both heroes lacked charity, the results of Gauvain's lack are less serious. There is also an inversion in the relationship of the two heroes to their victims. The Red Knight, simply by virtue of being a knight, is of a higher status than Perceval: by killing him in a manner neither knightly nor charitable, Perceval ironically moved closer to becoming a knight himself. The Red Squire, however, is of a lower social status than Gauvain, who lowers himself in brawling with an inferior. Perceval reduced what should have been a knightly encounter to a hunting incident; Gauvain reduces his own knighthood by precipitating and participating in an unknightly fight. The crucial difference here is that Perceval was unaware of the values he demeaned, while Gauvain's apologies show him all too conscious of his error.

It will not be necessary to pursue the analysis of the Gauvain section with the detail of the preceding pages, though it offers a rich field for further examples of Chrétien's talents as ironist and comic writer. Once that basic intent is clearly established, and the aesthetic and moral point of view from which the narrative is to be observed is seen to be defined in the Hermit Episode, the remaining sections of the romance offer little difficulty on that score. Furthermore, Frappier's appreciation of Chrétien's irony and humor in these sections is an excellent guide in this respect. [291] However, it is possible to have the impression from his commentary that the elaboration of the "univers disloqué" in which various adventures take place without logical connection and are strangely intermingled has little purpose except to agree with "l'inconstance de son personnage Gauvain." [292] My intention in these pages will be to show that, on the contrary, Chrétien was following a thoroughly conscious and rational plan both in relation to the values represented by Gauvain and in relation to the frequent parallelistic structure which binds this section to the Perceval section; and that his basic strategy remained the use of ironic and comic techniques.

The major episodes bring Gauvain into a relationship with a female figure. In Gauvain's first adventure, he pledges life-long service to a little girl for whom he has already fought in a tournament. This brought into play the *sine qua non* of knighthood, prowess. As we saw, Gauvain's service in that episode was subject to ridicule in that its object was a parody of a courtly lady. [293] The second major episode saw Gauvain discomfited in a situation where successful seduction was at stake rather than a more distant love-service. Again, it was in terms

[291] *Perceval*, pp. 122-35.
[292] *Ibid.*, p. 122. Frappier attributes the "juxtaposition plutôt incohérente" of adventures which give rise both to laughter and admiration to Chrétien's source, but feels "qu'il s'est probablement abstenu de remédier à ce désordre, et qu'il l'aurait même accentué, car la vision d'un univers disloqué s'accordait avec l'inconstance de son personnage Gauvain." (p. 122 f.).
[293] *Supra*, pp. 207-11.

of the standards of knighthood and courtliness that Gauvain was ridiculed. [294] At this point occurs the Hermit Episode, with its introduction of a new aesthetic and moral point of view, which is first applied in the Greoreas Episode.

The next feminine figure of major importance is that of the Orguelleuse de Logres, whom Gauvain finds under an elm admiring herself in a mirror (6676-9). He spurs his horse toward her only to be greeted with a proud, disdainful.

> "Mesure,
> Mesure, sire, or belemant,
> Que vos venez mout folemant!" (6684-6)

We learn from the ensuing conversation—which consists mainly of the lady reading Gauvain's mind and his surprised acquiescence—that he expected simply to pick her up and carry her off on the neck of his horse. [295] Instead, he unhesitatingly accepts her service even though she presents her sovereignty in the most unattractive and disdainful manner:

> "Et neporquant, se tu osoies,
> Mener avuec toi m'an porroies...
> ....
> Je iroie tant avuec toi
> Que tu antre tes braz me taingnes:
> Et diaus et honte et mescheance
> T'avenist an ma conpeignie." (6711-9)

He is refused even the most superficial satisfaction, that of helping her mount the horse he has just brought her:

> "Ce ne te lest ja Deus conter"
> Fet la pucele, "an leu ou vaingnes,
> Que tu antre es braz me taingnes:
> Se tu avoies rien tenue
> Qui fust sor moi, de ta main nue
> Ne menoiiee ne santie,
> Je cuideroie estre honie." (6840-6)

And the same pattern of meek and minimal services repulsed occurs again when he wishes to help her on with her coat (6874-94).

Gauvain's service to the *male pucele* is one long series of humiliations. Paradoxically, he came up to her after his pride and desire to augment his reputation led him to abandon the wounded Greoreas. In fact, he endures only the *male avanture et pesance et diaus et honte*

---

[294] *Supra*, pp. 213-20.

[295] "En somme, Gauvain se proposait de kidnapper la demoiselle; dessein curieux chez celui qui passe pour le modèle de toute courtoisie!" (Frappier, *Perceval*, p. 124, n. 1). What is even more curious is that this is precisely the crime for which Gauvain forced Greoreas to spend a month eating with the dogs, his hands tied behind his back (7109-31): Greoreas had kidnapped and raped a girl.

et mescheance she has predicted. Typical of this is the farcical mis-adventure at the *Guez Perilleuz*. He has just defeated the companion of the *male pucele*. Having handed over his victim to the *notonier*, Gauvain endures her sarcasm. He may be proud of his victory, but the other man was weak from wounds, or the outcome would have been different:

> "Mout fussent voz bordes cheües,
> N'eüssiez or mie tant jangle,
> Plus fussiez muz que maz an angle." (8426-8)

But her sarcasm is purposeful: she wants something from Gauvain, and is preparing the way. If he will do the same thing that her friend did,

> "Adonc por voir tesmoigneroie
> Que vos vaudriiez miauz que il
> Ne ne vos avroie plus vil." (8440-2)

The appeal is to two of the most potent motives in Gauvain: care for his reputation, and success with the ladies. He grants her request without hesitation or qualification. As the ladies of the nearby Château des Merveilles tear their hair in fear of his approaching death, Gauvain is led to the bank of a river. Without any sarcasm, the Orguelleuse points to the deep ford and its high banks, on the other side of which, she says, her friend used to pick flowers for her. Innocently, Gauvain asks:

> "Pucele, comant i passoit?" (8485)

I knew it, says she, you are not courageous enough to undertake this:

> "Que nus, se trop n'est corageus,
> N'ose passer por nule painne." (8496 f.)

Gauvain, a perfect victim now, rides closer to the river, looks at the deep water below and the steep bank above ... but also notices that the river is narrow:

> Quant mes sire Gauvains la voit
> Si dit que ses chevaus avoit
> Maint greignor fossé tressailli
> Et panse qu'il avoit oï
> Dire et conter an plusors leus
> Que cil qui del Gué Perilleus
> Porroit passer l'eve parfonde
> Qu'il avroit tot le pris del monde. (8503-10)

Openly boasting and silently weighing the potential gain in reputation, Pride goeth to its fall. Gauvain backs off for a running start, comes bounding back for his jump,

> ... mes il faut,
> Qu'il ne prist mie bien son saut,
> Einz sailli droit anmi le gué. (8513-5)

Fortunately, the horse saves the knight: it finds its footing again and jumps up the high bank. In doing so, it does something impossible. The Orguelleuse has described this as a *gué parfont Don les rives si hautes sont* (8479 f.). When Gauvain looks at it, he repeats the description and adds one specification:

> "Je ne sai pas ou li guez soit;
> L'eve est trop parfonde, ce dot,
> Et la rive haute par tot
> *Si qu'an n'i porroit avaler.*" (8486-9)

If it is impossible to go down the bank because it is too steep, is it likely that the horse would climb up? Likely or not, he does, and in a single jump:

> Et ses chevaus a tant noé
> Qu'il prist terre de quatre piez,
> Si s'est por saillir afichiez:
> Si se lance si que il saute
> Sor la rive qui mout fu haute. (8516-20)

This unreality is immediately followed by thoroughly realistic detail. After the effort of his jump, the horse refuses to budge. Gauvain must dismount, take off the saddle, and dry it and the horse: a squire's job. In the meanwhile, the *male pucele* has disappeared.

One aspect of the unreality in the situation is that the Orguelleuse lied in saying that her friend used to jump over the *gué* at her request. As Gauvain soon learns, he is the only knight to have come out of the river alive (8588-91). This lie, in turn, is part of her whole manipulation of Gauvain, which played on his main motives in the same manner and according to the same principle by which Blancheflor manipulated Perceval. [296] Psychologically, Gauvain follows the same principles of masculine reaction as Perceval. [297] The contrast with the Belrepeire episode suggests the third implication of this unreality. As has already been noted in another connection, Perceval's foolishness in that episode was nonetheless an adequate reaction to a realistic and practical necessity. [298] Gauvain's acceptance of the relationship with the Orguelleuse de Logres has no relevance to any kind of social or political reality such as came into play in the Belrepeire and Escavalon episodes. Indeed, until the final revelation of her story, the only contact Gauvain has with a certain reality is to fall into a river.

On the other hand, there is an obvious literary pattern reflected in this relationship, a pattern Chrétien had already used in an earlier romance. Without a word of complaint, Lancelot had accepted the necessities imposed by the love-service: [299] the humiliation of the cart

---

[296] *Supra*, pp. 161 ff.
[297] See also *supra*, p. 231, n. 279.
[298] *Supra*, p. 219 f.
[299] On the varieties of love-service in Chrétien's romances, and their sources, see Cross and Nitze, *Lancelot and Guenevere*, pp. 79-98.

(with a moment's hesitation, never repeated), Guenièvre's icy and un-explained disdain after the duel with Meleagant, and the command to fight *au noauz* at the Tournament of Noauz. In the same way, Gauvain accepts the repeated humiliation imposed by the *male pucele*; as he played the role of the graciously condescending knight with the *pucele as manches petites,* the role of the knight renowned for his prowess in the hunt of the white doe, the role of the courtly seducer in Escavalon, so here Gauvain plays the role of the courtly knight who is all service to the lady who is his sovereign. [300] At one point, in truth, he mildly complains. After a particularly impressive display of her sarcasm, Gauvain says:

> "Bele amie,
> Vos diroiz ce que buen vos iert;
> Mes a demeisele n'afiert
> Que ele soit si mesdisanz
> Puis que ele a passé dis anz,
> Einz doit estre bien anseigniee
> Et cortoise et bien afeitiee." (7200-6) [301]

But this meek complaint is haughtily dismissed:

> "Chevaliers par male avanture,
> De vostre anseignemant n'ai cure;
> Mes alez et si vos teisiez..." (7207-9)

Though his complaint does not alleviate his situation, it does serve to reveal his consciousness that there is something wrong with the situation.

Chrétien's irony aims at a larger target than the hero, however: it is the pattern he represents which is also in question, the pattern of an extreme and socially useless love-service. I think this is suggested by the sudden inversion in the relationship. Gauvain learns from Guiromelant that the Orguelleuse lied to him, and also that she had left Guiromelant for a less worthy knight. By the end of the conversation with Guiromelant, Gauvain has broken her "spell". When Guiromelant offers to lead him to a crossing place for the river into which he recently jumped, Gauvain refuses:

> "Ja n'i querrai ne gué ne pont
> Por rien nule qui m'an avaingne.
> Einz que a mauvestié le taingne

---

[300] "... in the romances, the stress is on *service* to a lady and in its implications, not on love as passion." Jackson, *The Literature of the Middle Ages,* p. 96 (emphasis in the original). That the idea of service is stressed does not, of course, exclude the presence of passion also, as in *Yvain.* One may also question whether it is service to the *lady* which is all-important in that romance: after all, Yvain is of greater service to a large number of ladies than to Laudine during his adventures.

[301] Gauvain's use of the word *cortoise* here should be cause for reflection. His relationship to the Orguelleuse is obviously an aspect of what modern critics, since Gaston Paris, call "courtly love." But he considers her behavior not *cortoise*: in this passage at least, the word means something like "courteous, polite, civil." It refers to social manners, not "courtly love" ... at least as Gauvain uses it.

> La dameisele felenesse,
> Li randrai je bien sa promesse,
> Si m'an irai tot droit a li." (8908-13)

He has not only broken her psychological hold on him, but something
else as well:

> Lors point et ses chevaus sailli
> Outre l'eve delivremant;
> Que point n'i ot d'anconbremant. (8914-6)

Suddenly, what Gauvain could not do before is easy: *point n'i ot
d'anconbremant.* [302] And when he reaches her on the other bank of the
river, the Orguelleuse's status as a proud and absolute superior is
inverted. She becomes a humble, infortunate young woman who
explains her previously haughty disdain as spite levelled at all men
in revenge for the sorrow caused by one. He learns, finally, that all the
humiliation he endured had only one purpose, to anger him to the point
that he would kill the Orguelleuse and rid her of a burdensome life. [303]

---

[302] As usual, when Chrétien has his characters do something "impossible",
it is done twice; *supra,* p. 109, n. 184.

[303]
> "Biaus sire," fet ele, "ore escoute
> Por quoi j'ai esté si estoute
> Vers toz les chevaliers del mont
> Qui aprés aus menee m'ont.
> Jel te dirai, s'il ne t'enuie:
> Cil chevaliers cui Deus destruie,
> Qui de la d'outre a toi parla,
> S'amor an moi mal anplea,
> Qu'il m'ama, et je haï lui;
> Car il me fist si grant enui
> Qu'il ocist, nel celerai mie,
> Celui a cui j'estoie amie.
> Puis me cuida tant d'enor feire
> Qu'a s'amor me cuida atreire;
> Mes onques rien ne li valut;
> Que au plus tost que il me lut
> De sa conpeignie m'anblai
> Et au chevalier m'assanblai
> Cui tu me ras gehui tolue,
> Dont il ne m'est a une alue.
> Mes de mon premerain ami
> Quant morz de lui me departi,
> Ai si longuement esté fole
> Et si estoute de parole
> Et si vilainne et si musarde
> Qu'onques ne me prenoie garde
> Cui j'alasse contraliant,
> Einz le fesoie a esciant
> Por ce que trover an volsisse
> Un si ireus que jel feïsse
> A moi irestre et correcier
> Por moi trestote depecier,
> Que pieç'a volsisse estre ocise.
> Biaus sire, or pran de moi justise

The application of psychology reduces the figure of the Lady as sovereign to that of a pitiful wretch. [304]

The Castle of Marvels

After displaying the purposelessness of Gauvain's prowess, seduction, and love-service, Chrétien shows him, in the last episode he wrote, apparently trapped by that most elusive of knightly ideals, *courtoisie*. [305] This is the adventure of the Roche de Chanpguin, ruled by yet another female figure, Yguerne, the Queen with white hair. That this castle is somehow a parallel to that of the Fisher King has long been

---

> Tel que ja mes nule pucele
> Qui de moi oie la novele
> N'ost dire a nul chevalier honte." (8927-63)

[304] Compare the similar deflation by a practical, realistic explanation in *Cligès*, above, pp. 61 ff.

Another type of courtly love is exemplified by the relationship between Guiromelant and Clarissant, Gauvain's sister. After his disillusion with the Orguelleuse, Guiromelant has fallen in love with Clarissant, though he has never seen her except across the river which runs before the Roche de Chanpguin. As Clarissant later tells her brother, *C'est de loing que s'amie sui* (9017):

> "Mes si message m'ont proiiee
> Tant que je li ai otroiiee
> M'amor, n'an mantiroie mie;
> De plus ne sui ancor s'amie." (9023-6)

Theirs is an *amor de lonh* à la Jaufré Rudel. The practical difficulties of this kind of love are suggested by Guiromelant's assumption that Clarissant hates her brother as much as he does (8793-6), which she denies completely (9027-42)

The entire scene is one of complex dramatic irony which touches both knights. Guiromelant is put in the awkward position of having violently denounced Gauvain (who killed Guiromelant's cousin, and whose father killed Guiromelant's father—according to Guiromelant) only to learn toward the end of their conversation that it is Gauvain to whom he has been speaking. At the same time, Gauvain hears himself violently denounced without making any protest (other than a mild irony only the reader can appreciate: ll. 8802-4; see Frappier, *Perceval*, p. 133), and agrees to take a love-token from this sworn enemy to Clarissant before identifying himself. Afterwards, of course, he must carry out the promise, and indirectly ask the sister whether she shares Guiromelant's hate for him—his own sister might be an enemy! Again, Gauvain's habit of not identifying himself puts him in awkward positions.

In meeting Guiromelant, Gauvain comes face to face with another aspect of his own values (as in meeting the Orguelleuse: see Frappier, *op. cit.*, p. 125). Why did not Chrétien have Gauvain himself represent this aspect of courtly love? I think because it would have been out of character. Gauvain represents a Northern French version of courtly love, more concerned than the Provençal with prowess and social values (see Frappier, "Vues sur les conceptions courtoises...," pp. 144 ff.; cf. Moshé Lazar, "Les éléments constitutifs de la *cortezia* dans la lyrique des troubadours," *Studi mediolatini e volgari*, VI-VII [1959], 67-96; p. 76, where he stresses the social implications of *mezura*).

[305] Still useful on "courtesy" is Henri Dupin, *La courtoisie au moyen âge* (*d'après les textes du XIIe et du XIIIe siècle*), (Paris: Picard, 1931). On the distinctions between courtesy and courtly love, and the Provence and Northern French versions of the latter, see Frappier, "Vues sur les conceptions courtoises..." and Lazar, "Les éléments constitutifs de la *cortezia*...." Lazar's *Amour courtois et "fin'amors" dans la littérature du XIIe siècle* (Paris: Klincksiek, 1964) unfortunately reached me too late to be used in this study.

recognized, [306] but the meaning of this parallelism has yet to be discussed. On the most obvious level, Gauvain, in surviving the test of the Bed of Marvels (in which he is first the target of hundreds of arrows, and then a lion's prey), seems to find success where Perceval failed. In fact, this success leads to an even greater one as Chrétien presents what seems to be a veritable courtly apotheosis of his hero: he is hailed by hundreds of maidens, *vaslet,* and Yguerne herself as their king and savior. But this soon turns into a "royauté charmante et dérisoire!" [307] as Gauvain learns that the "elect" in this adventure is condemned to remain forever within the walls of his kingdom.

But Gauvain is more than trapped: after he learns this, he is brought to enjoy it. What is in question here is the manner in which this is done. When Gauvain first learns that his apotheosis is also his incarceration, he shows his displeasure unmistakably to the *pucele* who is serving him. [308] She informs Yguerne, who reassures her. She will visit the knight (whose name she does not know):

> "Ja si grant ire el cuer n'avra
> Que tost ne l'an aie fors mise
> Et grant joie an leu d'ire mise." (8090-2)

The means by which the old Queen comforts the angry knight and puts joy in his heart are delightful, but hardly extraordinary. She engages him in light conversation. In courteous progression, she asks whether he is a member of Arthur's household (Yes), a member of the watch (No), a member of the Round Table? The last question is ambiguously phrased:

> "... estes vos, dites le moi,
> De çaus de la Table Reonde,
> Qui sont li plus prisié del monde?" (8124-6)

To complacently accept the flattery of being "one of the most praised knights in the world" would be immodest and improper. Gauvain avoids the trap with proper delicacy:

> "Dame," fet il, "je n'oseroie
> Dire que des plus prisiez soie,
> Ne me faz mie des meillors,
> Ne ne cuit estre des peors." (8127-30)

He does not claim to be of the most praised ... but does not deny it; he does not consider himself one of the best ... but leaves his reputation to be understood by others. One of the rewards of such social delicacy is its recognition. Yguerne compliments Gauvain on his subtlety:

---

[306] Kellermann, *Aufbaustil und Weltbild...,* p. 217; Frappier, *Perceval,* p. 129.
[307] Frappier, *Perceval,* p. 129.
[308] This may be Clarissant. Yguerne calls the maiden *Bele niece* (8065); if this is not a mere formula (as *biaus niés* can be), it indicates that Gauvain has been served by his sister all along.

> "Biaus sire,
> Grant corteisie vos oi dire
> Qui ne vos ametez le pris
> Del miauz ne del blasme le pis." (8131-4) [309]

Once these nameless introductions are over, the conversation turns to gossip. The guest is placed in the satisfying position of relating court news to the charming old Lady. She first asks how many sons King Lot had of his wife. This is an odd question. Yguerne should know the answer, since as we learn later, King's Lot's wife is living with her. Gauvain names the four sons, himself first of all. This might be considered a perfect opportunity for him to reveal his identity. Given the fact that the Queen probably knows the answer, one might consider that she had guessed at his identity, or hoped he would be one of King Lot's sons. In any case, the opportunity is there for Gauvain to name himself without seeming to boast—but he doesn't.

They continue, as Gauvain, in answer to a question, describes the two Yvains, sons of King Urien:

> "Cil sont a la cort anbedui
> Mout preu, mout sage et mout cortois." (8162 f.)

The tone of the conversation—light, superficial, and amusing in its superficiality—is indicated as the structural pattern of the last line is repeated, three lines later, in response to a question about Arthur's health:

> "Miauz [se contient] qu'il ne fist onques ancore
> Plus sains, plus legiers et plus forz." (8166 f.)

Gauvain's courtesy has perhaps carried him to the edge of absurdity: few men become lighter on their feet or stronger as they age. Yguerne twits him by a self-denying exaggeration:

> "Par foi, sire, ce n'est pas torz;
> Qu'il est anfes li rois Artus:
> S'il a çant ans, n'a mie plus,
> Ne plus n'an puet il pas avoir." (8168-71)

It is perhaps not quite just to simply declare that the old lady has lost her sense of time: [310] she seems quite self-possessed, perceptive of her guest's realities, and thoroughly in control of the situation. It is more in keeping with her character and the context to see this as a light, but intended, irony. At least for the reader, the irony is double,

---

[309] To consider this as evidence that Gauvain's fault lay in that "il ne se voulait pas meilleur" (Wagner, *"Sorcier" et "magicien"...*, p. 84; and Frappier, *Perceval*, p. 114) is to miss the point of the character and Chrétien's manner of presenting it. Gauvain does not wish himself better because he considers himself the best. But he is also courteous, and therefore wears at least a social modesty which prevents any open statement to that effect.

[310] "La bonne dame a perdu le sens du temps terrestre. Fourquet, "L'œuvre et la source...", p. 301.

since the Arthur we have seen is far from the sprightliness Gauvain
ascribes to him.

This reference to the Arthurian world as the reader knows it leads
into the next subject of conversation, Guenièvre—certainly a rife
subject for gossip in that world. But Gauvain's description has nothing
to do with the "reality" Chrétien's readers know. On the contrary, his
emphasis is exactly the opposite of that reality:

> "Dame, voir, ele est tant cortoise
> Et tant est bele et tant est *sage*
> Que Deus ne fist loi ne langage
> Ou l'an trovast si *sage* dame.
> Des que Deus la premiere fame
> Ot de la coste Adan formee,
> Ne fu dame si renomee,
> Et ele le doit mout bien estre:
> Tot ausi con li *sages* mestre
> Les petiz anfanz andoctrine,
> Ausi ma dame la reïne
> Tot le monde ansaingne et aprant;
> Que de li toz li biens desçant
> Et de li vient et de li muet." (8176-89)

That Guenièvre is courtly and beautiful, no reader of the *Lancelot*
would deny, but that she is, as Gauvain says three times, *sage,* is
dubious. And since her major appearance in Chrétien's fictional universe is in the *Lancelot,* one may also have certain doubts about
Guenièvre "indoctrinating" little children as a teacher—with the
doctrine of courtly love, presumably? The irony is reinforced by the
reference to Eve (which does not actually name her: Adam's wife):
she is presented by Gauvain only as the first woman, but she was also
the first woman to deceive her husband (albeit with a snake rather
than a man) and the cause of his fall.

Gauvain has become so entranced by the pleasures of social conversation that it bears him of its own momentum farther and farther
from reality. This is quite within Yguerne's purpose, to comfort her
guest and reconcile him to the situation in which he finds himself:
imprisonment. When she assures him that he will not be angry when
he leaves her, he answers:

> "Dame" fet il, "bien vos an croi,
> Que einçois que je vos veïsse,
> Ne me chaloit que je feïsse,
> Tant estoie maz et dolanz.
> Or sui si liez et si joianz
> Que je nel porroie plus estre." (8200-5)

That he is a prisoner of the castle who will leave only temporarily and
by special permission, that he has (again) placed in jeopardy his honor
by acceding to a situation which may prevent the fulfillment of the
lance-quest, these do not seem to weigh on him at all as he accepts,
now, the invitation to dinner:

> "Dame, je ne quier ja changier
> Por nule chanbre cest palés;
> Que l'an me dit que onques mes
> Chevaliers n'i manja ne sist."   (8218-21)

The last phrase reminds us of the custom of the Roche de Chanpguin which originally trapped him, but the first two lines are the result of the wiles of a white-haired Queen whose pleasant conversation has led Gauvain to accept his incarceration. [311]

This quest, however, may be secondary. Gauvain has already failed the same test as Perceval: the test of asking a certain question at a certain time. Having obtained permission to leave the castle temporarily, he meets Guiromelant, who asks:

> "Mes de la reïne chenue
> Me dites se vos la veïstes
> Et se vos point li anqueïstes
> Qui ele est et dont ele vint."   (8726-9)

Gauvain must admit that he did not, and then learns that he was speaking to Arthur's mother. Furthermore, he learns that his own mother and sister also are in the castle. The import of this unasked question is not revealed in the unfinished romance, but we cannot doubt its importance since it would have led to a familial recognition (as would have Perceval's), and since this is the second appearance of the motif in the Gauvain section. [312]

For this is Gauvain's second failure of the same test. The first occurred while the *notonier* was leading Gauvain to the Roche de Chanpguin, and is even closer to the Perceval analogue. As the two men arrive at the steps of the castle,

> Truevent sor un trossel de gles
> Un eschacier tot seul seant
> Qui avoit eschace d'arjant;
> A neel estoit bien doree,
> Et fu de leus an leus bandee
> D'or et de pierres precïeuses.
> N'avoit mie ses mains oiseuses

---

[311] When confronted again with the "reality" of his imprisonment later on, Gauvain will protest, but accept Yguerne's rule nonetheless (8330-9).

[312] The similarity in questions has been noted by Kellermann (*Aufbaustil und Weltbild...*, p. 20), and Stefan Hofer, "La structure du *Conte del Graal* examinée à la lumière de l'œuvre de Chrétien de Troyes," in *Les romans du Graal...*, pp. 15-25; p. 22.

The fact that Yguerne is also Gauvain's grandmother has not been noted, as far as I know. The relationship is briefly indicated at one point, when Yguerne and Gauvain's mother are together:

> Et la vieille reïne sist
> Delez sa fille...   (9045 f.)

Chrétien seems to have intended a familial elaboration for Gauvain similar to Perceval's.

> Li eschaciers, car il tenoit
> Un quanivet et s'antandoit
> A doler un baston de fresne. (7650-9)

The similarities between this figure and the Fisher King are remarkable. Both are wounded, and in similar ways; both, as we learn shortly, are wealthy; [313] both are engaged in pass-times (the *eschacier*'s, like the Fisher King's, presumably forced on him by his disability): fishing and whittling. More important, however, is their similarity in function and the technique Chrétien uses in both cases. Both exist to arouse curiosity, but neither succeeds in drawing a question from the hero:

> Li eschacier de rien n'aresne
> Çaus qui par devant lui s'an vont,
> Ne cil nul mot dit ne li ont. (7660-2)

Gauvain does not respond to the strange apparition, even though his guide calls attention to the figure:

> Et li notoniers a lui tire
> Mon seignor Gauvain et dit: "Sire,
> De cest eschacier que vos sanble?" (7663-5),

to which Gauvain answers flippantly:

> "S'eschace n'est mie de tranble,"
> Fet mes sire Gauvains, "par foi;
> Que mout m'est bel ce que je voi." (7666-8)

Like Perceval watching the procession of strange objects in the castle of the Fisher King, Gauvain is interested by what he sees, but does not react even when his guide insists:

> "Enon Deu," fet li notoniers
> Il est riches li eschaciers
> De mout granz rantes et de beles.
> Vos oïssiez ja teus noveles
> Qui vos enuiassent mout fort,
> Se ne fust ce que je vos port
> Conpeignie et si vos condui." (7669-75)

And so Gauvain and the *notonier* went up the castle steps, and we shall never know who this cripple is, or what bad news he might have imparted to Gauvain: in the section of the romance Chrétien completed, there is no cousin or Hideous Damsel to inform Gauvain or us of what might have happened if ....

Nevertheless, the basic identity of the two situations is unmistakable: similarly crippled men, associated with mystery intended to

---

[313] Frappier, noting the similarities in wound and wealth in a footnote, asks: "Cet énigmatique personnage ... a-t-il quelque affinité avec le Roi Pêcheur? On ne peut l'affirmer." (*Perceval*, p. 128, n. 1). Alone, the similarities of wound and wealth may not be convincing. A more extended comparison, not of the mysterious figures alone, but of their function in their contexts, suggests a more positive answer, especially when this similarity is seen as only one case among many correspondences between the Perceval and Gauvain sections.

arouse curiosity, both failing in obtaining a response from the hero. The *eschacier* parallel is not as elaborated as the Fisher King Episode, but the basic elements are there. In the procession of mysterious objects, it was the author himself who stressed the mystery; here, it is another character speaking to the hero. The Fisher King addressed Perceval most courteously, the *eschacier* is silent. [314] A major difference between the two scenes is the question of motives. Perceval's silence was due to an ignorance of social manners compounded by misinterpreted advice. The same obviously cannot be true of Gauvain. Was it a proud reluctance to be the first to address another person? Was it fear of committing an indiscretion—not unlike Perceval's fear of being impolite?... These are no more than speculations, however: what is more certain is the identity of outcome, whatever the motives. Chrétien has established a context which suggests and leads to the anticipation of a question. That Gauvain does not ask the question leads to the same conclusion as his earlier adventures: the success of the great courtly figure at the Castle of Marvels is undercut, as were the earlier successes, by a failure which is essentially the same failure as Perceval's failures in his attempts to become a courtly knight.

The last scene Chrétien completed gently ironizes at the expense of Gauvain's habit of involving himself with ladies from whom he can obtain no satisfaction. He and his sister Clarissant sit side by side on the Wondrous Bed in pleasant conversation. The situation is reminiscent of the episodes with the sister of the King of Escavalon, and also of Perceval's first evening with Blancheflor. Gauvain knows it is his sister, but she is still unaware of his identity. The two are observed by the two Queens, Yguerne and Gauvain's mother, who also do not know his identity. It is a mark of the knight's nobility, says Yguerne, that he has chosen the most beautiful and *la plus sage* (9055) in the palace:

> "Et pleüst Deu que il l'eüst
> Esposee et tant li pleüst
> Con fist a Eneas Lavine!" (9057-9)

The irony is particularly marked by the *significatio per similitudinem*. In the medieval tradition, Dido represented a destructive kind of love, Lavinia an ennobling kind: [315] how ennobling would a marriage with one's sister be! But this, of course, is only for the reader's benefit. Gauvain's mother answers in heartfelt agreement and equal ignorance:

> "Ha! dame," fet l'autre reïne,
> "Deus li doint si metre son cuer
> Qu'il soient come frere et suer
> Et qu'il l'aint tant et ele lui
> Qu'une chose soient andui!" (9060-4)

---

[314] The similarity in episodes is even greater if the *eschacier* and *notonier* are recognized as two aspects of the Fisher King; the latter inherits the role of guide to the castle as well as the association with water and a boat.

[315] Jackson, *The Literature of the Middle Ages,* p. 99 f.

In the last pages he wrote, Chrétien uses the same techniques he developed in *Cligès:* here, the inversion of the metaphorical and literal levels. [316] The element to which reality is compared is, unbeknownst to the speaker but to the delight of the informed reader, the reality itself. It is also, of course, dramatic irony: the reader is unlikely to have forgotten Guiromelant's information that the young lady is Gauvain's sister. Just in case he has, Chrétien reminds him of the fact at the beginning of the scene (9005 f.). In fact, Chrétien stresses the point at length:

> An sa proiiere antant la dame*   *Gauvain's mother
> Qu'il l'aint et qu'il la praingne a fame;
> Cele ne reconoist son fil;
> Come frere et suer seront il;
> Que d'autre amor point n'i avra.
> Quant li uns de l'autre savra
> Qu'ele est sa suer et il ses frere,
> S'an avra grant joie sa mere
> Autre qu'ele n'i antant. (9065-73)

There are two points here. The first is that Gauvain's refusal to reveal himself misleads his mother and grandmother to false expectations: how happy they would be to know it is he. The other point Chrétien stresses, that *autre amor n'i avra point* than that between brother and sister, does not seem necessary in the context of a courtly romance: the reader, by now, can trust that the author's taste will avoid prurience and incest. The emphasis, then, is not on the absence of incest, but on the fact of innocence. Here is a pair of young people sitting side by side on a bed under the happy eye of observers to whom they seem made for each other; but they will remain innocent. The visual image and the outcome are the same as those of Perceval's meeting with Blancheflor: they too seemed made for each other to the admiring observers, they too remained chaste. Though Gauvain, as we well know, is an able conversationalist where Perceval was mute, the result, once more, is the same.

Conclusion

That stylistic irony and comedy exist in Chrétien's *Perceval* did not need proving; nor would the exercise of reducing all the instances of irony to the forms promulgated in the texts of grammar and rhetoric prove much more than perverse ingenuity. Some of the ironies in *Perceval* fit quite comfortably in those traditional categories, and are therefore of no particular theoretical interest. Others represent the same techniques developed by Chrétien in *Cligès,* or are further extensions thereof. The technique of stressing the unimportant introductory phrase of indirect discourse occurs in a passage where amplification is the basic principle. [317] The ironization of traditional material is far less

---

[316] *Supra,* pp. 70 ff., 76-80, 108.
[317] *Supra,* p. 143.

extensively used than in *Cligès*: weak examples of ironized symbolism are the references to Eve and Lavinia. [318] I find no *topoi* as such in *Perceval*. On the other hand, ironization of contemporary literary material is more frequent: *amor de lonh* is ironized both lyrically and in action; [319] the paradigmatic figures of the jealous lovers, both indicated by "allegorical" names, also belong here. [320] There are at least three important cases of the ironization of lyricism. [321] Inversions of the level of language are quite frequent. [322] The interruption of the fictional contract occurs at least four times, possibly five. [323]

A device Chrétien uses a number of times in *Perceval* but which I did not find in *Cligès* is midway between style and composition. A certain level of discourse and reference is maintained in a more or less extensive development, only to lead to a brief, sudden reduction in level at the end (I think of this as the "final bump" technique): the Orguelleus' jealous tirade is followed by the one-line statement that he then sat down to eat; [324] when Perceval is talking to his lady after the meeting with his cousin, the Orguelleus' whirlwind entrance and threatening speech lead to an invitation to listen to a story. [325] The same principle is operative in the reduction of Perceval's emotional upheaval when he can't see the Fisher King's castle to a question of finding lodging. [326] Some of these are reinforced by stylistic devices, others not. Extended to a structural principle, this technique is at the basis of Chrétien's undercutting by psychological analysis of the Orguelleuse de Logres figure. [327]

A particular development of the principle of parallelism is the technique of the descriptive pivot, of which a few examples were noted in the Perceval section. [328] They serve as signs indicating the relevance of two or more episodes to each other, and seem to be used especially to relate episodes within the same section. However, they bear an obvious kinship to the extensive parallel descriptions of Belrepeire and Escavalon, which juxtapose scenes from the two sections. Performing the same function is the identity of "allegorical" names: the Orguelleus de la Lande and the Orguelleuse de Logres. These two figures present opposite sovereignties, that of the man over the woman, that of the woman over the man. The technique of role inversions (a structural irony already developed in *Cligès*) [329] is one of Chrétien's

---

318 *Supra*, pp. 246, 249.
319 *Supra*, pp. 188 ff., 243, n. 304.
320 *Supra*, pp. 135, 178, n. 164; 182 ff., 238 ff.
321 *Supra*, pp. 159 f., 174 f., 189; cf. 142 f. (prophecy ironized).
322 *Supra*, pp. 123, nn. 28 and 29, 134, 141 f., 145, 193 f., 250.
323 *Supra*, pp. 180, n. 172(?), 188 ff., 240 ff.
324 *Supra*, p. 135; food is a frequent source of irony or comedy; pp. 135, n. 55, 174 f., 185, n. 188.
325 *Supra*, p. 184.
326 *Supra*, p. 167 ff.
327 *Supra*, p. 241 f.
328 *Supra*, pp. 118, 147 and n. 91, 164, 169, n. 136, 177, n. 158, 182, 219.
329 *Supra*, p. 107 and n. 175.

favorites in *Perceval.* Three obvious examples are: Perceval, the martial hero, is ruled by Blancheflor; Perceval, who was disappointed at Arthur's pensiveness, becomes pensive himself in the snow-drops episode; and the complete inversion of the Gauvain-Orguelleuse relationship.

The wide variety of these ironic techniques tends only to prove that if the techniques which produce a particular irony can be analyzed to a fair degree of exactitude, irony itself is a particular cast of mind which will use any available technique of style or construction to make itself understood. The only characteristic all these examples share is that of incongruity of some kind.

The same principle of incongruity is at the basis of the comic effects studied in these pages: an action is incongruous with the character who performs it, or with his intention, or with the situation in which he finds himself. Though a final analysis of comedy might well yield the same conclusion as for irony—that it is profoundly unanalyzable—a simple, categorical listing of the most frequent bases of Chrétien's comedy may be useful.

1. *Automatism.* The less automatism functions as direct expression of individual character, the closer it approaches pure farce. The most farcical examples are associated, not with Perceval, whose automatism is always a function of his character, but with Gauvain: his jump into a river,[330] and the blow he lands on the Red Squire.[331] Two unelaborated touches which come close to farce are the knocking off of Arthur's cap by Perceval's horse[332] and the sudden raising of drawbridge at the castle of the Fisher King.[333]

Most of the automatism in the romance is Perceval's, of course: the constant references to his mother are the most obvious and frequent examples. After he comes under the aegis of Gornemant, the automatism changes form. It no longer leads to verbal expressions but to inner recall in problematic situations. In these situations, he either does not know what the advice meant and how to carry it out (Anguingueron, Clamadeu),[334] or carries it out incongruously (his silence in the Fisher King Episode, which, though not comic in itself, follows the pattern of comic automatism, and is itself followed by the comedy of overimbibing). This automatism is the basic structure of Perceval's "progress", and leads to the thematic link between the two sections of the romance: when Perceval meets Gauvain, he resolves to accept a third guide ... but events interrupt the sequence. Before that happens, however, we have seen the principle of the *chastoiement* itself become an automatism.[335]

---

[330] *Supra,* p. 239 f.
[331] *Supra,* p. 235 f.
[332] *Supra,* p. 138.
[333] *Supra,* p. 175.
[334] *Supra,* p. 163 f.
[335] *Supra,* p. 195 f.

Both of the following categories are really subdivisions of automatism: the misidentification of objects and persons is usually the result of a mental habit which does not take cognizance of a new reality.

2. *Misidentification of objects.* The first example in the romance is also the finest: Perceval's reduction of the knightly lance and hauberk to the situation of hunting. [336] Later, there are his taking the Tent for a minster, [337] and his reduction of knightly sword fighting to the arms practice of footmen. [338] All of these are reductive in a social sense. Gauvain also misidentifies the lance and uses an inappropriate horse in the White Doe episode; instead of being reductive, however, these errors work in the opposite direction, that of attempting to raise the hunting situation to the level of knightly adventure. The effect on the character is the same, however: he is reduced in the reader's eyes. [339] The basic principle of inverse reductiveness is the same in a more comically elaborated episode, Gauvain's use of the chessboard as a shield and the transformation of the chess pieces into artillery ammunition by the sister of the King of Escavalon. [340]

Perceval has another kind of difficulty with objects when he is unable to remove the armor of the Red Knight: [341] this is rather a misuse of objects (tugging, instead of unfastening) than a misidentification.

Similar to the misidentification of objects is the misidentification of a situation: when asked what he would do in knightly combat if his lance shattered, Perceval is ready to jump on his opponent and fight with his fists. [342] When Perceval is faced with mystery in the castle of the Fisher King, he reduces the situation to an over-simplified rule. [343] When the hermit presents him with other mysteries or paradoxes, he reduces the situation by retaining only the most familiar, immediate, and unimportant matter. [344]

3. *Misidentification of persons.* One reason the Five Knights Episode is such brilliant comedy is that it combines a number of comic techniques. The misidentification of objects is preceded by the misidentification of persons—the knights are first taken for devils, then for angels—and the change from devils to angels is itself automatic. [345] Gauvain, at the Tintaguel Tournament, is mistaken for a merchant and a money-changer (or the ladies ironize at his expense by feigning to mistake him as such). In the same episode, Gauvain's service of the

---

[336] *Supra,* pp. 122 ff.
[337] *Supra,* p. 131.
[338] *Supra,* p. 150 f.
[339] *Supra,* pp. 211 ff.
[340] *Supra,* pp. 216 ff.
[341] *Supra,* p. 145.
[342] *Supra,* p. 150.
[343] *Supra,* pp. 171 ff.
[344] *Supra,* p. 224.
[345] *Supra,* p. 120.

pucele as manches petites may be considered a misidentification of a
little girl as a courtly Lady. [346]

A variation on misidentification is simply the lack of identification:
both Perceval and Gauvain do not identify themselves, though for
different reasons. The occasion when Perceval first identifies himself
may be comic at his expense. [347] With Gauvain, it is the absence of
identification which leads him into a number of awkward and/or comic
situations. [348]

4. *Erotic suggestiveness.* These effects depend largely on verbal
suggestiveness, but Chrétien combines them with action. In the Tent
Maiden Episode, Perceval climbs on the maiden ... to kiss her twenty
times. [349] Later, he invites Blancheflor to bed with him, kisses and
caresses her ... with the same negative result. [350] In so far as his
abstraction in the snow-drops episode (and its resultant automatism)
recalls those earlier episodes, it also belongs here. [351] Three episodes
in the Gauvain section partly depend on this source of comic effect: the
interrupted affair with the sister of the King of Escavalon, [352] the
Orguelleuse's prohibition that Gauvain touch her, [353] and the last scene
in the romance where Chrétien exploits the erotic potential of the knight
and maiden sitting next to each other, though more delicately than in
the previous episodes. [354]

5. *Pensiveness.* The first scene in which we see this state (Perceval's
first arrival at Arthur's court) is not comically elaborated, though it
does lead to a moment of farce when Perceval's horse knocks off
Arthur's cap. [355] In the Snow-drops Episode, however, the state of
pensiveness is the basis of comic elaboration: it is because he is
abstracted that Perceval falls into the automatic pattern of fighting and
returning to his pensiveness. [356]

Gauvain is too self-conscious to be pensive.

6. *Manipulation.* On the surface, this seems to be the opposite of the
previous category: the pensive person is unaware of his surroundings,
while the manipulation of others is a conscious activity. But it is not
the manipulator who is comic (unless his plan misfires, as does Fénice's
in *Cligès*) but the person who is being manipulated. In a sense, then,
the object of manipulation is passive in the other's hand. So, Perceval
is manipulated by Blancheflor into fighting for her when she seems to

---

[346] *Supra,* pp. 209 ff.
[347] *Supra,* pp. 179 ff.
[348] *Supra,* pp. 213-18, 243, n. 304, 244-7, 249 f.
[349] *Supra,* p. 132 f.
[350] *Supra,* pp. 158 ff.
[351] *Supra,* p. 189 f.
[352] *Supra,* pp. 213 ff.
[353] *Supra,* p. 238.
[354] *Supra,* p. 249 f.
[355] *Supra,* p. 137 f.
[356] *Supra,* pp. 190-3.

try to dissuade him from fighting, [357] Gauvain is manipulated by the Orguelleuse who uses the same technique as Blancheflor, [358] and Yguerne manipulates Gauvain by flattering his desire to be courteous and to be appreciated as such. [359]

More interesting than these categorizations is the function of both irony and comedy in *Perceval*. It was suggested at the beginning of this chapter that their main purpose was to provide a modification to the impetus of the heroic form which Chrétien was using as the structural skeleton of his romance. This has been amply demonstrated in detail, especially for the first part, but it is worth summarizing. If we consider only the action of the Perceval section, disregarding all effects of irony and comedy, we seem to witness the progress of a youth from the zero level of an almost total lack of socialization until he reaches, in his acceptance by the Arthurian court, a full level of manhood as defined by his society: knighthood. [360] At that point, he seems to be regarded as a full-fledged member of society, perhaps even equal to the character who embodies Arthurian ideals most fully, Gauvain. This, it must be said, is the most widely accepted interpretation current today. [361] Our analysis has demonstrated two things. First, that the psychological impulses behind Perceval's behavior remain constant through all the episodes, and that they are modified—not replaced— by the imposition of restraint, beginning with the Gornemant episode. This restraint is an attempt to prevent Perceval's permanent impulses from having the harmful effects which have been shown earlier. Furthermore, this restraint itself is shown to have harmful or risible effects since Perceval is unable to apply it properly. Nevertheless, this restraint does not replace his original impulses: he still performs the same kind of reductiveness with the hermit as with the five knights and with Gornemant.

The second major conclusion of our analysis of the Perceval section is both more important and more elusive. It lies in the concept of aesthetic distance. As in *Cligès,* the reader of *Perceval* has a privileged view of the hero, though the techniques by which this is obtained are usually not made as obvious by stylistic emphases as in the earlier romance. The reader has been privy to the entire story of Perceval, a fact which gives him a different view of the character than is possible for a court which knows only the externals of his victories as reported by his victims. Specifically, the reader is aware of a character permanently marked by its origin, groping in what may, under the circumstances, be called a violent hesitation, to find a proper mode of behavior in a completely strange social world. [362] The reader is also aware of

---

357 *Supra,* p. 162.
358 *Supra,* pp. 238-43.
359 *Supra,* pp. 244-7.
360 The most consistent and extreme example of this approach is the already cited article by Stanton de V. Hoffman, "The Structure of the *Conte del Graal.*"
361 Thus Frappier, *Perceval,* p. 70 f.
362 That the analysis of comedy should lead to a suggestion of the tragic is in the nature of literary things as arranged by first rate comic writers.

two specific failures which, given the dynamics of Chrétien's "heroic" world, must lead to at least a temporary disaster. Chrétien's rhetoric (the word here is equivalent to "literary structure") is one in which the reader is essential: if he does not play his role properly, he goes awry, like the hero, and takes the romance with him. His role is that of an acute observer whose attitude is a compound of respect, sympathy, and judgment.

These modifications refer to Chrétien's first hero and to the structure of his section. They also affect the linkage of the two sections. In *Cligès,* we found that a secondary character (Alis) provided both a narrative link between the sections and a thematic one. [363] In *Perceval,* the narrative link is provided by a secondary character who appears only for that purpose: the Hideous Damsel. The thematic link is in the meeting of the two heroes themselves, and the readiness of Perceval to accept Gauvain as the third stage of the *chastoiemant* comedy. With Gauvain, we follow not the attempts of Perceval to adhere to new values, but the very values he wished to embrace.

The modifications brought by irony and comedy to the character of Gauvain are somewhat different from those in the Perceval section. They follow the same principle in the episodes which precede the Hermit Episode, in that Gauvain is found risible by contrast to what he wants to be. A Knight at the service of a Lady is not comic ... but when the Lady is a shrewd little girl? The incongruity between desire and fulfillment is even more obvious in the Escavalon Episode. Even in these two episodes, however, Gauvain falls into difficulties as a result of following courtly imperatives. This is even more true in those episodes which follow the Hermit Episode. Gauvain not only follows courtly imperatives: they lead him to courtly situations *par excellence.* The situations themselves are extreme paradigms of courtly relationships, absolute and self-sufficient until undercut by a psychological realism which reduces them to normal patterns of human behavior. [364] Thus, the standards by which Perceval was found risible are ridiculed in turn as Gauvain acts according to them in situations that reflect them perfectly. It is both the character and his ideals that are affected. [365]

Perceval is constructed on two kinds of structure. It combines the dual structure of *Cligès* with the heroic pattern Chrétien used so successfully in *Erec et Enide* and *Yvain.* A major difference is that in *Cligès,* the two parts were sequentially discrete (except for the second-

---

[363] *Supra,* pp. 82-5.

[364] We actually see this happen only with the Orguelleuse de Logres, and, to a lesser extent, in the Guiromelant-Clarissant relationship. I assume Chrétien intended to do the same in the Roche de Chanpguin Episode: the indications are the repeated opposition of Gauvain's imprisonment and his desire to leave ... with his grandmother's permission.

[365] An aspect of the Gauvain section I have not discussed adequately is the atmosphere of fantasy in which it is bathed. I would equate this with the use of magic in *Cligès,* which was an indication of the unreality of the courtly lovers' solution.

ary figure of Alis). It is generally agreed that Perceval was to return to the stage at some point. [366] This in itself suggests an attempt to unite the two parts more closely than in *Cligès*. Another means Chrétien used to bind together the adventures of the two heroes is the technique of parallelism. As has been shown in detail, the parallelisms result in the two heroes performing the same acts, usually for different reasons. As was the case in *Cligès,* these parallel events are generally not elaborated to the same extent: a brief interlude may refer to a major episode, as the hunt of the white doe refers to Perceval's meeting with the five knights. Furthermore, a given episode may refer to more than one point in the Perceval section. The general purpose of the system of parallelism is clear, however: it is to have two very different heroes, sometimes diametrically opposed, perform the same acts.

What may be a unifying technique structurally is paradoxical from the point of view of meaning. To have the *vaslet sauvage* and the epitome of courtliness perform identical acts may satisfy our aesthetic pleasure at recognizing this identity, but, intellectually, it proposes an identity of opposites. The absence of socialization, with all it entails in energy, ineptness, and even brutality, is no better or worse than a socialization so complete that it produces complete identification of character with social values....

At this point, one must proceed with caution. That the romance is unfinished robs us of a climax, satisfactory or not, which would provide a vantage point from which to interpret the whole work. It is possible that Chrétien intended to provide a resolution in which this antithesis would have been resolved. Given the irony which pervades this work, I find this doubtful: the ironic spirit is not given to completely satisfying solutions, and Chrétien had not provided such a solution since his first romance. The modest reunion which concludes *Yvain* is a triumph of psychological realism over heroic satisfaction. Psychological realism cannot conceive of Perceval becoming Gauvain, or Gauvain becoming Perceval, or a perfect fusion between the two. It is my impression that Chrétien did not conceive of human character enduring radical change; at best, he showed a limited adaptation of the individual to the requirements of his social context.

If the conflict of values elaborated within the romance was not to be finally resolved within the narrative, this means that the unity of the work is to be found in a point of view which can understand the two aspects of the conflict as two parts of a whole. This suggests that the romance provides materials for meditation from a point of view external to the romance, but inferred from it.

Within the limits imposed by the incomplete state of the romance, it is possible to glimpse an opposition whose terms are adequate to

---

[366] I would urge an equally general recognition that any statement more specific than that is pure speculation. The speculation that happens to appeal most to me is a negative one of Pauphilet's that has generally been ignored. For good literary reasons, he believes that Perceval would never have returned to the castle of the Fisher King: *Le legs du moyen âge...,* p. 177 f.

both major characters. Those episodes centering around Perceval are elaborated on the basis of a conflict between his crude energy and the normative standards of society. These standards are also part of the definition of manhood which Perceval himself desires to attain: knighthood, in Chrétien's romances, is manhood from both the psychological and social viewpoints. The conflict, then, is not only between individual ignorance and social standards, but exists within the psychology of the hero. In the case of Gauvain, this conflict does not exist: the acme of courtly knighthood is the perfect embodiment of certain conventional social ideals, and there is nothing in him which lies beyond these. His adventures lead him into situations which are paradigmatic of those ideals, in which one might expect Gauvain to be fully triumphant. Nevertheless, each of his adventures leads to humiliation and a revelation of inadequacy. Thus, both the inability of the individual to adhere to social values and the individual entirely defined by social values are objects of risibility: neither represents a goal acceptable to the author.

That Perceval is ridiculed for his lack of socialization indicates that its values—heroism, a certain poise, courtesy—are not themselves derided in the Gauvain section: it is the manner or the purpose of their application which is wrong. The defense of helpless women, recommended to Perceval by all his advisors, is the subject of Gauvain's first adventure. His behavior is formally perfect: it follows both the conventions of his literary role and its social values. The only false note is the incongruity between the assumed urgency of the general principle and the actual woman in question: the *pucele as manches petites*. The parallel descriptions of Belrepeire and Escavalon suggest a standard of realism and the social usefulness of knighthood: where Perceval is socially ludicrous but useful, Gauvain is polished but destructive. With the Orguelleuse de Logres, the conventions which rule Gauvain's behavior are eventually shown as quite irrelevant to the actual character and motivations of the Lady. In the Roche de Chanpguin episode, this irrelevance is pervasive: he knights five hundred *vaslez,* many of them too old to bear arms; he is seen in a situation suggestive of love, but it is his sister to whom he speaks; and his triumphs here lead to imprisonment, an imprisonment which his delight in an old lady's courtesy leads him to regard with equanimity.

All of Gauvain's adventures are vitiated by their irrelevance to realistic considerations, an irrelevance which has its source in his thoroughgoing socio-literary formalism. Perceval's behavior, though sometimes adequate to reality (he obtains the armor he wants, successfully defends Belrepeire, etc.), is ludicrous because of its distance from accepted social values. This juxtaposition suggests a point of view as different from that of Gauvain's completely courtly world as of the *Gaste Forez*; in the context of *Perceval* studies, it is surprising by its very normality. Our analysis found one particular point of contact where both the moral and literary concerns of the author were fused, and where a moral and literary connection between the Perceval and Gauvain sections was being established; the transition from the Hermit Episode to the Greoreas Episode. The former represented the nadir of Perceval's adventures, but it also recalled a concept broached in the Prologue: charity, not as a theological concept, but as a practical form of human relationship, as Perceval himself receives it in the form of patience, kindness, understanding, and firmness from the hermit. Charity, as the Prologue suggested, which is a requirement for fruitful interchange among men. Charity, then, in the sense in which it is equivalent to consideration, practical courtesy, a realistic helping of the other.

This moral point of view recognizes both components of the antithesis of the romance. It views the other as an individual with individual needs. It also recognizes the necessity of society in mutual dependence. It also differentiates the reader in whom it exists from both Perceval and Gauvain, and places him at an aesthetic distance from which he can enjoy their adventures, heroic and comic.

———

CONCLUSION

As was indicated in the Preface, this dissertation is in part the report of an experiment. It was begun on the basis of a specific hypothesis; that the works of medieval writers are to be studied in terms of the techniques found in the medieval school tradition. That these techniques were initially important and of continued usefulness is undeniable. It is equally undeniable that this importance and usefulness are limited. Even the romance which is characterized by the greatest dependence on such techniques, *Cligès,* has been shown to contain an individual rhetoric which, though it includes those techniques, is elaborated far beyond their conceptions. This became especially obvious in the *Perceval* chapter, where even the localized ironies of style could often not be adequately analyzed in those traditional terms: it was only within the context of the autonomous literary work that the tone and intention of style could be deduced. Chrétien de Troyes knew the techniques taught in the schools of his time; he used them greatly toward the beginning of his career, less as he developed, but always adapted them to his own purposes.

That is a question of form: much the same can be said of Chrétien's use of literary materials. One of the characteristics of medieval literature which strikes the modern reader most is its dependence on traditional materials; an implied corrolary of this is the apparent reduction of the creative freedom available to the individual writer. This impression has been confirmed by a misappreciation of Ernst Robert Curtius' epoch-making work, in which medieval literature often seems to consist of a dreary repetition of clichés: baptizing them with the scholarly name of *topoi* and tracing them back to classical sources did not prevent a suggestion that the main virtue of medieval writers was an unimaginative assiduity. Such was far from Curtius' intention. The Preface of his second edition states quite clearly his concern with the constants of European culture and a purpose which is admirably extra-literary: "Ce livre ne vise pas que des buts scientifiques, il témoigne aussi d'un souci de maintenir la civilisation occidentale." [1] Literary critics and scholars should take their cue from this open avowal. When a *topos* occurs in a medieval work, its identification as such is merely the scholarly basis of the critic's job, which is to inquire into the purpose and function of that particular *topos* in that particular work. It was a finding of our study of *Cligès* that such materials—*topoi,*

---

[1] *La littérature européenne...,* p. x.

name symbolism, literary references to the classical tradition—were used ironically. The implications of such usage are wide-ranging. The medieval author of sufficiently powerful imagination was not bound by his tradition: instead, it provided him with a treasury of materials which he could shape to his own satisfaction within the context of an individual work of art.

The same is true of Chrétien's use of a more recent literary tradition in *Cligès* and especially *Perceval*. Whether the source of what we call courtly love is found in Provence or Northern France, it is not an attitude which informs Chrétien's work so much as it provides the narrative stuff towards which his romance suggests an attitude compounded of sympathy and judgment. Gauvain's adventures in particular have been seen to embody certain relationships archtypical of this tradition. Far more than the occasional use of classical material in *Cligès,* these courtly relationships form the structural basis of the Gauvain section, but they are not presented on their own terms. Just like the *topoi* of *Cligès,* the courtly relationships of *Perceval* are offered for observation and judgment, not acceptance or identification. They are materials, not purposes; their pretensions are the characters', not the author's. Chrétien de Troyes, in *Cligès* and *Perceval,* is not a courtly writer in the sense that he propagandizes the ideals of courtly love, but only in using them as literary subjects toward which he suggests an attitude which is primarily ironic.

This attitude, which the author suggests the reader share with him toward his material, is determined by the techniques of aesthetic distance. All the forms of irony and comedy used by Chrétien serve to inform the reader and to maintain him at a certain intellectual, emotional, and moral distance from the characters of his story—most often both purposes are served simultaneously. It is the normal experience in looking at paintings to find an optimal distance from the canvas which provides the best rapport with the work of art. Something of the same is true in literature. There are literary experiences—particularly those of adolescence—in which the identification of reader and hero is complete, and the customary realities fall into oblivion. [2] More common for mature readers is a sympathy which does not cancel out a certain level of simultaneous analytic thinking and judgment. For most readers, there is likely to be an inverse relationship between the intensity of analytic activity and the degree of identification. [3] Irony is a means of increasing the proportion of intellectual analysis; comedy (at least in Chrétien) suggests not so much analytic activity as moral judgment. Both establish aesthetic distance. If used only as an occa-

---

[2] Fortunately, this remains a frequent mode of experiencing lyric poetry, at any age.

[3] A distinction must be made between experiencing literature and analyzing it. The primary experience of tragedy, for example, is empathy; but when we analyze the play, it is likely to be on the basis of a remembered empathy rather than a present one. In the ironic mode, the two processes are not antithetical, but exist more or less simultaneously with a weakening of emotional identification.

sional stylistic device, this merely provides a momentary relief of identification. Used continually, and erected into the systematic basis of structure in which the reader is expected to notice, juxtapose, and compare repeated parallels, it has the effect of drawing the reader away from empathy (if this was a possibility) toward the stance of an observer whose pleasure is at least partly derived from his own intellectual activity.

It is from this point of view that Chrétien suggests we watch the unfolding of his romances,[4] a point of view continually indicated by the individual ironies and comic moments. As such, it is primarily an aesthetic matter: the romance offers for observation an autonomous world of fiction whose realities are radically different from those to which the observing reader is accustomed. Paradoxically, the acceptance of this autonomy has led to the discovery of a greater work. Our stress on his romances as constituting independent systems of literary notation with their sole source in a unique imagination has led to a view of these romances as dealing with the delicate balance within the individual between the contradictory demands of his own nature and those of society—a balance our own time finds as delicate and precarious as the twelfth century.

Without detracting from the importance of this central concern, I would rank Chrétien's main gift to the reader as lying elsewhere. Though aesthetic distance and moral judgment are logically separable in analysis, they are identical in the actual experience of reading. In life, pleasure and moral concerns are usually contradictory. In the art of Chrétien de Troyes, the reader's imaginative life is expanded in a universe of structured fantasy offered for his delight from a perspective which unites pleasure and moral awareness. The full enjoyment of these romances is savored from a distance which both defines and reaffirms the reader's moral and aesthetic freedom.

---

[4] I do not hesitate to affirm this of *Yvain* as well as of *Cligès* and *Perceval*, though it is not true of *Erec et Enide*. One romance presents unique problems among Chrétien's works: I reserve judgment on the *Lancelot*.

BIBLIOGRAPHY

This bibliography contains only those works quoted or referred to in the preceding pages. General bibliographical guides relevant to Chrétien de Troyes are: *A Critical Bibliography of French Literature* (under the general editorship of David C. Cabeen), Vol. I, *The Mediaeval Period*, ed. U[rban] T[igner] Holmes, 2nd ed. (Syracuse University Press, 1952); and Robert Bossuat, *Manuel bibliographique de la littèrature française du moyen âge*, in "Bibliothèque elzévirienne, Nouvelle série. Etudes et documents." (Melun: Librairie d'Argence, 1951; two supplements for the years 1949-53 [published in 1955] and 1954-60 [published in 1961]). There are two annual bibliographies: "A Bibliography of Critical Arthurian Literature," (begun by J.J. Parry and continued by P.A. Brown), usually in the June issue of *Modern Language Quarterly* (1940-61); and the *Bulletin bibliographique de la Société Internationale Arthurienne* (since 1949). Finally, there are two essays on our author in particular: John R. Reinhard, "Chrétien de Troyes: A Bibliographical Essay," in *Essays and Studies in English and Comparative Literature* (Ann Arbor: University of Michigan Press, 1932); and Wilhelm Kellermann's *état present* (as of 1935): "Wege und Ziele der neueren Chrestien de Troyes-Forschung," in *Germanisch-romanische Monatsschrift*, XXIII (1935), 204-228. More recent surveys will be found in Jean Frappier's *Le Roman Breton, Introduction, Des origines à Chrétien de Troyes* (Paris: Centre de Documentation Universitaire, 1950), pp. 114-123, and in the *Note Bibliographique* of his *Chrétien de Troyes, l'homme et l'œuvre* (see below).

DICTIONARIES

Foerster, Wendelin. *Kristian von Troyes: Wörterbuch zu seinen sämtlichen Werken.* ("Romanische Bibliothek," Vol. XXI). Halle (Saale): Niemeyer, 1914.

Godefroy, Frédéric. *Dictionnaire de l'ancienne langue française et de tous ses dialectes du IX° au XV° siècle,* 10 vols. Original edition: Paris, 1880-1902; reprinted: Vaduz (Lichtenstein) & New York: Scientific Periodicals Establishment & Kraus Reprint Corp., 1961.

Meyer-Lübke, Wilhelm. *Romanisches etymologisches Wörterbuch.* 3rd ed. ("Sammlung Romanischer Elementar- und Handbücher," III Reihe, Vol. 3). Heidelberg: Carl Winters Universitätsbuchhandlung, 1935.

Tobler, Adolf, and Lommatzsch, Erhard. *Altfranzösisches Wörterbuch.* 6 vols. Berlin: Weidmann, 1926-65.

Von Wartburg, Walther. *Französisches etymologisches Wörterbuch, Eine Darstellung des galloromanischen Sprachschatzes.* 17 vols. Bonn: Klopp, 1928-64.

Texts

Bede. *De schematibus et tropis Sanctae Scripturae.* In J.P. Migne, *Patrologiae cursus completus, series latina,* Vol. XC, 175 ff.; also in Halm (below).

Cassiodorus, Senator. *Expositio in Psalterium.* In J.P. Migne, *Patrologiae cursus completus, series latina,* Vol. LXX.

Charisius. See Keil (below).

Chrestien de Troyes. See Chrétien de Troyes.

Chrétien de Troyes. *Der Percevalroman (Li Contes del Graal),* ed. Alfons Hilka ("Christian von Troyes sämtliche erhaltene Werke," ed. Wendelin Foerster, Vol. 5). Halle (Saale): Max Niemeyer Verlag, 1932.

— *Philomena, conte raconté d'après Ovide,* ed. Ch[arles] de Boer. Paris: Paul Geuthner, 1909.

— *Les Romans de Chrétien de Troyes édités d'après la copie de Guiot* (*Bibl. nat. fr. 794*), II, *Cligès,* ed. Alexandre Micha. ("Classiques Français du Moyen Age," Vol. 84). Paris: Champion, 1957.

— *Les Romans de Chrétien de Troyes...,* I, *Erec et Enide,* ed. Mario Roques. ("CFMA," Vol. 80). Paris: Champion, 1955.

— *Les Romans de Chrétien de Troyes...,* IV, *Le chevalier au lion (Yvain),* ed. Mario Roques. ("CFMA," Vol. 89). Paris: Champion, 1960.

— *Les Romans de Chrétien de Troyes...,* III, *Le chevalier de la charrete,* ed. Mario Roques. ("CFMA," Vol. 86). Paris: Champion, 1958.

— *Yvain (Der Löwenritter),* ed. Wendelin Foerster; 4th revised edition. ("Grosse Auflage"). Halle (Saae): Max Niemeyer Verlag, 1912.

Christian von Troyes. See Chrétien de Troyes.

[Cicero]. *Ad C. Herennium. De ratione dicendi (Rhetorica ad Herennium),* ed. & trans. Harry Caplan. Cambridge, Mass. & London: Harvard University Press & William Heinemann Ltd., 1954.

Diomedes. See Keil.

Donatus. See Keil.

Eneas, roman du XIIe siècle, 2 vols., ed. J.-J. Salverda de Grave. ("Classiques Français du Moyen Age," Vols. 44 & 62). Paris: Champion, 1929 & 1964.

Faral, Edmond. *Les arts poétiques du XIIe et du XIIIe siècle, recherches et documents sur la technique littéraire du moyen âge.* ("Bibliothèque de l'Ecole des Hautes Etudes," Vol. 238). Paris: Champion, 1958.

Fortunantianus. See Halm.

Geoffroi de Vinsauf. See Faral.

Halm, Karl Felix von. *Rhetores latini minores.* Leipzig: Teubner, 1863.

Hugh of St. Victor. *De grammatica.* "Le *De grammatica* de Hughes de Saint-Victor," ed. Jean Leclerq in *Archives d'Histoire Doctrinale et Littéraire du Moyen Age,* Vol. XVIII (1943), pp. 263-322. Paris: Librairie philosophique J. Vrin, 1943.

Isidore of Seville. *Isidori Hispalensis episcopi etymologiarum sive originum libri XX,* ed. W[illiam] M. Lindsay, 2 vols. Oxford, 1911.

Julian of Toledo. *De vitiis et figuris,* ed. W[illiam] M. Lindsay. ("St. Andrews University Publications," No. XV). Oxford, 1922.

Keil, Heinrich, ed. *Grammatici latini.* 8 vols. (Vol. VIII ed. Hermann Hagen). Leipzig: Teubner, 1857-80.

Marie de France. *Les lais de Marie de France,* ed. Jeanne Lods. ("Classiques Français du Moyen Age," Vol. 87). Paris: Champion, 1959.

Martianus Capella. *De nuptiis Philologicae et Mercurii,* ed. Adolphus Dick. Leipzig: Teubner, 1925.

Matthew of Vendôme. See Faral.

Pompeius. See Keil.

Quintilian. *The Institutio oratoria of Quintilian.* 4 vols., trans. H.E. Butler. Cambridge, Mass., & London: Harvard University Press & William Heinemann Ltd., 1958.

Sacerdos. See Keil.

Victor, C. Julius. See Halm.

Secondary Sources

Abelson, Paul. *The Seven Liberal Arts, a Study in Mediaeval Culture.* New York: Columbia University Press, 1906.

Baldwin, Charles Sears. *Medieval Rhetoric and Poetic (to 1400) Interpreted from Representative Works.* New York: Macmillan Co., 1928.

Becker, Ph[illipe] A[uguste]. "Von den Erzählern neben und nach Chrestiens de Troyes," *Zeitschrift für romanische Philologie,* LV (1935), 385-445.

Bergson, Henri. *Le rire: essai sur la signification du comique.* (Paris: Presses Universitaires de France, 1947).

Bernheimer, Richard. *Wild Men in the Middle Ages, A Study in Art, Sentiment, and Demonology.* Cambridge, Mass., & London: Harvard University Press & Cumberledge, 1953.

Bertolucci, Valeria. "Commento retorico all' *Erec* et al *Cligès,*" *Studi medio-latini e volgari,* VIII (1960), 9-51.

— "Di nuovo su *Cligès* e *Tristan,*" *Studi Francesi,* XVIII (1962), 401-13.

Bezzola, Reto R. *Le sens de l'aventure et de l'amour (Chrétien de Troyes).* Paris: Editions de la Jeune Parque, 1947.

Biller, Gunnar. *Etude sur le style des premiers romans français en vers (1150-75).* ("Göteborgs Högskolas Arsskrift," Vol. IV). Göteborg, 1916.

Bloch, Marc. *La société féodale,* 2 vols. Vol. I: *Les classes et le gouvernement des hommes.* ("L'Evolution de l'humanité"). Paris: Albin Michel, 1949.

Bowra, C. M[aurice]. *Primitive Song.* New York: New American Library, 1963.

Clerval, A[lexandre]. *Les écoles de Chartres au moyen âge, du Ve au XVIe siècle.* Paris: Picard, n.d.; 1895?

Cohen, Gustave. *Un grand romancier d'amour et d'aventure au XIIe siècle, Chrétien de Troyes et son œuvre,* 2nd ed. Paris: L. Rodstein, 1948.

Colby, Alice Mary. "The Style of the Portraits in the Works of Chrétien de Troyes." Columbia Dissertation (unpublished), 1962.

Cross, Tom Peete, and William Albert Nitze. *Lancelot and Guenevere: A Study on the Origins of Courtly Love.* ("The Modern Philology Monographs"). Chicago: The University of Chicago Press, 1930.

Curtius, Ernst Robert. *La littérature européenne et le moyen âge latin*, 2nd ed., trans. Jean Bréjoux. Paris: Presses Universitaires de France, 1956.

De Trooz, Ch[arles]. "La critique de Virgile dans les commentaires de Servius," *Musée Belge*, XXXII (1929), 229-61.

Dupin, Henri. *La courtoisie au moyen âge (d'après les textes du XIIᵉ et du XIIIᵉ siècle)*. Paris: Picard, 1931.

Emmel, Hildegard. *Formprobleme des Artusromans und der Graldichtung. Die Bedeutung des Artuskreises für das Gefüge des Romans im 12. und 13. Jahrhundert in Frankreich, Deutschland und den Niederlanden.* Bern: Franck, 1951.

Faral, Edmond. *Recherches sur les sources latines des contes et romans courtois du moyen âge.* Paris: Champion, 1913.

Fierz-Monnier, Antoinette. *Initiation und Wandlung. Zur Geschichte des altfranzösischen Romans im zwölften Jahrhundert von Chrétien de Troyes zu Renaut de Beaujeu.* ("Studiorum Romanicorum Collectio Turicensis," No. V). Bern: Francke, 1951.

Fotich, Tatiana. *The Narrative Tenses in Chrétien de Troyes, A Study in Style and Stylistics.* ("Catholic University of America: Studies in Romance Languages and Literature," Vol. XXXVIII). Washington, D.C.: The Catholic University of America, 1950.

Foulet, Lucien. *Petite syntaxe de l'ancien français*, 3d ed. ("Classiques Français du Moyen Age"). Paris: Champion, 1958.

— "Sire, Messire," *Romania*, LXXI (1950), 1-48, 180-221.

Fourquet, Jean. "Le rapport entre l'œuvre et la source chez Chrétien de Troyes et le problème des sources bretonnes," *Romance Philology*, IX (1955), 298-312.

— *Wolfram d'Eschenbach et le Conte del Graal; les divergences de la tradition du Conte del Graal chez Chrétien et leur importance pour l'explication du Parzival.* ("Publications de la Faculté des Lettres de l'Université de Strasbourg," Fasc. 87). Paris: Les Belles Lettres, 1938.

Fourrier, Anthime. *Le courant réaliste dans le roman courtois en France au Moyen Age.* Vol. I: *Les débuts (XIIᵉ siècle).* Paris: Nizet, 1960.

Fowler, David C. *Prowess and Charity in the "Perceval" of Chrétien de Troyes.* ("University of Washington Publications in Language and Literature," Vol. XIV). Seattle: University of Washington Press, 1959.

Franz, A. "Die reflektierte Handlung im *Cligès*," *Zeitschrift für romanische Philologie*, XLVII (1927), 61-86.

Frappier, Jean. *Chrétien de Troyes, l'homme et l'œuvre.* ("Connaissance des Lettres," Vol. 50). Paris: Hatier, 1957.

— "Le Graal et l'Hostie (*Conte del Graal*, vv. 6413-6431)," in *Les romans du Graal...* (see below).

— "Le personnage de Gauvain dans la *Première Continuation de Perceval* (*Conte du Graal*)," *Romance Philology*, XI (1957-8), 331-44.

— *Le roman breton. Chrétien de Troyes: Cligès.* Paris: Centre de Documentation Universitaire, 1951.

— *Le roman breton. Chrétien de Troyes: Perceval ou le conte du Graal.* Paris: Centre de Documentation Universitaire, 1961.

— *Le roman breton. Yvain ou le Chevalier au lion.* Paris: Centre de Documentation Universitaire, 1952.

— "Le tour *je me sui* chez Chrétien de Troyes," *Romance Philology,* IX (1955-6), 126-133.

— "Vues sur les conceptions courtoises dans les littératures d'oc et d'oïl au XIIᵉ siècle," *Cahiers de civilisation médiévale,* II (1959), 135-156.

Gautier, Léon. *La chevalerie.* Paris: Delgrave, 1884.

Gérold, Théodore. *La musique au moyen âge.* ("Classiques Français du Moyen Age," Vol. 73). Paris: Champion, 1932.

Grant, Mary A. *The Ancient Rhetorical Theories of the Laughable: The Greek Rhetoricians and Cicero.* ("University of Wisconsin Studies in Language and Literature," No. 21). Madison, Wisc.: University of Wisconsin Press, 1924.

Grose, Francis. *Military Antiquities Respecting a History of the English Army from the Conquest to the Present Time,* 2 vols. Picadilly: Stockdale, 1812.

Grosse, R. *Der Stil des Chrestiens von Troies.* ("Französische Studien," No. 1). Altenburg, 1881.

Grosser, Dorothy. "Studies in the Influence of the *Rhetorica ad Herennium* and Cicero's *De inventione.*" Cornell Dissertation (Unpublished), 1953.

Guiette, Robert. "D'une poésie formelle en France au moyen âge," *Revue des sciences humaines,* LIV (1949), 61-68.

Gwynn, Aubrey. *Roman Education from Cicero to Quintilian.* New York: Russell & Russell, 1926 & 1964.

Haarhoff, Theodore. *Schools of Gaul, A Study of Pagan and Christian Education in the Last Century of the Western Empire.* Oxford, 1920.

Hatzfeld, Helmut. "Deuten Stilelemente in Chrétiens *Perceval* auf eine strukturelle Einheit?" in *Medium Aevum Romanicum, Festschrift für H[ans] Rheinfelder,* ed. Heinrich Bihler & Alfred Noyer-Weidner. Munich: Hueber, 1963. Pp. 140-160.

Hauvette, Henri. *La "Morte vivante".* Paris: Boivin, 1933.

Heinemann, S. "Zur stilgeschichtlichen Stellung Chrétiens," in *Mélanges de linguistique et de littérature romanes à la mémoire d'Istvan Frank.* ("Annales Universitatis Saraviensis." Philosophie-lettres. Vol. VI.) University of Saarbrücken, 1957.

Hilka, Alfons. *Die direkte Rede als stilistischer Kunstmittel in den Romanen des Kristian von Troyes.* Halle: Niemeyer, 1903.

Hoepffner, Ernst. "Jean Fourquet, *Wolfram d'Eschenbach et le Conte del Graal,*" rev. *Romania,* LXV (1939), 397-413.

Hofer, Stefan. "La structure du *Conte del Graal* examinée à la lumière de l'œuvre de Chrétien de Troyes," in *Les romans du Graal...* (see below), pp. 15-25.

Hoffman, Stanton de V. "The Structure of the *Conte del Graal,*" *Romanic Review,* LII (1961), 81-98.

Imbs, Paul. "L'élément religieux dans le *Conte del Graal* de Chrétien de Troyes," in *Les romans du Graal...* (see below), pp. 31-53.

— "Perceval et le Graal chez Chrétien de Troyes," *Bulletin de la Société Académique du Bas-Rhin,* LXXII-LXXIV (1950-52), 38-79.

Jackson, W[illiam] T.H. *The Literature of the Middle Ages.* New York: Columbia University Press, 1960.

Jankélévitch, Vladimir. *L'ironie ou la bonne conscience,* 2nd ed. Paris: Presses Universitaires de France, 1950.

Jullien, Emile. *Les professeurs de littérature dans l'ancienne Rome et leur enseignement depuis l'origine jusqu'à la mort d'Auguste.* Paris: Leroux, 1885.

Kellermann, Wilhelm. *Aufbaustil und Weltbild Chrestiens von Troyes im Percevalroman.* ("Beihefte zur Zeitschrift für romanische Philologie," No. 88.) Halle (Saale): Niemeyer, 1936.

Köhler, Erich. *Ideal und Wirklichkeit in der höfischen Epik. Studien zur Form der frühen Artus- und Graldichtung.* ("Beihefte zur Zeitschrift für romanische Philologie," No. 97). Tübingen: Niemeyer, 1956.

— "Zur Discussion über die Einheit von Chrestiens *Li contes del Graal,*" *Zeitschrift für romanische Philologie,* LXXV (1959), 523-539.

Küchler, Walther. "Über den sentimentalen Gehalt der Haupthandlung in Crestiens *Erec* und *Yvain,*" *Zeitschrift für romanische Philologie,* XL (1919), 83-99.

Lazar, Moshé. "Les éléments constitutifs de la *cortezia* dans la lyrique des troubadours," *Studi mediolatini e volgari,* VI-VII (1959), 67-96.

— *Amour courtois et "fin' amors" dans la littérature du XIIe siècle.* ("Bibliothèque Française et Romane... Faculté des Lettres de Strasbourg," Série C: Etudes Littéraires, Vol. VIII). Paris: Klincksieck, 1964.

Lehmann, Paul. "Die *Institutio oratoria* des Quintilianus im Mittelalter," *Philologus,* LXXXIX (1934), 349-383.

Lejeune, Rita. "La date du *Conte du Graal* de Chrétien de Troyes," *Moyen Age,* LX (1954), 51-79.

Les romans du graal aux XIIe et XIIIe siècles. ("Colloques Internationaux du Centre National de la Recherche Scientifique, III: Strasbourg, 29 mars-3 avril 1954"). Paris: Editions du Centre National de la Recherche Scientifique, 1956.

Levy, Raphael. "The Motivation of *Perceval* and the authorship of *Philomena,*" *Publications of the Modern Language Association,* LXXI (1956), 853-862.

Lewis, C.D., trans. *The Aeneid of Virgil.* Garden City, N.Y.: Doubleday Anchor, 1952.

Linker, Robert White, trans. *The Story of the Grail.* Chapel Hill: University of North Carolina Press, 1952.

Lyons, Faith. "La fausse mort dans le *Cligès* de Chrétien de Troyes," in *Mélanges de linguistique et de littérature romanes offerts à Mario Roques,* 4 vols. Paris: Didier, 1950. Vol. I, pp. 167-177.

— "Sentiment et rhétorique dans l'*Yvain,*" *Romania,* LXXXIII (1962), 370-377.

Manitius, Karl. "Zur Überlieferung des sogenannten Auctor ad Herennium," *Philologus,* C (1956), 62-66.

Marrou, Henri-Irénée. *Histoire de l'enseignement dans l'Antiquité.* Paris: Editions du Seuil, 1948.

— *Saint Augustin et la fin de la culture antique.* ("Bibliothèque des Ecoles Françaises d'Athènes et de Rome". Fasc. 145(bis). Paris: Boccard, 1949.

Micha, Alexandre. *"Eneas* et *Cligès,"* in *Mélanges de philologie romane et de Littérature médiévale offerts à Ernst Hoepffner...,* ("Publications de la Faculté des Lettres de l'Université de Strasbourg"). Paris: Les Belles-Lettres, 1949. Pp. 237-243.

— *"Le Perceval* de Chrétien de Troyes," in *Lumière du Graal, études et textes présentés sous la direction de René Nelli.* Paris: Cahiers du Sud, 1951.

— *La tradition manuscrite des romans de Chrétien de Troyes.* Paris: Droz, 1939.

— *"Tristan* et *Cligès," Neophilologus,* XXXVI (1952), 1-10.

Misrahi, Jean. "Bezzola, Reto R. *Le sens de l'aventure et de l'amour,"* rev., *Romance Philology,* IV (1950-51), 348-361.

Mollard, A. "L'imitation de Quintilien dans Guibert de Nogent," *Moyen Age,* V (1934), 81-87.

— "La diffusion de l'*Institution oratoire* au XII⁰ siècle," *Moyen Age,* V (1934), 161-175, and VI (1935), 1-9.

Nitze, William A. "The Character of Gauvain in the Romances of Chrétien de Troyes," *Modern Philology,* L (1952-3), 219-225.

— "The Guinganbresil Episode in Chrétien's *Perceval," Romania,* LXXII (1951), 373-380.

— *Perceval and the Holy Grail: An Essay in the Romance of Chrétien de Troyes.* ("University of California Publications in Modern Philology," Vol. XXVIII, No. 5). Berkeley & Los Angeles: University of California Press, 1949.

Paetow, Louis John. *The Arts Course at Medieval Universities with Special Reference to Grammar and Rhetoric.* ("The University Studies," Vol. III, No. 7). Urbana-Champaign, University [of Illinois] Press, 1910.

Painter, Sidney. *French Chivalry: Chivalric Ideas and Practices in Mediaeval France.* Baltimore: Johns Hopkins Press, 1940.

Paré, G[érard], A. Brunet, & P. Tremblay. *La renaissance du XII⁰ siècle: les écoles et l'enseignement.* ("Publications de l'Institut d'Etudes Médiévales d'Ottawa," Vol. III). Paris & Ottawa: Vrin & Institut d'Etudes Médiévales, 1933.

Paris, Gaston. *Mélanges de littérature française du moyen âge.* Paris: Champion, 1912.

Pauphilet, Albert. *Le legs du moyen âge, études de littérature médiévale.* Melun: Librairie d'Argences, 1949.

Rand, E[dward] K. "Ovid and the Spirit of Metamorphosis," in *Harvard Essays on Classical Subjects,* ed. Herbert W. Smyth. Boston: Houghton Mifflin, 1912. Pp. 207-238.

Riché, Pierre. *Education et culture dans l'occident barbare, V⁰-VIII⁰ siècles.* ("Patristica Sorboniensia," Vol. IV). Paris: Editions du Seuil, 1962.

Riffaterre, Michael. *Le style des Pléiades de Gobineau, essai d'application d'une méthode stylistique.* New York: Columbia University Press, 1957.

Robertson, D[avid] W., Jr. "Chrétien's *Cligès* and the Ovidian Spirit," *Comparative Literature,* VII (1955), 32-42.

— "The Doctrine of Charity in Medieval Literary Gardens: A Topical Approach through Symbolism and Allegory," *Speculum,* XXVI (1951), 24-49.

Roger, M. *L'enseignement des lettres classiques d'Ausone à Alcuin; introduction à l'histoire des écoles carolingiennes.* Paris: Picard, 1905.

Roques, Mario. "Pour l'Introduction à l'édition du *Roman de Perceval* de Chrétien de Troyes," *Romania,* LXXXI (1960), 1-36.

Salmon, Paul. "Ignorance and Awareness of Identity in Hartmann and Wolfram. An element of Dramatic Irony," *Beiträge zur Geschichte der Deutschen Sprache und Literatur,* LXXXII (1960), 95-115.

Spitzer, Leo. "Kellermann, Wilhelm, *Aufbaustil und Weltbild Chrestiens von Troyes im Percevalroman,*" rev., *Modern Language Notes,* LV (1940), 222-226.

Thurot, C[harles]. *Notices et extraits de divers manuscrits latins pour servir à l'histoire des doctrines grammaticales au Moyen Age.* ("Notices et extraits des manuscrits...," Vol. XXII, Part 2). 1868.

Van Hamel, A.G. "*Cligès* et *Tristan,*" *Romania,* XXXIII (1904), 465-489.

Volkmann, Richard. *Hermagoras oder Elemente der Rhetorik.* Stettin: Nahmer, 1865.

Waddell, Helen. *Mediaeval Latin Lyrics.* New York: Henry Holt, 1929.

Wagner, Robert Leon. "*Sorcier*" et "*magicien*", contribution à l'étude du vocabulaire de la magie. Paris: Droz, 1939.

Whitney, Marian P. "Queen of Mediaeval Virtues: Largesse," in *Vassar Mediaeval Studies,* ed. Christabel Forsyth Fiske. New Haven: Yale University Press, 1923. Pp. 181-215.

Wilmotte, M[aurice]. *Le poème du Graal et ses auteurs.* Paris: Droz, 1930.

Wood, William S. "The Plot Structure in Four Romances of Chrestien de Troyes," *Studies in Philology,* L (1953), 1-15.

Zumthor, Paul. *Histoire littéraire de la France médiévale, VIᵉ au XIVᵉ siècle.* Paris: Presses Universitaires de France, 1954.

ACHEVÉ D'IMPRIMER
AUX « PRESSES DE SAVOIE », AMBILLY-ANNEMASSE (H.-S.),
EN AOÛT 1968.